Checklist for Writing to Sh<!-- cut -->

- **Reconsider the Assignment**
    - A. What words in this assignment provide cues for writers?
    - B. How can I make my draft respond more directly to this assignment?

- **Consider Audience**
    - A. What information do readers need?
    - B. What is unclear to readers of my draft?

- **Identify Your Thesis**
    - A. What point do I want to make about this subject?
    - B. Will readers be able to tell what this paper is about?

- **Check Organization**
    - A. What organizational pattern(s) does this paper employ?
        analysis
        cause and effect
        comparison
        general to specific
        order of importance
        spatial order
        time order
    - B. Is there enough variation in organizational pattern?

- **Evaluation Cohesion**
    - A. Are my references clear?
    - B. Have I used conjunctions effectively
    - C. Does my punctuation contribute to cohesion?

- **Edit**
    - A. Have I attended to conventions of spelling, punctuation, capitalization, usage, and format?
    - B. Have I proofread my writing carefully?

Writing AND Learning

Writing and Learning

SECOND EDITION

Anne Ruggles Gere
University of Michigan

MACMILLAN PUBLISHING COMPANY
New York

Copyright © 1988, Macmillan Publishing Company,
a division of Macmillan, Inc.

Printed in the United States of America

All rights reserved. No part of this book may be reproduced or transmitted in any form or by any means, electronic or mechanical, including photocopying, recording, or any information storage and retrieval system, without permission in writing from the Publisher.

Earlier edition copyright © 1985 by Macmillan Publishing Company.

Macmillan Publishing Company
866 Third Avenue, New York, New York 10022

Library of Congress Cataloging-in-Publication Data

Gere, Anne Ruggles, 1944-
   Writing and learning.

   Includes index.
   1. English language—Rhetoric. I. Title.
PE1408.G485 1988   808'.042   87-18492
ISBN 0-02-341460-X

Printing: 1 2 3 4 5 6 7   Year: 8 9 0 1 2 3 4

ISBN 0-02-341460-X

Acknowledgements

Applied Science and Technology Index. From *Applied Science and Technology Index*, 1971, page 1475. Copyright © 1971, 1972 by The H.W. Wilson Company. Material reproduced by permission of the publisher.

Book Review Digest. Copyright © 1971 by The H.W. Wilson Company. Material reproduced by permission of the publisher.

Book Review Index. Selected from *Book Review Index, 1986 Cumulation,* edited by Gary C. Tarbert (copyright © 1986 by Gale Research Company; reprinted by permission of the publisher). Gale Research, 1983, p. 248.

David Brewster. *The Best Places,* page 161. Sasquatch Publishing Company, 1981. Reprinted by permission.

David Brewster. "Revising the Downward Drift of American Education." From *The Weekly* (12/8/82). Reprinted by permission.

J. Bronowski. *The Ascent of Man.* From *The Ascent of Man* by J. Bronowski. Copyright © 1973 by J. Bronowski. By permission of Little, Brown and Company.

Paul Connolly. *On Essays.* Pages 1–2, "What Is an Essay?" (Introduction) from *ON ESSAYS: A Reader for Writers* by Paul H. Connolly. Copyright © 1981 by Paul H. Connolly. Reprinted by permission of Harper & Row, Publishers, Inc.

Frank Conroy. "Savages." From STOP-TIME by Frank Conroy, pages 16–20. Copyright © 1965, 1966, 1967 by Frank Conroy. All rights reserved. Reprinted by permission of Viking Penguin Inc.

Malcolm Cowley. Excerpt from "Truman Capote," WRITERS AT WORK, FIRST SERIES, ed. by Malcolm Cowley. Copyright © 1957, 1958 by The Paris Review, Inc. All rights reserved. Reprinted by permission of Viking Penguin Inc.

John Daly. "Development of an Apprehension Measure." From *Research in the Teaching of English* 13:1, pp. 37–44. Reprinted by permission.

John A. Daly and Wayne G. Shamo. "Writing Apprehension and Occupational Choice." From the *Journal of Occupational Psychology* 49, 1976, pp. 55–56. Reprinted with the permission of The British Psychological Society.

Dictionary entry. Copyright © 1982 by Houghton Mifflin Company. Reprinted by permission from *The American Heritage Dictionary, Second College Edition*.

Joan Didion. "Why I write." Reprinted by permission of Wallace & Sheil Agency, Inc. Copyright © 1976 by Joan Didion. First appeared in The New York Times Book Review.

Loren Eiseley. *The Star Thrower*. Copyright © 1978 by The Estate of Loren C. Eiseley. Reprinted by permission of Times Books/The New York Times Book Co., Inc.

Donald Hall. "Land of One Thousand Seasons." From *YANKEE Magazine* (November 1985). Reprinted by permission.

Humanities Index, Vol. 5 (April 1978–March 1979). Copyright © 1978,1979 by The H.W. Wilson Company. Material reproduced by permission of the publisher.

H.W. Janson. *History of Art.* Reprinted from the book *History of Art* by H.W. Janson, first edition. Published by Harry N. Abrams, Inc., New York, 1962. All rights reserved.

Suzanne Britt Jordan. "The Lean and Hungry Look." From *Newsweek* 92 (1978), pp. 32–33. Reprinted by permission.

Harper Lee. *To Kill a Mockingbird.* Excerpt on page 293 from TO KILL A MOCKINGBIRD by Harper Lee (J.B. Lippincott). Copyright © 1960 by Harper Lee. Reprinted by permission of Harper & Row, Publishers, Inc.

Aldo Leopold. *A Sand County Almanac.* From *A Sand County Almanac, with Other Essays on Conservation from Round River* by Aldo Leopold. Copyright © 1949, 1953, 1966; renewed 1977, 1981 by Oxford University Press, Inc. Reprinted by permission.

Deborah Luepnitz. "Can Men Mother?" From *Child Custody.* Reprinted by permission.

John McPhee. Excerpt from *Coming into the Country* by John McPhee. Copyright © 1976, 1977 by John McPhee. Reprinted by permission of Farrar, Strauss and Giroux, Inc.

Meteorological and Geoastrophysical Abstracts. "Radar Forecast Aide," by Waldheuser and Hughes. From *Meteorological and Geoastrophysical Abstracts,* January–April 1970, Vol. 21, No. 1, pages 76–77. Copyright by the American Meteorological Society. Reprinted by permission.

New York Times Index. From the *New York Times Index.* Vol. 58, 1970, pages 1899–1900. Copyright © 1970 by The New York Times Company. Reprinted by permission.

James O'Brien. "The Future for Satellite-Derived Surface Winds." First published in *Oceanus 24,* the magazine of the Woods Hole Oceanographic Institution, in 1981, pages 28–29. Reprinted by permission.

Psychological Abstracts. This citation is reprinted with permission of *Psychological Abstracts* and the PsycINFO Database (copyright © by the American Psychological Association), and may not be reproduced without its prior permission. Further information may be obtained by addressing requests to: PsycINFO, American Psychological Association, 1200 Seventeenth Street, N.W., Washington, D.C. 20036.

Reader's Digest Version. Reprinted from "The Reader's Digest Bible," copyright © 1982 by The Reader's Digest Association, Inc. Reprinted by permission.

Readers' Guide to Periodical Literature. From *Readers' Guide to Periodical Literature,* Vol. 30 (March 1970–February 1971). Copyright © 1970, 1971 by The H.W. Wilson Company. Material reproduced by permission of the publisher.

Revised Standard Version Bible. The Scripture quotations contained herein are from the *Revised Standard Version Bible,* copyright 1946, 1952, 1971 by the Division of Christian Education of the National Council of the Churches of Christ in the USA, and are used by permission.

Tom Robbins. *Another Roadside Attraction.* Excerpt from *Another Roadside Attraction* by Tom Robbins, page 311. Copyright © 1971 by Thomas E. Robbins. Reprinted by permission of Doubleday and Company, Inc.

Theodore Roethke. From "The Visitant," copyright 1950 by Theodore Roethke, from *The Collected Poems of Theodore Roethke,* reprinted by permission of Doubleday and Company, Inc.

Carl Sandburg. "Fog" from *Chicago Poems* by Carl Sandburg. Copyright © 1916 by Holt, Rinehart and Winston, Inc.; copyright 1944 by Carl Sandburg. Reprinted by permission of Harcourt Brace Jovanovich, Inc.

May Swenson. "The Universe." From *New and Selected Things Taking Place* by May Swenson. Copyright © 1963 by May Swenson. First appeared in *The Hudson Review.* By permission of Little, Brown and Company in association with the Atlantic Monthly Press.

Judy Syfers. "I Want a Wife." From *MS* magazine, December 31, 1971. Reprinted with permission.

Lewis Thomas. *The Lives of a Cell.* From *The Lives of a Cell* by Lewis Thomas, page 75. Copyright © 1974 by Lewis Thomas. Reprinted by permission of Viking Penguin Inc.

Susan Allen Toth. "Cinematypes." From *Harper's Magazine,* May 1980, pages 99–100. Reprinted by permission.

Susan Allen Toth. "Science." From *Blooming: A Small-Town Girlhood,* pages 84–87. Copyright © 1978, 1981 by Susan Allen Toth. Reprinted by permission of Little, Brown and Company.

Barbara Tuchman. *Practicing History,* page 48. Copyright © 1981. Reprinted with the permission of Alfred A. Knopf, Inc.

Barbara Tuchman. "'This Is the End of the World': The Black Death." From *A Distant Mirror: The Calamitous 14th Century* by Barbara Tuchman, pages 92–97. Copyright © 1978 by Barbara Tuchman. Reprinted by permission of Alfred A. Knopf.

Carll Tucker. "Fear of Dearth." From *Saturday Review,* 1979.

John Updike. "Central Park." Copyright © 1956 by John Updike. Reprinted from *Assorted Prose,* by John Updike, by permission of Alfred A. Knopf, Inc. Originally appeared in *The New Yorker.*

John Updike. "Three Boys." In *Five Boyhoods* by Martin Levin. Copyright © 1962. Reprinted by permission.

Jung Waser et al. *Chem One,* pages 427–428. Copyright © 1980 by McGraw-Hill Book Company. Reproduced with permission.

E.B. White. *Essays of E.B. White* (first paragraph p. 71)—Allen Cove, February 8, 1975—in ESSAYS OF E.B. WHITE. Copyright © 1975 by E.B. White. Originally appeared in *The New Yorker.*

E.B. White. *Letters of E.B. White.* Letter to Alison Marks, April 20, 1956 (p. 417) in LETTERS OF E.B. WHITE, Collected and Edited by Dorothy Lobrano Guth. Copyright © 1976 by E.B. White. Reprinted by permission of Harper & Row, Publishers, Inc.

Tom Wolfe. *The Right Stuff.* Excerpt from *The Right Stuff* by Tom Wolfe, pages 148–149. Copyright © 1979 by Tom Wolfe. Reprinted by permission of Farrar, Strauss and Giroux, Inc.

Ann Wotring. "Two Studies of Writing in High School Science," pages 28–30. National Writing Project, School of Education, University of California–Berkeley. Reprinted by permission.

*For Margaret Dies Ruggles
and to the memory of Sumner Eugene Ruggles
who gave me love and words;
also
for Margaret Chamberlain Gere
and to the memory of Brewster Huntington Gere
who gave me Budge*

Preface

The French saying "plus ca change, pluc c'est la même chose" [the more things change, the more they stay the same] describes this second edition of *Writing and Learning*. There are a number of new features, some of the original material has been rearranged, and parts have been deleted or updated. But the essence of the first edition remains unchanged.

New features include a chapter that suggests ways to prepare for a writing course. This chapter raises questions about habits, experiences, and attitudes toward writing, explains the writing process, makes connections between reading and writing, and suggests specific tools and procedures for approaching a composition class. Another new feature is the inclusion of more samples of writing from both students and professional writers. These samples demonstrate the various types of writing discussed in the book. Much of the student writing includes both drafts and revisions, which allow readers to see how the processes of writing and learning occur. The handbook has been expanded to include more information useful to student writers.

Rearrangement of material has brought sections on drafting and revising closer together. Portions on drafting emphasize writing as a means of learning, a way of discovering new connections, a process of developing ideas. Sections on revising emphasize writing as a means of showing one's learning to others. Here issues of thesis, organization, audience awareness, and conventions of standard written English become important. Part One surveys both writing to learn and writing to show learning, and it also suggests many strategies for evaluating one's own writing. Written selections have been updated to include more contemporary material.

Although there are many changes, the central assumptions of the book remain unchanged: writing is a recursive process that occurs over time; what is learned in a writing course should have application in other courses; learning is a complex and ongoing process; and learning to write is not the same as writing to show learning. This edition, like the first, combines the best of traditional approaches with innovations based on current theory and research in composition. It includes writing assignments from many disciplines, and it assumes that writing and learning cannot be separated. Learning in history or physics or art involves more than mastering subject matter, and effective

Preface

writing requires knowledge as well as control of the conventions of writing. This book presents writing as a series of choices rather than as rules that must be followed slavishly. In so doing, it emphasizes that without learning there is no writing, and that without writing, learning is impoverished.

I have learned as much from revising *Writing and Learning* as I did from writing the first edition. Once again, many people helped along the way. A more detailed explanation of sources appears in the Instructor's Manual, but I would like to acknowledge a number of individuals here: John Daley in Chapter One; Roy Hughes D. Gordon Rohman and Ann Wotring in Chapter Two; Barry Kroll in Chapter Three; Ken Davis, Michael Halliday, Requa Hasan, Philip Phenix, and Mike Rose in Chapter Four; Stephen Dunning and Frances Yates in Chapter Five; Mike Rose in Chapter Six; George Lakoff and Mark Johnson in Chapter Seven; Richard Larson in Chapter Eight; Chaim Perelman in Chapter Nine; Arthur Stern in Chapter Ten; Frank O'Hare in Chapter Eleven; Walker Gibson and Martin Joos in Chapter Twelve; Virginia Tiefel and Paula Walker in Chapter Thirteen; George Dillon, Mina Shaughnessy, and Eugene Smith in the handbook.

My debts to colleagues are larger but more difficult to specify. Spending a summer as a visiting professor at the University of New Hampshire provided an opportunity for extended conversations with Bob Connors, Don Murray, and Tom Newkirk—conversations that enlarged my thinking about teaching writing. With them, as with George Dillon and Eugene Smith, valued friends and colleagues at the University of Washington, I could not always tell where their thoughts left off and my own began. Jeff Carroll, now of the University of Hawaii, added much to my learning as he completed his own graduate school career. As was true for the first edition, members of my writing group responded helpfully to drafts, and many of the suggestions of Marcia Barton, Sandra Silberstein, and Kate Vangen all have been incorporated into these pages. Students whose work appears in the text are acknowledged by name, but I continue to learn from all I teach.

Tony English, my editor at Macmillan, provided me the tonic of laughter along with many insightful comments and continuing support. A number of reviewers offered helpful suggestions along the way: Michael Feehan, The University of Texas at Arlington; Jerrie C. Scott, University of Florida; Peter Owens, Southeastern Massachusetts University; Ted W. White, Cochise College; Catherine A. Curtis, University of Houston; Ronald H. Dow, University of Maine at Presque Isle; Martha Coultas Strode, Spoon River College; Ann B. Dobie, University of Southwestern Louisiana; and Charles V. O'Brien, Rochester Community College. Roy Angell's careful reading of the first edition gave me many useful ideas and Meg Schreiber's indexing helped make them accessible.

This edition, like the first, is dedicated to the older generation, symbolizing my continuing gratitude to those who embodied the love on which Budge and I base our own lives. I am particularly grateful to my mother whose grace under the pressure of debilitating illness instructs me in living that seeks not merely to endure but to prevail.

A. R. G.

Contents

PART ONE AN OVERVIEW — 1

    Chapter One **Getting Ready for Writing and Learning** — 3
    Examine Habits, Experiences, and Attitudes   3
        Recollect Experiences   4
        Be Conscious of Writing Habits   4
        Assess Attitudes Toward Writing   6
    Think of Writing as a Process   8
        Writing to Learn   8
        Writing to Show Learning   9
    Read Like a Writer   10
        Predict   11
        Respond   11
        Collect   11
    Look at Previous Writing   12
        Keep a Writing Folder   13
    Start a Journal   13
        Record   13
        Practice   14
        Experiment   14
        Learn   14
    Locate the Best Place and Time   14
    Gather Writing Tools   15
        Get a Dictionary   15
    Examine This Book   15

Readings

Catch Her in the Oatmeal
Dan Greenberg   25

A Farewell to Porridge
Dan Greenberg   25

    Chapter Two **Discovery: Writing to Learn** — 17
    Prewriting   17
    Journals   18
        Collect   19
        Imitate   21
        Experiment   26

Contents

Just Forget It
Monica Caoli 36

Readings

To Kill A Mockingbird
Harper Lee 44

Baseball
Jeff Carroll 48

Language Essay
Eva Godwin 60

The Generic Essay
Eva Godwin 63

The Unfortunate Encounter
Monica Caoli

Readings

History of Art
H.W. Janson 76

Oceanus
James O'Brien 78

Writing Apprehension
John Daley and Wayne Shamo 81

Learning a Foreign Language
Mike Anderson 89

Observe 30
Explain 33
Drafts 35

Chapter Three Development: Writing to Show Learning 39

Assignments 39
    Taking Cues from Assignments 40
    Asking Questions of Assignments 42
Audience 43
    Seeing Your Audience 45
    Asking Questions 46
    Audience in College Writing 52
Thesis 53
    Developing Your Thesis 53
    Stating Your Thesis 54
    Placing Your Thesis Statement 55
Revising 57
Reseeing the Whole 59

Chapter Four Redevelopment: Evaluating Writing to Show Learning 69

Peer Response 69
    Writing Groups 70
Consider Audience Priorities 74
    Arts and Humanities 75
    Natural Sciences 78
    Social Sciences 80
Evaluate Organization 83
    Time Order 83
    Spatial Order 84
    Order of Importance 84
    Analysis 84
    General to Specific 84
    Cause and Effect 84
    Comparison 85
    Identify Organizational Patterns 85
    Mix Organizational Patterns 85
    Outline 89
Evaluate Cohesion 93
    Cohesive Ties of Reference 94
    Cohesive Ties of Conjunction 99
    Cohesion in Your Writing 102
Evaluate Format 103
    Standard Form for College Papers 104
Evaluate Conventions 105

Contents

PART TWO APPLICATIONS — 107

Readings

Savages
Frank Conroy 110

This is the End of the World
Barbara Tuchman 114

Can Men Mother?
Deborah Anna Leupnitz 123

I Kings 1:1–38
The Bible 127

Fun Anger
Jim Lawton 131

Revenge Can Be Sweet
Jim Lawton 136

Chapter Five Reporting Events — 109

Getting Ready to Report Events 110
    Memory 110
    Collecting 114
Writing to Learn 119
    Memory 119
    Gather 121
    Select 126
Selecting for a Draft 131
    Summary 133
Writing to Show Learning 133
    Reconsider the Assignment 133
    Consider Audience 133
    Identify Your Thesis 134
    Check Organization 135
    Evaluate Coherence and Cohesion 135
    Editing 136

Readings

That Lean and Hungry Look
Suzanne Britt Jordan 142

Land of One Thousand Seasons
Donald Hall 146

The '60s—A Time for a College Education
Monica Caoli 156

Revision of The '60s
Monica Caoli 161

Chapter Six Supporting Assertions — 141

Getting Ready to Support Assertions 142
    Definition 142
    Illustration 145
Writing to Learn 148
    Definition 149
    Illustration 153
    Defining and Illustrating in a Draft 156
    Summary 158
Writing to Show Learning 158
    Reconsider the Assignment 159
    Consider Audience 159
    Identify Your Thesis 160
    Check Organization 160
    Evaluate Coherence and Cohesion 161
    Editing 161

Readings

Three Boys
John Updike 169

Cinematypes
Susan Allen Toth 174

The Way It Should Be
Adam Cooney 184

Chapter Seven Analyzing Information — 165

Getting Ready to Analyze Information 166
    Metaphor 166
    Categories 167
    Parts and Wholes 168
    Similarities and Differences 172
Writing to Learn 176
    Think Metaphorically 176

Contents

Looking for an Answer in MEDITATION
Adam Cooney 189

Categories 179
Using Parts and Wholes 180
Similarities and Differences 182
Summary 186

Writing to Show Learning 186
Reconsider the Assignment 186
Consider Audience 187
Reconsider Method of Analysis 188
Check Organization 188
Editing 189

Readings

Science
Susan Allen Toth 196

Fear of Dearth
Carll Tucker 199

The Redesigning of a Deathtrap
Robert Johnson 207

The Death of a Friend
Robert Johnson 213

Chapter Eight Explaining Causes and Effects 193

Getting Ready to Write about Causes and Effects 194
Chain Outlines 195
Questions about Events or Processes 195
Cause-Effect Pattern 196
Effect-Cause Pattern 199

Writing to Learn 201
Chain Outline 202
Questions about Events and Processes 203
Develop Organizational Plan 206
Summary 209

Writing to Show Learning 209
Reconsider Assignment 209
Consider Audience 210
Check Organization 211
Evaluate Coherence and Cohesion 212
Editing 212

Readings

Reversing the Downward Drift
David Brewster 219

I Want a Wife
Judy Syfers 222

Problems and Solutions
Patrick Johnson 232

Drug Abuse
Patrick Johnson 241

Chapter Nine Arguing Proposals 217

Getting Ready to Support Propositions 218
Consider Audience
Collect Information
State and Define Terms of Proposition

Writing to Learn 224
Ask Five "W" Questions 224
Who 224
What 225
When 225
Where 226
Why 226
Collect Evidence 227
State Your Proposition 228
Define the Terms of Your Proposition 229
Specify Causes 231
Summary 235

Contents

Writing to Show Learning   236
- Reconsider the Assignment   236
- Consider Audience   236
- Avoid Fallacies   237
- Check Organization   239
- Evaluate Coherence and Cohesion   240
- Editing   241

PART THREE THE STRUCTURE OF WRITING   249

Chapter Ten Paragraphs   251

Deciding Where Paragraphs Begin and End   251
- Identify Important Parts   253

Types of Paragraphs   256
- Introductory Paragraphs   257
- Transitional Paragraphs   259
- Topical Paragraphs   260
- Concluding Paragraphs   261

Revising Paragraphs   263
- Revising for Purpose   263
- Revising for Organization   266
- Revising for Cohesion   269
- Revising for Style   271

Chapter Eleven Sentences   275

Perspective on Sentences   275

Combining Sentences   276
- Modification   276
- Coordination   279
- Subordination   280

Revising Sentences   281
- Revising for Clarity   282
- Revising for Variety   290
- Revising for Symmetry   295
- Revising for Economy   297
- Imitate   299

Chapter Twelve Word Choice and Style in Writing   301

Denotation and Connotation   301
- Abstract and Concrete Language   303
- Cliches   304

Consider Your Audience   305
- Jargon   305
- Pretentious Language   306

Euphemisms 307
Sexist Language 308
Style in Writing 309
Tone 309
Voice 309
Personna 309
Casual, Informal, and Formal Styles 311

PART FOUR SPECIAL APPLICATIONS 315

Chapter Thirteen Getting Ready to Write Research Papers 317
Length and Time 317
Plan 317
Develop a Topic 318
Gather Information 319
Interviews 320
Library Resources 322
The Search Strategy 323
Paper References 329
Nonpaper Resources 340
Evaluating Library Resources 341
Plagiarism 342
Note Cards 343
Assimilate Information 345
Annotate Readings 345
Create Dialogues 345
Paraphrase 348
Summarize 350
Documentation 350

Chapter Fourteen Writing Research Papers 353
The First Draft 353
Writing to Show Learning 353
Reconsider the Assignment 354
Consider Audience 354
Develop an Organizational Plan 355
Consider Subheadings 355
Insert Quotations 356
Documentation 358
Placement of Footnotes 359
Sample Endnotes 360
Form Guide for Footnotes 360
APA Parenthetical Citations 362
Form Guide for APA Parenthetical Citations 363

Contents

MLA Parenthetical Citations   363
Form Guide for MLA Parenthetical Citations   364
Bibliography   365
Form Guide for Bibliographies   366
List of Works Cited (APA Style)   366
Form Guide for List of References (APA Style)   367
List of Works Cited (MLA Style)   367
Form Guide for Works Cited (MLA Style)   368
Sample Research Paper (APA Style)   370
Sample Research Paper (MLA Style)   389

Chapter Fifteen **Writing on Demand**   403

The Essay Examination   403
     Getting Ready to Write Essay Exams   404
     Allocate time   404
     Read the Question Carefully   404
     Plan Your Answer   405
     Accommodate Length   406
     Short Answers   407
     Long Answers   408
The Business Letter   409
     Getting Ready to Write a Business Letter   409
     Sample Business Letter   410
     Format   411
The Résumé   413
     Getting Ready to Write a Résumé   413
     Format   413
     Sample Résumé   414

PART FIVE HANDBOOK OF USAGE AND GRAMMAR   417

Perspective on Conventions   418
Parts of Speech   419
     Noun   420
     Pronoun   420
     Verb   421
     Adjective   422
     Adverb   422
     Preposition   422
     Conjunction   422
     Interjection   422
Sentences   422
     Complements   423
     Modifiers   424
     Phrases   425

Contents

        Clauses   426
        Sentence Types   427
        Tense, Number, and Person   428
        Aspect   429
        Mood   429
        Voice   430
        Agreement   430

Usage   431
        Dialect   432
        Puzzling Usages   433

Punctuation   437
        Punctuating to Enclose   437
        Punctuating to Separate   441
        Punctuating to Join   443
        Punctuating to End   444
        Punctuating to Show Omission   445
        Punctuating with the Apostrophe   445

Mechanics   446
        Capitalization   446
        Abbreviations   447
        Hyphens   448
        Italics   449
        Numbers   450

Spelling   451
        Self Assessment   452
        Learning Appropriate Rules   454
        Confusing Homophones   455
        Eliminating Word Confusions   458
        Eliminating Misspelled Words   464

Author and Title Index   467

Subject Index   496

Writing AND Learning

Copyright © Charlie Ott, The National Audubon Society Collection/Photo Researchers, Inc.

PART ONE

AN OVERVIEW

Chapter One

Getting Ready for Writing and Learning

THE first page of a book, perhaps the first day of a new course, the prospect of the first blank sheet of paper sitting before you—it seems a time for new resolve ("This time I'm going to do it right. No more procrastinating for me") or reassurances ("I know I'm a good writer. I always did well in high school"). You may be feeling curious ("How do people write anyway? Is it worth all the trouble?") or anxious ("What if I don't have a gift for writing?") or resigned ("Learning to write better will be good for me. It will help me get higher grades in all my courses"). In the classroom you may eye other students, wondering whether they know as much or as little as you do. You may intend to evaluate the instructor, to determine what this individual will expect of you, whether you will be able to get a good grade, what you will learn from the course. You may look at this textbook, trying to decide whether it contains "the way" to improve your writing.

Looking at other students, at the instructor, or at the text ignores the most important resource—*yourself*. This may be your first writing course or your last, you may be taking this course by choice or by requirement, and the word "writing" may fill you with dread or delight, but what you bring to the course and what you choose to do will determine how much your instructor or this book can help you. Let's take a look at what you bring and what you can do before you actually begin a course on writing.

Examine Habits, Experiences, and Attitudes

Whether you have come to this course directly from high school or after an absence of many years, you bring with you experiences, habits and attitudes that are part of your preparation. You may enjoy writing and look forward to taking composition courses, or you may think of writing instruction as disagreeable medicine to be choked down. A five-page paper on a topic of

An Overview

your choice due anytime before the end of the term may strike you as either terrifying or wonderful. You may have written a great deal for your own pleasure, or your writing may have been limited to what teachers and employers have required of you. You may be a writer who needs the discipline of deadlines in order to produce something, or you may find it easy to complete a piece of writing simply because you care about the topic.

Recollect Experiences

All of these feelings and ways of proceeding derive from the experiences, habits and attitudes you have developed over time. The sources of many of them are probably buried in your subconscious. Becoming more aware of your experiences, habits, and attitudes will make it easier for you to improve your writing. It is easy to follow old patterns without being fully aware of where they come from or how they shape writing. Answering the following questions will help you see how your experiences shape the writer you are today.

1. What is the first thing you can remember writing?
2. How old were you?
3. Did you write this on your own or in school?
4. Did anyone help you?
5. What happened to this first piece of writing?
6. What do you remember writing after it?
7. What is the most important piece of writing you have completed?
8. Has most of your writing been done in school or outside it?
9. What rules have you been taught about writing?
10. Do you remember any writing teacher especially well?
11. Can you describe this person?
12. Did you ever have to write as a punishment? Explain.
13. What, in your opinion, is the best thing you have ever written?
14. What is the worst?
15. Have you ever received any sort of recognition for your writing?
16. Can you recall a time when your feelings about writing changed sharply?

Be Conscious of Writing Habits

As you responded to these questions, you undoubtedly discovered long-forgotten experiences that contribute to your habits and attitudes about writing. You may assume that you have no particular habits of writing, but if you look more closely at what you do, you will probably discover that you have many distinctive habits of writing. Generally, habits remain least visible to the individual practicing them. I once had an instructor who habitually rose to his toes at the end of each sentence, and I am sure he never realized that his students noted the number of rises per lecture more carefully than his statements about history. Your writing habits may be equally invisible to you, but a little thought can make you more aware of them. To bring your habits of writing to a more conscious level, answer the following questions.

Getting Ready for Writing and Learning

1. How often do you write?
2. Where do you usually write?
3. What conditions are necessary for you to write? (quiet, music, food, equipment, what?)
4. When you have a long-term writing assignment how do you handle it? Do you subdivide it into parts, do it all at once, or what?
5. What do you do the night before a writing assignment is due?
6. Do you revise your writing? If yes, when and how?

If you compare your answers with those of other students, you will probably find both similarities and differences. You may begin writing with an elaborate set of rituals such as cleaning off the desk or sharpening pencils while someone else plunges in immediately, writing feverishly until a first draft is completed. Both of you may share the habit of writing while listening to music or of revising with scissors and tape. Interviews with successful professional writers demonstrate that there are no "right" habits for writing. Ernest Hemingway claimed that he wrote best early in the morning while standing. He wore an oversized pair of loafers and stood with the typewriter chest-high opposite him. Joan Didion reports that she sometimes pins selections of her writing on the wall, leaving them for a month or two until she takes them off to rewrite them. Becoming more aware of your own habits of writing can help you strengthen the useful ones and eliminate the ones that keep you from doing your best work.

One habit common to many writers is *procrastination*. Writers always need more time. Think about the last essay exam you took. As the designated time period drew to a close, a few people were still scribbling furiously, and the instructor finally had to wrest their papers away from them as the students for the next class poured into the room. Or recall a paper written outside class: The night before the due date, a flurry of activity probably burst forth, a flurry marked by lost sleep and a typewriter clacking into the night. What you have observed and experienced is typical of most writers, and organizing time helps minimize the pressures associated with writing.

Experts in time management claim that procrastination results from fear, and if you tend to put off writing assignments, you may want to consider fear's role in your actions. Does writing make you anxious? Are you afraid to begin because you know that you cannot write very well? Or do you fear that even your very best efforts may not be sufficient? An exceptionally honest student wrote this about his delaying tactics:

```
    Most of my papers are begun the night before they
are due. It is not that I don't have time to get
started earlier, but the late start gives me an excuse
for writing a bad paper. I can always say that I got a
low grade because I did the paper on the last night
and didn't have time to make it good.
```

An Overview

The surest way to confirm your anxieties about writing is to procrastinate on a writing assignment; the hastily written paper will undoubtedly be returned with negative comments and a low grade, which combine to make you feel even more fearful of writing.

If you procrastinate writing and if your procrastination stems from anxiety about writing, you may take some comfort in the fact that you are not alone in either. Many writers confess to cleaning closets and scrubbing floors before they begin to write. Often this procrastination can be helpful because it allows the writer to think about the writing task, to incubate ideas. Nearly all writers find it hard to start writing because a blank page stands at the beginning of every writing task. Having achieved success with one piece of writing provides no guarantee (although it can help) of success with another.

If you have difficulty getting started with writing, you may want to consider ways of breaking your habit. These are admittedly contrived, but they have worked for a number of students:

- Set an artificial deadline, pretending that a paper is due in a few days before the actual deadline so that you will have time to put it away and look at it with some perspective.
- Write a draft immediately, beginning as soon as the assignment is given, long before you understand the topic or what you want to say about it.
- Break the writing task into very small parts, so small that no one task will overwhelm you.
- Make a balance sheet that lists "Why I am putting off writing" on one side and "Benefits of getting writing done" on the other, and list everything you can think of for each category: the results will usually speak for themselves.
- Find out, from close observation of your own writing habits, when your "prime time" for writing is; it varies among individuals, but find out when you write most easily, and protect that time for writing.
- Pay close attention to how you use your time; you may even want to make a time log for a day, and note what you do within each half-hour period. The results of that log may help you find more time for writing.

Time alone cannot produce effective writing, and there are many occasions when time is arbitrarily limited, as in an essay exam or an in-class writing assignment. However, conscious organization of time, like prewriting and taking account of the general context of writing, can make writing less mysterious and more like something that you can control.

Assess Attitudes Toward Writing

As you look at your responses to the preceding questions, you may see some habits that you would like to change. Perhaps you do not always want to begin writing assignments on the night before they are due or perhaps you would like to revise your writing more frequently and extensively. A closer look at your attitudes toward writing may help you understand—and change—

Getting Ready for Writing and Learning

some of your habits. The following statements deal with your attitudes toward writing. Indicate the degree to which each statement applies to you by writing (1) strongly disagree, (2) disagree, (3) uncertain, (4) agree, or (5) strongly agree with the statement. Even though some of the statements seem repetitious, try to respond to all of them.

1. I avoid writing.
2. I have no fear of my writing being evaluated.
3. I look forward to writing down my ideas.
4. I am afraid of writing essays when I know they will be evaluated.
5. Taking a composition course is a very frightening experience.
6. Handing in a composition makes me feel good.
7. My mind seems to go blank when I start to work on a composition.
8. Expressing ideas through writing seems to be a waste of time.
9. I would enjoy submitting my writing to magazines to be considered for publication.
10. I like to write my ideas down.
11. I feel confident in my ability to clearly express my ideas in writing.
12. I like to have my friends read what I have written.
13. I'm nervous about writing.
14. People seem to enjoy what I write.
15. I enjoy writing.
16. I never seem to be able to clearly write down my ideas.
17. Writing is a lot of fun.
18. I expect to do poorly in composition classes even before I enter them.
19. I'm no good at writing.
20. Discussing my writing with others is an enjoyable experience.
21. I have a terrible time organizing my ideas in a composition course.
22. When I hand in a composition, I know I am going to do poorly.
23. It's easy for me to write good compositions.
24. I don't think I write as well as most people.
25. I don't like my compositions to be evaluated.
26. I like seeing my thoughts on paper.

As you can probably tell from these statements, your responses indicate something about your apprehensions regarding writing, To compute your score, follow these steps:

- Reverse the values of your responses to statements numbered 2, 3, 6, 9, 10, 11, 12, 14, 15, 17, 19, 20, and 23. That is, if you responded with a 5, change it to a 3; if you responded with a 4 change it to a 2; change 3 to 1; 2 to 4; and 1 to 5.
- When you have completed the reversals, add the totals of all your responses (the highest possible total is 130).

Higher scores indicate a higher degree of apprehension about writing, but computing your score is less important then considering how your attitudes toward writing influence your habits and experiences. If, for example, your

An Overview

score indicates a high degree of writing apprehension, you might consider whether you have habits (such as putting off work) that contribute to apprehension. Perhaps you can identify an experience—a particularly negative comment by a teacher, for example—that makes you feel apprehensive about writing. Becoming conscious of the attitudes underlying your habits and experiences will prepare you to get the most out of this book and to become a better writer.

Think of Writing as a Process

If you bring some anxiety to writing, it may be because you think you don't have a "gift" for writing. Many people assume that writing ability is genetically determined, like the ability to curl up the sides of your tongue, and that the world is populated by "born" writers and the other people. Actually, anyone can learn to write clear and effective prose, and the first step is recognizing that most writing isn't done in one sitting; it is a process. Specifically, it is a process of moving from writing that aids learning to writing that shows learning. In the early stages of a writing project, most of your writing aids learning. It is writing for which you are the primary audience. You write for yourself. You collect information and ideas, explain them to yourself, and write drafts that help you discover which aspects you wish to emphasize. As you gain control over your material and decide what you want to say, you move toward writing to show learning. This part of the process gives more attention to organization, coherence, audience, conventions of standard written English, and it ends in a finished piece of writing.

Occasionally writing consists almost entirely of writing to show learning. Essay exams, in-class writing assignments, and other testing situations leave little time for writing to learn. They insist that you move immediately to demonstrating learning in writing. Even in these situations, however, it is possible to do some writing for yourself prior to demonstrating learning in writing. And a regular habit of writing to learn will make it easier when you must move immediately to demonstrating learning with writing.

Writing letters to friends, for example, is almost always "writing to show learning," but if you want to see the learning/show learning relationship, try writing a letter in draft and copying it two days later. You will almost always change something to "show" learning better.

WRITING TO LEARN

The earliest part of writing does not involve phrasing the perfect first sentence for an opening paragraph. It is a messy business of making lists, scrawling notes on the back of a napkin when ideas occur to you, using various procedures to learn more about your subject, and frequently it does not involve writing at all. When you know you will be writing about a given issue, your mind usually goes to work long before you sit down with a piece of paper. You may begin thinking about ways to approach your subject, finding additional information, or talking with a friend about your plans for writing. You may also go to the library and find resources or you may locate and interview an expert on your topic, taking notes as you do so. You may jot a few notes into your journal or play with an organizational plan, but this writing will not be intended for anyone but you to read because it is part of the way you write to learn.

Even when you begin drafting, the process of writing to learn continues. Many writers have commented on how they learn as they write. Eudora Welty claims: "Writing... is one way of discovering sequence in experience, of stumbling upon cause and effect in the happenings of a writer's own life. This has been the case with me." William Stafford says of writing: "It's like any discovery job; you don't know what's going to happen until you try it." Robert Tucker, a student, explained his experience with a research paper in history this way:

```
    It was through the writing, the physical and mental
act of putting down my thoughts, that I began, in a
haphazard manner, to get a grasp on my subject. It was
also through the act of writing that I began to dis-
cover new dimensions of my topic, new dimensions which
ultimately led to a major change of subject. In this
way my subject, initially inspired by an eccentric
customs collector, grew into an examination of the
economic motivations in the settlement of the Puget
Sound. This rather significant jump was to a large
part achieved through the act of writing.
```

Although they express it differently, all of these writers share the view that writing aids learning, that writing leads to the discovery of new ideas and to seeing new relationships.

Writing to Show Learning

Writing to learn makes it possible to show learning in writing. Much of the writing you will do in college and at work—essay exams, reports, term papers, briefs, lab reports, memos—will ask you to demonstrate what you have learned. The success of that demonstration will depend on writing to learn in the terms already described, but it will also depend on revising your writing to show your knowledge to best advantage. When you have begun to see what you want to say (frequently this becomes clear at the very end of a first draft), it is time to start thinking about how to present your ideas to others. It is time to start thinking about revising.

Revising can be described as the most important (and frequently most neglected) part of writing. Novelist Doris Lessing has said that many mediocre novels miss greatness because authors are unwilling or unable to revise them.

An Overview

James Michener explains the importance of revision this way: "I have never thought of myself as a good writer. Anyone who wants reassurance of that should read one of my first drafts. But I'm one of the world's great revisers."

Revising takes many forms. It means thinking about the audience for your writing. Who will read your work and why? It also means developing an overall plan for the writing that will make your ideas clear. Often the organization of a first draft will reflect your process of discovery, but that may not be the best way to present your ideas to someone else. A chronological account of your visit to a welfare agency, for example, may not be the most effective way to organize a sociology paper on public assistance programs. Revising also gives attention to the style of language, to the structure of paragraphs, and to the shape of sentences. Finally, it shades into concern for the conventions of standard written English, for spelling, punctuation, capitalization, and the other forms that show learning to its best advantage.

Writing to learn and writing to show learning are never, of course, entirely separate processes. Writers frequently consider issues of demonstrating learning while writing to learn, and writing to show learning often leads to new understandings. In drafting, for example, you may start thinking about what an audience will need to know in order to understand your point and change a word or a phrase to make your meaning clearer. But understanding the differences between writing to learn and writing to show learning is central to seeing writing as a process.

Read Like a Writer

In one sense you have been preparing for this course since you learned to read because reading contributes directly to writing. At the moment you learned to symbolize a barking four-legged animal by the letters D-O-G, you entered a world where letters carry meaning. In learning a meaning for D-O-G, you gained the capacity to enter worlds not limited by time and space. Reading enables you to participate in events of the past, to share the ideas and experiences of people long dead, and to travel to distant parts of the globe. Reading also enables writing because it involves you in making meaning.

You make meaning on many levels when you read. Much of this happens so quickly you may not be aware of it, but as you read, you predict the next syllable, the next word, the next phrase, the next sentence, the next paragraph in a continuing process of making meaning. Seeing the letters S-L-I-C may lead you to predict that the word is "slick" but if the final letter is "e," you quickly change your mind. In a similar way, you postulate meanings for groups of words, continually shifting as you encounter new information, and developing an ever larger sense of what the entire selection means. When you were younger, perhaps you read a book that asked you to make decisions as you went along ("If you think the soldier took the sword turn to page 54" "If you think the dragon flew out of the cave turn to page 72"). Books like these make explicit the processes of predicting, responding, and collecting that enable readers to make meaning, and these same processes occur in writing.

As you write a word or sentence you reach ahead to the next one, making predictions about where your ideas will take you. At the same time you read back over what you have written, and your response to it helps you shape what you will write next. These processes of predicting and responding enable you to collect an ever-developing idea of what you mean. This continuing development explains why you so frequently know what you really want to write about when you write the last sentence of your first draft. Not only does reading resemble writing, it also aids writing directly. As you read, you absorb a great deal of knowledge about how language works, knowledge that helps you when your writing poses questions of usage, decisions about organization, issues of style, and the other choices that emerge every time you write.

The reading you have already done can help you write, but you can use reading to greater effect by becoming a more active composer through predicting, responding, and collecting.

Predict

When you begin a book or chapter or article start by trying to figure out what each might be about before you start reading the first page. Look at the title and decide what it tells you about the work that follows. Look at the table of contents (for a book) or the headings (for an article or chapter). Turn to the end and see what conclusions appear or what sources are listed. When you begin reading the first pages, compare your initial predictions with what you actually find, and continue your pattern of predicting. As you finish one paragraph or one section, try, before you continue, to decide what will come next, and compare your prediction with what you find.

Respond

Talk back to your reading. This does not mean just highlighting or underlining important ideas, although that may be helpful. Write your responses in the margins. Your marginalia should include questions ("How does this point fit with what was said on page 32?"), observations ("This description is like Schwartz's"), criticisms ("Piaget's theory doesn't support this idea"), and anything else that occurs to you as you read. Feel free to draw arrows across pages, to make diagrams, to use any form that records your conversation with the text. For too long, many of us have feared making marks in books, and composing in reading has been diminished as a result.

Collect

Pay attention to your developing ideas of what the whole book or chapter or article means, noting the places where you were mistaken as well as the places where you could see clearly what the next move would be. At the same time, think of your reading as a resource you can draw upon for writing and start collecting pieces of language that will be useful to you. If you see an especially

An Overview

fine turn of phrase, make note of it; perhaps you will be able to incorporate it into your own writing later. Notice how other writers make connections between ideas and add to your collection of transitions. Look at opening paragraphs by two different authors and notice how they establish their individual voices immediately. Observe how word order can indicate a writer's perspective on a subject (subordination such as "Although these incidents were important," tells you that what the writer's main point comes after the comma). Pay attention to endings and see how other writers draw their ideas together.

Look at Previous Writing

Over the years you have written and this experience helps prepare you for the writing ahead. One of the ways to keep track of your progress is to look at where you have been. Growth charts on the back of the kitchen door, childhood pictures in a family album, and once fashionable clothes that look comical in the light of current styles—in these and many other ways we look back at our former selves. In the same way, looking at what you composed last week, last month, last year, or many years ago provides perspective on your development as a writer. Perhaps you or your parents have saved samples of your childhood drawing or writing. If you look at them carefully, you may see the beginnings of patterns that still characterize your writing today. Perhaps your drawings emphasized small mechanical devices and you find considerable attention to detail in your more recent writing, or perhaps your early writing consisted of lists (of friends or favorite toys or, even, shopping lists), and you find lists useful in the beginning stages of current writing projects.

If you have samples of more recent writing, look at them to see what you can say about yourself as a writer. Does your writing indicate that you need to give more attention to the mechanics of spelling, punctuation, and usage? Put large diagonal marks between sentences and see what they show about sentence length. Are most of your sentences the same length or do you vary length? Here is a sample from Craig Jackman's paper:

```
    Both of them decided to hit the hay early. / One
o'clock came quickly. / Then the plan went into effect.
/ Jeff, Chris, Cal and Alex crept into Mike's room as
quiet as mice. / Then Alex clamped his hand on Mike's
mouth. / The rest of them secured his hands and feet.
/ Quickly they hauled his squirming body outside. /
Mike was finally able to yell for help when they threw
him in the back of the truck. / But then it was too
late.
```

Once he had analyzed his own writing this way Craig realized that he needed to vary the length of his sentences more.

Getting Ready for Writing and Learning

In addition, Craig saw that he needed to introduce more variation in sentence patterns because most of them followed a straight SUBJECT-VERB pattern. What about variation in your sentence patterns? Do you use a mixture of types of sentences or do you have a favorite? Look at your introductions and conclusions. What can you say about your strategies for beginning and ending writing? Read a few of your paragraphs aloud and then describe the voice you hear.

Keep a Writing Folder

If you have not been in the habit of keeping copies of your writing, begin now. Establish a folder in which you keep copies of everything you produce for each writing project—notes, lists, drafts, discarded sections, and successive approximations of the final piece. When you hand a paper in to an instructor, make a copy for yourself and add it to a folder. Not only will this protect you against lost papers, but it will give you a new perspective on your own writing. By the end of this term or this year, you will be able to look back at a substantial amount of your own writing, and in the process of looking back you will see how you have developed as a writer.

Start a Journal

If you have ever kept a diary or journal, you bring another form of preparation to writing. You may have simply recorded the events of the day or you may have written about issues that disturbed you, but your journal contributed to your writing because it extended your resources beyond what you could retrieve from your mind at a given moment. Journals also provide a place to record the language of others, a place to practice writing, to experiment, and to learn. Now is an excellent time to start or restart a journal.

Record

Memory, as you have no doubt noticed, is fallible. You may have a brilliant idea while riding the subway, walking across campus, or eating lunch. It may be inspiration you are sure you will be able to use, but if you don't jot it down quickly it will probably be impossible for you to recall it when you want it. Like facts that you crammed into your head before a test, good ideas for writing fade quickly. If you develop the habit of capturing them in a journal you will increase your resources for writing.

Journals can also serve as storehouses for the language of others. When you read like a writer, you will start finding bits of language—a turn of phrase, a fine sentence, a telling description—that you want to remember. Perhaps this bit of language can serve as a model or perhaps it can be incorporated into something you write. If you preserve it you will have it when you need it, and a journal can be an excellent storehouse for memorable language. It doesn't matter whether you clip and paste, xerox, or copy by hand, the crucial thing is to record language that strikes you.

An Overview

PRACTICE

If you haven't done any extended writing for a while—for a summer or for a number of years—you may feel a certain stiffness, not just muscular but mental. Writing regularly in a journal (remember the French *jour* meaning "day") will help you write more easily. Even if you have done a fair amount of writing recently, daily entries in a journal will warm you to the tasks set by your composition instructor. Like calisthenics, journal writing may not always be significant, but it exercises faculties that facilitate other forms of writing.

EXPERIMENT

Good writers, like good athletes or good artists, push against the boundaries of the old—the old style, the old forms. Perhaps you are not in the habit of writing sentences with several modifiers following the main clause, as in: *He dipped his hand in the bichloride solution and shook them, a quick shake, fingers down, like the fingers of a pianist above the keys.* Journals offer a safe place to experiment, to take risks, to extend your repertoire as a writer. Without this kind of pushing against boundaries, it will be too easy for your writing to settle into comfortable but old and tired patterns.

LEARN

Perhaps most important, writing in a journal can help you learn. Writing helps you assimilate ideas and find out where you still have questions. To see this for yourself, go to a lecture class or read a chapter in a book taking notes in your usual way. When the class is over or when you have finished the chapter, turn to your journal and write an explanation of what you have just learned, summarizing main points and explaining important details. You will probably find that what seemed easy to follow in reading or listening is much harder to reproduce in your journal. It is easy to confuse recognition with assimilation and assume that because we can follow a lecture or a chapter in a book that we actually understand the material. Writing in a journal guarantees that you will not confuse passive reception with active learning.

Locate the Best Place and Time

Looking at what you have written will lead you to understand how you write best. Although there are some general similarities in most people's writing processes—similarities that will be explored in this book—there are also individual differences. Some people make extensive written preparation while others do more preparing in their heads. Rituals such as sharpening pencils or getting a cup of tea may be essential to you and not matter at all to someone else. You may write best in a crowded room under the protection of background noise, or you may need a quiet place where you will not be interrupted. Although it is true that you can write anywhere—standing in

Getting Ready for Writing and Learning

line, riding a bus, or eating lunch—try to find the place where you can do your best work.

At the same time that you can identify the places where you write most comfortably, start paying attention to the time of day that is most productive for you. Some writers work best early in the morning before they begin daily activities, and others report that they do their best writing late at night after a full day of thinking about what they will say. Some writers attend to different parts of the process during different times of the day, drafting in the morning, for example, and saving editing for evenings. Your best time may be morning, afternoon, or evening, but whenever it is, try to arrange a schedule that protects it from interruptions.

Gather Writing Tools

If your typewriter ribbon has given out at midnight the night before a paper is due, you already know the importance of having an adequate supply of writing tools on hand. You can have this experience or you can collect writing tools now. If your drafts are handwritten, be sure you have plenty of paper (do you prefer lined or blank?) and pens (or do you prefer pencils? What about erasers?). If you allow yourself a generous supply of materials you may find that your drafts feel less strained and squeezed. If you use a typewriter for final drafts, be sure you have an extra ribbon of the same color, plenty of typing paper, and correction fluid (unless you use erasable paper). You will probably also want tape and scissors for cut-and-paste revisions. If you use a word processor, buy an extra disk along with a spare wheel/ribbon for your printer, and be sure you have an adequate supply of computer paper.

GET A DICTIONARY

Tools for writing include books as well as materials for inscribing words. Writers use a variety of reference books, but the essential one is a dictionary. Not only can a dictionary tell you the correct spelling of a word, it can also provide information on parts of speech, pronunciation, forms, definition, level of usage, related forms, synonyms, and etymology. For a full explanation of what a dictionary entry contains and how to use it, turn to the Handbook at the back of this book.

Examine This Book

If you read this book like a writer, you will begin by examining the Table of Contents to see what is included; you will notice the Index and Handbook in the back, you will see the questions and suggestions on the end papers, and you will scan a few chapters to see what they contain. You will look at the headings, the exercises, the excerpts of writing, and the lists of questions and suggestions. As you look at the Contents, you will see that this book is divided into five parts, and you will determine what makes each part different from the others. Finally, you will read the Preface at the front of this book.

Copyright © Grant Haist, The National Audubon Society Collection/Photo Researchers, Inc.

Chapter Two

Discovery: Writing to Learn

A five-page paper on character development in *The Great Gatsby* is due on Friday.

Explain the influence of the Stamp Act on the American Revolution.

Write a research report on some aspect of kinship in these groups.

You have received or will receive many assignments like these, assignments that ask you to demonstrate what you have learned. Most required writing in college serves to "test" your knowledge; it asks you to write to show learning. Writing outside college often requires the same demonstration. Effective reports, briefs, and memoranda demand that you understand certain ideas and convey your understanding through writing.

Many people faced with a writing task sit down immediately and try to compose the first sentence. Usually they stare at a blank piece of paper, chew their fingernails, and become more and more anxious because the first sentence simply won't come. They write a few words, scratch them out, crumple up the paper and begin again—and again, and again, and again. A few sessions like this convince many individuals that they lack a gift for writing, that inability to produce fine prose at one sitting means one simply is not a writer.

Prewriting An alternative to this defeatist conclusion is to recognize the value of writing to learn as a prelude to writing to show learning. The very earliest stages of writing to learn can be called *prewriting*. That is, writing that precedes an actual draft. It provides a way of easing into the task of writing without the pressure of having to produce a draft immediately.

The prewriting phase of writing uses writing as a means of exploring a

An Overview

subject, of discovering various approaches, of seeing things in a new way, and of finding contradictions. The prewriting phase of writing to learn also fosters getting a subject right for yourself, not settling for someone else's ideas or interpretations. The essayist E. B. White has explained the importance of putting a subject in your own terms:

New York
April 20, 1956

Dear Miss Marks:

I'm very grateful for your letter. My theory of communication is different from yours. I think there is only one frequency and that the whole problem is to establish communication with one's self, and, that being done, everyone else is tuned in. In other words, if a writer succeeds in communicating with a reader, I think it is simply because he has been trying (with some success) to get in touch with himself—to clarify the reception. . . .

Sincerely,

E. B. White

In the process of communicating with one's self about a subject, ideas begin to emerge, the very ideas that remain so elusive when one starts too soon with the first sentence. "All there is to writing is having ideas," wrote Robert Frost. "To learn to write is to learn to have ideas." If you have struggled over a first sentence, you know how difficult "having ideas" can be. When prewriting relieves the pressure of producing the first sentence immediately, writers can concentrate on communicating with themselves about a subject, and with "having ideas."

Prewriting, then, can help you learn in these ways:

- Understand your subject better by putting it in your own words.
- Generate new ideas about your subject.
- Express what you think about your subject.

Journals

Journals provide a place to preserve prewriting. It is easy to undervalue the prewriting phase of writing to learn and to discard all the phrases, observations, and ideas scrawled in the process of communicating with one's self. After all, these unfinished pieces of writing will not be handed in for a grade; they will not become part of a polished report or essay. Yet, these rough sketches and half-shaped thoughts are the material out of which good writing develops, and they need to be preserved.

The poet Theodore Roethke described a journal as a *greenhouse* because it is a place where ideas can grow. The prewriting phase of writing to learn can take many forms, but keeping all of them in a journal enables you to go back and develop them so they can grow. Because journals ought to preserve writing, they are best kept in bound books rather than spiral notebooks from which pages can be torn easily. Because they do not make it easy to tear pages out, bound books retain all the false starts and half-developed thoughts that contribute to growing ideas.

A writer's journal is not a diary of daily events. Rather, it preserves thoughts and impressions significant to the writer. The writing in journals can take many forms, among them *collections* of others' words, phrases, or longer writings that are meaningful or appealing; *imitations* that attempt to capture the style of another person's writing; *experiments* with different forms of writing; *observations* about people, places, and events that the writer wants to remember and perhaps use later; and *explanations* to one's self that help clarify some experience.

COLLECT

Perhaps you have collected photographs, souvenirs, postcards, or programs of events you attended. These collections help you recall your past by representing particular places or persons or events. At the same time they may lead you to new insights about your earlier years.

You might, for example, look at a photograph taken when you were very young and allow it to take you back to that time and place as the author of this journal entry did:

```
    I am wearing the crepe paper costume that won
first prize in the local children's parade. The mono-
chrome print does not show the pink and white of my
hoop skirt and parasol, but I remember the colors
along with the awkward feeling of walking in that wire
contraption while holding an umbrella over my head. At
the same time I marvel that my New Hampshire grand-
mother, a reserved and severe woman, created this
southern belle get-up. There must have been an extrava-
gant and uninhibited side to her that I missed as I
grew up across the street from her prim clapboard
house.
```

Like collectors of bottle caps or coins, writers are always on the look-out for an interesting bit of language. Perhaps it is an unusual *word*, one you have never seen before and would like to remember. Journal entries like the ones that follow can help you preserve words you may want to use later.

Sclaff: A golf term for hitting the ground instead of the ball (I remember learning that term on the greens).

An Overview

Bordereau: A detailed accounting (a word I read in a book recently).
Hippocampus: A Greek word for sea horse (I don't remember where I found that word, but I like its sound).

Language collections in journals can include *phrases or sentences* that strike you as unusual or interesting. Here are some examples:

"*the two long men*"— a phrase my daughter used years ago to describe her father and another six-footer.
"*dip your lights*"—seen on a traffic sign in Hong Kong.
"*Time flies like an arrow and fruit flies like a banana*"—heard someone say this in class.

Journals can also contain collections of longer pieces of language—sayings, graffiti, quotations from reading, and other selections that you would like to keep. The following excerpts were recorded in a writer's journal:

```
   --to my mind it is a mistake to think of creative
activity as something unusual. I hold that the creative
activity is normal to all living things. Creation is
the finding of order in what was disorderly, and this
is a characteristically human activity. (I copied this
from Jacob Bronowski's A Sense of the Future because I
thought I might quote it later.)

   We are always saying farewell in this world, always
standing on the edge of loss, attempting to retrieve
some meaning, some human meaning from the silence,
something which was precious and is gone. (I found
this in Adlai Stevenson's eulogy for Eleanor Roosevelt
and copied it because I was mourning the death of a
friend and these words expressed some of what I felt.)
```

Longer selections of language collected in journals can remind you of different styles, ideas you would like to think about, or they may be passages you want to quote in your own writing. Here, for example, is a selection from *The Right Stuff* by Tom Wolfe:

All these people with their smiles of sympathy didn't ask for much. A few words here and there would do fine. *Do good work.* Nevertheless, that didn't make these public appearances any better for Cooper. He was in the same boat with Gus and Deke, who was also no Franklin D. Roosevelt when it came to public appearances. Everybody latched on to you during these trips, congressmen and businessmen and directors and presidents of this and that. Every hotshot in town wanted to be next to *the astronaut.* For the first ten or fifteen minutes it was enough for them to breathe the same air you breathed and occupy the same space as your famous body. But then they began looking at you . . . and waiting . . . Waiting for what? Well, dummy!—waiting for you to say a few words! They wanted something hot! If you were one of the seven greatest pilots and seven bravest men in America, then obviously you must be fascinating to listen to. *Riveting*—that was what you were supposed to be. A few war stories, man! And you would sit there with the clutch in, furiously trying to think of something, anything, and it would make you gloomier and gloomier. Your light no longer shone 'round about you.

(I copied this passage because it demonstrates Wolfe's ability to capture a conversational voice in his writing. The processes of copying it and reading it aloud help me see ways of using more rhythms of speech in writing.)

E X E R C I S E

1. Find a phrase or a sentence—a sign or a bumper sticker or an advertising slogan or some graffiti—that you like and copy it into your journal with a brief explanation of why you want to keep it.
2. Select a passage from your reading and copy it into your journal. It can be from a newspaper, a book, or a magazine article. Write yourself a note about why you like it.

IMITATE

When you were a child, you probably delighted in wearing adults' shoes. As you clomped around with your feet flapping inside, you may also have taken pleasure in measuring your feet against the grown-up standard. Trying to use someone else's language is like wearing someone else's shoes. If done for an extended time, it can be crippling to limp around in another's words, but as play it can be delightful. Imitation is a form of walking in another's language, and it can help you discover more about writing.

One way to do an imitation is to select a passage by a published author and follow the same sentence patterns to write about an entirely different subject. Here is an excerpt from Mark Twain's *Adventures of Huckleberry Finn*:

> It was a mighty nice family, and a mighty nice house, too. I hadn't seen no house out in the country before that was so nice and had so much style. It didn't have an iron latch on the front door, nor a wooden one with a buckskin string, but a brass knob to turn, the same as houses in town. There warn't no bed in the parlor, nor a sign of a bed; but heaps of parlors in towns has beds in them. There was a big fireplace that was bricked on the bottom, and the bricks was kept clean and red by pouring water on them and scrubbing them with another brick; sometimes they wash them over with red water-paint that they call Spanish-brown, same as they do in town. They had a big brass dog-irons that could hold up a saw-log. There was a clock on the middle of the mantlepiece, with a picture of a town painted on the bottom half of the glass front, and a round place in the middle of it for the sun, and you could

see the pendulum swinging behind it. It was beautiful to hear that clock tick; and sometimes when one of these peddlers had been along and scoured her up and got her in good shape, she would start in and strike a hundred and fifty before she got tuckered out. They wouldn't a took any money for her.

Here is an imitation of the Twain passage using McDonald's as the subject:

```
                McDonald's Takes Me In
    It was a mighty nice burger and a mighty nice
rest'raunt too. I never seen no rest'raunt in the
country before that was so nice and had so much style.
It didn't have no little wood sign in front nor a
ordinary lamp post, but these big gold arches that let
everybody know where it set. There was a big counter
that was smooth on top and the surface was kept clean
and white by spraying blue water on it and swishing it
around with a little sponge; sometimes one of the
girls in the fancy red cap opened up the straw-spitter
or the napkin-maker and looked it over. They had big
machines that lighted up and went buzzing and ringing
and had a drawerful of money. There was a sign in the
middle of the wall behind the counter with a picture
of this clown painted on one side by the 'scription of
"Ronald" and you could see the menu beside him. It was
grand to see that clown smile, and sometimes when one
of these girls had been waiting on a young'un standing
in front of that counter, she would hand him a placemat
she must've made special with that clown drawn on it.
They wouldn't a took no money for that clown.
```

As you can see, this imitation closely followed Twain's sentence patterns and the general tone of his prose, even though the topic was very different.

But the topics for imitation need not be literary. A student in computer sciences selected this passage from *Another Roadside Attraction* by Tom Robbins:

> His voice is like a steel dog barking bricks.
> I have never heard the voice before but I know instantly to whom it belongs. Forty Hell's Angels roared up my colon. Parked their bikes in my diaphragm. Swaggered into my esophagus, ordered beer from my larynx and began shoving my tongue around.

Here is the imitation she wrote:

Discovery: Writing to Learn

> The sound of the computer was like a mechanical hummingbird with nowhere to go.
> I have seen very few computers before, but I sensed at what purpose this one was aimed. The program was typed into the memory. Computed its values in some obscure microchip. Wandered back to my terminal. Creaked and coughed from my keyboard, and began printing my results.

The value of imitation does not lie in perfection. The authors of the two examples above were not completely satisfied with what they had written, but both learned about writing through borrowing another writer's language.

E X E R C I S E

Here are some selections written in varying styles. Try writing imitations of them, following their sentence patterns and general style as closely as you can.

On an afternoon in the spring of 1938, foreseeing a change in my life, I rode the subway down to Cortland Street, visited Peter Henderson's seed store, and came away with a mixed order of flower and vegetable seeds. The bill was $19. Peter Henderson is long gone, and times have changed—but not the warm, receptive earth, yielding to the advances of the sun. Today, with so much wrong with the planet, with everyone discouraged and uneasy and some desperate, almost the only things that can dispell the gloom for me are the bright and fradulent pictures in a seed catalogue and the glad cry that issues from a box of day-old chicks arriving on an April morning from the hatchery. Our 1975 orders went off in the mail three weeks ago. The seeds came to $67, up from $19. A baby chick this spring will cost me thirty-three cents, up five cents from the 1974 chick. Even so, there is hardly a better buy around: the seed, the exploded egg, the perennial promise that they hold. In the years that have intervened since 1938, we have not missed a springtime of this wild dreaming and scheming. We are hooked and are making no attempt to kick the habit.

—E. B. White, *Essays*, 1977

We have been praising this restaurant for years, and in many ways it is the model of fine restaurants in the Northwest: an owner who does all the cooking and is an assertive, omnipresent personality; a menu that ranges throughout European cuisines (the chef is Czech) and prices; a sure way with fresh, local ingredients; decor that is minimalist without being ostentatiously so; refined simplicity all around. In some moods, particularly when repairing here after a disappointing visit to the latest new restaurant, this can seem like the only truly fine, absolutely reliable dining spot north of San Francisco. (A foolish exaggeration, to be sure.)

—David Brewster, *The Best Places*

An Overview

> Working a typewriter by touch, like riding a bicycle or strolling on a path, is best done by not giving it a glancing thought. Once you do, your fingers fumble and hit the wrong keys. To do things involving practiced skills, you need to turn loose the systems of muscles and nerves responsible for each maneuver, place them on their own, and stay out of it. There is no real loss of authority in this, since you get to decide whether to do the thing or not, and you can intervene and embellish the technique any time you like; if you want to ride a bicycle backward, or walk with an eccentric loping gait giving a little skip every fourth step, whistling at the same time, you can do that. But if you concentrate your attention on the details, keeping in touch with each muscle, thrusting yourself at the last moment by sticking out the other foot in time to break the fall, you will end up immobilized, vibrating with fatigue.
>
> —Lewis Thomas, *Lives of a Cell*

A more mechanical form of imitation is to create an actual diagram of the language being used and fill the frame with language from another topic. A frame can be created by taking out all the substantive words and indicating the type and form of words to be inserted in the blanks. Here is a pattern frame of the imitated Robbins passage:

```
_____   _____   _____ like a _____   _____  _____
(possessive pronoun)   (noun)    (verb)         (adjective)  (noun)   (-ing verb)
_____   _____ have never _____ the _____ before but _____
 (noun)    (pronoun)                (verb)      (noun)                (pronoun)
_____  instantly to _____   _____   _____ Forty _____
 (verb)                 (pronoun)    (pronoun)    (verb)          (adjective)
_____  _____ up _____   _____   _____ Parked _____
 (noun)    (verb)      (possessive pronoun)       (noun)          (possessive pronoun)
_____ in _____   _____ . _____ into _____
 (noun)     (possessive pronoun)  (noun)   (past tense verb)    (possessive
_____   _____ , _____   _____ from _____
 pronoun)    (noun)     (past tense verb)  (noun)       (possessive pronoun)
_____ and began _____   _____   _____ around.
 (noun)              (-ing verb)  (possessive pronoun)  (noun)
```

EXERCISE

Write an imitation of the Robbins selection using this pattern frame.

Still another way to imitate is to rewrite familiar material in the style of an author whose work you know well. This is more difficult task, but if you choose an author with a very distinctive style, the results can be amusing, as the following versions of "The Three Bears" by Dan Greenberg illustrate:

Catch Her in the Oatmeal

If you actually want to hear about it, what I'd better do is I'd better warn you right now that you aren't going to believe it. I mean it's a true *story* and all, but it still sounds sort of phony.

Discovery: Writing to Learn

Anyway, my name is Goldie Lox. It's sort of a boring name, but my parents said that when I was born I had this very blond hair and all. Actually I was born bald. I mean how many babies get born with blond hair? None. I mean I've *seen* them, and they're all wrinkled and red and slimy and everything. And bald. And then all the phonies have to come around and tell you he's as cute as a bug's ear. A bug's ear, boy that really kills me. You ever seen a bug's ear? What's cute about a bug's ear, for Christ's sake. Nothing, that's what.

So, like I was saying, I always seem to be getting into these very stupid situations. Like this time I was telling you about. Anyway, I was walking through the forest and all when I see this very interesting house. A *house* you wouldn't think anybody would be living way the hell out in the *goddam forest*, but they were. No one was home or anything and the door was open, so I walked in. I figured what I'd do is I'd probably horse around until the guys that lived there came home and maybe asked me to stay for dinner or something. Some people think they *have* to ask you to stay for dinner even if they *hate* you. Also I didn't exactly feel like going home and getting asked a lot of lousy questions. I mean that's all I ever seem to do.

Anyway, while I was waiting I sort of sampled some of this stuff they had on the table that tasked like oatmeal. It would have made you puke, I mean it. Then something very spooky started happening. I started getting dizzier than hell. I figured I'd feel better if I could just rest for a while. Sometimes if you eat something like lousy oatmeal you can feel better if you just rest for a while, so I sat down. That's when the goddam *chair* breaks in half. No kidding, you start feeling lousy and some stupid chair is going to break on you every time. I'm not kidding. Anyway I finally found the crummy bedroom and I lay down on this very tiny bed. I was really depressed.

I don't know how long I was asleep or anything, but all of a sudden I hear this very strange voice say, "Someone's been sleeping in *my* sack, for chrissake, and there she is!" So I open my eyes and here at the foot of the bed are these three crummy *bears*. Bears! I swear to God. By that time I was *really* feeling depressed. There's nothing more depressing than waking up and finding three *bears* talking about you, I mean.

So I didn't stay around and shoot the breeze with them or anything. If you want to know the truth. I sort of ran out of there like a madman or something. I do that quite a little when I'm depressed like that.

On the way home, though, I got to figuring. What probably happened is these bears wandered in when they smelled this oatmeal and all. Probably bears *like* oatmeal, I don't know. And the voice I heard when I woke up was probably something I dreamt.

So that's the story.

I wrote it all up once as a theme in school, but my crummy teacher said it was too whimsical. Whimsical. That killed me. You got to meet her sometime, boy. She's a real queen.

—in the style of J. D. Salinger, *Catcher in the Rye*

A Farewell to Porridge

"And the porridge. How about the porridge?"

"That too. I really love the porridge too."

"It was supposed to be a surprise. I made it as a surprise for you. But someone has eaten it all up."

An Overview

"You sweet. You made it as a surprise. Oh, you're lovely," I said.

"But it is gone."

"It is all right," I said. "It will be all right."

Then I looked at my chair and you could see someone had been sitting in it, and Mama Bear looked at her chair and someone had been sitting in that too, and Baby Bear's chair was broken.

"We will go upstairs," I said, and we went upstairs to the bedroom, but you could see that someone had been sleeping in my bed, and in Mama Bear's too, although that was the same bed, but you have to mention it that way because that is the story. Truly, and then we looked in Baby Bear's bed and there she was.

"I ate your porridge and sat in your chairs and I broke one of them," she said.

"It is all right," I said. "It will be all right."

"And now I am lying in Baby Bear's bed."

"Baby Bear can take care of himself."

"I mean that I am sorry. I have behaved badly and I am sorry for all of this."

"*Sa ne fait rien,*" said Mama Bear. "It is nothing." Outside it had started to rain again.

"I will go now," she said. "I am sorry." She walked slowly down the stairs. I tried to think of something to tell her, but it wasn't any good.

"Good-bye," she said.

Then she opened the door and went outside and walked all the way back to her hotel in the rain.

—in the style of Ernest Hemingway, *A Farewell to Arms*

EXERCISE

Select a children's story with which you are very familiar, and try rewriting it in the style of either Salinger or Hemingway.

Revising whole pieces of writing is a complex process that requires many different strategies. As you revise a single piece of writing, you may not draw on all of these strategies, but knowing all the alternatives will help you make revision something more than correcting spelling or merely recopying a draft.

Experiment

Prewriting to learn in journals can take many forms. You may find that you make *lists* regularly—of topics you want to cover in a piece of writing, of possible titles for your work, of concluding sentences you might use. Perhaps your lists tend to be vertical like this search for a title:

Learning to Live with My Sister
Beautiful Sisters
Bella Sorella
Two Sisters
Sister to Sister

Discovery: Writing to Learn

Try listing in another form. Below, for example, is a circular list a student made as part of her prewriting for a paper in a landscaping class. Because she conceived her project visually and could think of it best in terms of areas of the yard, this student found it easier to list the items around the central words *yard*, *deck*, and *walkway*. Prewriting this way helped her see how all the aspects of her project could work together.

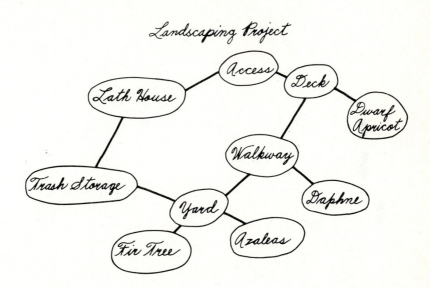

Another type of circular list is illustrated on p. 28. As you can see, these circular lists allow the writer to distinguish more important from less important ideas. For example, "colors of the rainbow" is subordinate to "rainbow prism," which in turn is subordinate to the question of why rainbows form. Yet, the circular form does not require the writer to rank all the ideas that radiate from the central idea of rainbows but permits a mixture of freedom and structure.

Clustering is another form of listing. To list in clusters, write your topic in a word or phrase in the center of a sheet of paper and draw a circle or square around it. When you think of a main idea related to that topic, write it in a word or phrase. Connect it to the topic in the center. As you think of subtopics or facts or details related to the main idea, cluster them around the main idea in similar fashion.

Variations on lists are, of course only one of many forms you can try in a journal. Take risks and try new things. If you have never written a poem, try one in your journal. Here is the form for what is called a *biopoem*, a poem that can help you learn more about a subject by assembling specified information about it. Biopoems follow this format:

line 1. first name
line 2. four traits that describe character.
line 3. relative of . . . (brother, sister, daughter, or whatever).

27

An Overview

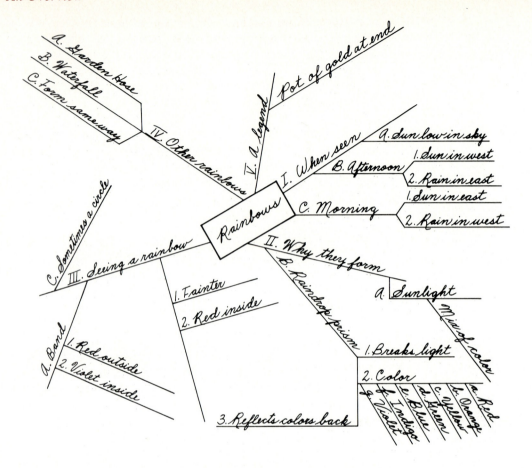

line 4. lover of . . . (three things, people, or whatever).
line 5. who feels . . . (three items).
line 6. who needs . . . (three items).
line 7. who fears . . . (three items).
line 8. who gives . . . (three items).
line 9. who would like to see . . . (three items).
line 10. resident of . . . (place).
line 11. last name.

Biopoems can be a very helpful way of expanding thoughts on a person, either real or imaginary. The following, for instance, is a biopoem on Dr. Heidegger, a character in a short story by Nathaniel Hawthorne.

```
Doctor
Eccentric, curious, singular, old
Friend of Medbourne, Killigrew, Wycherly, Bascoigne
Lover of Sylvia, magi, a rose
Who feels isolated, alone, old
```

Discovery: Writing to Learn

```
Who needs friendship, experimentation, love
Who gives medicine, free champagne, second chances
Who fears his own youth,
Who would like to see results, happiness, youth
Resident of Massachusetts,
Heidegger.
```

The students who wrote this were able to examine what they knew about Dr. Heidegger by answering the biopoem's questions. Consequently, they realized they were interested in Heidegger's relationships with other people and decided to use a combination of narrating and explaining to discuss these relationships. Biopoems need not be limited to people, however. They work equally well with inanimate entities because they, like metaphorical questions, provide a way of seeing the inanimate subject from a new perspective. Here, for example, is a biopoem written in a geology class:

```
                    Mount Stuart

Mount
Pinnacle, jagged, smooth, cold
Home of glaciers, pikas, and Black Rosy Finches
Friend of climbers and photographers
Lover of spectacular sunrises, St. Elmo's Fire
and melancholy sunsets
Who feels the crunch of crampons, the nestle of clogs,
the smooth running of a lead rope
Who needs trespassers who care
While fearing pitons, bolts, and candy wrappers
Who gives spectacularly steep North Ridges and
gentle sloping south facing couloirs
Loves to see summer's heat cooled by autumn's spread
  of color
blanket with the silence of snow
Resident of the Cascades
Stuart
```

The student who wrote this biopoem generated a number of ideas about the mountain as he wrote. Thinking from the mountain's point of view helped him see geological features as more than just "there." He began to think about how humans change mountains and about how fragile mountains can be. His knowledge of climbing gave him a special vocabulary to use in his poem, but as he began evaluating what he had written, he realized that it was not climbing but a more ecological question that really interested him. This insight led him to write an argument in which he tried to convince his readers of the importance of protecting mountains and their natural surroundings.

An Overview

EXERCISE

Try writing your own biopoem about a person or thing you are currently studying.

1. After you have written the biopoem, list all the new ideas you thought of.
2. Write a paragraph explaining how the exploration associated with the biopoem could shape your writing on this subject.

There are many other forms you can experiment with in your journal. This list suggests some of them:

True confessions	Telegrams
Obituaries	Dialogues
Profiles of friends	Interviews
Satires	Role playing
Children's stories	Paraphrases
Advertisements	Editorials
Reviews	

No matter what form you use, the experience of putting language in new configurations will help you see your subject in a new way, will help you learn about it.

EXERCISE

1. Interview someone in your class and then write a biopoem about that person.
2. Select one of the forms from the list above and write a selection in your journal using that form.

OBSERVE

Use your journal to record your own observations or insights. Perhaps you see an unusual person on the bus and want to note his or her appearance, or perhaps you overhear a bit of conversation that you would like to return to later, or perhaps you have come to a new understanding that you don't want to lose. Journals can contain these and many other forms of observation.

The process of writing about what you observe will lead you to understand more thoroughly, to see more clearly. Anais Nin, in her journal, explains how writing contributes to her perceptions: "When I write afterwards, I see much more, understand better, I develop and enrich." Nin's statement underlines the connection between writing and learning. By writing one enlarges upon experience.

Observation need not be written in paragraph form. You may find it useful

Discovery: Writing to Learn

to simply jot down *bits* of language. One of the most careful observers of nature, Henry David Thoreau, kept a journal in which he wrote about what he saw, and many of his observations appeared in incomplete sentences. Here, for example, is an excerpt from his 1846 journal in which he describes a fish he is observing:

> A regular graceful fish with coppery red reflections—the back and belly curving very slightly and regularly from end to end the width of the body being nearly the same for some distance.
> Above dusky—olivaceous—head above dark blue—snout blue—(scales on the sides edged with black and a black membrane covering their base with golden and red copper reflections lighter above redder below) (below and on belly lustrous red copper—) P.V.A. fins reddish but dusky at extremities. . . .
> —Henry David Thoreau, Journal, 1846

In writing about this fish Thoreau's powers of observation were heightened, and by recording this account in his journal he was able to return to it later as he observed and compared this fish with others.

Observations in journals often, of course, appear in more fully developed form. They may be extended sections of *prose* that show relationships, and develop ideas. The excerpt below, another from Thoreau's 1846 journal, shows how observations can be expressed in connected prose:

> In some parts of the river, the water willow when it is of large size and entire—is the lightest and most graceful of all our trees seeming to float upon the water masses of finely cut foliage being piled upon one another—occasionally the slight grey stems seen between. It has more than any a foreign aspect. It reminds us of Persian luxury and of the trim gardens and artificial lakes of the east.
> —Henry David Thoreau, Journal, 1846

Here Thoreau goes beyond a recording of details to create an image of the willow tree floating in the river and to draw comparisons between it and exotic parts of the world.

Extended prose observations frequently become links between one idea and another. Sometimes, as in the case of Thoreau, it is a matter of seeing a new relationship (between willow trees and Persia), and at other times it means developing a new thought. Here, for example, is a selection from Thomas Edison's journal. He begins by describing a dog:

> The dog wagged its tail continuously. This is evidently the way a dog laughs. I wonder if dogs ever go up to flowers and smell them—I think not—flowers were never intended for dogs and perhaps only incidentally for man. Evidently Darwin has it right. They make themselves pretty to attract the insect world who are the transportation agents of their pollen—pollen freight via Bee line.
> —Thomas Edison, Journal

An Overview

Edison's movement from wondering about dogs smelling flowers to the playful turn of phrase about the "Bee line" is typical of journal entries that begin in observation.

Observations do not always begin with what is physically present. Frequently they offer commentary on some aspect of the writer's life or experience. Like observations of physical things, these journal entries move from one topic to another, develop a thought, and lead to an *insight* the writer did not have at the beginning of writing. The following excerpt, written by a student named Jordan Kleber, demonstrates how insights emerge from this kind of observation:

```
    The problem with video games is that they are so
attractive. Their attraction is the same as that of
soap operas and glass-bottomed boats. They offer an
opportunity to observe, and even influence, a function-
ing world without risk or responsibility. Unlike the
threatening, complicated, and uncontrolled real world,
they provide a refuge of simplicity. These refuges are
dangerous because they stunt growth. It is in facing
and surviving threats and complications that we grow.
```

As you can see, Kleber begins with a simple observation about the attraction of video games, moves through a comparison, points out some dangers, and concludes with an insight about human growth. When he began writing about video games, Kleber did not know that he would be led to think about conditions necessary to growth, but in noting the dangers of refuge from risk and responsibility, he came to an insight about how threats and complications contribute to human growth.

EXERCISE

Take some common object from nature—a leaf or a piece of fruit or a rock—and record what you see. Compare your observations with someone else's observations of a similar object.

Sit in one corner of a room—a classroom, a room in your house, a dorm room, whatever—and write a journal entry about what you observe. Then move to another corner and do the same thing. What differences do you find?

Begin a journal with an observation about life such as "The problem with VCR's is . . ." or "The problem with college athletics is . . ." and write until you come to an insight that goes beyond the terms of your original observation.

Discovery: Writing to Learn

EXPLAIN

When you attend a class or read a chapter in a book, you probably have little difficulty following what is said. But if you had to explain the same material to someone else, how well would you do? Many students find that what seemed perfectly clear when they were listening or reading is much less simple when they try to explain it. They discover that they have forgotten key concepts or terms, that they are missing a crucial connection, that they don't understand nearly as well as they thought they did. What they could comprehend passively escapes them when they have to demonstrate their knowledge.

The move from passive to active understanding does not occur automatically, and writing can aid it. Your journal is a place to explain to yourself information you think you know. Explaining information to yourself is not the same as taking notes in class or jotting as you read. It is writing in which you can talk with yourself about what you are studying, ask questions, and clarify important points. The selection below, written by a student in a chemistry class, demonstrates how explaining to one's self in writing aids learning:

(1) We learned about the spectrograph. Goldstein devised
(2) this apparatus to measure the mass of protons. A current
(3) of protons is sent into a chamber with a negatively
(4) charged plate. This plate has a hole in the middle, so
(5) the protons will speed forth in a straight line. Then
(6) neon atoms then bump off the electron-from a proton?
(7) I'm totally confused. I don't know what is sent into the
(8) apparatus to start - electrons, atoms? / The plate is pos-
(9) itively charged, which means that negatively charged
(10) ions must be sent into the apparatus, to shoot
(11) through the hole, be bumped with neon and
(12) ~~become protons~~ neon becomes positively charged ions. Neon's elec-
(13) tron is bumped off and it becomes a ~~but how does~~
(14) ~~one turn a negative ion into a proton by introduc-~~
(15) ~~ing neon?~~ positively charged ion.
(16) *See *below* Anyhow, the neon ions are then deflected by a mag-
(17) netic field outside the apparatus. The variables of mass
(18) and charge are the most significant. Those with
(19) higher charge have a higher deflection, (farther to

33

An Overview

*the right, closer to the negative magnetic field.) The (20)
heavier ones deflect less, and a ratio can be set up (21)
to balance between mass and charge to see how (22)
they can land in different places. Using known (23)
elements, a scale was set up so unknowns could (24)
be calibrated. Each proton has the same mass, but (25)
different atoms have different numbers of pro- (26)
tons, thus different masses and different readings on (27)
the spectograph.* ~~This is wrong, because individual~~ But (28)
~~protons have the same mass.~~ Wait—were talking about (29)
an atom (30)

with the electrons bumped off (31)

*So each atom has a different mass, thus the different (32)
readings. O.K. The charge is simply how many more pro- (33)
tons than electrons or visa versa. It is simply a rep- (34)
resentation. Despite the real change, this is +1* (35)

*Millikan's drum had one neg. and one pos. plate and (36)
a negative charge on the oil drop. The drop was attracted (37)
up toward the plate, but pulled down by gravity and (38)
the other charge, so it became stationary.* (39)

    As Tim's explanation to himself demonstrates, writing about what you read and study allows you to become a more active participant in your learning—to start living the material: it forces you to look more closely at what you are studying. It is not always easy to admit in writing that you do not understand something, to cross out and try to explain in a different way, but the process of doing so aids learning.

    Students who regularly write explanations to themselves do not need to cram before exams. Because they have used writing to learn, they do not need to stack lists of words in their heads. And instructors of students who do this kind of explaining note that students who write to learn get better grades than do those who rely on rote memory.

Discovery: Writing to Learn

Drafts Prewriting in a journal, whether it is collecting, imitating, experimenting, observing, explaining, or some other form, helps accomplish what E. B. White describes as establishing communication with one's self before trying to respond to assignments that require communication with others. This process of writing to learn leads to writing that shows learning; it prepares you for five-page papers, for explanations of issues studied, for research reports, and for the other writing assignments that come with college classes.

The term "prewriting" suggests that this form of writing to learn precedes actual writing, but early drafts also qualify as prewriting to be collected in journals. When you receive a writing assignment you may begin to "have ideas" by clustering words and phrases, by making lists of things to include, by paging through your journal to find ideas and language you can use. Monica Caoli, for example, was given this assignment:

> Describe and narrate an event or situation that you reacted to in a negative way—with, for example, disapproval, anger or disbelief.
>
> Your general purpose is to express a sense of your own involvement with your environment—in this case your reaction to it—and to share your experience with the reader. Remember that your readers expect to see, feel and understand something that they have no direct knowledge of; so you must try to be as precise and clear as possible.
>
> Your audience, as already implied, is a general one—its distinguishing characteristic being that it has no direct connection to you or the action that unfolds in your text. One conclusion you may draw as you imagine your audience: Take nothing for granted, but assume your reader must be *shown* the important elements of your text.

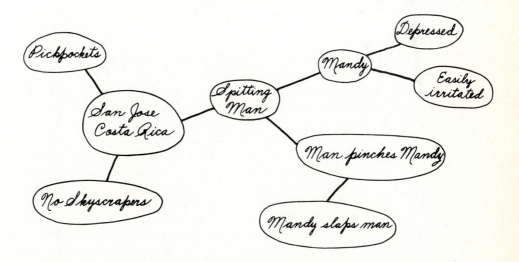

Monica began by clustering her ideas, as shown in the accompanying illustration. After thinking a little more about the incident, Monica wrote this draft in her journal.

An Overview

Just Forget It

Costa Rica is a beautiful country. I have many pleasant memories of my stay there. I lived there for five months with a Costa Rican family as a foreign exchange student. I lived in Tibas, San Jose.

San Jose is the capital. Downtown San Jose is unlike the major cities in the United States in that it isn't nearly as developed, although it is the largest city in Costa Rica. There are no towering skyscrapers, no subways, and little air pollution. San Jose is, however, similar to big urban cities in that one must be careful, even in the middle of the day, of crime and certain people that wander the streets.

I have always known that one must hold his money carefully for fear of pick-pockets. I have learned that wearing exposed necklaces is dangerous for fear of someone running up to you and pulling the valuable necklace from your neck until it breaks off your neck. But there was one experience that I witnessed that I could never have been prepared for or imagined could happen.

Mandy was a tall, slender girl. She could be quite nice sometimes, but was rather pessimistic. Her mother had died a year ago and she had had a hard time adjusting. But during her time in Costa Rica she had begun to approve. As we walked around together looking for souvenirs one day, we talked and became closer friends. She began to smile more and seemed to reach out to me. Mandy being caucasian, stood out from the dark-skinned people of Costa Rica. Sometimes men stared at her and made little comments, but she was already used to it. It didn't bother her anymore. This particular day, however, she was being harrassed a little more than usual. A man came up to her and pinched her. She turned around and slapped him. She was now getting very irritated. From her expression, I could see that she was thinking--why can't you guys leave me alone? It felt very degrading to be treated so indecently. It was very crowded on the sidewalk corner where we waited to cross the street. Very slowly, as if in a dream, I saw the man--the same man that had pinched Mandy earlier--stand alongside of Mandy. I turned only to see Mandy turn in surprise to see a face above her right shoulder. The man puckered his lips, flexed his cheek muscles, and shot out a shower of saliva on Mandy's cheek,

Discovery: Writing to Learn

right next to her right eye. I was shocked. Mandy was shocked. My first instinct was to run, and we ran. When we felt we were safe, we stopped. I took a look at her. Tears were rolling down her face. I still couldn't believe what had happened. Whey did he do that? How could he do that? Then I was angry. I helped Mandy clean up and I could see she was really hurt. She felt disgraced and humiliated. It was hard to think for a while. We slowly relaxed. "It's okay," I told her. "Just forget about it."

It was just a very unfortunate incident. The man had reacted furiously to her slap and that was it. Incidents like this are just better forgotten.

As you can see, this draft contains errors ("approve" for improve), awkwardness (the shift from "one" to "you" in paragraph two), confusing statements (the sentence about the necklace suggests that thieves break victims' necks), rough transitions (the shift from "treated so indecently" to "It was very crowded" does not work well), the one long paragraph needs to be broken into smaller sections, and the ending is abrupt. Despite its awkwardness, this draft has strengths. The description of San Jose creates a strong contrast between this and other metropolitan areas, the description of Mandy gives the reader a clear sense of the impression she created as she walked down the street, and the girls' reaction to the spitting incident seems very authentic. Monica will be able to develop this draft into a finished response to the assignment.

EXERCISE

Reread the assignment to which Monica responded. In your journal cluster ideas about an incident in your own life. Then write a draft about this incident. Your objective in this draft is to "have ideas," so do not concern yourself with spelling or transitions or smooth phrasing or introductions and conclusions.

Copyright © Charlie Ott, The National Audubon Society Collection/Photo Researchers, Inc.

Chapter Three

Development: Writing to Show Learning

Writing to learn postpones the first sentence of the final draft, but it does not eliminate it. After writing has served to generate new ideas, to underline contradictions, and to create new perspectives on a subject, it becomes the vehicle for demonstrating learning. Insights discovered in a journal and developed in early drafts need to be refined and incorporated in revised and polished final drafts that address assignments such as "A five-page paper on kinship relationships among the Yoruba is due on Friday" or "Write an essay about your formal education. What have you learned in school and how is this learning different from your out-of-school education?"

Just as writing to learn occurs in stages and extends over time, so the process of writing to show learning has multiple dimensions. These include a careful examination of the writing *assignment* to determine exactly what it requires; thoughtful consideration of the audience to determine what expectations and predispositions potential readers may hold; identifying and clarifying the *thesis* or central idea of the writing; and *revising* the entire piece to address issues of organization, style, paragraphing, and sentence structure; and *editing* for language mechanics.

Assignments

Many people write without any specific requirement that they do so. They write because they are moved to express an idea, to capture an important moment, to convince someone about an issue. You have probably done some voluntary writing of your own over the years. Commonly, however, people also write in response to an assignment. Assignments take a variety of forms and can be given by a teacher in school or an employer at work. Wherever and however they appear, assignments are inescapable obligations to write. They require you to start writing, and—because they usually contain a deadline—to stop writing as well.

An Overview

TAKING CUES FROM ASSIGNMENTS

Any writing assignment, whether given in school or at work or in a voluntary organization, contains a number of cues to the writer, cues that indicate what is expected in the final product. After an initial reading of the assignment, writers can begin by writing to learn or prewriting in journals. Whether it takes the form of collecting, imitating, experimenting, observing, or explaining, this prewriting helps generate and develop writing that can respond to the assignment. As the first draft evolves into writing that shows learning, however, it is time to reconsult the original stimulus for writing and, with rough draft in hand, to reexamine the assignment for cues as to how the writing should be shaped and what it should include.

Many assignments contain "key" words or phrases that indicate something about what shape the writing should take or what it should include. Words such as "describe," "explain," "evaluate," and "argue" appear in college writing assignments across the disciplines, and they help you understand what qualifies as a good response. Not only do they indicate what should be included in the content of the writing, they frequently suggest how the writing could be shaped or organized. Here, for example, are several assignments that contain cues about how writers should proceed.

COMMUNICATIONS ASSIGNMENT

Locate on television a thirty- to sixty-second institutional spot commercial. It should be one produced by a major "Fortune 500" corporation. Note that companies such as Dupont, General Motors, General Electric, Oil Companies (Chevron, Amoco, Shell, Exxon, computer and business machine manufacturers (Xerox, IBM, Honeywell) are producing such commercials. They tend to cluster around news and public affairs programs, especially at the 6:00 P.M. and 11:00 P.M. newscasts (network and local), and during prime-time news specials.

Briefly describe the advertisement chronologically—what it showed first, next, and so on: in short, write a running description. In it, name the subject it discusses—a case study of some corporation's success, some technological feat, its overall importance as an industry, criticism a company is trying to live down, whatever. Also describe the visual or aural effects used (music and the like).

As you read the assignment, the word *describe* appears several times and suggests itself as a cue, but what kind of description is called for? A further cue appears in *chronologically* and *running*. What this assignment is asking for is a narrative description, one that uses *seriation*, or listing in order. Narrating or summarizing the main idea is required by "name the subject it discusses," and "also describe . . ." cues the writer to include visual and aural effects.

CHINESE CIVILIZATION ASSIGNMENT

Briefly evaluate the importance of the foreigner in Chinese history from the Sung to the present. How did the foreigner's role and the Chinese reaction to him or her change over time?

Development: Writing to Show Learning

Two key words appear in this assignment. The first is *evaluate,* which suggests that the writer make some judgment about foreign-Chinese relations during the designated time period. It would not be enough to list events to complete this assignment, as the question asks for an explanation of these events. The second cue word is *change,* which suggests that the explanation of foreign-Chinese relations should emphasize the changes that occurred over time rather than focusing on a specific period of time.

POLITICAL SCIENCE ASSIGNMENT
It is often charged that Marxism in practice has failed to deliver on what it promises in theory. Can the same charge be made against liberal democratic ideology? Take a position on this question and write an essay designed to convince your readers of your position.

This assignment asks the writer to take a position—that liberal democratic ideology does or does not deliver on its theoretical promises—and to write a persuasive defense of that position. The key word here is *convince,* which indicates that the writer must go beyond explaining what a liberal democratic ideology is to argue that it does or does not fulfill its promise. A successful response to this assignment would consider issues on both sides of the question, work from reliable information, and anticipate counterarguments to ensure that claims for the opposite position are answered.

LITERATURE ASSIGNMENT
One of the continuing qualities of the fiction we have been reading this quarter is the repeated presence of the phenomenon of role reversal. By this I mean that characters are created to carry traits in their personalities that contradict the usual assumptions about the types of people they seem to be. They are placed into situations that go against the natural roles of their types. For example, in *The Maltese Falcon* the villain Gutman is described as one would expect the traditional jolly fat man to be—and we all know how harmless jolly fat men are. But Gutman would do any villainous deed to get the black bird. Over and over again, characters seem to be set against their types. I would like you to ponder the books we have read and write an essay about the ways in which our authors use role reversal. What is the effect of the hunter being turned into the hunted? What is the effect of the beautiful young college girl being a foul-mouthed, aggressive female? What about the mother who is the working mainstay of the family—and the father who is an alcoholic slob? What of the cowboy woman who is more man then the men are? What of the worn-out spy and his innocent, comic girlfriend? Of course, some of our characters are pure in their roles. The Great White Hunter. The Noble Policeman. The Heroic Cowboy.
I am giving you an inchoate topic. Ponder it, and come to terms with the phenomenon by giving it shape, producing a thesis, and arguing a case. Lastly, demonstrate your knowledge of the material.

This assignment gives you considerable information but fails to specify how the writing should proceed. In fact, that is the major problem of the assignment

An Overview

because this task asks the writer to explore, to develop an idea about role reversals in fiction. In the process of exploring, you would probably prewrite about several of the books read and think of several different ways of looking at the question of role reversal. The major task is not to narrate or explain, although some of both may be necessary, but to explore the various forms of role reversal in an attempt to produce a central idea or thesis. "To argue a case" as it appears in this task implies offering justification for the thesis that comes out of exploration.

EXERCISE

The following assignment comes from a political science class. Read it carefully, and write a paragraph in which you explain the cues it provides and how you would approach it.

> Discuss the erosion in the authority of a person or an institution with which you are familiar. You can take your case study from history or your immediate environment. You are not required to do library research. You are, however, expected to deal with a situation that you know well. Should you choose a private person, you should keep the person anonymous. The problems you analyze must be generalizable.
>
> First, discuss why the person or the institution had authority, and how much. Second, discuss the reasons behind the erosion of his or her authority. Third, recount the events that diminished this person's authority.

ASKING QUESTIONS OF ASSIGNMENTS

In addition to providing clues about the shape and content writing should take, assignments can give you further information about how to proceed. This is as true of an assignment given by an employer as of one given by a teacher. The key in both cases is to ask questions that will help you understand completely the writing task and use all of the resources available to you. The person who asks you to write, whether an employer or a teacher, usually has some expectations of what you should write, even if the details are not included in the assignment. By asking questions such as the following, you can learn more about these expectations and at the same time clarify your own thinking about the writing at hand.

1. *Can I restate the assignment in my own words?* Putting the assignment in your own words certifies that you understand it, whereas simply reading it might permit you to overlook some parts.
2. *Who is the audience for my writing?* As I have said, the instructor is usually your audience, but some assignments designate an audience. For example, a geology professor may ask you to explain earthquakes to the people of your state. This audience of nonexperts requires you to consider how much average citizens know about earthquakes, what

Development: Writing to Show Learning

their interest in earthquakes is, what features of your state's geology will interest them, and what terms they will understand. An employer may ask you to write a memo about a new product for the sales force or for a press release. Even though your topic is the same in both cases, the difference in audience will shape your writing.

3. *What questions do I have about this assignment?* Making an assignment is itself a writing task, and what is clear to the writer may not be evident to the reader. Accordingly, do not hesitate to raise questions if you think an assignment fails to tell you everything you need to know.

4. *Can I immediately write something about this assignment?* Here I do not mean restating the assignment but making an initial response, writing a few sentences or a few paragraphs or a list (depending on how long the final writing will be and how much time you have) that will aid you in collecting your thoughts and discovering what you know about the topic.

5. *What do I need to do before beginning to write a response?* Here again the time allowed and length of the assignment will determine how much you can do before actually writing a draft, but even an essay exam can be improved by taking a few moments to formulate ideas, and considerable prewriting should precede an extended assignment.

6. *What can I do to/for the reader on this subject?* This is in many ways the most central question of all writing. To ask this question is to ask why write on this subject at all and can lead you to ask some hard questions of yourself. Another way to ask the same question is "What do I have to say that merits the time and attention of my reader, and how do I hope to influence that reader through my writing?" Sometimes you will not be able to answer this question immediately, but if you keep it in mind throughout your writing, it can serve as an internal monitor/editor.

EXERCISE

Ask questions about a writing assignment you have been given recently. The assignment can be from any class, and it can be for any type of writing, from essay exam to research report, as long as it asks for several paragraphs of prose. The questioning should begin with the preceding six questions, the general questions to be asked of any assignment. Then read the assignment closely, and find the key words or images that indicate what shape and content should be included in the writing. Write a paragraph explaining what you find.

Audience

Near the end of her novel *To Kill a Mockingbird*, Harper Lee describes an encounter between Scout, the main character, and her reclusive neighbor, Arthur (Boo) Radley. Scout and her brother Jem have spent years speculating about Boo and scheming ways to see him, but he remains in his house except

43

for the October night when he saves their lives. Scout walks Boo back to his house after the rescue, and the narrative continues:

> I turned to go home. Street lights winked down the street all the way to town. I had never seen our neighborhood from this angle. There were Miss Maudie's, Miss Stephanie's—there was our house, I could see the porch swing—Miss Rachel's house was beyond us, plainly visible. I could even see Mrs. Dubose's.
>
> I looked behind me. To the left of the brown door was a long shuttered window. I walked to it, stood in front of it, and turned around. In daylight, I thought, you could see to the post office corner.
>
> Daylight... in my mind, the night faded. It was daytime and the neighborhood was busy. Miss Stephanie Crawford crossed the street to tell the latest to Miss Rachel. Miss Maudie bent over her azaleas. It was summertime, and two children scampered down the sidewalk toward a man approaching in the distance. The man waved, and the children raced each other to him.
>
> It was still summertime, and the children came closer. A boy trudged down the sidewalk dragging a fishing-pole behind him. A man stood waiting with his hands on his hips. Summertime, and his children played in the front yard with their friend, enacting a strange little drama of their own invention.
>
> It was fall, and his children fought on the sidewalk in front of Mrs. Dubose's. The boy helped his sister to her feet, and they made their way home. Fall, and his children trotted to and fro around the corner, the day's woes and triumphs on their faces. They stopped at an oak tree, delighted, puzzled, apprehensive.
>
> Winter, and his children shivered at the front gate, silhouetted against a blazing house. Winter, and a man walked into the street, dropped his glasses, and shot a dog.
>
> Summer, and he watched his children's heart break. Autumn again, and Boo's children needed him.
>
> Atticus was right. One time he said you never really know a man until you stand in his shoes and walk around in them. Just standing on the Radley porch was enough.
>
> The street lights were fuzzy from the fine rain that was falling. As I made my way home, I felt very old, but when I looked at the tip of my nose I could see fine misty beads, but looking cross-eyed made me dizzy so I quit. As I made my way home, I thought what a thing to tell Jem tomorrow. He'd be so mad he missed it he wouldn't speak to me for days. As I made my way home, I thought Jem and I would get grown but there wasn't much else left for us to learn, except possibly algebra.

Although Scout's claim about having little left to learn seems exaggerated, it contains some truth because she has learned to see things from the perspective of another. Standing on the Radleys' porch allowed her to see her neighborhood as Boo saw it, and as she absorbed this view, Scout saw the world in a new way. Developing the ability to see things from another's viewpoint is one of the most difficult tasks that humans undertake.

Learning to stand in another's shoes is an essential part of writing to show learning because it is in taking that stance that one becomes aware of how

Development: Writing to Show Learning

an audience sees what one says. Conferences between students and writing instructors frequently illustrate the difficulty of seeing from the audience's perspective. The dialogue during the conference goes this way:

Teacher: I can't quite figure out what you are saying in this paper. Could you explain it to me?
Student: Well, what I mean is . . . (what follows is a clear oral presentation of the ideas that appear garbled in the paper).
Teacher: So that's what you are saying. Why didn't you write that?

    This dialogue probably raises in your mind the question of why the student did not write the oral version in the first place. When I first began having such conversations with students, I wondered the same thing myself, but I gradually realized that in addition to giving students a chance to *say* what they meant, these conversations helped the students become more conscious of their audience. When what the students wrote was ambiguous, it was often because they had difficulty putting themselves in the audience's place; they had difficulty "seeing" the audience or imagining what the audience might need. However, when we talked, I became a visible audience; they could "see" me in a way they had not been able to see their audiences as they wrote. Furthermore, even without intending to, I indicated where more explanation was needed, or when statements did not make sense. With a raised eyebrow or quizzical look I told them what I, the audience, required.

    Developing the ability to "see" your audience when that audience is not physically present is integral to demonstrating learning in writing. Even if you know a great deal, that knowledge will not be apparent unless you can put it in a form accessible to your reader.

SEEING YOUR AUDIENCE

When you meet new people, you always, sometimes unconsciously, size them up. You notice their clothing, hairstyle, posture, and general bearing. Even before a person speaks, you will have drawn some tentative conclusions, and once talk begins, you continue to shape your impressions. My students claim that they can tell a great deal about an instructor just from attending the first day of class and often base a decision about a course on that single observation. They assert that one hour with an instructor gives them information on his or her background, values, knowledge, and personality. In practical terms, they feel they have insight into the instructor's attitude toward students, preparation for teaching the course, expectations of students, and temperament.

    Ability to size people up is a survival skill for writers as well as for students on the first day of class. The difference is that the writer's audience is invisible. Writers must transform the shadowy figure called *audience* into something they can visualize clearly. This transformation is easiest if an audience is specified for writing, and here college writing often poses a special problem because it so rarely specifies an audience. I have looked at many assignments from a variety of disciplines, and I can predict that you will be asked to summarize events, explain causes, argue in favor of a given position, or explore a topic, but you will rarely be asked to do this for a clearly identified audience. To see the difference that an audience can make in an assignment, consider the following two assignments from a geology class:

1. In this course we have discussed several theories about glacial growth. Write an explanation of them.
2. In a recent paper in the *Journal of Geology*, Professor I. C. Thymes of the University of Northern Svalbard stated that we are now nearing the end of the present interglacial age and will notice a steady deterioration of the climate during the next several decades, alterations that will herald the beginning of the next glacial age. You are called by the local TV station as a person knowledgeable about ice-age matters and are asked for a brief evaluation of this item for broadcast on the 6:00 P.M. news. In formulating your response, be sure to examine this prediction and the scientific basis for it.

As you can see, the first question does not specify an audience, and the student must discuss the information asked for with no guidance as to how much to explain or how much detail to include. The second question, on the other hand, names the general public as audience. A student responding to this assignment will need to define his or her terms carefully, as not everyone who listens to the 6:00 P.M. news will know what "greenhouse effect" or "interglacial age" means. The student will probably also want to consider climatology, explaining that Professor Thymes' statement is part of a larger argument regarding the future of the earth's climate. Thus, it is clear that the task of writing is usually easier when the audience is identified.

But whether or not the audience is known, the task of "seeing" your reader remains. Knowing that your writing is intended for the school board or the viewers of the 6:00 P.M. news can provide some guidance, but you must still visualize the audience for yourself in the same way that you must when no audience other than your instructor is designated. This act of visualizing resembles what Scout experienced as she stood on the Radleys' front porch, seeing the world as another saw it.

Asking Questions

Another way to visualize your audience is to ask yourself questions about that audience. Whether you are writing for a diverse group such as members of the sales force or for your instructor, a few moments of conscious probing can help you see the audience more clearly. The following questions are designed to help you with that process.

1. What values does this audience hold? Values are expressed in beliefs about family, religion, money, society, politics, work, or education. They derive from a complex assortment of education, age, health, income, ethnic background, and environment. As you have probably already discovered, it is often difficult to be absolutely certain of the values held by people you know well,

Development: Writing to Show Learning

much less a distant audience, but you can make your audience less vague by speculating on these factors. In particular, you can think about the values your audience is likely to hold about your subject. For example, a politically liberal, agnostic audience in a university community would have a different view of geology than would religious fundamentalists who view the principles of evolution as heresy, and affluent and educated suburbanites would be interested in different aspects of possible climate changes than would second-generation immigrant farmers trying to make a living in the fields of Iowa.

2. What does my audience know about this topic? Once you have generally defined your audience's values regarding your subject, you can begin to think in more specific terms about the audience's probable knowledge of your subject. Even though you can assume that an audience knows a considerable amount about the subject, you still need to determine what the instructor knows about your topic. For example, if you were writing about busing within a given school district for a political science instructor unfamiliar with that district, you would need to supply background information about the district, its population, the history of school busing there, and the particular issues facing the district. You could assume that the instructor would be familiar with the larger issues of equal opportunity education, legal precedents, and political implications. But if you were writing to members of the school board in that district, you could assume that your audience would already know most of the background information. Instead, you might find it necessary to explain in detail the very things—equal opportunity education, legal precedent, and political implications—that you could assume your instructor knew. As you can see, thinking about what your audience knows (and needs to know) can help you plan the general shape of your writing because it helps you decide what to include and exclude.

3. Does my audience have any strong opinions about my topic? As you have probably already learned, knowledge and opinion are not the same thing. Given the same set of information or knowledge, two different people can develop opposite opinions, and you have undoubtedly encountered some people who have little regard for information and express this with "Don't confuse me with the facts." Accordingly, it is important to think of your audience in terms of opinions as well as knowledge.

Thinking about your audience's values can give you a general idea of its opinion about your topic. For example, you could probably assume that auto workers from the Midwest would be opposed to lowering tariffs on imported automobiles, whereas a middle-income car buyer on the West Coast might favor reduced tariffs that would allow a lower purchase price. In other cases you may have direct indications of your audience's opinion. The representative to whom you write to enlist support for the proposed university budget may have a record of voting against appropriations for higher education, and so you can assume that your audience will have a negative view of your request. Knowing this, in turn, can help you plan what you will say to change the representative's mind. Instructors frequently provide indications of their opinions, and you may want to consider these as you write in response to assignments.

Sometimes you may know or be able to guess the audience's reason for having a strong opinion. In the case of the auto worker whose livelihood is threatened by imported automobiles, the explanation is obvious. A representative opposed to supporting higher education may base his opinion on personal values, views of constituents, the stance of his political party, or pressures from other legislators. Knowing something about the reasons for your audience's opinion can strengthen your argument against them.

4. What effect do I want to have on my audience? The answer to this question explains why writers address audiences and what they hope to accomplish by doing so. The answer to this question requires that you visualize how the audience will respond after reading what you have written. In some cases this is relatively easy: The representative will be persuaded by your argument and vote in favor of the proposed university budget, and the car buyer will see the societal value of a higher tariff on imports. However, writing does not always have such obvious purposes, and so writers need to think hard about the effects they seek.

This kind of thinking is not so much an effort of will as an exercise in taking another's viewpoint. To consider what effect your writing should have on its audience requires that you take an imaginative journey into the mind of that audience. As you know from your own reading, the effects of writing are mostly internal. Occasionally writing may move you to laugh or even to take action, but usually the response occurs entirely inside your head. Accordingly, the final and most difficult task of seeing your audience is to project yourself into the audience's mind and determine what will cause that audience to be moved, to understand the information you present, to enjoy your account, or to give you a good grade.

Answering these four questions is never, of course, easy, but practicing can improve your accuracy. One way to begin practicing is to apply the questions to finished pieces of writing. Like biologists who dissect in order to understand an organism's inner workings, you can learn to see your own audience by considering how other writers have seen theirs.

The following three selections by Jeff Carroll all deal with the throw in baseball, but each is written for a different audience. Read each and decide what kind of audience is being addressed.

Baseball #1

It takes more than desire to win. It takes more than the kind of dedication we see in the weekend athlete, who is dedicated mainly to a good time and competent performance. What it takes to be a winner is skill.

Skill is very different from ability. Ability is what you bring to the game; you could call it "the state of your mind and body." You aren't exactly born with it, but you grow up with abilities. Skill, on the other hand, is learned—and learned and learned until it becomes as automatic as brushing your teeth.

Development: Writing to Show Learning

Take the basic unit of any baseball game—the basic move: the throw. The throw of the baseball connects all parts of the game. If you can't throw the baseball, you might as well try bowling. No position on the field, from behind the plate to right field, is exempt from demanding the very special skill of throwing the ball.

And you sure can't learn it from watching the game from the stands or on TV. Sure, the fans in the stands think it's all quite simple. In their minds they go through all the little things in the game. It's a part of being a fan, of course, but can you imagine a fan coming down out of the stands, taking the glove away from the third baseman and really throwing a man out at first base?

No way, unless he's awfully lucky—and even luckier if he hasn't caught a hard ground ball in the pit of the stomach. The best third basemen have practiced several years of their lives away picking the ball off the turf, reaching into the glove and with a motion that is learned and relearned until it is forgotten pulling the ball out, fingers across the seams, and firing it to second or first. And what I mean by "forgotten" is that once you start thinking about what you're doing, you fall apart; skill is not something you draw on—it draws on you and makes you play the game right.

You can't think about the placement of your feet, the flex in your legs, the angle of your arm as it draws back in that second or less you have to make these moves. The man is streaking toward the base and you have to get the ball there first. So somehow you pull the ball back and let it fly, and it whips out of your hand and takes off for the glove of your teammate.

The "somehow" of all this can be explained in that one word—skill. Everybody's got the ability to throw the ball, but only the ones who like to learn with their bodies and minds the way some of us do—40 hours a week, an hour for lunch—are going to make it into the real center of the game of baseball. That center is "the bigs," the major leagues.

Baseball #2

Many baseball fans love a high-scoring game. There's nothing like the home-run or the extra base hit to make an afternoon, nothing like a stolen base, or a circus catch to deep center field. But there are just as many fans out there who go to the game to watch other things, which we could call games-within-the game. Taken together, they wrap the game on the field in as much entertainment as any Vegas floor show. From the time the fan finds his seat, he can enjoy any of the following:

"Pitchers Taking Batting Practice" is a game to see who among the men of the mound can actually *hit the ball* that day. Those pitchers from the American League never have to bat, of course, and for them batting practice is sheer fantasy, taking their bats between the brawny-armed, sharp-eyed sluggers the team depends on for runs. National League pitchers do have to bat, and for them batting is a more serious task. Nevertheless, you can pick out the pitcher by the way he squints at the slow balls, steps back from the medium-speed pitches, and closes his eyes at the hard ones.

"Wasting Time in the Bullpen" is another pitcher's delight, abetted by second- and third-string catchers. The bullpen is normally in deep left or right field, behind the fences or outside the foul lines; starting and relieving pitchers hang out there, occasionally answering the call to warm up and play the game, but

An Overview

more often finding ways to pass the two or three hours of game time. They work, for instance, on gum chewing, juggling and balancing baseballs, and composing and rehearsing insults and banter (depending on whose park they're sitting in). Watch for naps. Watch for a thoughtful discussion and vivid demonstration of tobacco-spitting.

"The Batter's Ritual at Home Plate" has, according to the batter, everything to do with the success of the batter, but it is easy to miss particularly if your chili dog is starting to run. The ritual can begin with cleaning of spikes or severe rotating of the neck, and proceeds through a variety of steps leading up to the pitch. Of special interest to the batter is the set of his cap and the unrestricted comfort of the shoulders under the shirt—watch for much adjusting here—and then the preliminary swings of the bat can trace any number of lovely geometric shapes in the air—spirals, figure-eights, ellipses. Watch, too, for the optional dialog among batter, catcher, and umpire, the subject of which has been reported to be weather, relatives, the pitcher, good restaurants in town.

"The Peanut Vendor as Hero" has lately become over-publicized on TV because the networks have begun to show this fellow tossing bags around his back and fifteen rows up, all for glory and a buck. But there are still the finer points not to be missed; the handicap of the big aluminum box he carries in front, making him lean backwards for nine innings as he staggers up and down the aisles, his hand stuffed with dollar bills also making change from that big cloth belt around his waist, and his uncanny ability to get in front of you when something finally happens down on the field. Heroes get away with this sort of thing, though; no harsh word has ever been spoken against a peanut vendor.

And the game goes on. No big plays. No big moments. Just practice, or napping in the bullpen, or figure-eights in the air, or peanuts. And the games go on.

Baseball #3

There are people in Italy who can't stand soccer. Not all Canadians love hockey. A similar situation exists in America, where there are those individuals—you may be one of them—who yawn or even frown when somebody mentions baseball. It doesn't matter that the game goes hand in hand with mom and apple pie; some people don't like those items either. Baseball to them means boring hours watching grown men in funny tight outfits standing around in a field staring away while very little of anything happens. They tell you it's a game better suited to the nineteenth century—slow, quiet, gentlemanly. These are the same people—you may be one of them—who love football because there's always something happening, and it's bone-crunchingly *active*—a contact sport that glorifies "the hit."

By contrast, baseball seems abstract, cool, silent, still—the skeptic says the game could be played by two men with counters, a board, and dice between them. To the skeptic let it be said: basball can only be known in person.

On TV the game is fractured into a dozen perspectives, replays, close-ups. The geometry of the game, however, is essential to understanding it. And only at the park can the skeptic (or the innocent) truly test his dislike of the game. You must choose a seat—there are several philosophies about this—because this is your own view; no TV screen flashing ten angles can give you this sense

Development: Writing to Show Learning

of place. You will contemplate the game from one point as a painter does his subject; you may, of course, *project* yourself into the game. It is in this projection that the game affords so much space and time for involvement. The TV won't do it for you.

Take, for example, the third baseman. You sit behind the third base dugout and you watch him watching home plate. His legs are apart, knees flexed. His arms hang loose. He does a lot of this. The skeptic still cannot think of any other sport so still, so passive. (Perhaps golf.) But watch what happens every time the pitcher throws: the third baseman goes up on his toes, flexes his arms or brings the glove to a point in front of him, takes a step right or left, backward or forward, perhaps he glances across the field to check his first baseman's position. Suppose the pitch is a ball. "Nothing happened," you say. I could have had my eyes closed."

The skeptic and the innocent must play the game. And this involvement in the stands is no more intellectual than listening to music is. Watch the third baseman. Smooth the dirt in front of you with one foot; smooth the pocket in your glove; watch the eyes of the batter, the speed of the bat, the sound of horsehide on wood. If football is a symphony of movement and theatre, baseball is chamber music, a spacious interlacing of notes, chords and responses.

As you no doubt concluded, the audience for "Baseball #1" is people who actually play the game. The individuals to whom this selection is addressed value athletics in general and baseball in particular. They know a great deal about baseball, its forms and strategies, and they know how to throw a ball. This audience believes there is a distinct difference between those who "know" baseball and those who don't. In writing this selection Jeff Carroll sought to remind his audience of the distinction between skill and ability, the distinction between their own skills and those of major league players.

The audience for "Baseball #2" consists of people who don't play baseball but value the recreational experience of attending games. They know the basic rules of the game and may even keep score on the forms provided in game programs, but they know little about the fine points of the game. They can recognize an error and a double play, but they would have difficulty anticipating a fielder's choice play. The audience for this piece believes that baseball is the appropriate national sport, that it provides wholesome family entertainment, and that the home team ought to win the world series. In this selection Jeff sought to recreate for fans some of what they experience as they watch a baseball game.

"Baseball #3" takes as its audience persons who are neither players nor fans of baseball. These people value sports that provide a great deal of action, physical contact, and speed. Accordingly, they know very little about baseball and they hold the strong opinion that some other sport—such as football—should be the national sport. Jeff's purpose in writing this selection was to persuade this audience to reconsider baseball, to give it enough attention to see the action in it.

To write each of these selections, Jeff asked himself these questions:

1. What values does this audience hold?

An Overview

2. What does my audience know about this topic?
3. Does my audience have any strong opinions about this topic?
4. What effect do I want to have on my audience?

The process of answering this question enabled him to "see" the three audiences he addressed.

EXERCISE

Although few college writing assignments specify audiences, you will sometimes be given assignments that do, and the following are examples. Read each and answer the four questions about audience. Then write a paragraph for each showing how the audience influences what you would write.

1. You are a British subject who has been invited to colonial America in 1775 so that you may visit, in turn, the city of Philadelphia, a Massachusetts homestead near Lexington, and a Virginia plantation. After these three visits but before your departure, you wish to share your impressions and discoveries with a friend back home in England. Write him or her a letter, describing your views of the life, politics, land, and people who live here.
2. You live in a state that emphasizes economic education for schoolchildren, and you have been asked, because of your background in economics, to explain Keynesian economics to a group of seventh graders. What will you say?
3. A charitable foundation in your city has expressed its willingness to increase its support of the arts, and you are the curator of the local art museum. You have an opportunity to purchase Jackson Pollock's *One* but will need financial help from the foundation. How will you describe the painting to the members of the foundation?

AUDIENCE IN COLLEGE WRITING

Answering questions about your audience's opinions, knowledge, and values and considering the effect you wish to have provides information about specific readers, but much of the writing you do in college will not have a specific audience such as residents of the community next to a nuclear power plant or sixth graders studying the Civil War. True, you will be writing for an instructor who has a certain area of expertise, who has priorities and who, no doubt, holds strong opinions about some issues, but this instructor will also represent the academic community.

All members of the academic community value writing that is well organized and coherent, that moves the reader smoothly from one point or sentence to another. They assume that writers will give adequate attention to details of spelling and punctuation, and to conventions of standard written English. They also attach value to evidence that authors have done their homework,

Development: Writing to Show Learning

know what they are talking about, and give attention to neatness and accuracy of presentation. Accordingly, even if you do not know the details of what your instructor/audience values, knows, and believes, you can always write with the purpose of demonstrating that you should become a member of the academic community.

Thesis

One of the benefits of writing to learn is that it helps you discover what you want to say about a subject. Often the last sentence of a first draft indicates what the writing is really about. You may start your first draft confident that you know exactly what you want to say, but the process of writing can take you in unexpected directions so that you depart from your original plan. Such departures are part of the learning that accompanies writing, but transforming your writing into a demonstration of learning for others requires that you make your main point clear. This main point is your *thesis*.

A thesis differs from a subject. It makes a point about the subject, it gives the subject focus, it transforms a general subject into *your* subject. The subject may be, for example, the language of advertising, but when you develop a thesis such as "Shopping is confusing because brand names have so little to do with the products they represent," the language of advertising becomes *your* subject.

DEVELOPING YOUR THESIS

The process of transforming a subject into a thesis takes time, and writing to learn provides the best means of accomplishing the transformation. As you prewrite in your journal about your subject and write a first draft you will begin to develop ideas and one of these may become your thesis. Here, for example is part of Troy Alstead's first draft about violence in sports:

```
     Society frowns on people beating each other up.
We've made laws against it. A person can go to jail or
be sued for intentionally hurting someone else. Fight-
ing is a good way to get kicked out of school. Despite
all these rules, we encourage kids to beat each other
up on the football field and in the boxing ring. Is
that right?
     I remember my football coach in high school yelling
at us to go out there and make sure we hurt someone.
I've seen players carried off the field on a stretcher,
their faces twisted in pain. I saw the fight on TV
where a boxer died from the constant pounding his head
took. Should we allow that to happen? Should we allow
people to make money off those things?
```

An Overview

>   Of course we should. It's called "freedom." Responsible adults can put themselves in that kind of danger if they want. We would be taking away people's rights if we decided boxing was illegal because of the dangers to the fighters.

In this draft the writer explores his subject in several ways. He begins with the contradiction between society's laws against violence and the socially sanctioned violence of sports, then he recalls his own experiences of participating and watching violence in sports, and this leads him to the question of whether this violence should be allowed. The process of asking and answering the question leads him to what will become his thesis.

STATING YOUR THESIS

Your thesis tells your readers what your writing is about. It is like an announcement or advance notice for your writing. Troy Alstead, who wrote the draft about violence in sports, put his thesis this way:

>   Although recent deaths and serious injuries to professional boxers have raised questions about outlawing the sport, our society must continue to allow people the freedom to choose, even if the choice includes violent sports.

In this one sentence the author states his main idea and makes clear what position he takes with regard to violence in sports. Statements such as "Many people argue that violent sports such as boxing should be outlawed," or "People choose to box just as they choose to design clothes or sell real estate," would give readers much less advance notice about the writing that follows.

A student writing about her experiences as a biker used this thesis statement:

>   On the block where I grew up there was an unwritten law that every kid should have a bike, and my family lived by that law. I got my first 10-speed when I was ten, and I've been biking ever since.

These two sentences give the reader a clear idea of what the paper will discuss, and prepare the way for a history of riding experiences, different bikes, equipment, and, throughout, the pleasure that the writer takes in biking. If that student had begun with a statement such as: "I commute to school by bike

Development: Writing to Show Learning

and enjoy touring with local bike clubs," or "Biking is good exercise and a great way to release tension," the reader would have a much less clear idea of what the paper discusses.

In introducing a discussion of the climate in New England, Donald Hall writes:

> New York has people, the Northwest damp, Iowa soybeans, Texas money, and New England seasons. Convention speaks of four; the observant New Englander numbers at least a thousand, and on a good day our spendthrift climate runs through seven or eight.

In these two sentences Hall informs the reader about what will follow. He advertises his intention to explain the thousand or more seasons that one can observe in New England. The reader expects, then, the discussion of climactic variations on a March day and an explanation of the 227 seasons of winter that appear in succeeding pages.

EXERCISE

1. In each of the pairs below identify the best thesis statement and explain why you think it is best.
    - Ia. In this paper I will discuss the relationship of nutrition to learning.
    - Ib. More than a source of calories, food helps us learn.
    - IIa. Reducing an employee's personal space can lead to a decrease in that individual's productivity.
    - IIb. Personal space is carefully guarded in the workplace because many people believe it influences productivity.
2. Develop a thesis statement for one of the subjects below:
    a. preservation of historic buildings
    b. the rise of special interest politics
    c. cable TV
    d. pornography
    e. space exploration
    f. beautification projects

PLACING YOUR THESIS STATEMENT

Once you have developed and stated your thesis, you can organize your writing to highlight it. In some cases this means putting the thesis statement at the beginning. Donald Hall, for example, begins his discussion of New England seasons with the thesis statement given. Because he does this, readers know from the first sentence exactly what point Hall intends to make. This organization leaves no ambiguity about the writer's intentions.

Sometimes, however, it is more effective to insert the thesis statement later in the writing. Here is the first paragraph of the paper on violence in sports:

An Overview

> A few days after receiving a knock-out blow to the head in a boxing ring, a professional boxer died from a massive brain hemmorrhage. He was not the first to die from injuries suffered in a boxing match, and many people have begun to argue that boxing should be outlawed. Even Howard Cosell, long-time boxing announcer, recently denounced boxing as too violent.

Then he brought his thesis statement in, beginning the second paragraph with it. By waiting until the second paragraph to introduce his thesis statement, this writer was able to establish a context for it. He introduced the issue of boxing, gave examples of the problem of violence in boxing, and cited individuals' responses to this violence. In doing all of this, he created a counterbalance to his thesis about the importance of individual freedom. Instead of simply asserting his position, he began by showing an opposing perspective, thereby demonstrating the need to argue his own position.

A thesis statement need not appear as a first sentence of a paragraph. Just as it is effective to delay the thesis statement until a second or later paragraph, so it can be effective to put the thesis statement in the middle of a paragraph. See, for example, this first paragraph from Mie Yanase's paper about being in but not of a culture:

> Natives of Tokyo call themselves "Edokko," which means "a child of Edo." (Tokyo was known as "Edo" during the feudal period.) I joined the millions of other Edokkos when I was born in Ochnomizu, Tokyo, on December 6, 1968. But I was not born a genuine "Edokko" since my parents were foreigners. My father immigrated from Korea, and my mother was a second generation Korean living in Tokyo. I was born a foreigner and have spent most of my life under that title. I was a Korean living in Japan for the first 18 years of my life; I am currently a Japanese living in the United States.

The thesis statement appears in this sentence: "I was born a foreigner and have spent most of my life under that title," and it is placed effectively between explanations of Japanese culture and the writer's individual experience.

EXERCISE

Identify the thesis statement in each of the following passages:

Development: Writing to Show Learning

Some scout-masterish philosophers argue that the appeal of jogging and other body-maintenance programs is the discipline they afford. We live in a world in which individuals have fewer and fewer obligations. The work week has shrunk. Weekend worship is less compulsory. Technology gives us more free time. Satisfactorily filling free time requires imagination and effort. Freedom is a wide and risky river; it can drown the person who does not know how to swim across it. The more obligations one takes on, the more time one occupies, the less threat freedom poses. Jogging can become an instant obligation. For a portion of his day, the jogger is not his own man; he is obedient to a regimen he has accepted. —Carll Tucker, *Fear of Dearth*

Caesar was right. Thin people need watching. I've been watching them for most of my adult life, and I don't like what I see. When these narrow fellows spring at me, I quiver to my toes. Thin people come in all personalities, most of them menacing. You've got your "together" thin person, your mechanical thin person, your condescending thin person, your tsk-tsk thin person, your efficiency-expert thin person. All of them are dangerous.
—Suzanne Britt Jordan, "That Lean and Hungry Look"

At a time when everyone's mind is on the explosions of the moment, it might seem obtuse of me to discuss the fourteenth century. But I think a backward look at that disordered, violent, bewildered, disintegrating, and calamity-prone age can be consoling and possibly instructive in a time of similar disarray. Reflected in a six-hundred-year-old mirror, a more revealing image of ourselves and our species might be seen than is visible in the clutter of circumstances under our noses. The value of historical comparison was made keenly apparent to the French medievalist Edouard Perroy, when he was writing his book on the Hundred Years' War while dodging the Gestapo in World War II. "Certain ways of behaving," he wrote, "certain reactions against fate, throw mutual light upon each other." —Barbara Tuchman, *A Distant Mirror*

Revising

Writing to show learning is not, of course, simply a matter of finding and placing a thesis statement. The process of developing, stating, and placing sentences that announce the main point of a piece of writing are part of the much larger process called *revising*. If you take the word "revision" apart, you find that it is composed of "vision" which refers to seeing and "re" meaning again. To revise is to see again.

Many famous writers testify to the importance of revising in their own work. Most of their statements are a variation of "writing is revising" and detail the importance of revising in their achievements. Some, like the essayist S. J. Perelman, take a wry view. Perelman claimed that he wrote thirty-seven drafts before he was satisfied with his work: "I once tried 33, but something was lacking, a certain. . . . On another occasion I tried 42, but the final effort was too lapidary." In a more serious vein Ernest Hemingway told an interviewer that he revised continually until the manuscript was in galley proofs, and asserted: "I rewrote the ending to *A Farewell to Arms,* the last page of it, thirty-nine times before I was satisfied."

An Overview

Revising is not a new concept, as the words of classical rhetorician Quintillian reveals: "Erasure is quite as important a function of the pen as actual writing. . . . For we have to condemn what had previously satisfied us and discover what had escaped our notice." Quintillian's word *discover* suggests the invention that lies at the heart of revising. To see again is to see something new, and that is a process of invention. But here the task has more to do with finding focus and creating organization than it does with finding something to say.

Revising can be both difficult and disheartening because it often means rethinking a whole approach or reorganizing an entire paper or discarding major sections of a first draft. One way to make revising somewhat easier is to recognize its analogue in speech. You have probably said, "What I mean is" or "I meant to say" many times and then gone on to "revise" what you said. Revising writing proceeds from the same impulse to make language clear and effective, but it is much more than a mechanical process of changing a few words: it is reseeing at every level.

Another way to minimize the difficulties of revising is to recognize its multidimensional nature. There are many forms of revision in writing, one of which is *reseeing the whole* through discovering what a paper is really about and developing a thesis statement. This may happen as you write the last line of a first draft and realize what you wanted to say, or it may occur to you as you are in the middle of writing. Reseeing the whole usually involves major changes in emphasis or major additions or deletions to the first (or second or third) draft. Another form of revision is *organizing* or placing information so it can be easily comprehended by the reader. Here the emphasis is on arranging parts of writing so that they work together effectively and on ensuring that there are logical relationships among the ideas introduced. A third and related form of revision focuses on *cohesion,* or connections among the parts of writing. The word *cohesion* means sticking together, and when you revise for cohesion, you focus on the "glue" in your writing. A fourth type of revision concerns *style,* which is related to structure and cohesion because all three are part of the overall effect created by a piece of writing. These four—reseeing the whole, organizing, creating cohesion, and attending to style—are forms of conceptual revision because they are concerned with the largest dimensions of writing.

Another level of revision concentrates on the shape of individual paragraphs, sentences, and words, considering clarity, interest, and variety. Still another level of revision attends to the correctness and conventions of writing. Here the concern is with spelling, punctuation, capitalization, usage, and format. *Editing* is often the word used to describe this level of revision. All these forms of revision are important, and no one deserves more emphasis than another.

Often revision proceeds in the order I have described, moving from the large question of the main idea to progressively smaller-scale issues and concluding with conventions of spelling, capitalization, and usage. But writing has a way of doubling back on itself, so that we revise as we are discovering and discover as we are revising. For example, you have probably found yourself stopping to correct spelling or to think about how to punctuate a sentence even when you are in early stages of drafting.

Reseeing the Whole

Although at times you may have to resee writing just after you have completed it (toward the end of an essay exam, for example), the best practice is to distance yourself from writing before trying to resee it. If you write a draft and put it away for a few days, you will have a fresh perspective when you return to it. Another way to obtain distance from your writing is by soliciting the views of others. Showing your draft to a friend, reading it to a writing group, or participating in a conference with your instructor can change your view of a draft. When you have gained some distance from your draft, return to the assignment that prompted the writing. The assignment usually suggests reasons or purposes for the writing required, and rereading the draft in light of the assignment can help you determine whether you have fulfilled these purposes.

Asking a series of questions about your draft can often help determine whether the draft is fulfilling the purposes of the assignment and the purposes you developed as you wrote in response to the assignment. These questions include:

1. What is the purpose of this assignment? What am I supposed to do?
2. Does my draft do what the assignment asks?
3. What purposes do I have for this writing?
4. Is my purpose clear?

Another way to resee a draft is to consider your audience. The four audience questions that appeared earlier can also be asked about a draft, because thinking about the audience for writing provides another way of seeing the draft:

1. What values does this audience hold?
2. What does my audience know about this topic?
3. Does my audience have strong opinions about this topic?
4. What effect do I want to have on my audience?

Finally, you can revise your drafts by focusing on the draft itself and trying to determine what the draft is doing and how it might do it better. To do this effectively, you need to pretend that you are reading a draft by someone else and ask these questions as if you had never seen the writing before:

1. What question does this essay try to answer?
2. What is the answer to this question? Respond by completing the following sentence: "In this essay the writer (asserts) (maintains) (argues) that. . . ."
3. What are the major reasons supporting this assertion? Respond by completing the following sentence: "To support this thesis, the author makes the following points. . . ."

An Overview

4. What conclusions does the author draw? Respond by completing the following sentence: "The author concludes. . . ."

To see how all of these questions aid revising, consider the following assignment, which was given in a writing class:

> Language enables us to learn about our world: we develop understanding of molecules, mollusks, and misery through language. At the same time language helps us to learn about itself. We frequently have experiences that help us understand language better. In your next paper I would like to write about an experience in which you came to some insight or understanding about language. Your audience will be people like yourself, college-educated individuals interested in language.

Here is a draft Eva Godwin wrote in response to this assignment:

Language Essay

Have you ever thought how much simpler America would be if we all spoke English? I am not referring to Asian Americans or Hispanic citizens or others who want to preserve their ethnic heritage. What I am referring to is the people who feel compelled to distort and contort our perfectly functional language. I am talking, of course, about the business people, advertisers, and promoters who decided somewhere along the line that it would be a good idea to create new names for every new product entering the market.

We no longer have plastic containers for storing leftovers; we have Tupperware. I do not carry a checkbook with a calculator built into it, but a Cal-cu-clutch. Children do not eat cereal for breakfast they eat Captain Crunch or Lucky Charms or Wafflos. First there was the chocolate bar; now there are Kit-Kats, Summits, and Wachamacallits. People no longer drive a Model A or a Model T, but Civics, Camaros, Tercels, or Futuras. What in the world is a Camaro or a Tupper? Do they have any meaning besides an automobile or a plastic dish? What is wrong with calling something by its proper name? Whatever happened to simplicity? Imagine how confusing all of this must be to foreigners!

"Well, after I fed the kids their <u>Trix</u>, I drove them to school in the <u>Citation</u>. Later <u>I</u> stopped at the grocery store and picked up some <u>Ruffles, Doritos,</u> <u>Fiddle Faddle</u>, and <u>Dr. Pepper</u> for the party tonight. I got home in time to <u>Lysol</u> the bathroom and run the

Electrolux over the carpet before the children returned from school."

How would anyone who is not a native understand all of this? "Do you wear or eat Ruffles? Who is Dr. Pepper? And what kind of sadistic parent would feed children Tricks?"

In a way I get a secret thrill out of generic products. I find peace, somehow, in their simplicity. I know what is in the package, and you know what is in the package. There is something gratifying about picking up a six-pack of beer and knowing it is just what the label says.

After she had completed this draft, the author waited for two days. Then she began evaluating her work by asking questions. First she considered questions about the assignment.

1. What is the Purpose of the Assignment?

    This assignment asks me to explain a personal experience that taught me something about a language. Recounting a moment of insight or new understanding seems to be part of the purpose.

2. Does my Draft do what the Assignment asks?

    I do talk about language here and show how I have come to appreciate generic brands, but the first paragraph does not seem right; it seems too general and impersonal.

3. What Purposes do I have?

    In addition to fulfilling the requirements of the assignments, I want to amuse people. I want my readers to see how funny the advertisers' made-up names are and through their laughter to recognize the value of generic brands. I think the generic brands come in too late, and I need to start the humor sooner to make my purpose really clear. Maybe it would help to change the title to "The Generic Essay."

By answering these questions about purpose, the author began to resee her draft and to plan changes. She decided to change the first paragraph because it did not serve her purpose well. Instead, she decided to do more with the quotation containing all the brand names because she had actually heard that conversation.

An Overview

Next she considered her audience and responded to questions about her readers.

1. What Values does my Audience hold?

    If my readers care about language, they will probably value clarity of expression and the precise use of words.

2. What does my Audience know about this Topic?

    My readers will probably be middle-class people who are familiar with brand names, and they will not need extensive introductions or explanations of words like Trix and Tupperware. They will also know about generic words.

3. Does my Audience have Strong Opinions about this Topic?

    Many readers may not have thought about brand names enough to have strong feelings against them, but they probably do not have strong preferences for them, either.

4. What Effect do I want to have on my Audience?

    I want to convince my audience that the language of advertising is phony, and I want to do it in a humorous way.

Finally the author reread her draft from the perspective of a reader and answered questions about it from this viewpoint.

1. What Question does this Essay try to Answer?

    This essay tries to answer the question of what we can learn from the language of advertising.

2. What is the Answer to the Question?

    In this essay the writer argues that much advertising obstructs the central function of language, which is communication.

3. What are the Major Reasons Supporting this Assertion?

    To support this thesis, the author makes the following points: product names invented by advertisers are unnecessarily complicated, and many of these names bear no relationship to the products to which they are attached.

4. What Conclusions does the Author draw?

   The author concludes that generic brands are superior to advertisers' name brands because they communicate their contents clearly.

By asking these questions about her draft, this student was able to resee the whole essay and realized that her point was to show how name brands prevent communication by failing to refer to the product they represent. She began rewriting and produced the following revision:

The Generic Essay

After several minutes of contemplation, I gave up trying to decide between Cheerios and Grape Nuts, and settled on some store-brand bran flakes. The frustration I felt when attempting to choose between Grape Nuts, which have nothing to do with grapes, and Cheerios (what is a Cheerio?), reminded me of a conversation I had overheard while waiting in line at the post office. There were two women in front of me discussing their plans for the day. One of them, who seemed to be the more talkative of the two, reeled off a list of phrases that made as much sense as ear muffs in July! "Well, after I fed the kids their <u>Trix</u>, I drove them to school in the <u>Citation</u>. Later I stopped at the grocery store and picked up some <u>Ruffles</u>, <u>Doritos</u>, <u>Fiddle Faddle</u>, and <u>Dr. Pepper</u> for the party tonight. Hopefully, I'll get home in time to <u>Lysol</u> the bathroom and run the <u>Electrolux</u> over the carpet before the children get home."

How could anyone who is not a native understand all of that? "Should you wear or eat Ruffles? Who is Dr. Pepper? Is Electrolux anything like shock therapy? And what kind of sadistic parent would feed children Tricks?"

The answers to these questions must lie somewhere in the minds of promoters and advertisers who decided long, long ago that product brand names should be as distantly related to product description or usage as possible. Somewhere along the way, somebody decided that plain English was not effective enough for marketing purposes, so new words were contrived to name every new product entering the marketplace.

My grandmother never owned a refrigerator; she had a <u>Frigidaire</u>. We don't have plastic containers for

An Overview

storing leftovers, but Tupperware. Originally you could only buy a Model A or a Model T. Now the highways are crowded with Camaros, Tercels, and Futuras, as well as several kinds of felines and equines (Cougars, Bobcats, and Lynx; Pintos, Mustangs, and Colts). Some of these names could be said to portray a certain desirable image or relationship between the product and its referent. I can see a correlation between the swiftness of a horse and an automobile, (after all, they are said to have "horsepower"), but what is a Camaro? I've never heard anyone use it in conversation to mean anything besides an automobile, and it's not even in the dictionary.

It seems that the names advertisers and promoters put on new products have gotten so unrelated to the items that most cannot be linked to the product without prior knowledge of their relationship. If you made two lists, one of products, the other of names, and then gave them to some person who had never heard of these items (the hypothetical child raised by wolves in the wilderness), he or she would never be able to properly match the names with the products. What do Lucky Charms have to do with breakfast cereal, or Tupper with plastic dishes?

I get a secret thrill out of generic products. I wish we had generic everything. Shopping would become so much easier if you didn't have to sort through aisles of eye-catching packages and screaming slogans. I wouldn't have to choose between Cheerios and Grape Nuts. With their simple wrappers and "bare bones" labeling, generics don't mislead consumers or make false connections through association with nonrelated items and made-up words. I know what is in the package, you know what is in the package. There is something satisfying about picking up a six-pack of beer and knowing it is just what the label says.

These two drafts demonstrate how revising helps writers resee their topics. As a result of asking and answering questions, the author developed her main idea about the confusion caused by brand names. The revisions she makes to highlight this main idea enable her readers to understand her views on brand names. Her writing shows new learning, and she is able to help readers see brand names through her eyes.

Development: Writing to Show Learning

EXERCISE

Compare the two drafts of "The Generic Essay."

1. How does the effect of the first paragraph differ in the two drafts?
2. List at least three statements that appear in the first draft and have been deleted in the second. How do these deletions improve the second draft? (Consider audience and purpose in particular.)
3. List at least three statements that do not appear in the first draft but are added in the second. In what ways do these additions help answer the essay's central question?
4. What discoveries has the author made in writing the revised version?

Here is the final draft of the paper Monica Caoili began as an early draft in her journal (see page 36 in Chapter 2). Read it through carefully and answer the questions that follow.

```
            The Unfortunate Encounter

     San Jose, Costa Rica, is unlike the major cities
of the United States in that it isn't nearly as de-
veloped, although it is the largest city as well as
the capital city of Costa Rica. There are no towering
skyscrapers, no subways, and little air pollution. The
buses and taxis serve as the main means of transporta-
tion. The air is somewhat humid. Walking along the
streets and passing through the parks, you smell the
aroma of fresh fruit and freshly baked bread until car
exhaust and noise interrupt the peace, as the city
comes to life. Clusters of litter are scattered here
and there along the sidewalks. The people are a sea of
dark skin and black hair, except for the few mestizos
(mixed) and foreigners sprinkled among them. A girl
with blonde hair and blue eyes is a rare sight and a
treat for the men. Accordingly, the men react with
stares and smiles, sometimes going as far as reaching
out to touch her.
     All girls must be wary and cautious if planning to
go downtown. Miniskirts and shorts are very inviting
and all girls, blonde hair or not, seen exposing them-
selves to that extent are asking for extra attention.
     Mandy was a tall thin girl. She had very prominent
cheek bones. Her blue skirt exposed her bony knees and
clung to her small hips. She was window shopping with
```

65

her friend Monica. Mandy smiled very little and when she did, her lips and teeth seemed to smile, but her eyes did not. She was seventeen. Her mother had died only months ago and although she had never been a very optimistic person, her mother's death had caused her to become negative, sarcastic, and irritable. She was still hurting, but this stay in Costa Rica was to help her by getting away from home for a while.

Mandy was attracting attention. Her hair was a light brown, but her skin was bone white and her eyes hazel. As she passed through the streets, she talked to Monica, who although an American too, blended in with the general populace, being of Philippine descent, with brown skin and black hair.

Costa Ricans who have never been to America only know of Americans from what they have seen on TV and in the movies. On TV they see only women who are very attractive, rich and "friendly." They assume that American women are all that way. So when they see an American woman walking their way, often times the men can't help but take notice and wonder if what they've seen is really true.

Mandy should have been more careful. Her skirt was a little too short. She had been advised about not asking for "extra attention," unlike other ignorant tourists who arrive and must discover their mistakes the hard way. Mandy tried to ignore the comments, but her face betrayed a look of irritation. As she approached a particularly crowded sidewalk, the man closed in on her from behind. His clothes were ragged. He smelled of alcohol and sweat. He drew his right hand from his pocket and reached for her skirt. Then quickly with her flesh and skirt between his forefinger knuckle and thumb, he pinched her. A look of satisfaction spread across his face. Mandy whirled. Shocked. Violated. She had had enough. She drew breath from between clenched teeth, glared angrily, and struck his arm fiercely. She turned and proceeded on her way.

"Mandy, he looks very familiar. I think he's been following us" spoke her companion as their casual stroll shifted to a hurried walk.

"God, I think so too."

The man was irritated. His look of satisfaction was gone. Nobody treated him like that. He quickened his pace, pushing himself through the crowd of people who stood waiting to cross the street. "She's not going to get away with this," he thought to himself. "Who do these Americans think they are anyway?" He was now so close to her that Mandy could feel his breathing on her neck. Her curls brushed across his cheek as she turned her head. Her eyes opened wide in surprise. He stared into her eyes. The man puckered his lips and sucked in his cheeks. Monica had turned around also, but before either Mandy or Monica could react, the man jolted his face forward, releasing a burst of saliva so thick that it plastered itself below Mandy's right eye in a glob of thick slime on her cheek.

She reached up her right hand and touched her cheek. A tear welled in her eye. Her face now reeked of tobacco. She was stunned. She was humiliated. "That man spat on me! That man SPAT on me!" she thought to herself over and over. She was disgraced. Disgusted. The stench was unbearable. Monica could only stand with her mouth agape. She felt helpless. She did not know what to do. They could not believe what had just happened. The people around them only looked at Mandy sympathetically. There were no policemen around. No one took any action toward the man. The saliva was now dripping down Mandy's face. Monica grabbed Mandy's arm, pulled her away, and they fled, bewildered and confused.

The man did not pursue them. He turned to continue along his way as his smile returned to his face.

---

1. Notice that she has moved to a third-person account. How does this change affect the whole piece?
2. What is the thesis of this selection? If you can't find a single sentence to quote, write a sentence of your own that captures the essence.
3. How do changes in title, introduction and ending support this thesis?
4. In what ways have the weaknesses of the first draft been eliminated?

EXERCISE

Revise the draft you wrote in response to the assignment on page 35. In your revision consider the same event or situation from a different viewpoint, one that is more objective. For example, if you are a central participant in your first draft, shift your role of narrator to that of less immersed observer.

Copyright © Tony Ganba, The National Audubon Society Collection/Photo Researchers, Inc.

Chapter Four

Redevelopment: Evaluating Writing to Show Learning

In writing to show learning the final step occurs as you submit your revised draft to an instructor. Previously you may have given the instructor drafts of the work-in-progress and received comments to help you revise, but at this point the instructor, assessing both the quality of the writing and the knowledge evident in it, assigns a grade. For many students this final step is a mysterious and intimidating one. You may have heard myths about instructors who throw stacks of student papers down the stairs and assign grades according to where each lands. (Such instructors may, like Big Foot and the Loch Ness Monster, exist, but the vast majority spend hours evaluating student essays in very responsible fashion.) Perhaps you spend time trying to figure out exactly what the instructor expects because you worry about your grade point average.

These uncertainties and anxieties are natural, but there are alternatives to concentrating on them. Instead of worrying about what an instructor expects, you can spend time and energy evaluating your own writing. There are a number of ways to conduct self-evaluation of writing. These include participating in writing groups; determining the priorities of your audience; and assessing the organization, cohesion, format, and mechanical conventions of your writing. Self evaluation of writing will enable you to *revise* writing to fit audience priorities, organize ideas effectively, and to *edit* for mechanics. This chapter explains how to evaluate your own writing.

Peer Response

One of the myths associated with writing is that it occurs entirely in isolation. Our language reflects this myth in descriptions of the "the writer's garrett," and in real estate advertisements for "secluded cottage ideal for writer." In these and other ways we perpetuate the mistaken idea that writers always work alone. Every writer must, of course, spend some time alone to inscribe words on paper, but biographies of and interviews with professional writers reveal that most of them work within a community. Many share their work-in-progress with others. Sometimes the sharing occurs in a formal group that meets regularly. Ben Franklin, for example, organized a club called Junto which required each member to bring an original composition for group critique once a month, and similar writing groups have existed in this country ever since. Other writers rely on more informal systems of peer response. They meet in cafes, public buildings, and one another's homes to read their work aloud to one another and receive suggestions for revisions.

Like these writers, you may find response from peers a valuable aid to revising. There are, of course, many ways to solicit suggestions from peers. You can simply hand a piece of your writing to friends and ask them to critique it; you can arrange to exchange drafts with someone in your class; your instructor may direct pairs of students to fill out an evaluation form about one another's papers, or you can participate in a writing group. All forms of peer response help you evaluate and revise your writing by giving you an actual audience. You have an opportunity to identify passages that although perfectly clear to you, confuse your readers. Peers can give you an indication of the effect of the whole piece, of sections that work especially well, and of questions that your writing raises—all of which give you specific ideas for revising.

WRITING GROUPS

One of the most effective forms of peer response occurs in writing groups because these groups provide an immediate indication of how several authors respond to your writing. Writing groups consist of five to seven individuals who all have work in progress. There are many ways for writing groups to proceed, but here are the guidelines I recommend:

1. *The group meets once a week for two hours.* It is important to meet regularly and promptly. The regularity keeps you in the habit of writing, and the promptness ensures that a two-hour commitment will not slide into three or more hours.

2. *Each week each group member brings work in progress to read.* Merely attending the writing group meeting does not constitute satisfactory participation. Although responding to others' writing is important, it is even more important to get responses to your own work.

3. *Each member is allocated an equal portion of the two hours.* Designate a timekeeper for the group, and divide the total time (120 minutes) by the number of people in the group (usually four, never more than five). It is the

Redevelopment: Evaluating Writing to Show Learning

timekeeper's responsibility to make sure that the group stays on schedule, allowing an equal amount of time for each member.

4. Each member's allocated time is divided into half for reading and half for group response. The timekeeper is responsible for dividing each individual's time into two parts and should stop the reading if it goes too long. For example, if your group contains four persons, each should be allowed to read for only fifteen minutes.

5. Work in progress is read aloud once; the author pauses long enough for the group members to write their initial responses; and then the author reads the writing a second time. During the second reading, the group members take detailed notes on their responses. I recommend reading aloud rather than exchanging papers for silent reading because oral reading prevents you from fussing with small features on the page and keeps your attention focused on the larger effects of writing. In addition, writers often benefit from reading their own work aloud. Oral reading can reveal a problem that will remain undetected in silent reading. When you listen to others' writing, *write your responses* so that you can recall for the author actual words and phrases. At the end of the first reading, write an overview of the whole piece, such as "This is about making decisions, but I don't understand which side the author is on. The word *aphasia* sticks out in my mind." Or "This is a good clinical description of bulimia, but I don't care about it because I can't see the victims clearly enough. All this vomiting makes me feel sick." Sometimes the second reading will answer the questions raised by the first one. Notes taken during the second reading should be more detailed. Record words, phrases, and even whole sentences that strike you as positive, negative, or that raise questions. My own system of recording looks like this:

- −certain traditions
- ?hissing fits
- +proud in stateliness
- +our valiant attempt for . . . perfect garden
- +cache
- −imposing precious rarities
- +vetch
- −it sounds too closely like wretch
- −such bright yellow heads
- +its leaves toss into salad
- ?tickle our minds to silliness
- ?an old trick
- −proudly shout
- ?throve a patch
- ?there was magic
- −muddled attempts toward perfection

My system is to catch as much of the language as I can so that I will be able to tell the author precisely what I am referring to, and I use a "+" for language that strikes me positively, a "−" for things I do not like, and a "?" for sections about which I am uncertain. Feel free to develop your own system, but make sure you can tell the author the actual words that prompted your response.

6. Group members give oral responses to the author immediately after the second reading. Each member has an equal amount of time to make verbal comments, and each person speaks in turn, with no comment from the other members of the group. Because the purpose of the writing group is to give the author as much audience response as possible, do not waste time talking among yourselves. Try to begin your response with "After the first reading I thought . . ." and then proceed with the list of responses collected during the second reading.

7. Oral responses are from the perspective of the audience; they do not offer advice. Your job is to give the author genuine responses to the writing but not to tell the author how to rewrite. That is the writer's job. Your task is to respond to what you hear in the language. If you hear obvious errors, feel free to mention them, but concentrate on responding to rather than directing the author. Writing groups exist to help the writer improve the text, not to do it for him or her.

8. The author remains silent as the group members respond and writes down all comments for future reference. This is perhaps the hardest part of the writing group procedures because most writers want to say, "No, you're wrong. I didn't say that at all" or "You don't understand; that's not my point." We all feel very defensive about our writing and resent criticisms of it. But the best way to profit from the group's comments is to bite your tongue and take careful notes. Often several group members will agree on the same points in a given piece of writing, and as you read these comments later, you may agree with what group members have said, even when it is painful.

9. Writers may not apologize for their work. Because writing groups deal with work in progress, it is easy to fall into a pattern of excusing the work before you begin reading. Comments such as "I really didn't have time to finish this" or "I've had a lot of trouble with this, and I don't like it very well" or "What I'm trying to do here is . . ." should not be tolerated because they attempt to prejudice the audience, and the writing group's function is to behave as much as possible like a real audience.

Established writing groups frequently develop their own procedures, but these guidelines offer a starting place for new groups. One issue these procedures do not address is how writing groups are formed, how individuals sort themselves into groups. If writing groups meet outside of class, logistics play a major role because groups need members with the same two hours free. Other considerations in forming groups include balancing gender, background,

Redevelopment: Evaluating Writing to Show Learning

personality and writing experience so the group has a diverse membership. If a group does not work well because of personality conflicts, your instructor can help you reformulate your group. If logistics make out-of-class meetings difficult—for commuting students, for example, you might try meeting during class time, or perhaps adding an hour before or after class to make two hours available.

If you participate regularly in writing groups for a class you may find that you want to continue meeting with other writers to get responses to work in progress. Many students find that they need writing groups to help them see what they are saying, to give their revisions direction, and to continue their development as writers.

Here is an example of how a classroom writing group can work. Susan read this selection from her paper about a frightening experience. The first part of the paper describes how she disobeyed her grandparents when she visited their pig farm and then found herself trapped inside the pen about to be attacked by the pigs. Fortunately her grandfather arrived in time to rescue her from the pen, and in the conclusion she reflects on her experience:

```
       It was about a month before I would go near the
pen again, even with Grandma. I was terrified of them.
But gradually my fear of them lessened and once again
I was out there helping feed them. Although I did get
over my fear of the pigs, it took me a long time to
recover from the fear of being in trouble and no one
being there to help me. My ordeal at the pig pen had
lasted only ten minutes, but it seemed like an eternity
before Grandpa had saved me. After my ordeal I had a
recurring dream that I was stranded in the woods and
some villainous force was pursuing me, but there was
no one to rescue me. I would awaken drenched in sweat
and trembling with fright. I hated being left alone
and I rarely ventured anywhere by myself. As I grew
older the dream became less frequent and eventually it
disappeared. However, even today I am leery of going
out, especially at night, by myself. The fear is not
that intense but nonetheless it is still there, and it
is something that I must deal with in order to live.
```

When Susan read this selection to her writing group, her peers commented that this selection seemed flat in comparison with the detailed description of her terror in the pig pen and of the grandparents' farm. In particular, they felt that the description of the dream did not include enough information and that the final sentence did not live up to the rest of the piece. They also stated that they were confused by the repetition of "them" in the first sentences.

An Overview

In response to these comments, Susan rewrote the second sentence to read "I was terrified of the pigs," and she expanded the description of the dream this way:

> Trying to reach the edge of the woods, I would run and run as fast as I could, hoping that someone would save me. But no one heard my cries for help. I was all alone. I never found out if I made it out of the woods, if I was rescued, or, worse yet, if I was caught by my assailant. I always awoke before my dream ended, my body drenched with sweat. I needed a night light on before I would go to sleep. Even then, I often lay in bed fighting the urge to sleep so that I would not dream. As I grew older the dream became less frequent and eventually it disappeared. However, I was still fearful of being out in the dark and needing help when there was no one there to help me. This is not an intense fear now but I still think about needing help and finding none. I was lucky when Grandpa rescued me, but will I be lucky again?

This revision demonstrates how comments from a writing group can enable a writer to improve a draft. Comments from her peers helped Susan see the need to add detail to the last part of her paper and to strengthen the ending. Without the writing group she might not have had such clear ideas about where and how to revise.

EXERCISE

Form and participate in a writing group, following the guidelines already outlined. After you have attended at least two sessions, write a review of your experience in the group giving special attention to what you have learned about writing.

Considering Audience Priorities

Writing groups and other forms of peer response can provide you with an immediate audience, one that will indicate general strengths and weaknesses and point to places where clarity of detail is needed. This type of evaluation is helpful for general revision, but it does not always address evaluative concerns of individual disciplines. Criteria for what constitutes a good piece of writing vary as one moves from, say, business administration to literature to physics. Thinking about the criteria for assessing quality of writing within a given discipline is not easy until you have worked in the discipline for a while, but the following analogy may help.

Redevelopment: Evaluating Writing to Show Learning

Exercises in values clarification ask participants to become more conscious of the values or criteria that guide their daily choices. Perhaps you have participated in an exercise such as imagining that you are involved in an emergency in which only a few people from a group can survive; brief biographies of each group member are provided; and your task is to decide who should be allowed to live. Another exercise asks you to list your favorite activities and then indicate whether they are solitary and/or involve spending money. Other exercises include deciding whether economic freedom, religious freedom, or political freedom is the most precious; determining whether income tax evasion or drug dealing is the more serious crime; examining the contents of your own wallet or the messages conveyed by your clothing. The rationale behind all of these exercises is that many people are unaware of the values or criteria that guide their life choices, and a better understanding of these criteria helps people make better decisions.

Becoming aware of a discipline's values is a long and complex process just as clarifying one's personal values is. There are no exercises to reveal what constitutes evidence in a given field, how an argument is made, or, even, the preferred forms for written presentations. Part of college education, however, involves becoming more familiar with these criteria, and writing aids the process. As you write in various classes you begin to learn the priorities of philosophy, as opposed to mathematics.

Consider, for example, William Golding's novel *Lord of the Flies*. This is a book that might be read in any number of classes, and the approaches taken to it suggest some of the criteria of different disciplines. For example, students in a literature class might read the book to examine its development of character, to analyze its structure, or to consider its thematic development of the question of evil. Students would be expected to examine how language is used to achieve the effects observed. A sociology class may read the book to consider group behavior among the boys on the island, and a psychology class might be asked to write about the degree of deviant behavior demonstrated by the boys.

As you think about the courses you are taking, you can probably identify some of their priorities. At most colleges, departments are grouped together because they share certain values. Becoming more conscious of these priorities can help you evaluate your own writing.

ARTS AND HUMANITIES

Areas of study in the arts and humanities include art and art history, communications, foreign languages, classics, film studies, drama, literature, music, philosophy, and religion. As you take courses in these departments, you will find that they emphasize individual interpretation, the uniqueness of objects of study, direct perception, and intrinsic or innate qualities. Accordingly, courses in literature or art emphasize the distinctive features of a poem or painting, encourage interpretation by the teacher and students, and scrutinize the work in question. Even though they share values, each area of study within

An Overview

the humanities has its own set of priorities. In literature the features of language are important, whereas considerations of line, space, and color figure prominently in considerations of art. Consequently, writing in the humanities reflects these values, as seen in the following passage:

> The twentieth century may be said, so far as painting is concerned, to have begun five years late. Between 1901 and 1906, several comprehensive exhibitions of the work of Van Gogh, Gauguin, and Cézanne were held in Paris. Thus, for the first time the achievements of these masters became accessible to a broad public. The young painters who had grown up in the "decadent," morbid mood of the 1890s were profoundly impressed, and several of them developed a radical new style, full of violent color and bold distortions. On their first public appearance, in 1905, they so shocked critical opinion that they were dubbed the *Fauves* (the wild beasts), a label they wore with pride. Actually, it was not a common program that brought them together, but their shared sense of liberation and experiment. As a movement, Fauvism comprised numerous loosely related, individual styles, and the group dissolved after a few years.
>
> Its leading member was Henri Matisse (1869–1954), the oldest of the founding fathers of twentieth-century painting. *The Joy of Life* (fig. 770), probably the most important picture of his long career, sums up the spirit of Fauvism better than any other single work. It obviously derives its flat planes of color, heavy undulating outlines, and the "primitive" flavor of its forms from Gauguin (see colorplate 69); even its subject suggests the vision of Man in a state of Nature that Gauguin had pursued in Tahiti (see fig. 761). But we soon realize that these figures are not Noble Savages under the spell of a native god; the subject is a pagan scene in the Classical sense—a bacchanal, like Titian's (compare colorplate 41). Even the poses of the figures have for the most part a Classical origin, and in the apparently careless draughtsmanship resides a profound knowledge of the human body (Matisse had been trained in the academic tradition). What makes the picture so revolutionary is its radical simplicity, its "genius of omission": everything that possibly can be, has been left out or stated by implication only, yet the scene retains the essentials of plastic form and spatial depth. Painting, Matisse seems to say, is the rhythmic arrangement of line and color on a flat plane, but is not *only* that; how far can the image of nature be pared down without destroying its basic properties and thus reducing it to mere surface ornament? "What I am after, above all," he once explained, "is expression . . . [But] . . . expression does not consist of the passion mirrored upon a human face . . . The whole arrangement of my picture is expressive. The placement of figures or objects, the empty spaces around them, the proportions, everything plays a part." But what, we wonder, does *The Joy of Life* express? Exactly what its title says. Whatever his debt to Gauguin, Matisse was never stirred by the same "decadence" of our civilization. He had strong feelings about only one thing—the act of painting: this to him was an experience so profoundly joyous that he wanted to transmit it to the beholder in all its freshness and immediacy. The purpose of his pictures, he always asserted, was to give pleasure.
>
> —H. W. Janson, *History of Art*

Redevelopment: Evaluating Writing to Show Learning

The value placed on individual interpretation is evident in two ways. In the first paragraph the author suggests the individuality of paintings by Van Gogh, Gauguin, and Cézanne and then shows how their work influenced the individualistic styles of the Fauvists. Implicit in this paragraph is the idea that individual interpretation is encouraged in art. A more pervasive emphasis on individual interpretation appears throughout the whole passage. The author includes a number of statements—the degree of influence of Van Gogh, Gauguin, and Cézanne on the Fauvists, what united the Fauvists, the importance of *The Joy of Life,* and the meaning of Matisse's painting—that could be subject to debate, but little justification is offered for any of these statements. That is, the author proceeds on the assumption that his interpretation is sufficient in itself.

Throughout this discussion, the uniqueness of paintings is described in positive terms. The first paragraph emphasizes the innovations of the two groups. The lengthy paragraph on Matisse points toward his uniqueness in several ways. *The Joy of Life* is compared with paintings by Gauguin, Titian, and the classical artists, but the point of these comparisons is to show how *The Joy of Life* departs from them. The author establishes the unique quality of *The Joy of Life* as its "radical simplicity" and spends considerable time showing how this uniqueness is achieved. ("Whatever his debt to Gauguin, Matisse was never stirred by the same agonized discontent with the decadence of our civilization.")

In his discussion of *The Joy of Life,* the author offers direct perception of the painting. The explanation of flat planes of color, heavy outlines, primitive flavor, and apparently careless draftsmanship all derive from the author's own close examination of Matisse's work. Another direct perception appears in the quoted statements by Matisse. The author does not summarize Matisse's words but offers them directly to the reader.

The author's concern with innate or intrinsic qualities of painting is evident throughout this selection. In the first paragraph he uses phrases such as "decadent morbid mood," "bold distortions," and "sense of liberation and experiment" to describe the paintings. The final sentences of the second paragraph are directed to a close examination of the essence or intrinsic quality of *The Joy of Life,* and the concluding statement that Matisse's purpose in painting was "to give pleasure" summarizes the author's view of what is intrinsic to Matisse's work in general.

E X E R C I S E

Much writing in the humanities is based on criteria of individual interpretation, uniqueness of object of study, direct perception, and attention to intrinsic quality. Select a passage used in a humanities course, and analyze it in terms of these four criteria. Write an essay in which you explain how these four criteria are manifested.

An Overview

Natural Sciences

The departments usually grouped under natural sciences include astronomy, biology, botany, chemistry, some areas of engineering, geology, mathematics, physics, and zoology. Courses in this area emphasize factual descriptions of the physical world and living things. Hypotheses, principles, generalization, laws and theories are advanced to amplify and/or support factual descriptions, and these formulations are tested through observation and experimentation. Evidence and verification result from observation and experimentation. Many courses in the natural sciences include laboratory experiences so that you will learn how to collect your own evidence and verification. Within the natural sciences, the life sciences and physical sciences are concerned with all matter-energy systems, and life sciences deal with only those systems that are alive. One of the interesting problems of life sciences is to decide how to characterize something as alive. If you have taken courses in the natural sciences, you have already seen natural science priorities in action. Rather than focusing on the unique qualities of an object, as you might in the humanities, you are encouraged to see the piece of igneous rock or the slab of shale as part of the exploding and folding of layers over time so that you can move to generalizations about the earth's crust. As you have probably already noticed, writing in the natural sciences is influenced by the area's priorities, as the following selection demonstrates:

> It appears technically feasible to measure surface winds from a satellite. In the summer of 1978, the National Aeronautics and Space Administration (NASA) launched Seasat, which was equipped with several experimental instruments. Almost 100 days later, after 1,502 orbits, there was a power failure. On board was a scatterometer, a radar instrument capable of deducing estimates of the wind speed and direction in an ocean patch about 50 kilometers on each side. We are not quite sure exactly how the instrument works, but we do know it sends a radar beam to the ocean and measures the amount of back-scattered radar energy. It is supposed to measure the intensity of the wavelets in the ocean patch. Wavelets are very small 5- to 10-centimeter waves that ride on the back of bigger waves. The premise is that the intensity, strength, and quantity of these little waves are related to the wind speed at the same place and time. Some of the data from Seasat have been carefully examined by oceanographers and meterologists and there is cautious agreement that the scatterometer is capable of measuring wind speed in many weather situations to within 2 meters per second (approximately 5 miles per hour). The wind scatterometer is also capable of measuring wind direction except it always has a 180-degree bias—for example, it cannot tell north from south or east from west. Most meterologists can remove this bias by looking at a standard satellite view of the earth and noting the position of storm centers.
>
> A wind scatterometer mounted on an orbiting spacecraft would estimate the surface wind speed and direction below its path as it moved around the earth. If the orbit were adjusted to altitudes of about 2,400 kilometers, the satellite could cover the entire globe in a few days. For the first time in our history, we would have global distribution of wind estimates every week or so. These would be used in a variety of ocean models to simulate ocean surface currents

on many space and time scales. In essence, we would be able to estimate the distribution of ocean currents over an entire ocean and their changes on a day-by-day basis. The wind field derived from the radar reflection from the tiny wavelets would in turn be used to derive pictures of the ocean movement. This cannot be done from buoys and ships, since an enormous number of platforms would be required, but appears to be possible from satellites. Thus we would be measuring the wind at the surface of the ocean from an instrument located 2,400 kilometers in the sky.

—James O'Brien, *Oceanus*

The value placed on factual description is evident throughout this passage. Specific information on the time and circumstances of the work are given immediately, and precise terms such as "after 1,502 orbits" and "2,400 kilometers" appear throughout. The scatterometer is described in terms of its function, and wavelets are explained in terms of their size and location. Likewise, the benefits and limitations of Seasat data are explained. Subjective interpretation is not part of this description. Adjectives, so common in the humanities selection, are used very sparingly, and the author seems to be carefully avoiding any subjective response to the items described.

With the first two words, "It appears," the author gives prominence to the criteria of advancing hypotheses, and the whole selection emphasizes the tentative nature of what is being advanced ("we are not sure," "cautious agreement," "180-degree bias," and the continuing use of "would" in the second paragraph all demonstrate this tentativeness). Despite the cautions observed, the whole point of the passage is to suggest a principle for measuring surface winds, and the basis of this suggestion lies in the statement "The premise is that the intensity, strength and quantity of these little waves are related to the wind speed at the same place and time." It is this hypothesis that supports the factual descriptions of what has been measured by the scatterometer.

Much of this passage is devoted to explaining how the theory that satellites can measure surface winds has been tested. The factual description and statement of hypotheses provide the background for the discussion of the tests conducted. The narrative that begins "In the summer of 1978" and ends "five miles per hour" recounts the experimental work that provides the basis for the claims made. This article does not contain much actual evidence or verification, but the statement that data have been carefully examined tells us that evidence does exist.

EXERCISE

Much of the writing in the natural sciences is based on these criteria of factual description of the physical world and living things, advancement of hypotheses, principles, generalizations, laws or theories, testing formulations through observation and experiment, and collecting evidence or verification from observation and experiment. Select a passage used in a natural science course, and analyze it in terms of these four criteria. Write an essay in which you explain how these four criteria are manifested.

An Overview

SOCIAL SCIENCES

In the social science group you will find departments such as anthropology, economics, geography, history, linguistics, political science, psychology, and sociology. As the word *science* suggests, some aspects of the social sciences resemble those of the natural sciences: observation, evidence, and verification all contribute to generalizations or theories, much as they do in the natural sciences. But because the social sciences deal with various aspects of human life, there is less emphasis on facts and more on interpretative understanding of how human beings act. In economics, for example, everything turns on the question of how humans, who have unlimited wants, deal with limited resources. Descriptions of various approaches to production and consumption suggest systems of behavior that respond to the central idea of unlimited wants and limited resources. Indeed, the economic chaos of recent years demonstrates that economics is not a science based on fact. Writing in the social sciences reflects concern with systems of behavior, as the following article demonstrates:

Writing Apprehension and Occupational Choice

The importance of perceived communication demands in an individual's selection of a vocation has been suggested recently by Daly & McCroskey (1975), using a model predicting decisions on the basis of maximization of rewards. Individuals very anxious about speaking were found to select jobs perceived to have low demands for speech communication. The opposite was true for non-anxious individuals. The present report extends that finding to apprehension of writing. Previous work with this variable has found it predictive of message encoding behavior (Daly & Miller, 1975a), enrollment in advanced writing courses (Daly & Miller, 1975b) and the successful encoding of counter-attitudinal messages (Toth, 1975). It was hypothesized that individuals with high writing apprehension would perceive jobs with low writing requirements significantly more desirable than those with high perceived writing requirements. The opposite prediction was made for individuals low in writing apprehension. Individuals with low writing apprehension should also report actually selecting specific occupations with higher perceived writing requirements than those selected by subjects with high apprehension.

METHOD

Ninety-five undergraduate students completed the writing apprehension measure (Daly & Miller, 1975c), as well as instruments similar to those used by Daly & McCroskey (1975) to assess the perceived writing demands and perceived desirability of various occupations. Subjects also indicated the perceived writing demand of their actual vocational choice. The ten highest and ten lowest occupations in terms of writing requirements were retained from an original pool of 31. In terms of writing requirements, the combined mean for high writing positions ($\bar{X} = 6.6$) was significantly ($F = 1663.2$, $P < 0.0001$) greater than the mean for low writing occupations ($\bar{X} = 2.9$). Subjects were classified as high or low in writing apprehension on the basis of a mean split. Individuals with scores above 56 (on the 20 item measure) were classified as high apprehensive ($n = 48$) while those with scores below 57 were labeled low apprehensive ($n = 47$).

Results

A two-way analysis of variance with one repeated measure was computed for the perceived desirability scores of the retained vocations. One factor was the level of subject apprehension while the other (the repeated measure) was the level of writing requirements. As hypothesized a significant interaction was observed ($F = 30.2$, d.f. $= 1, 93$, $P < 0.0001$) with the means in the directions posited above. Individuals with high apprehension found occupations with low writing requirements ($\overline{X} = 3.1$) more desirable ($t = 5$, $P < 0.001$) than those with high writing requirements ($\overline{X} = 2.1$). On the other hand, there was only a marginally significant trend for low apprehensives to see high writing occupations ($\overline{X} = 3.1$) more desirable ($t = 1.5$, $P = < 0.1$ than low writing occupations ($\overline{X} = 2.8$). In addition, high writing apprehensives ($\overline{X} = 2.6$) saw all occupations as significantly less desirable ($F = 4.8$, d.f. $= 1, 93$, $P < 0.05$) than low writing apprehensives ($\overline{X} = 3.0$). Overall, jobs with low writing requirements ($\overline{X} = 3.0$) were seen as significantly more desirable ($F = 8.7$, d.f. $= 1, 93$, $P < 0.005$) than those with high writing requirements ($\overline{X} = 2.6$). The second hypothesis was also supported. Low apprehensives indicated significantly ($F = 8.1$, d.f. $= 8.1$, d.f. $= 1, 93$, $P < 0.01$ higher ($\overline{X} = 4.9$) writing requirements than did high apprehensives ($\overline{X} = 4.1$).

Discussion

Results indicate the probable importance of perceived communication demands in the decisions people make about various occupations. For both spoken and written communication the apprehension data now show the importance of individual differences in this factor for occupational decision-making. The less than significant difference on desirability for the low apprehensive individual has at least two explanations. First, it is possible that highly apprehensive individuals are more sensitive to writing demands than are low apprehensives. Secondly, the low apprehensive may feel that a position with low writing requirements may be moulded into one with high requirements. Once a level of communication is established, it may be difficult to decrease the demand but relatively easy to expand the requirements.

—John A. Daly and Wayne G. Shamo,
"Writing Apprehension and Occupational Choice"

Because of their relationship with the natural sciences, these social scientists seek to test the hypotheses that people who feel apprehensive about writing desire occupations that require little writing and that people who feel little such apprehension prefer occupations that require significant amounts of writing. Likewise, factual description and numbers (ninety-five students, twenty-item measure) are given prominence throughout the article, and the results of the study are described as supporting the two hypotheses.

Yet, despite its similarity to natural science writing, this article uses the criteria of social science. Unlike natural science, which uses instruments to measure physical features, the instruments described in this article are designed to measure human behavior and opinion. Interpretation of results is given considerable attention in the article, and statistics provide the basis for this interpretation (the ten highest and the ten lowest occupations in terms of writing . . .). Although the statistical procedures are given considerable attention, they are not an end in themselves but a means to discovering more about how people (in this case, those with large or small degrees of apprehension about writing) act. One of the implications of this article, and of most writing in the social sciences, is that the people investigated in this study are typical and that their behavior may be generalized to other human beings.

The values or criteria of a discipline are sometimes built into the questions asked within that discipline. A phrase such as "effective political leadership" signals that the issue under consideration is political, concerned with how power influences people's behavior, and thus an effective response to this question will include political considerations.

In other cases the question does not specify priorities but assumes that the students will know that they are. For example, here is a question from a literature class.

> Analyze the relationship between theme and setting in Faulkner's *A Rose for Emily*.

Terms such as *theme* and *setting* have specific meanings for literature students, and the word *setting* refers to a much smaller range of features than it would, say, in a geography class. Here is an excerpt from one response:

```
    The site of action is a once-grand gothic structure
that is now an "eyesore among eyesores" with its "stub-
born and coquettish decay." Progress for the town is a
dilemma, with cotton gins, garages, and gasoline pumps
appearing on the once most select street in town.
Details of the house's interior parallel the inability
of old southern aristocrats to move with the times.
There is a close, dank smell of dust and disuse, and
the house is filled with shadows.
```

As you can see, the writer draws on the general values or criteria of the humanities in this excerpt. The author offers his own interpretation of Emily's house and of progress in the town. The uniqueness of Emily and her house are suggested by the comment on southern aristocrats unable to move with the times. Considerable direct perception, in the form of quotations from the fiction, are present in this account, and the author has arranged these details in a way that shows his views on the intrinsic quality in the story. The decay evident in the house contributes to both setting and theme.

This process of identifying and responding to the (often unstated) criteria of a discipline is an important part of expository writing because the ability to speak to these criteria makes writing more comprehensible to the specialists in that discipline. Identifying priorities might be described as a subtle form of audience analysis, determining what an instructor wants to hear, and it is

Redevelopment: Evaluating Writing to Show Learning

that, but only in part. The greater part of identifying criteria moves toward learning to think in the way that specialists in a given discipline do, and writing to reflect such priorities enhances learning in any subject.

Even though you may not be immediately able to describe the criteria of a given discipline, being aware that disciplines differ in terms of the value they assign to individual interpretation, uniqueness, direct perception, intrinsic qualities, factual description, hypotheses, generalizations, or experimental verification can help you evaluate your own writing.

EXERCISE

Here are two questions, the first from an economics class and the second from an English literature class:

1. As a general rule, the elasticity of supply is greater in the long run than in the short run. Construct examples of situations in which supply might be virtually zero in the long run and almost infinite in the short run.
2. In what ways are Mark Twain's *Huckleberry Finn* and William Howell's *The Rise of Silas Lapham* specifically romantic works?
   a. List the criteria you can identify in each question.
   b. Compare your list with someone else's. What are the differences?
   c. How do the priorities that you have identified reflect the criteria of economics and literature?

Evaluate Organization

One of the comments you may hear in your writing groups is "I like this selection because it really flows" or "This piece doesn't seem to flow very well." Even though they don't offer much concrete help, comments like these address organization in writing, another aspect of writing that you can evaluate for yourself. Organization consists of placing information so that it can be easily comprehended by the reader. To see the importance of organization, clip out your favorite comic strip, then separate the individual frames of the strip, and rearrange them randomly. The scrambled version demonstrates the importance of organization because most comic strips make little sense when the frames are rearranged.

TIME ORDER

Organization plays an even more important part in writing, because readers have nothing except lines of words to guide their understanding. If writing wanders randomly, readers have no way to make sense of it. As a reader yourself, you probably know that predictable patterns help you follow another writer's prose. For example, if you read "I was a junior in high school when I bought my first bike," you expect that the selection will continue by following *time order*. You expect the following sentences to chronicle what happened to

An Overview

the first bike, what the author experienced with that and subsequent bikes, what the author learned about bicycling in the intervening time. You might also find bicycling equipment listed in the order in which it was purchased.

SPATIAL ORDER

Reading a sentence such as "The clothes bikers wear look pretty silly to people who don't know anything about the sport," leads you to expect a description of bicycling clothes. You look for a discussion of tight-fitting shorts, of gloves without fingers, of helmets with chin straps, of cycling cleats, and of jerseys with pockets in the back. The author might follow *spatial order* by beginning with the helmet and working down to the cleats. This organizational pattern enables the reader to assimilate information about equipment with the more familiar physical structure of the body.

ORDER OF IMPORTANCE

A sentence such as "People who want to do more than ride bikes down the sidewalk will need special equipment" could also lead into a description of bicycling accessories and clothing, but the reader might expect the organizational plan to follow *order of importance*. Items could be introduced in terms of their importance to safety, beginning with helmets and progressing to toe clips and knee pads.

ANALYSIS

A sentence such as "There are several kinds of helmets to choose from," by contrast, creates an expectation of *analysis*. As you read this sentence, you expect that the following sentences will classify helmets according to criteria such as safety, durability, or comfort. You look for details that will distinguish one helmet from another.

GENERAL TO SPECIFIC

Reading a sentence such as "There seems to be an unwritten law stating that every kid on the block will have a bike," sets up an expectation of a series of specific statements to support this generalization. This movement from *general to specific* will probably include examples of the kinds of bikes kids have, accounts of interactions among various bikers on the block, and an explanation of how the block—with potholes or smooth concrete—treats bicyclists.

CAUSE AND EFFECT

Your expectations shift again if you read a sentence such as "Enrolling in college caused me to use my bike for commuting as well as pleasure touring."

Redevelopment: Evaluating Writing to Show Learning

This kind of sentence suggests a *cause and effect* pattern of development. You read watching for an account of how the author used bicycling as a form of transportation to and from college classes, and you expect to see an explanation of the distance between the author's home and college, a list of the benefits of bike commuting, and possibly a discussion of other (rejected) modes of transportation.

Comparison

A sentence such as "I was transformed from an ordinary biker to a true biker," arouses yet another set of expectations. Reading this sentence leads you to look for a *comparison* between ordinary and true bikers. You know that this kind of sentence will introduce features that distinguish the two types of bikers from one another, and it may even lead to a comparative analogy such as "Ordinary bikers are the seeds from which true bikers grow."

Identify Organizational Patterns

Patterns that enable you to anticipate what will come next in your reading are patterns you can use to organize your own writing. You can employ these structures to help your readers follow the development of your ideas:

- time order
- spatial order
- order of importance
- analysis
- general to specific
- cause and effect
- comparison

As the explanation of reading illustrates, each of these patterns takes a different direction, and patterns are not dictated by subject matter. For example, you could approach the topic of developing from an ordinary bicyclist into a true bicyclist with a time order pattern, tracing the series of events that led from early and ordinary biking experiences to more recent "true" experiences. Or you could employ a classification pattern, using "ordinary" and "true" bicyclists as the two categories, listing features that divide individuals into one category or the other.

Mix Organizational Patterns

Just as several organizational patterns can be used with the same subject matter, so one piece of writing can employ multiple patterns. Beginning with a time order pattern does not mean that you must adhere to that pattern exclusively throughout a whole piece of writing. Time order can be your dominant structure even when you use description or comparison or cause and effect patterns in the same piece of writing. It is rare indeed for a writer

An Overview

to follow a single pattern of development because it is difficult to sustain a single pattern and because readers find it tedious.

In evaluating the organization of your writing, you can use these patterns to determine whether your writing delivers on the promises it makes, whether it gives your readers a structure to follow. The following example illustrates how a mixture of organizational patterns can be identified in writing:

```
                        Charge It

     I squeezed her hand to see if I could get a re-
sponse from my mom. I couldn't. I held on a while
longer as we strolled down to the elevator. I knew she
was getting sick of me, and I couldn't blame her. We
had been together all day. I squeezed again and asked
if it would be okay if I went walking around by myself.
She replied positively and suggested that I should go
and buy a new pair of school shoes. I thought, "Me
charge? You bet! I have never done that before." She
placed the credit card in my hand, rattled off some in-
structions and gave me a gentle push towards the chil-
dren's shoes.
     As I walked on, I stopped and just stood there
looking at the card. I really couldn't understand how
a credit card worked, but then again I didn't really
care. I let my fingers ride over the numbers feeling
the grooves between each ridge, I pretended that
braille was my second language. My hand was a little
bit larger than the card. I turned it over, and looked
at where my mom had signed her name like an autograph.
I can always tell my mom's handwriting, large loops
here, small ones there, and don't forget the umlaut
over the "a."
     I finally found a pair of shoes that struck my
fancy. I got my size (which was larger than my normal
size since I had to grow into them) and went up to the
counter. The salesman had that "hatred of children"
look on his face especially when I handed him the
credit card and said "Please charge it." Once I had my
shoes in my hands, I held them with a sense of ac-
complishment.
     Because I was so proud of myself I started to gal-
lop along looking for my mother. I pretended that I was
on the range, darting through the make-up counter,
trotting through the accessories and paying no atten-
tion to anything. I guess I should have, since I
knocked down a fat lady. She sat there, staring up at
```

Margin annotations: Time order · Description · Time order

Redevelopment: Evaluating Writing to Show Learning

Cause and effect me with indignation, her packages sprawled out on the floor, her rolls of fat peeking out of her polyester blouse, her face resembling a pug bulldog. I tried to explain myself. She wouldn't listen. I gave a good effort to help her up, but that made matters worse. I ran her panty hose. I could tell that it was time to gallop away by the way her facial muscles contorted.

    I ran for the open elevator, barely making it. I knew my mom was in the housewares department on the second floor, so I pushed "2." I swear that everybody was staring at my temples pounding. I was so hot. Relief came when the doors opened and there she was, standing at the cashier, wearing her Monday ensemble.

Time order I walked to her. Handing her my shoes we exchanged a few words (nothing to do with the fat lady incident). She picked up her packages and told me to follow. I trailed behind her; slowly I slid the card out of my pocket. I looked at it and laughed.

As "Charge It" demonstrates, it is possible to combine a mixture of organizational patterns in a single piece of writing. By adding description and cause and effect patterns to the dominant time order structure, the author creates texture and adds interest to the writing. Too much variety and too many changes of pattern can, however, make writing less effective. The following essay demonstrates how lack of a dominant pattern of organization diminishes the quality of writing:

My Best Course

General to specific   Of the classes I have taken at the university, Economics 100 is my favorite. The class is an introductory course in the field of economics. It is taught by Professor Thomas, who is an excellent lecturer, which really helped add to my interest level in the class. As a result of this class I have decided to major in economics.

Description   When friends ask me why I believe Economics 100 is such a good course, I tell them that the material is interesting and informative. Even at the introductory level the concepts presented are useful in everyday life. This information gives you an understanding of how and why our economic system functions.

    In the beginning of the class I learned about microeconomics which is the study of supply, demand, and

An Overview

<table>
<tr><td>Time
order</td><td>the forces that affect these. The supply and demand for microeconomics is for the individual firm or industry. The last three weeks of the course will be spent on the subject of macroeconomics. Macroeconomics is the study of factors that affect the whole economy. This material is presented in a basic and interesting fashion by Professor Thomas. Anytime he discusses a topic, he uses examples that have meaning in everyday life.</td></tr>
<tr><td>Description</td><td>The tests given in Economics 100 are the multiple-choice variety. This is nice for me because I have always had trouble with essay tests. On the seven weeks that we don't have tests, we have quizzes. These quizzes cover material taken up in the preceding week's lectures. The quizzes consist of problems and short-answer questions. The quizzes count for 10 percent of my grade, and the rest is split evenly between the two midterms and the final.</td></tr>
<tr><td>Comparison</td><td>Although Economics 100 is only an introductory course in economics, the material covered is not as simplistic as I have found in other introductory courses. I am taking Sociology 110 from Professor Sneed, and this class is a big waste of time because the material presented is so basic that the class is bored. It is a class where I am learning almost nothing.</td></tr>
<tr><td>Comparison</td><td>I have taken other interesting informative classes. In each class the instructor has done much to help both my understanding and enjoyment. These classes are good, but I feel that Economics 100 has a little more to offer the student.</td></tr>
<tr><td>Classification</td><td>In the bad classes I have taken, I feel it was the way the information was organized and presented that made the class bad. One chemistry teacher I had spent all the time disagreeing with the text and expanding on it. By the end of the term only half the class was left. This showed me that there was definitely something wrong with his approach to teaching the class. This experience discouraged me from going into chemical engineering, which had been my intended major.</td></tr>
<tr><td>General to specific</td><td>There is no doubt in my mind that Economics 100 is the best course I have taken at the university. It will take quite an effort on the part of any instructor to top the efforts made by Professor Thomas to make the class as interesting and informative as he did.</td></tr>
</table>

Redevelopment: Evaluating Writing to Show Learning

EXERCISE

Imagine that the author of "My Best Course" came to you for advice on revising the organization of the paper. What changes would you recommend?

OUTLINE

Analyzing and revising structural patterns offer one method for evaluating organization in your writing. Another way to determine whether your writing is well organized is to make an outline of it. The formal outline has often been recommended as a way of planning before you write, but it can be even more effective to make an outline after you have written. The process of outlining your own work can show you where organization falters. The standard form for outlines appears in the next paragraph. Topic outlines use words or short phrases, and sentence outlines employ complete sentences. For outlining your own work, topic outlines are usually adequate because the content is familiar.

Outlines usually have three or four types of headings. Capital Roman numerals indicate the main divisions of the outline. Capital letters indicate the subparts of these main divisions, and arabic numerals signal the breakdown of information listed under second-level headings. Lower-case letters can be used for subjects of the third-level headings, so that the final structure looks like this:

```
I.
    A. (Rules of formal outlining dictate that if
       there is a I,A there must be a I,B.)
       1.
       2.
    B.
II.
    A.
    B.
    C.
```

The following essay can be outlined to demonstrate how this technique enables you to examine organization.

Learning a Foreign Language

My great-grandmother is ninety years old. She came to America in 1952 with other members of my family. She never learned to speak English. She really didn't have to because the people she associated with all spoke Greek. When I was younger I would visit her very

89

often but I never could understand what she said. I learned some Greek words and phrases as I got older. Yet I never pursued my education in the Greek language. My father would always say "You should go to Greek school so you can speak with your great grandmother because she is old and isolated." I never took him seriously. It seemed as though I always had something better to do.

It was not until I went to Greece that I realized the importance of my learning the Greek language. In the summer of 1980, my family and I went to Greece for six weeks. We first arrived in Athens on June 1. My uncle, who lives in Ionnina, met us and showed us around Athens for the good part of a week. I didn't feel too uncomfortable around my uncle, even though he spoke Greek, because my parents were always there to translate for me.

We left Athens to spend some time with my relatives in Ionnina. The time spent there with my cousins was when I realized how much Greek I needed to learn. I can remember the first time I met my cousins. It was our first day there. They were all three to four years younger than me, but they were at home, like having the field advantage. I blurted out "Hello, I'm Mike. How are you?" It didn't come out quite as well as I had expected and they began to laugh. Before we arrived, my cousins had taken a few English lessons, and they responded, "Hello, how are you?" Since they were younger, I felt as though they were way ahead of me. We all knew words in each others' language but we couldn't put things together. They tried to make me feel at home yet I still felt somewhat isolated. I finally knew how my great grandmother felt in Seattle. After realizing this I just decided to go for it, open up and take chances speaking Greek. The rest of the time spent with my cousins was a learning experience for everyone. They introduced me to all of their friends and we hit it off well. It worked out so that I had to speak Greek or not communicate at all. Granted I made mistakes, and probably sounded like a two year old, still everyone understood what was going on. I was helped by nearly everyone I met.

My great-grandmother could not believe the difference in my Greek when I got back. Since then I speak Greek every chance I get and I visit my great-grandmother as often as possible. I still only speak with novice expertise but I can carry on an intelligent conversation with my great-grandmother. I just wish I would have learned a little bit earlier because she won't be around much longer.

Mike made the following outline of his essay:

    I. Great-grandmother speaks only Greek
        A. Mike speaks little Greek
        B. Father recommends Greek school
            1. Grandmother isolated
            2. Mike too busy
   II. Visit to Athens
        A. Uncle speaks only Greek
        B. Parents translate
  III. Visit to Ionnina
        A. Young cousins speak little English
        B. Mike feels isolated
            1. Mike understands isolation great-grandmother feels
            2. Mike decides to learn Greek
   IV. Return to U.S.
        A. Mike speaks Greek
        B. Mike visit great-grandmother frequently

In making this outline, Mike realized that the basic organizational structure of his essay was sound, but the first paragraph needed some restructuring to make clear the relationship between the great-grandmother's speaking only Greek and her isolation. He realized that there was a potential contradiction between the statement about her not needing English and the one about her isolation. He knew it was important for him to highlight the isolation issue because he returned to it in the third paragraph.

EXERCISE

Make an outline for the following essay (or for a selection of your own writing) and then explain organizational changes suggested by your outline.

Making Friends

"I'm sure you have all noticed that there is a new boy in the class," is the way teachers always seemed to start off my first day in a new school. I know this line quite well. I've moved fourteen times during my lifetime. Eight times in the middle of the school year.

An Overview

The first thing I would try to do is make new friends. Making new friends can be difficult, but it doesn't need to be. Some people will say "Act natural, be yourself." I've always had a problem with this. I could never figure out what is "natural." Or what "being yourself" really meant. After a few years of experience I found that being myself is being whoever I needed to be to fit into my surroundings.

When I learned that I could be anyone I wanted to be, making new friends became much easier.

I remember my dad coming to class on my first day of fourth grade. While talking to the teacher my dad, to the amazement of all the fourth graders started beeping. Turning off his beeper my dad left to call a real estate client. Naturally all the guys wanted to know what the beeping meant. After some hesitation I quietly informed them that my dad was a secret agent. Needless to say, I had twenty instant friends.

Although stretching the truth might help, it is not the safest way to make friends. Because once the lie is found out popularity tends to drop rapidly. And this tactic only seems to work well before the seventh grade.

I found that adapting to the new surroundings was a good way to make friends. For instance, when I went to a public school in Los Angeles I tried to act poorer than I was. The families of the kids I liked best didn't have much money. I thought they would be uncomfortable around me if they knew my family was middle class. So I would slip out of the house in old clothes or change in a department store on the way to school. The problem was that I always had to think of excuses for not inviting friends to my house. My mom and dad thought I was acting strange, so they sent me to a private school.

I've also learned that association with various groups is an easy way to make friends. I would usually join the sports crowd. But I also associated with the strictly scholastic type on occasion. But once, in the eighth grade, I hung around the "stoners." We would just smoke cigarettes, sometimes marijuana, and act like jerks. I was glad we moved during eighth grade.

Now and then I think that maybe I would have liked to live in the same neighborhood for seventeen years and develop one long-lasting friendship. But that would probably have been boring. And without the many different friends I've made, I wouldn't have been able to experience the many different aspects of life that I have.

Evaluate Cohesion

Cohesion refers to the capacity of writing to stick together. Writing that lacks cohesion has a disjointed feeling. The selection that appears below illustrates this feeling.

On Becoming Human

Leo Buscaglia taught a college course on love at the University of California at Berkeley during the 1960s and early 1970s. Students learned to care for themselves. Buscaglia learned along with the students. He oversees a few graduate students in the field. Buscaglia has written several books, including <u>Because I Am Human.</u> Buscaglia had an encounter with a four-year-old Indian boy named David. Buscaglia contends that adults never talk with children. They either talk at them or else over their heads. Buscaglia and David had a conversation about the things David could do. David's responses were, "I can spit" and "I can cry." Asked why he could do these things, David replied, "Because I am a boy." Leo Buscaglia was the keynote speaker for the Northwest Residence Life Conference in January. His keynote address was given in the Hub Auditorium. Tickets to the address were free. The auditorium was filled to capacity. The speech was videotaped by Housing and Food Services and is available for viewing. Leo Buscaglia is a very powerful, intimate speaker. A young man introduced Buscaglia; when Buscaglia climbed onto the stage, he received a warm bear hug. Leo admits to being a "great toucher" and attributes it to his Italian background. He wants everyone he meets to feel warmth. In his love class at U.C. Berkeley he had a "voluntary mandatory" requirement that each of his students come to his office to meet him personally. Buscaglia wanted to know each student as an individual. He said they were intimidated.

An Overview

You probably had difficulty following this essay, and your difficulty stems from the fact that it lacks cohesive ties. Cohesive ties are words that signal connections among different parts of a piece of writing. Cohesive ties can be divided into several types. The most common and easiest to use are *reference ties,* words that refer ahead or back to other words in writing. Pronouns, adverbs, and comparatives can work as cohesive ties in reference.

COHESIVE TIES OF REFERENCE

Pronouns. You no doubt know the definition of pronouns as "words that take the place of nouns." Although this definition is helpful, I think it is more useful to think of pronouns in terms of what they *do*: they help create coherence in writing. There are several types of pronouns that can serve as cohesive ties. Among them are personal pronouns, indefinite pronouns, demonstrative pronouns, and relative pronouns.

Personal Pronouns

I	you	he	them
me	they	him	their
mine	we	his	theirs
my	us	she	it
you	our	her	its
yours	ours	hers	

Personal pronouns refer to beings or objects.

Indefinite Pronouns

all	each	much	several
another	each one	neither	some
any	either	nobody	somebody
anybody	everybody	none	someone
anyone	everyone	no one	something
anything	many	one	
both	many a	other	

Indefinite pronouns make only third-person (he, it, they, and the like) references.

Demonstrative Pronouns

this	these
that	those

Demonstrative pronouns focus on or point to something that has appeared earlier.

Relative Pronouns

who	whose	that
whom	which	what

Redevelopment: Evaluating Writing to Show Learning

Relative pronouns introduce clauses that act as nouns or modifiers and refer to other clauses or sentences. For example:

```
The carpenter, whose assistant did all the work,
came to collect his check.
```

The two following sentences demonstrate how pronouns work as reference ties:

```
There were two women in front of me discussing
their plans for the day. One of them, who seemed to be
the more talkative of the two, reeled off a list of
phrases that made about as much sense as ear muffs
in July.
```

The pronoun *them* ties the second sentence to the first because it is clear that *them* refers to the *two women*. Pronouns cannot provide cohesion unless their referent is clear. One way to evaluate cohesion in your writing is to check for unclear pronoun references.

Unclear reference occurs when the pronoun can refer to more than one noun, when the number of noun and pronoun do not agree, or when the pronoun is too far away from the noun to which it refers. This sentence from "On Becoming Human" illustrates the first type of unclear reference:

```
A young man introduced Buscaglia; when Buscaglia
climbed onto the stage he received a warm bear hug.
```

He refers to one of the two males mentioned, either Buscaglia or the young man who introduced him, but *he* cannot function as a cohesive tie because there is no way of telling which male received the hug. One way to remove the ambiguity is to rewrite the sentence this way:

```
The young man who introduced Buscaglia received a
warm bear hug from the speaker when Buscaglia climbed
up onto the stage.
```

The relative pronoun *who* functions as a cohesive tie to link the young man with the act of introducing, and the repetition of Buscaglia's name removes all uncertainty about who gave and received the hug. An alternative revision of this sentence would be

An Overview

> A young man introduced Buscaglia; when Buscaglia climbed onto the stage he gave the young man a warm bear hug.

Here the repetition of "the young man" solves the reference problem.
The final sentence in "On Becoming Human" contains another reference problem:

> Many of them were intimidated.

We can assume that *them* refers to the *student* mentioned in the previous sentence, but *them* is a plural form and cannot be tied with the singular *student*. This use of *they* may derive from vague uses of the pronoun in common speech; utterances such as "They say it will rain tomorrow," or "When will they stop taxing us?" appear frequently in conversation. Shifting the pronoun from plural to singular or shifting the noun from singular to plural can solve the problem and create a cohesive tie between the two sentences:

> Buscaglia wanted to know all of his students. He said they were intimidated.

As you probably noticed, aligning the pronoun and referent makes the two sentences clearer, but they still do not sound very good. Additional cohesive ties of pronoun reference would improve them considerably. Consider this revision of the two sentences:

> Buscaglia wanted to know all of his students, something that was very intimidating for many of them.

Here the indefinite pronoun refers to *something,* the concept of Buscaglia's wanting to know all of his students, and creates a cohesive tie between the wanting to know and the feeling of intimidation. Earlier passages in "On Becoming Human" can likewise be improved by introducing cohesive ties of reference:

> Buscaglia has written several books, including <u>Because I Am Human</u>. Buscaglia had an enounter with a four-year-old Indian boy named David.

Redevelopment: Evaluating Writing to Show Learning

As they stand, the two sentences have no apparent relationship to each other. However, if we introduce cohesion through reference, the relationship will become clear:

```
    Buscaglia has written several books, including
Because I Am Human. The idea for this book stemmed
from an encounter that Buscaglia had with a four-year-
old boy named David.
```

The demonstrative pronoun *this* substitutes for the specific title mentioned in the previous sentence and links the title with the additional information about the genesis of the book. The same kind of improvement can be made by changing

```
    Leo Buscaglia taught a college course on love at
the University of California at Berkeley during the
1960s and early 1970s. Students learned to care for
themselves.
```

to

```
    Leo Buscaglia taught a college course on love at
the University of California at Berkeley during the
1960s and early 1970s. The purpose of this class was
for the students to learn to care for themselves.
```

Locating similar problems of reference in your own writing is one way to evaluate cohesion.

EXERCISE

1. Return to the second draft of "The Generic Essay," and read the third and fourth paragraphs. List all the pronouns in these two paragraphs that provide cohesive ties.
2. Return to the first two paragraphs of "My Best Course" and identify at least three places where cohesive ties of reference would improve the writing. Rewrite these sections.

Demonstrative adverbs. Demonstrative adverbs are another source of cohesion in writing. Four demonstrative adverbs serve to tie parts of sentences or whole sentences to one another. These adverbs are

97

An Overview

    here   there   now   then

Two sentences from "On Becoming Human" can be improved by adding cohesive ties of demonstrative adverbs.

```
    Leo Buscaglia taught a college course on love at
the University of California at Berkeley during the
1960s and early 1970s. Students learned to care for
themselves.
```

to

```
    Leo Buscaglia taught a college course on love at
the University of California at Berkeley during the
1960s and early 1970s. The students learned to care
for themselves.
```

Inserting the demonstrative adverb *here* connects the college course on love with the students in the course. The sentence

```
    He oversees a few graduate students in the field.
```

seems unrelated to the sentences on either side of it, but its relationship can be made clear by introducing a demonstrative adverb:

```
    Even now, he oversees a few graduate students in
the field.
```

The addition of *now* connects the present activity of supervising graduate students with the course that Buscaglia formerly taught.

Comparatives. Comparatives describe two or more elements in terms of *similarity, difference, quantity,* or *quality*. The most common forms of comparatives are formed by adding *-er* or *-est* to one-syllable adjectives and adverbs to produce such words as bigger, faster, oldest, and farthest. As well, there are other comparatives:
Comparatives link words and sentences through reference, as this sentence from "On Becoming Human" illustrates.

```
    He wants everyone he meets to feel warmth.
```

Redevelopment: Evaluating Writing to Show Learning

to

```
    He wants everyone he meets to feel more warmth.
```

Adding the comparative *more* here connects this sentence with the preceding one, which describes Buscaglia as a "great toucher." The *great* here suggests that Buscaglia touches more than most people do and thus connects it with his desire to give "more" warmth to those he encounters. As you find similar places to link words and sentences with comparatives you evaluate another dimension of cohesion.

COHESIVE TIES OF CONJUNCTION

Reference through pronouns, adverbs, and comparatives is one type of cohesive tie; another is *conjunction*. Conjunctions unite phrases, clauses or sentences that may not have a direct relationship, and conjunctions say something about the kind of relationship being established. Some conjunctions signal addition.

As you read through "On Becoming Human," you can see that it contains some conjunctions such as *and* and *or*. You can probably also see places where conjunctions could be added. For instance, the sentence,

```
    Students learned to care for themselves
```

could be linked by an *and* to

```
    Buscaglia learned along with the students.
```

Other conjunctions can be introduced by using words that signal more complex forms of addition. The sentence

```
    He wants everyone he meets to feel more warmth,
and in his love class at U.C. Berkeley he had a "volun-
tary mandatory" requirement that each of his students
come to his office to meet him personally.
```

can be linked by inserting "for example" before "in his love class." This "for example" shows that the explanation about the class is directly connected to the statement about Buscaglia's desire to make people feel more warmth.

Another kind of conjunction indicates opposition. For example, the sentence

99

An Overview

> Leo Buscaglia is a very powerful intimate speaker.

can be improved by introducing an adversative conjunction to link the opposing qualities of *powerful* and *intimate*. Writing "powerful yet intimate" signals that the two do not normally go together but that in this case the two qualities do coexist. Another kind of addition can also indicate a dismissal or opposition to uncertainty. The premise of the sentence

> Buscaglia admits to being a "great toucher" and attributes it to his Italian background.

relies on an ethnic stereotype with which not everyone might agree. The writer can acknowledge possible disagreement by inserting "in any case" or "at any rate" before

> he wants everyone he meets to feel warmth.

This insertion not only connects the two sentences more closely but also suggests some distance between the writer's and Buscaglia's views.

A third type of cohesive tie is *causal*, in which words show a cause-and-effect relationship between two ideas.

As you can see, "On Becoming Human" contains some causal ties. In David's response "because I am a boy," the *because* shows that being a boy causes him to be able to do things such as spit and cry. Additional causal ties could further improve this first page. The connection between the sentence,

> the auditorium was filled to capacity.

and

> The speech was videotaped by Housing and Food Services and is available for viewing.

could be signaled by connecting them with "consequently" or "because of this" or "for this reason."

A fourth type of conjunction is *temporal,* in which two sentences or parts of sentences are related by sequence; one thing precedes or follows another.

Adding words that signal temporal cohesion can enhance sections of "On Becoming Human." Among them are the sentences

Redevelopment: Evaluating Writing to Show Learning

       Buscaglia and David had a conversation about the
things David could do.

and

       David's responses were "I can spit" and "I can
cry."

---

which could be connected by inserting the temporal conjunction *when* at the beginning of the first sentence. By doing this, the writer indicates that the conversation and the responses occurred simultaneously. By contrast, adding 'first' to the sentence "David's responses were . . ." shows that David made a number of responses but that the first two concerned spitting and crying.

    Still another form of conjunction is supplied by *punctuation*. Commas, as you know, separate words in a series, and their separation simultaneously shows that the words listed belong together. Likewise, commas work with conjunctions such as *and, or,* and *but* to indicate two main clauses in a compound sentence, and in so doing, the comma points to the cohesion between the two parts of a sentence. The two sentences

       Students learned to care for themselves.

and

       Buscaglia learned along with the students.

---

could be connected by *and,* which would show their connection to each other. Another way to link two sentences is to use a ";" by itself. A semi-colon signals a logical relationship between two independent clauses. Thus:

       Buscaglia contends that adults never talk with
children; they either talk at them or over their heads.

The preceding sentence uses a colon (:), another form of punctuation that indicates cohesion. A colon can introduce a statement or a list, thus indicating the connection between the preliminary statement and the series that follows.

E X E R C I S E

Although this discussion has mentioned a number of revisions for "On Becoming Human," they have not been compiled, nor is the job complete. Rewrite the two paragraphs incorporating the suggestions noted here and adding as

An Overview

many additional cohesive ties as you think appropriate. Be sure to consider cohesive ties of reference using pronouns (personal, indefinite, demonstrative, and relative), adverbs, and comparatives, and conjunctions of addition, opposition, causation, and time, as well as punctuation.

Cohesion in Your Writing

Knowing words that signal reference and conjunctive cohesion is, of course, a first step toward evaluating cohesion in writing. An even more important step is to consider what you are writing about. To use cohesive ties to link ideas that do not have any relationship to one another makes writing worse, not better. To connect

```
Buscaglia learned along with the students.
```

and

```
He oversees a few graduate students
```

with a conjunction of opposites such as *yet, however,* or *nevertheless* would establish a causal relationship between the two sentences. And if your point were to show an incongruity between learning along with students and supervising graduate students, then this kind of cohesive tie would be appropriate. The final tests for cohesion in writing is whether the relationships signaled by cohesive ties are what you intend.

Spending considerable time on early stages of writing, determining what a writing task asks of you, deciding on strategies, and finding out what you know and need to know about the topic provide the best basis for deciding on cohesive relationships when you revise.

Cloze test. If you are interested in a mechanical measure of cohesion in your writing, you may wish to try a *cloze test.* Cloze tests were originally developed to measure reading ability, but they can also indicate the cohesion in writing. The principle of the cloze test is closure, or understanding well enough to predict what comes next. The reason that it can measure cohesion in writing is that it asks an unbiased reader to follow a piece of writing closely enough to predict what the writer will say. If someone who has not written on your topic can supply missing words in your writing, you will have a good indication that your writing will be cohesive when all the missing words are filled in.

To design a cloze test, retype or rewrite the last one hundred words of a piece of your writing, substituting a blank for every fifth word. The result should look like this:

Redevelopment: Evaluating Writing to Show Learning

On the bus ride _____(1)__, I became aware of _____(2)__ feeling I haven't had _____(3)__ intensely since I was _____(4)__ junior in high school: _____(5)__ was ready to go _____(6)__ again. In my _____(7)__ year, I ended my _____(8)__ season at the district _____(9)__, in which I was _____(10)__ the second day by _____(11)__ number two seed in _____(12)__ consolation rounds. I came _____(13)__ close to beating him, _____(14)__ ran out of time. _____(15)__ that match, I was _____(16)__ looking forward to wrestling _____(17)__. It was that feeling _____(18)__ was experiencing again, and _____(19)__ day in the future I _____(20)__ going to do this _____(21)__ sport of rapelling again.

E X E R C I S E

Make a cloze test with your writing, give it to several friends, and ask each to list the word that fits best in each numbered blank. Compare these lists with the words you actually used. If several people supply the word you actually used, you can be confident that your writing has sufficient coherence. However, if a number of people fail to guess the words you used, you may want to reexamine the coherence of your writing.

Evaluate Format

The format of most college writing will be dictated by the assignment, and reconsidering the format required should be part of evaluating your own writing.

The following assignment comes from an economics class:

> During the last six weeks of the term you will be required to hand in a reaction paper. The assignment is to locate a current newspaper or magazine article containing information, data, or speculation about the current economic situation. More than one article can be used for your paper. You should state the major points made in the article. This information should be related to the relevant theoretical material covered in class. The paper can proceed in several ways: you can contrast two theories using the current data; you can make predictions by combining theory and data; or you can find fault with the theory and/or predictions of the article to which you are reacting. Each paper should be two to four pages long and typed, and the material you are reacting to should be clipped to your paper. Special points that you wish to draw to my attention should be underlined.

The specifications for format are very general here. Beyond the stipulation of two- to four-page length and attached material, the instructor gives little indication of what format is expected. Many of the writing tasks you face in college will give no more direction about form than this assignment does, but you can assume that standard, double-spaced typewritten pages will be acceptable.

Some assignments, however, include more specific directions about format. This assignment was given in a sociology class:

> Your term paper should explore the institution of kingship from a comparative perspective in order to improve your understanding of authority and enhance your theoretical concepts for the analysis of social power. Your paper should contain two sections: an overview of the history of the kingdom chosen and an annotated bibliography of the sources you used. Use this outline for your writing: (1) a preface that introduces the kingdom selected and how it was chosen. Describe its location and the period of history to be studied. (2) a political and economic setting section that describes the major political, economic, and cultural features of the region surrounding the kingdom. (3) a historical sketch of the history of rule that lists successive rulers and summarizes external warfare and problems of internal control. (4) a structural analysis of the kingdom that describes the classes of people who comprised the kingdom and the institutional patterns governing their relations with one another. (5) a termination section that describes how the kingdom ended or evolved. (6) a theoretical analysis that employs whatever theoretical concepts or principles that seem useful in understanding the dynamics of authority and power in the kingdom under study. (7) a bibliography that annotates the sources you actually used: other sources relevant but not yet read or examined need only be listed in the standard format.

Here the form of the paper is specified according to section, and the writer is given a good deal of direction about how to put together the final draft. One student who completed this assignment explained that she had the general outline in mind from the time she began writing the paper, and the section divisions helped her plan her writing. However, she did not actually put her paper into the specified form until she was working on the final draft. If her experience is typical, and I think it is, writers have an internal sense of the eventual form in which they will write, but the actual shaping comes relatively late in the process of writing.

Sometimes instructors will provide very specific directions about form, as this sociology instructor did; directions for science reports, for example, often come with an outline for the parts to be included in the final paper. On other occasions the instructor will not provide specific directions, and you will need to determine what the conventional expectations for that class include. This process of learning about various forms adds, indirectly at least, to your understanding of the subject you are studying.

STANDARD FORM FOR COLLEGE PAPERS

In addition to the specifications given by an instructor, you can use general criteria to evaluate the format of all your college papers. Unless an instructor

Redevelopment: Evaluating Writing to Show Learning

gives you other directions, you can use the following guidelines for college writing.

Paper
- Use white, unlined, 20-pound, 8½ × 11 paper.
- If you use computer paper, be sure it has clear perforated edges.

Typing
- Type or word process your papers; do not turn in handwritten work unless your instructor asks for it specifically.
- Double-space the entire paper, including headings, quotations, and titles.
- Leave one-inch margins at the top, bottom, left, and right.
- Indent the first word of each new paragraph five spaces from the left margin.
- Number pages consecutively, beginning with page 2 (do not put a number on the first page).

Identification
- Be sure your last name appears on all pages. Type it before the number on each page.
- On the first page (or title page if your instructor requests one) type the following:

    Your name (and ID number if you have one)
    Assignment name or number
    Course title and number
    Instructor's name
    Date

Evaluate Conventions

Conventions refer to established forms of writing that enable readers to make sense of what they see. Conventions include spelling, punctuation, capitalization, sentence structure, word choice, and use of special forms such as abbreviations, hyphens, italics, and numbers. In the process of writing, these are among the last features to focus on. Shaping the organization of the whole piece, considering its audience, and ascertaining that there is cohesion all come before attention to conventions. But conventions need attention. One of the first things any reader will notice is a misspelled word. It is like a wrong note in an otherwise excellent piano recital. Other lapses in conventions elicit similar responses from readers. They will fix on the comma fault or inappropriate word choice, losing track of what the writing actually says.

One of the last things you need to do, then, is evaluate the use of conventions in your writing. If you have any doubts about specific conventions of writing, refer to the handbook section at the back of this book.

Copyright © Art Bilsten, The National Audubon Society Collection/Photo Researchers, Inc.

PART TWO

APPLICATIONS

Copyright © Myron Wood, The National Audubon Society Collection/Photo Researchers, Inc.

Chapter Five

Reporting Events

R EPORTING events occupies much of our everyday lives. We listen to news commentators retell world, national, and local events on the radio or television. As we meet others we relate past happenings, recount bits of gossip, and listen to the accounts of others. We hear snippets of conversation such as "When I moved to Boston. . . ." "And then she said. . . ." "He opened the door and. . . ." Often at the end of the day, we retell our day's experiences to a close friend or reflect on them privately. Many situations require recounting: responding to a friend who missed class and asks what happened; answering an interviewer who wants to know about previous work experience; and telling someone about a new film or play.

This process of recounting is a way of interpreting the world, because accounts of what happened provide an understanding of what has happened and what happens in general. When we give accounts of a day's activities, for example, we assign meanings to events and words, highlighting some items and minimizing others. The term *narrative* describes the process of recounting, whether it takes the form of reporting the day's events or writing a lab report, or presenting an overview of a historical period. Derived from the Latin *gnarus* meaning "to know," narrative is a means of learning because it requires an interpretation of events.

Recounting events transforms three-dimensional experience into linear language. It also involves selecting from a wide assortment of data and arranging this selection into a comprehensible order. For example, when someone who was absent asks what happened in class today, you do not give a fifty-minute account of every word spoken and every action taken. You select the statements and actions that strike you as being the most significant and describe them in some order. Your organization may be chronological, starting with what happened first and recounting events as they occurred. Alternatively, you may start with the assignment, thinking that the most important, or you

Applications

may start with something funny or unusual; whatever strategy you employ, you *interpret* the class for your friend. Both *selection* and *organization* operate as you interpret and recount events, whether orally or in writing.

Getting Ready to Report Events

Because we do so much narrating, it is easy to dismiss it as a skill we are all born knowing. After all, even a five-year-old child can tell a story. Yet an effective written account of events requires more than simply writing what you might say. When events come from your own experiences, memory plays an important part.

MEMORY

Reading the following selection carefully will show you how writers can draw on memory selectively and interpretively to recount experiences effectively. This selection, written by Frank Conroy, comes from the book *Stop-Time,* a memoir of Conroy's adolescence. It recounts an event that occurred while the ten-year-old Conroy was attending an experimental boarding school. As you read, notice how the details Conroy includes contribute to the effect he creates. What does he leave out?

Savages

Frank Conroy

A rainy day. All of us together in the big dorm except a fat boy named Ligget. I can't remember how it started, or if any one person started it. A lot of talk against Ligget, building quickly to the point where talk was not enough. When someone claimed to have heard him use the expression "nigger-lipping" (wetting the end of a cigarette), we decided to act. Ligget was intolerable. A boy was sent to find him.

I didn't know Ligget. He had no friends even though he'd been at school longer than the rest of us. There was some vagueness about his origins, probably his parents were dead and relatives cared for him. We knew he was in the habit of running away. I remember waking up one night to see three men, including a policeman, carrying him back to his bed. He fought with hysterical strength, although silently, as if he were afraid to wake the rest of us. All three had to hold him down for the hypodermic.

[*Notice how Conroy has dipped back in time to provide information about Ligget.*]

On this rainy day he didn't fight. He must have known what was up the moment he walked through the door, but he didn't try to run. The two boys assigned to hold his arms were unnecessary. Throughout the entire trial he stood quite still, only his eyes, deep in the pudgy face, swiveling from side to side as he followed the speakers. He didn't say anything.

The prosecutor announced that first of all the trial must be fair. He asked for a volunteer to conduct Ligget's defense. When it became clear no one wanted the job a boy named Herbie was elected by acclamation. It seemed the perfect choice: Herbie was colorless and dim, steady if not inspired.

[*The pace changes as Conroy moves into dialogue.*]

"I call Sammy as a witness," said the prosecutor. There was a murmur of approval. Sammy was something of a hero to us, as much for his experiences in reform school as for his fabulous condition. (An undescended testicle, which we knew nothing about. To us he had only one ball.) "The prisoner is charged with saying 'nigger-lip.' Did you hear him say it?"

"Yes. He said it a couple of days ago. We were standing over there in front of the window." Sammy pointed to the end of the room. "He said it about Mark Schofield." (Schofield was a popular athletic star, a Senior, and therefore not in the room.)

"You heard him?"

"Yes. I got mad and told him not to talk like that. I walked away. I didn't want to hear him."

"Okay. Now it's your turn, Herbie."

Herbie asked only one question. "Are you sure he said it? Maybe he said something else and you didn't hear him right."

"He said it, all right." Sammy looked over at Ligget. "He said it."

"Okay," said the prosecutor, "I call Earl." Our only Negro stepped forward, a slim, good-looking youth, already vain. (A sin so precocious we couldn't even recognize it.) He enjoyed the limelight, having grown used to it in the large, nervous, and visit-prone family that had spoiled him so terribly. He got a package every week, and owned a bicycle with gears, unheard of before his arrival.

"What do you know about this?" asked the prosecutor.

"What do you mean?"

"Did you ever hear him say what he said?"

"If he ever said that around me I'd kill him."

"Have you noticed anything else?"

"What?"

"I mean, well, does he avoid you or anything?"

Herbie suddenly yelled, "But he avoids everybody!" This was more than we had expected from old Herbie. He was shouted down immediately.

"I don't pay him no mind," said Earl, lapsing uncharacteristically into the idiom of his people.

The trial must have lasted two hours. Witness after witness came forward to take a stand against race prejudice. There was an interruption when one of the youngest boys, having watched silently, suddenly burst into tears.

"Look, Peabody's crying."

"What's wrong, Peabody?" someone asked gently.

Confused, overwhelmed by his emotions, Peabody could only stammer. "I'm sorry, I'm sorry, I don't know what's the matter. . . . It's so horrible, how could he . . ."

"What's horrible?"

"Him saying that. How could he say that? I don't understand," the boy said, tears falling from his eyes.

"It's all right, Peabody, don't worry."

Applications

"I'm sorry, I'm sorry."

Most of the testimony was on a high moral plane. Children are swept away by morality. Only rarely did it sink to the level of life. From the boy who slept next to Ligget: "He smells."

We didn't laugh. We weren't stupid boys, nor insensitive, and we recognized the seriousness of such a statement.

"His bed smells, and his clothes, and everything he has. He's a smelly, fat slob and I won't sleep next to him. I'm going to move my bed."

Sensing impatience in the room, the prosecutor called the prisoner himself. "Do you have anything to say?"

Ligget stood stock still, his hidden eyes gleaming. He was pale.

"This is your last chance, you better take it. We'll all listen, we'll listen to your side of it." The crowd voiced its agreement, moved by an instant of homage to fair play, and false sympathy. "Okay then, don't say you didn't have a chance."

"Wait a second," said Herbie. "I want to ask him something. Did you say 'nigger-lip' to Sammy?"

It appeared for a moment that Ligget was about to speak, but he gave up the effort. Shaking his head slowly, he denied the charge.

The prosecutor stepped forward. "All those who find him guilty say aye." A roar from forty boys. "All those who find him innocent say nay." Silence. (In a certain sense the trial was a parody of Freemont's "town meetings" in which rather important questions of curriculum and school policy were debated before the students and put to a vote.)

[*Notice how the punishment is introduced.*]

The punishment seemed to suggest itself. We lined up for one punch apiece.

Although Ligget's beating is part of my life (past, present, and future coexist in the unconscious, says Freud), and although I've worried about it off and on for years, all I can say about it is that brutality happens easily. I learned almost nothing from beating up Ligget.

There was a tremendous, heart-swelling excitement as I waited. The line moved slowly, people were taking their time. You got only one punch and you didn't want to waste it. A ritual of getting set, measuring the distance, perhaps adjusting the angle of his jaw with an index finger—all this had to be done before you let go. A few boys had fluffed already, only grazing him. If you missed completely you got another chance.

It wasn't hurting Ligget that was important, but rather the unbelievable opportunity to throw a clean, powerful punch completely unhindered, and with none of the sloppiness of an actual fight. Ligget was simply a punching bag, albeit the best possible kind of punching bag, one in human form, with sensory equipment to measure the strength of your blows.

It was my turn. Ligget looked at me blankly. I picked a spot on his chin, drew back my arm, and threw as hard a punch as I could muster. Instant disappointment. I hadn't missed, there was a kind of snapping sound as my fist landed, and his head jerked back, but the whole complex of movements was too fast, somehow missing the exaggerated movie-punch finality I had anticipated. Ligget looked at the boy behind me and I stepped away. I think someone clapped me on the back.

"Good shot."

Little Peabody, tear-stained but sober, swung an awkward blow that almost missed, grazing Ligget's mouth and bringing a little blood. He moved away and the last few boys took their turns.

Ligget was still on his feet. His face was swollen and his small eyes were glazed, but he stood unaided. He had kept his hands deep in his pockets to prevent the reflex of defense. He drew them out and for a moment there was silence, as if everyone expected him to speak.

[*See how the spontaneous second line reinforces the earlier point about how easily brutality happens.*]

Perhaps it was because we felt cheated. Each boy's dreams-of-glory punch had been a shade off center, or not quite hard enough, or thrown at the wrong angle, missing perfection by a maddeningly narrow margin. The urge to try again was strong. Unconsciously we knew we'd never have another chance. This wild freedom was ours once only. And perhaps among the older boys there were some who harbored the dream of throwing one final, superman punch, the knock-out blow to end all knock-out blows. Spontaneously, the line formed again.

After three or four blows Ligget collapsed. He sank to the floor, his eyes open and a dark stain spreading in his crotch. Someone told him to get up but it became clear he couldn't understand. Eventually a boy was sent to get the nurse. He was taken to the hospital in an ambulance.

X-rays revealed that Ligget's jaw was broken in four places. We learned this the day after the beating, all of us repentant, sincerely unable to understand how it had happened. When he was well enough we went to visit him in the hospital. He was friendly, and accepted our apologies. One could tell he was trying, but his voice was thin and stiff, without a person behind it; like a bad actor reading lines. He wouldn't see us alone, there had to be an adult sitting by him.

No disciplinary action was taken against us. There was talk for a while that Sammy was going to be expelled, but it came to nothing. Ligget never returned.

Now that you have an overall sense of this account, return for a second reading and find answers to the following questions:

1. Why does Conroy include the background information about Ligget's lack of friends and his running away?
2. What effect does the description of Herbie, Ligget's defender, have? How does it prepare you for Herbie's later "But he avoids everybody!" What about the description of Earl?
3. Why does Conroy insert his comment about brutality where he does? Would it be as effective if it came at another place?
4. What does the conclusion tell you about Freemont?

As you can see, Conroy's account does not include every detail of his experience. He acknowledges that he cannot remember some things, and he summarizes two hours of interrogation in a couple of pages of dialogue. He

Applications

selects from his memories. Although chronological order is dominant, Conroy moves freely from one time period to another. Notice how he weaves in the more distant past of Ligget's running away, of Sammy's experiences in reform school, of visits from Earl's family, of Freemont's "town meeting," and the recent past of his reflections on beating up Ligget. By *arranging* his account this way, Conroy controls his readers' perspective on the event.

Not all events you recount from memory will take such dramatic form as Conroy's. You may write about what happened in a laboratory experiment, or on a visit to a social service agency, or as you read a novel. Memory always plays some role in recounting events, even if it is merely remembering what you have read. Recounting events that you did not experience, however, draws on a broader range of skills. Chief among them is the ability to collect information.

COLLECTING

The first impulse of most students who need more information on a topic is to rush to the library and start reading books and articles on the subject. They begin recording information on notecards as they read. This is one way to gather information, but it is not the only one. Frequently you will be able to interview an expert on your topic or to find other sources of information. Regardless of your sources, recounting events that you have not experienced requires collecting even more information than you can use.

To see how a writer can recount events she did not experience, read the following selection by Barbara Tuchman. This selection comes from *A Distant Mirror—The Calamitous 14th Century,* an account of the plague that ravaged Europe during that period. As you read, notice the different types of information Tuchman includes. How does she move from one kind of information to another?

"This Is the End of the World": The Black Death

Barbara Tuchman

In October 1347, two months after the fall of Calais, Genoese trading ships put into the harbor of Messina in Sicily with dead and dying men at the oars. The ships had come from the Black Sea port of Caffa (now Feodosiya) in the Crimea, where the Genoese maintained a trading post. The diseased sailors showed strange black swellings about the size of an egg or an apple in the armpits and groin. The swellings oozed blood and pus and were followed by spreading boils and black blotches on the skin from internal bleeding. The sick suffered severe pain and died quickly within five days of the first symptoms. As the disease spread, other symptoms of continuous fever and spitting of blood appeared instead of the swellings or buboes. These victims coughed and sweated heavily and died even more quickly, within three days or less, sometimes in 24 hours. In both types everything that issued from the body—breath, sweat, blood from the buboes and lungs, bloody urine, and blood-blackened

Reporting Events

excrement—smelled foul. Depression and despair accompanied the physical symptoms, and before the end "death is seen seated on the face."

The disease was bubonic plague, present in two forms: one that infected the bloodstream, causing the buboes and internal bleeding; and was spread by contacts; and a second, more virulent pneumonic type that infected the lungs and was spread by respiratory infection. The presence of both at once cause the high mortality and speed of contagion. So lethal was the disease that cases were known of persons going to bed well and dying before they woke, of doctors catching the illness at a bedside and dying before the patient. So rapidly did it spread from one to another that to a French physician, Simon de Covino, it seemed as if one sick person "could infect the whole world." The malignity of the pestilence appeared more terrible because its victims knew no prevention and no remedy.

[*Notice the shift from the appearance and definition of the plague to a discussion of its effects.*]

The physical suffering of the disease and its aspect of evil mystery were expressed in a strange Welsh lament which saw "death coming into our midst like black smoke, a plague which cuts off the young, a rootless phantom which has no mercy for fair countenance. Woe is me of the shilling in the armpit! It is seething, terrible . . . a head that gives pain and causes a loud cry . . . a painful angry knob . . . Great is its seething like a burning cinder . . . a grievous thing of ashy color." Its eruption is ugly like the "seeds of black peas, broken fragments of brittle sea-coal! . . . the early ornaments of black death, cinders of the peelings of the cockle weed, a mixed multitude, a black plague like halfpence, like berries . . ."

Rumors of a terrible plague supposedly arising in China and spreading through Tartary (Central Asia) to India and Persia, Mesopotamia, Syria, Egypt, and all of Asia Minor had reached Europe in 1346. They told of a death toll so devastating that all of India was said to be depopulated, whole territories covered by dead bodies, other areas with no one left alive. As added up by Pope Clement VI at Avignon, the total of reported dead reached 25,840,000. In the absence of a concept of contagion, no serious alarm was felt in Europe until the trading ships brought their black burden of pestilence into Messina while other infected ships from the Levant carried it to Genoa and Venice.

By January 1348 it penetrated France via Marseille, and North Africa via Tunis. Shipborne along coasts and navigable rivers, it spread westward from Marseille through the ports of Languedoc to Spain and northward up the Rhone to Avignon, where it arrived in March. It reached Narbonne, Montpellier, Carcassonne, and Toulouse between February and May, and at the same time in Italy spread to Rome and Florence and their hinterlands. Between June and August it reached Bordeaux, Lyon, and Paris, spread to Burgundy and Normandy, and crossed the Channel from Normandy into southern England. From Italy during the same summer it crossed the Alps into Switzerland and reached eastward to Hungary.

[*See the quick movement from geographical spread to local devastation.*]

In a given area the plague accomplished its kill within four to six months and then faded, except in the larger cities, where, rooting into the close-quartered

115

population, it abated during the winter, only to reappear in spring and rage for another six months.

In 1349 it resumed in Paris, spread to Picardy, Flanders, and the Low Countries, and from England to Scotland and Ireland as well as to Norway, where a ghost ship with a cargo of wool and a dead crew drifted offshore until it ran aground near Bergen. From there the plague passed into Sweden, Denmark, Prussia, Iceland, and as far as Greenland. Leaving a strange pocket of immunity in Bohemia, and Russia unattacked until 1351, it had passed from most of Europe by mid-1350. Although the mortality rate was erratic, ranging from one fifth in some places to nine tenths or almost total elimination in others, the overall estimate of modern demographers has settled—for the area extending from India to Iceland—around the same figure expressed in Froissart's casual words: "a third of the world died." His estimate, the common one at the time, was not an inspired guess but a borrowing of St. John's figure for mortality from plague in Revelation, the favorite guide to human affairs of the Middle Ages.

[Tuchman's use of statistics adds to the enormity of the plague's effect.]

A third of Europe would have meant about 20 million deaths. No one knows in truth how many died. Contemporary reports were an awed impression, not an accurate count. In crowded Avignon, it was said, 400 died daily; 7,000 houses emptied by death were shut up; a single graveyard received 11,000 corpses in six weeks; half the city's inhabitants reportedly died, including 9 cardinals or one third of the total, and 70 lesser prelates. Watching the endlessly passing death carts, chroniclers let normal exaggeration take wings and put the Avignon death toll at 62,000 and even at 120,000, although the city's total population was probably less than 50,000.

When graveyards filled up, bodies at Avignon were thrown into the Rhone until mass burial pits were dug for dumping the corpses. In London in such pits corpses piled up in layers until they overflowed. Everywhere reports speak of the sick dying too fast for the living to bury. Corpses were dragged out of homes and left in front of doorways. Morning light revealed new piles of bodies. In Florence the dead were gathered up by the Compagnia della Misericordia—founded in 1244 to care for the sick—whose members wore red robes and hoods masking the face except for the eyes. When their efforts failed, the dead lay putrid in the streets for days at a time. When no coffins were to be had, the bodies were laid on boards, two or three at once, to be carried to graveyards or common pits. Families dumped their own relatives into the pits, or buried them so hastily and thinly "that dogs dragged them forth and devoured their bodies."

Amid accumulating death and fear of contagion, people died without last rites and were buried without prayers, a prospect that terrified the last hours of the stricken. A bishop in England gave permission to laymen to make confession to each other as was done by the Apostles, "or if no man is present than even to a woman," and if no priest could be found to administer extreme unction, "then faith must suffice." Clement VI found it necessary to grant remissions of sin to all who died of the plague because so many were unattended by priests. "And no bells tolled," wrote a chronicler of Siena, "and nobody wept no matter what his loss because almost everyone expected death . . . And people said and believed, 'This is the end of the world.'"

Reporting Events

In Paris, where the plague lasted through 1349, the reported death rate was 800 a day, in Pisa 500, in Vienna 500 to 600. The total dead in Paris numbered 50,000 or half the population. Florence, weakened by the famine of 1347, lost three to four-fifths of its citizens, Venice two-thirds, Hamburg and Bremen, though smaller in size, about the same proportion. Cities, as centers of transportation, were more likely to be affected than villages, although once a village was infected, its death rate was equally high. At Givry, a prosperous village in Burgundy of 1,200 or 1,500 people, the parish register records 615 deaths in the space of fourteen weeks, compared to an average of thirty deaths a year in the previous decade. In three villages of Cambridgeshire, manorial records show a death rate of 47 percent, 57 percent, and in one case 70 percent. When the last survivors, too few to carry on, moved away, a deserted village sank back into the wilderness and disappeared from the map altogether, leaving only a grass-covered ghostly outline to show where mortals once had lived.

In enclosed places such as monasteries and prisons, the infection of one person usually meant that of all, as happened in the Franciscan convents of Carcassonne and Marseille, where every inmate without exception died. Of the 140 Dominicans at Montpellier only seven survived. Petrarch's brother Gherardo, member of a Carthusian monastery, buried the prior and 34 fellow monks one by one, sometimes three a day, until he was left alone with his dog and fled to look for a place that would take him in. Watching every comrade die, men in such places could not but wonder whether the strange peril that filled the air had not been sent to exterminate the human race. In Kilkenny, Ireland, Brother John Clyn of the Friars Minor, another monk left alone among dead men, kept a record of what had happened lest "things which should be remembered perish with time and vanish from the memory of those who come after us." Sensing "the whole world, as it were, placed within the grasp of the Evil One," and waiting for death to visit him too, he wrote, "I leave parchment to continue this work, if perchance any man survive and any of the race of Adam escape this pestilence and carry on the work which I have begun." Brother John, as noted by another hand, died of the pestilence, but he foiled oblivion.

[*Watch the shift from Brother John to the masses of humanity in cities like Paris and Venice.*]

The largest cities of Europe, with populations of about 100,000, were Paris and Florence, Venice and Genoa. At the next level, with more than 50,000, were Ghent and Bruges in Flanders, Milan, Bologna, Rome, Naples, and Palermo, and Cologne. London hovered below 50,000, the only city in England except York with more than 10,000. At the level of 20,000 to 50,000 were Bordeaux, Toulouse, Montpellier, Marseille, and Lyon in France, Barcelona, Seville, and Toledo in Spain, Siena, Pisa, and other secondary cities in Italy, and the Hanseatic trading cities of the Empire. The plague raged through them all, killing anywhere from one-third to two-thirds of their inhabitants. Italy, with a total population of 10 to 11 million, probably suffered the heaviest toll. Following the Florentine bankruptcies, the crop failures and workers' riots of 1346–47, the revolt of Cola di Rienzi that plunged Rome into anarchy, the plague came as the peak of successive calamities. As if the world were indeed in the grasp of the Evil One, its first appearance on the European mainland in January 1348 coincided with a fearsome earthquake that carved a path of

Applications

wreckage from Naples up to Venice. Houses collapsed, church towers toppled, villages were crushed, and the destruction reached as far as Germany and Greece. Emotional responses, dulled by horrors, underwent a kind of atrophy epitomized by the chronicler who wrote, "And in these days was burying without sorrowe and wedding without friendschippe."

[*See how Tuchman brings the catastrophic events down to human scale.*]

In Siena, where more than half the inhabitants died of the plague, work was abandoned on the great cathedral, planned to be the largest in the world, and never resumed, owing to loss of workers and master masons and "the melancholy and grief" of the survivors. The cathedral's truncated transept still stands in permanent witness to the sweep of death's scythe. Agnolo di Tura, a chronicler of Siena, recorded the fear of contagion that froze every other instinct. "Father abandoned child, wife husband, one brother another," he wrote, "for this plague seemed to strike through the breath and sight. And so they died. And no one could be found to bury the dead for money or friendship... And I, Angelo di Tura, called the Fat, buried my five children with my own hands, and so did many other likewise."

There were many to echo his account of inhumanity and few to balance it, for the plague was not the kind of calamity that inspired mutual help. Its loathsomeness and deadliness did not herd people together in mutual distress, but only prompted their desire to escape each other. "Magistrates and notaries refused to come and make the wills of the dying," reported a Franciscan friar of Piazza in Sicily; what was worse, "even the priests did not come to hear their confessions." A clerk of the Archbishop of Canterbury reported the same of English priests who "turned away from the care of their benefices from fear of death." Cases of parents deserting children and children their parents were reported across Europe from Scotland to Russia. The calamity chilled the hearts of men, wrote Boccaccio in his famous account of the plague in Florence that serves as introduction to the *Decameron*. "One man shunned another... kinsfolk held aloof, brother was forsaken by brother, oftentimes husband by wife; nay, what is more, and scarcely to be believed, fathers and mothers were found to abandon their own children to their fate, untended, unvisited as if they had been strangers." Exaggeration and literary pessimism were common in the 14th century, but the Pope's physician, Guy de Chauliac, was a sober, careful observer who reported the same phenomenon: "A father did not visit his son, nor the son his father. Charity was dead."

Yet not entirely. In Paris, according to the chronicler Jean de Venette, the nuns of the Hôtel Dieu or municipal hospital, "having no fear of death, tended the sick with all sweetness and humility." New nuns repeatedly took the places of those who died, until the majority "many times renewed by death now rest in peace with Christ as we may piously believe."

As you return to reread this selection, note the variety and amount of information Tuchman has incorporated and answer the following questions

1. Consider the statistics Tuchman includes. Approximately how many numbers do you find in this selection and what is their effect?

Reporting Events

2. Tuchman has included a number of first person accounts—gleaned from a variety of sources. What do they add to this account?
3. How does Tuchman's inclusion of the different social groups and countries affected shape this account?

Writing to Learn

The early stages of writing to recount events draw on memory at the same time that they emphasize collecting new information and selecting the most important parts. As you retrieve information from memory and make selections about what to include in your drafts, you continue to learn about your subject.

MEMORY

Your memory contains a great deal more information than you may consciously realize. If you are writing about an event you have experienced, your memory will be a valuable resource. To get a sense of how much information you have stored in your memory, do the following exercise.

The first problem we encounter in thinking about selecting is where to find our material. Memory is a major source of material for narration. When you think of memory, you may be reminded of reciting lines from Shakespeare's *Hamlet* or repeating the Gettysburg Address. For many people *to memorize* means to learn by rote, to learn something word for word, and that is, of course, one definition. But a second and more inclusive definition of memory is the capacity to recall the general shape of information and events. For example, in telling someone what happened in class, you do not usually worry about reciting the instructor's exact words, but you do draw on the resources of your memory to explain the general shape of what occurred.

One hundred years ago memory training, particular of the rote memory sort, was prominent in American education. It was not unusual for an instructor to expect students to memorize a reading assignment and be ready to recite it verbatim in class. Today schools require considerably less memory training, which means that you probably do not fully recognize the power of your own memory. The following exercise illustrates:

EXERCISE

Go back as far as you can in memory, and visualize your first home, the first place in which you can remember living. Think about its color, the shape and location of rooms, and especially your favorite places in that home. Do you remember the window sills? What was under the kitchen sink? Where did you sleep?

1. Draw a floor plan of this house or apartment, and put x's in the places that were important to you.

Applications

2. Look at the picture you have drawn, and think about details of that home. Were there any closets? What did the kitchen smell like?
3. Show the picture to someone else, and tell that person about something that happened to you in that home. Use the picture to show exactly where the event occurred.
4. Write about the event you have just described. Your audience is someone outside your family, perhaps the person to whom you showed your floor plan.

If your experience is that of most students, you will probably find that drawing the plan and thinking about your early home brought back events you have not thought of in years. Students in my classes remember exactly what it felt like to fall out of bed and break an arm, what the blue tile in the bathroom looked like smeared with lipstick, and the way the kitchen smelled after the furnace exploded. They find that their memories contain many more details than they had suspected.

Most of the memories stimulated by this exercise take two forms: recounting events and supplying details. This combination of events and details comprises narrative, because making experience conscious requires the ability both to tell what happened, and happens, and to fill in details that make the events come alive. This excursion into memory also illustrates the close connection between narrating and learning because memory provides one way for us to know or bring to consciousness something about experience in this world.

Not every writing task you face will carry the same emotional freight as does the one based on your house plan, but the care in recounting and attending to detail evoked here provides a model for writing narrative. By learning to draw on the resources of your memory, you can increase the detail in your writing. As the preceding exercise suggests, one way to reach these resources is to make connections with concrete objects. Visualizing your childhood home probably helped you think of details that would have otherwise remained buried in your mind. Perhaps you have had the experience of being able to recall information during an exam by remembering where it was written on the page of your notes or by focusing on the place where you learned it.

Another way to draw on the resources of your memory is to recreate a memory chain that begins with some physical object and leads you to recall various experiences. Here, for example, is a memory chain that begins with a dish of concord grapes:

<pre>
                   concord grapes

    picking grapes in fall
    finding big milk snake--picking it up--terrible small
    Anthony the ring-necked snake I found when I was 11
      (he bit me)
    horseback riding in woods in Maryland (age 16)
    Robin, my crazy pony-horse
</pre>

Reporting Events

```
    stable cleaning
    special sneakers kept on back porch
    putting foot into a nest of wood spiders at 6:30
      a.m.--baby spiders flew all over the place--I
    became a shoe-shaker
```

Jim Lawton, who was assigned to write an account of an experience about to which he reacted in a negative way, began by creating this memory chain:

```
                    a hamburger
    catsup, onions, and all the trimmings
    food fights in the dining hall--getting covered with
      catsup
    fighting with my brother when we were in grade school
    wrestling team in junior high
    building up my "rep" in high school
    fight with Toby when I was a junior in high school
```

This chain helped Jim recall the event he eventually wrote about.

EXERCISE

Think about an event in your own life when you felt very afraid. If you have trouble recalling such an event, use a memory chain to get started. Write an account of what you remember about this experience, giving consideration to the specific sources of your fear and to the elements of fascination and thrill that may have accompanied feelings of fear.

GATHER

Of course your memory, like a computer, will be only as good as what you put into it. You can improve your writing not only by becoming more aware of how your memory works but by becoming also a collector of details. Increasing your powers of observation will increase your collection of information to use in writing. Many people, for example, can go for a walk and see nothing, but an observant writer found material for the following:

> The skunk track enters the woods, and crosses a glade where the rabbits have packed down the snow with their tracks, and mottled it with pinkish urinations. Newly exposed oak seedlings have paid for the thaw with their newly barked stems. Tufts of rabbit-hair bespeak the year's first battles among the amorous bucks. Further on I find a bloody spot, encircled by a wide-sweeping arc of owl's wings. To this rabbit the thaw brought freedom from want, but also a reckless abandonment of fear. The owl has reminded him that thoughts of spring are no substitute for caution.
>
> —Aldo Leopold, *A Sand County Almanac*

Applications

Becoming as observant as this writer will make your memory a rich resource for writing. The following exercise will help you enlarge your powers of observation, which in turn will feed your memory.

E X E R C I S E

1. Read the following selection, paying attention to the way that recounted events and descriptions are combined.

March 1956
   On the afternoon of the first day of spring, when the gutters were still heaped high with Monday's snow but the sky itself was swept clean, we put on our galoshes and walked up the sunny side of Fifth Avenue to Central Park. There we saw:
   Great black rocks emerging from the melting drifts, their craggy skins glistening like the backs of resurrected brontosaurs.
   A pigeon on the half-frozen pond strutting to the edge of the ice and looking a duck in the face.
   A policeman getting his feet wet testing the ice.
   Three elderly relatives trying to coax a little boy to accompany his father on a sled ride down a short but steep slope. After much balking, the boy did, and, sure enough, the sled tipped over and the father got his collar full of snow. Everyone laughed except the boy, who sniffed.
   Four boys in black leather jackets throwing snowballs at each other. (The snow was ideally soggy, and packed hard with one squeeze.)
   Seven men without hats.
   Twelve snowmen, none of them intact.
   Two men listening to the radio in a car parked outside the Zoo; Mel Allen was broadcasting the Yanks-Cardinals game from St. Petersburg.
   A tahr (*Hemitragus jemiaicus*) pleasantly squinting in the sunlight.
   An aoudad absently pawing the mud and chewing.
   A yak with its back turned.
   Empty cages labelled "Coati," "Orangutang," "Ocelot."
   A father saying to his little boy, who was annoyed almost to tears by the inactivity of the seals, "Father (Father seal, we assumed) is very tired; he worked hard all day."
   Most of the cafeteria's out-of-doors tables occupied.
   A pretty girl in black pants falling on them at the Wollman Memorial Park.
   "Bill & Doris" carved on a tree. "Rex & Rita" written in the snow.
   Two old men playing, and six supervising, a checkers game.
   The Michall Friedsam Foundation Merry-go-Round, nearly empty of children but overflowing with calliope music.
   A man on a bench near the carousel reading, through sunglasses, a book on economics.
   Crews of shinglers repairing the roof of the Tavern-on-the-Green.
   A woman dropping a camera she was trying to load, the film unrolling in the slush and exposing itself.
   A little black boy in aviator goggles rubbing his ears and saying, "He really hurt me." "No he didn't," his nursemaid told him.

Reporting Events

The green head of Giuseppe Mazzini staring across the white softball field, unblinking, though the sun was in its eyes.
Water murmuring down walks and rocks and steps. A grown man trying to block one rivulet with snow.
Things like brown sticks nosing through a plot of cleared soil.
A tire track in a piece of mud far removed from where any automobiles could be.
Footprints around a KEEP OFF sign.
Two pigeons feeding each other.
Two showgirls, whose faces had not yet thawed the frost of their makeup, treading indignantly through the slush.
A plump old man saying "Chick, chick" and feeding peanuts to a squirrel.
Many solitary men throwing snowballs at tree trunks.
Many birds calling to each other about how little the Ramble has changed.
One red mitten lying lost under a popular tree.
An airplane, very bright and distant, slowly moving through the branches of a sycamore.

—John Updike, *Assorted Prose*

2. Go for a walk, or sit quietly where you can observe and make a list of what you see.
3. Write a selection that imitates "Central Park." Use the same kind of introductory paragraph to explain the place and circumstances of your observation, and use the line "There I saw" to begin your listed observations.

To collect material for his account of the fight with Toby, Jim Lawton began listing what he could remember. Here is the beginning of his list:

```
Toby the biggest freshman
the school lunch room
a meatball thrown at the back of my neck
my friends in the junior class
froshing tradition at Gig Harbor High School
```

If your account is not an autobiographical one, you can collect information from other writers, just as Barbara Tuchman did before she wrote about the plague. Here, for example, is an article about gender and parenting.

Can Men Mother?

Deborah Anna Luepnitz

Nearly everyone agrees that, throughout the ages, whether or not it has been necessary, women have raised the children. In all the societies we know of—industrial and nonindustrial, pre- and post-revolutionary—women have had the primary responsibility for child care. The fact that women are anatomically equipped for *childbearing* does not explain why they have also had the task of caring for children who are weaned.

There have been several attempts to explain female-dominated child care.

Applications

One is that a woman's biological makeup creates not only the capacity for childbirth but also qualities of personality such as empathy. Alice Rossi, for example, contends that if men were to be primary caretakers of infants, they would require special training to make up for their lack of female hormones.[1]

The notion that biology alone accounts for women's history as primary caretakers was challenged by Harlow et al. in their 1970 experiments. They found that monkeys who grew up alone were unable to care for their own offspring. These animals, whose "instincts" were presumably intact, had been deprived of the benefit of social learning and thus did not know how to care for their babies.

There is an anthropological theory about mothering that holds that women have always raised the children not because they were driven by instinct but because childbirth and lactation made it impossible for them to do anything else. Indeed, in early societies women were pregnant most of the time, due to the absence of contraceptive devices. Many births were required, moreover, to ensure species survival since infant mortality was extremely high.

This argument may in fact be valid for *hunting* societies. It would have been inexpedient and dangerous for pregnant women to chase and kill large game. Pregnancy, however, has not prevented women in other kinds of societies from doing hard work. In agricultural societies, women have worked the fields with babies strapped to their backs and hips.[2] Certainly, in modern times there is no biological reason why one sex should care for the children while the other works in an office. Nonetheless, it continues to be the case—even in our relatively progressive nation, and even in contemporary Cuba and Sweden where women's equality is protected by law—that not only are women responsible for most of the home childcare, but they also constitute nearly 100 percent of all daycare workers.

The other major explanation for female-dominated childcare is the role-training argument. In other words, women mother because as girls they were pressured to play with "girl" toys and were rewarded for being gentle and soft whereas boys were made to play with "boy" toys and were rewarded for being aggressive and tough. Maccoby and Jacklin (1974) report fascinating research that shows the many and subtle ways in which parents and teachers prepare boys for achievement and girls for motherhood. This social pressure is maintained by other institutions, as well as by the mental-health establishment, as the classic study of Broverman et al. illustrated.[3]

Role-training theory has made a great contribution to our understanding of gender and has understandably dominated academic psychology. Psychoanalytic theory, however, which is not incompatible with learning theory, states that gender identity is achieved through a process more subtle and profound than social coercion. The analytic argument is that gender is formed not only through the *content* of what parents expect from boys and girls but also by the *structure* of the parent-child relationships from birth onward. A new contribution to the

---

[1] Alice Rossi, "A Biosocial Perspective on Parenting," *Daedalus,* Spring 1977, pp. 1–31.
[2] For a thorough review of this argument, see Nancy Choderow's *The Reproduction of Mothering* (Berkeley: University of California Press, 1978).
[3] I. Broverman, D. Broverman, F. Clarkson, P. Rosenkrantz, and S. Vogel, "Sex-Role Stereotypes and Clinical Judgments of Mental Health," *Journal of Consulting and Clinical Psychology* 34 (1970):1–7.

psychoanalytic argument is Nancy Choderow's powerful book, *The Reproduction of Mothering*. Choderow criticizes both the biological and the social-learning theories of mothering and emphasizes the relationship between the infant and its first perceived "other." The fact that in every case—in all societies we know of—the first "other" is a woman, is of profound significance. It creates an asymmetry that is the beginning of the difference between male and female psychology. Choderow contends that mothers experience a primary sameness with their infant girls and a primary "differentness" from their infant boys. Girls, nurtured by a same-sex parent, grow up with a sense of self as continuous with their first "other." Boys, nurtured by an opposite-sex parent, experience themselves as discontinuous with their first "other." Girls thus develop an ego that is predicated on *relatedness* to their emotional context and boys on *separateness* from theirs. The sex-role indoctrination that children later receive is thus an extension of the subtle psychological processes (largely unconscious) that have already occurred as a result of a family structure in which women mother. Choderow concludes that changing the social organization of gender will involve more than changing children's toys and textbooks. It is a much larger task than most social scientists imagine but nonetheless a change that Choderow sees as very desirable. If children were dependent from birth on people of both sexes, they would not develop "fears of *maternal* omnipotence and expectations of *women's* unique self-sacrificing qualities."[4] This, she believes,

> would reduce men's needs to guard their masculinity and their control of social and cultural spheres . . . and would help women to develop the autonomy which too much embeddedness in relationship has often taken from them.[5]

The question that Choderow does not directly confront is whether or not a man raised in the traditional family structure (that is, by an opposite-sex parent) *can* mother as well as a woman, and if so, what in her theory would explain this capacity.

No one has studied the family-of-origin experience of men who become active parents. The only study that speaks at all to this issue was done by Kelin Gersick in 1979. Gersick was interested in why some men chose to seek custody of their young children after divorce while other men did not. He found that men who sought custody described themselves as closer to their mothers than to their fathers and were more likely to have an older brother and a sister. He speculated that a child who follows both male and female siblings may be less bound by gender norms since the parents would have already focused their anxiety about creating sex-appropriateness in the older siblings.

Until recently, little thought has been given to developing men's potential for childcare. Some fascinating work done recently on fathers and infants has shown that infants show no preference for either parent in their display of attachment behavior (Lamb 1977). Most of the research on fathering, however, has dealt not with infants but with school-aged children being raised by their fathers after divorce. The best of these studies is reported in *Fathers Without Partners,* by Rosenthal and Keshet (1981). The authors studied 127 fathers

---

[4]Choderow, *Reproduction of Mothering,* p. 218.
[5]Ibid., p. 218.

with varying degrees of contact with their children after divorce. All fathers said that fathering had led to their own personal growth, as it required them to develop their empathy and emotional responsiveness, and to be less compulsive about their careers. Rosenthal and Keshet maintain that adults need children just as children need adults to be complete individuals. Unfortunately, their interviews included fathers only. Children were not interviewed nor was any direct assessment made of father-child interaction.

Santrock and Warshak (1979), on the other hand, did a study including both fathers and children after divorce. Their sample of sixty families consisted of one-third with mother custody, one-third with father custody, and one-third intact families. For our purposes, the most important of their comparisons were between children in father custody and mother custody. One clear result emerged: Children living with the same-sex parent were more socially competent than those living with the cross-sex parent. Boys living with fathers were more "mature," "social," and "independent" than girls living with their fathers. Conversely, girls living with mothers were more competent than boys living with mothers. Recall that in Hetherington's study of mother custody, the boys functioned more poorly than the girls.

Santrock and Warshak suggest that parents may simply find it easier to identify with same-sex children and therefore to become closer with them. In some cases, the cross-sex child may remind the custodial parent of the ex-spouse, and hostility may be transferred to the child. All clinicians have probably heard a divorced parent lamenting, "This child is the spitting image of my ex-spouse, and I'm afraid I see the same personality developing."

This fascinating set of issues and speculations about same-sex and cross-sex parenting is the most recent contribution of the divorce literature. All of this work, as well as Choderow's book, postdates the data-collection phase of this study. Thus the parents in this sample unfortunately were not asked about differences in the relationships with their sons and daughters. This is a rich area for future investigation.

EXERCISE

List items that you might include if you were collecting information for a paper on custody of children in divorce cases.

Select

Just as an oral account cannot reasonably include every detail of what happened (at Saturday's party or in class on Wednesday), so writers must choose certain bits of information and discard others as they recount events. The basis on which such decisions are made varies. Criteria of importance, personal preference, audience, purpose, humor, chronology, and variety can all contribute to decisions about what to include and what to discard in writing accounts of events. To see principles of selection and organization in operation, read the two following passages. The first, 1 Kings 1:38 is from the revised Standard Version of the Bible. The second shows the same passage as it appears in the *Readers Digest* condensed version of the Bible.

Reporting Events

Revised Standard Version

Now King David was old and advanced in years; and although they covered him with clothes, he could not get warm. ²Therefore his servants said to him, "Let a young maiden be sought for my lord the king, and let her wait upon the king, and be his nurse; let her lie in your bosom, that my lord the king may be warm." ³So they sought for a beautiful maiden throughout all the territory of Israel, and found Ab'ishag the Shu'nammite, and brought her to the king. ⁴The maiden was very beautiful; and she became the king's nurse and ministered to him; but the king knew her not.

5 Now Adoni'jah the son of Haggith exalted himself, saying, "I will be king"; and he prepared for himself chariots and horsemen, and fifty men to run before him. ⁶His father had never at any time displeased him by asking, "Why have you done thus and so?" He was also a very handsome man; and he was born next after Ab'salom. ⁷He conferred with Jo'ab the son of Zeru'iah and with Abi'athar the priest; and they followed Adoni'jah and helped him. ⁸But Zadok the priest, and Benai'ah the son of Jehoi'ada, and Nathan the prophet, and Shim'e-i, and Re'i, and David's mighty men were not with Adoni'jah.

9 Adohi'jah sacrificed sheep, oxen, and fatlings by the Serpent's Stone, which is beside En-ro'gel, and he invited all his brothers, the king's sons, and all the royal officials of Judah, ¹⁰but he did not invite Nathan the prophet or Benai'ah or the mighty men or Solomon his brother.

11 Then Nathan said to Bathshe'ba the mother of Solomon, "Have you not heard that Adoni'jah the son of Haggith has become king and David our lord does not know it? ¹²Now therefore come, let me give you counsel, that you may save your own life and the life of your son Solomon. ¹³Go in at once to King David and say to him, 'Did you not, my lord the king, swear to your maidservant, saying, "Solomon your son shall reign after me, and he shall sit upon my throne"? Why then is Adoni'jah king?' ¹⁴Then while you are still speaking with the king, I also will come in after you and confirm your words."

15 So Bathshe'ba went to the king into his chamber (now the king was very old, and Ab'ishag the Shu'nammite was ministering to the king). ¹⁶Bathshe'ba bowed and did obeisance to the king, and the king said, "What do you desire?" ¹⁷She said to him, "My lord, you swore to your maidservant by the Lord your God, saying, 'Solomon your son shall reign after me, and he shall sit upon my throne.' ¹⁸And now, behold, Adoniajah is king, although you, my lord the king, do not know it. ¹⁹He has sacrificed oxen, fatlings, and sheep in abundance, and has invited all the sons of the king, Abiathar the priest, and Joab the commander of the army; but Solomon your servant he has not invited. ²⁰And now, my lord the king, the eyes of all Israel are upon you, to tell them who shall sit on the throne of my lord the king after him. ²¹Otherwise it will come to pass, when my lord the king sleeps with his fathers, that I and my son Solomon will be counted offenders."

22 While she was still speaking with the king, Nathan the prophet came in. ²³And they told the king, "Here is Nathan the prophet." And when he came in before the king, he bowed before the king, with his face to the ground. ²⁴And Nathan said, "My lord the king, have you said, 'Adonijah shall reign after me, and he shall sit upon my throne?' ²⁵For he has gone down this day, and has sacrificed oxen, fatlings, and sheep in abundance, and has invited all the king's sons, Joab the commander of the army, and Abiathar the priest; and behold, they are eating and drinking before him, and saying Long live King

Applications

Adonijah!' ²⁶But me, your servant, and Zadok the priest, and Benaiah the son of Johoiada, and your servant Solomon, he has not invited. ²⁷Has this thing been brought about by my lord the king and you have not told your servants who should sit on the throne of my lord the king and you have not told your servants who should sit on the throne of my lord the king after him?"

28 Then King David answered, "Call Bathshe'ba to me." So she came into the king's presence, and stood before the king. ²⁹And the king swore, saying, "As the LORD lives, who has redeemed my soul out of every adversity, ³⁰as I swore to you by the LORD, the God of Israel, saying, 'Solomon your son shall reign after me, and he shall sit upon my throne in my stead'; even so will I do this day." ³¹Then Bathshe'ba bowed with her face to the ground, and did obeisance to the king, and said, "May my lord King David live for ever!"

32 King David said, "Call to me Zadok the priest, Nathan the prophet, and Benai'ah the son of Jehoi'ada." So they came before the king. ³³And the king said to them, "Take with you the servants of your lord, and cause Solomon my son to ride on my own mule, and bring him down to Gihon; ³⁴and let Zadok the priest and Nathan the prophet there anoint him king over Israel; then blow the trumpet, and say, 'Long live King Solomon!' ³⁵You shall then come up after him, and he shall come and sit upon my throne; for he shall be king in my stead; and I have appointed him to be ruler over Israel and over Judah." ³⁶And Benai'ah the son of Jehoi'ada answered the king, "Amen! May the LORD, the God of my lord the king, say so. ³⁷As the LORD has been with my lord the king, even so may he be with Solomon, and make his throne greater than the throne of my lord King David."

Readers Digest Condensed Version

Now King David was old and advanced in years, and although they covered him with clothes, he could not get warm. Therefore his servants said to him, "Let a young maiden be sought to wait upon my lord the king and be his nurse; let her lie in your bosom, that you may be warm." So they sought throughout all Israel and found Abishag the Shunammite, and brought her to the king. She was very beautiful, and she became the king's nurse and ministered to him; but the king knew her not.

Now Adonijah the son of David, born next after Absalom, exalted himself, saying, "I will be king." He was a very handsome man, and his father had never displeased him by asking, "Why have you done thus and so?" He prepared chariots and horsemen, with fifty men to run before him, and he conferred with Joab and with Abiathar the priest, and they followed him. But Zadok the priest, and Benaiah the commander of the king's bodyguard, and Nathan the prophet, and David's mighty men were not with him. Adonijah sacrificed sheep and oxen at En-rogel, outside Jerusalem, and he invited all his brothers except Solomon, and all the royal officials of Judah.

Then Nathan said to Bathsheba the mother of Solomon, "Have you not heard that Adonijah has become king and David does not know it? Go in at once to King David and say, 'Did you not swear to your maidservant, saying, "Solomon your son shall reign after me"? Why then is Adonijah king?'"

Bathsheba went to the king in his chamber, where Abishag was ministering to him. "My lord," she said, "you swore to your maidservant, saying, 'Solomon your son shall reign after me.' But now, behold, Adonijah is king. My lord the king, the eyes of all Israel are upon you, to tell them who shall sit on the throne after you. Otherwise, when my lord sleeps with his fathers, I and my son Solomon will be in danger."

"As the LORD lives," the king said, "as I swore to you that Solomon should reign after me, even so will I do this day." Then he summoned Zadok, Nathan, and Benaiah. "Take with you my bodyguard," he said, "and cause Solomon my son to ride on my own mule, and bring him down to Gihon; and let Zadok and Nathan there anoint him king over Israel; then blow the trumpet and say, 'Long live King Solomon!' For I have appointed him to be king over Israel and Judah in my stead."

"Amen!" said Benaiah. "May the LORD make his throne greater than the throne of my lord King David."

As you can see, the author of the condensed version has concentrated on selecting what seems most important. The standard by which importance is judged appears to be based on the centrality of the question of who should be king after David. The role of Nathan the prophet is given much less importance because mention of his absence at Adonijah's sacrifice (verse 10) and his plan to join Bathsheba's plea before David (verse 14) are eliminated, and his counsel to Bathsheba (verse 12) is abbreviated. Clearly the author has decided that Nathan's motivations and actions merit less attention than do other aspects of the account. In addition to diminishing Nathan's role, the author of the condensation elminates the protocol between Bathsheba and David (verse 28) and Bathsheba's response to David (verse 31) and shortens both David's instructions and Benaiah's response (verses 35–38). Although much is eliminated in the condensed version, the kingship question remains prominent.

We can speculate on how the author established the kingship question as most important. As you may know, David and Solomon were very prominent Hebrew kings and the biblical accounts of their reigns are very detailed. Accounts of conversations such as that between Nathan and Bathsheba and attention to court protocol (verses 28 and 35–38) are common. Because David had many sons, the question of who would succeed him was a major one, and the author of the condensation probably felt that this, rather than details of court life, was the most important part of this passage.

EXERCISE

The following article appeared in a popular magazine. Read it carefully, and decide which are the most important parts. The article contains approximately 525 words, and your task is to write a 250-word version of it that uses importance as the major principle of selection.

Skokie

In March 1977 a scruffy band of American Nazis decided to stage a half-hour parade in front of the village hall in Skokie, Illinois. They planned to wear storm trooper uniforms, display swastikas, and carry signs reading "Free Speech for White People." They had picked the right place to provoke anger—hence

Applications

attention. A refuge for survivors of Hitler's death camps, Skokie remains heavily Jewish today, and the village quickly passed ordinances to ban the Nazi rally.

Scenting a chance for massive publicity, the Nazis sought help from David Goldberger, a young Jewish lawyer who summed up his personal view of the group in two words: "Absolutely disgusting." Goldberger, though, happened to be legal director of the Illinois branch of the American Civil Liberties Union. To a lawyer duty-bound to protect the living Constitution, the Skokie uproar was a classic First Amendment case requiring a defense of free expression, even if the "victims" were people he detested. Goldberger agreed to represent the Nazis against Skokie in the spirit that his real client was the First Amendment and its ever-threatened rights for all Americans.

Lawyers for the village argued that a Nazi march would not protect free speech but would instead incite a riot. Pleading the case himself for lack of volunteer lawyers, Goldberger contended that Skokie's position was a surrender to a heckler's veto, that the Constitution required the village to permit the march—with adequate police to keep the peace—rather than abrogate the rights of the would-be marchers, offensive as they might be. In February 1978 a federal district court upheld the ACLU position, and the U.S. Supreme Court let the decision stand. In fact, the march never took place. Instead, the Nazis staged a demonstration in downtown Chicago.

But the vilification of David Goldberger had only begun. He was castigated from the pulpit of his parents' own synagogue. Wilder voices even accused him of being a neo-Nazi. As hostility mounted, Goldberger had to pull his kids out of school, travel under armed escort, and more than once evacuate his home in response to bomb threats. He had expected hostility. What surprised him was the lack of support from within the ACLU's own ranks for his position of principle. "I assumed that traditional supporters of the First Amendment would survey the situation, grumble at the philosophy and symbols of the Nazis, and then concede that the Skokie march was a tolerable cost for a great Constitution," he recalls.

Indeed, the ACLU's national membership fell by 15 percent in reaction to Skokie and has not fully recovered. "The threats and the name-calling were profoundly disturbing," says Goldberger, who resigned his ACLU post earlier this year to take an associate professorship of law at Ohio State. "But if I had to do it all over again, I would. I've been asked many times how a Jew can defend freedom for Nazis. I did it because I honestly believe that without the First Amendment, democracy has nothing to protect it. If you can frighten a lawyer out of a controversial case in this country, then neither the bar nor the legal system provides much safety for anyone."

—*Quest* (November, 1980)

After you have completed your 175-word version of this article, compare your notes with someone else's to see whether you selected the same ideas as most important. List the differences you find, and explain why you selected certain features as most important.

Perfecting your ability to select the most important ideas will make much of your college work easier. In reading as well as writing, you will frequently

Reporting Events

be expected to discern what merits attention, and many writing assignments will assume that you can make such selections. For example, here is a writing assignment from an economics class:

> Over the last six weeks of the term you will be required to hand in a reaction paper. The assignment is to locate a current newspaper or magazine article containing information, data, or speculation about the current economic situation. More than one article can be used for your paper, which should be a reaction to the published material. You should briefly state the major points made in the article and relate this information to the relevant theoretical material covered in class. The paper can follow one of several paths: you can contrast the two theories using the current data; you can make predictions by combining theory and data; or you can find fault with the theory and/or predictions of the article to which you are reacting. Your paper must, however, have a macroeconomic scope.

As you can see, this assignment asks students to identify "major points" from the newspaper articles selected and to relate them to "relevant theoretical material" from class work. Both of these aspects of the assignment require the ability to select the most important parts for narrating. The concluding directive to "have a macroeconomic scope" indicates the standard for selecting ideas, but beyond this, it is the student's responsibility to decide what to include. Of course, the need to select important parts does not end with graduation. In your future employment, you are likely to be asked to summarize meetings, report on your activities or the activities of those you supervise, or read and distill the writing of others. Your success in all of these tasks will depend on your ability to select the most important parts.

Selecting for a Draft

After he had listed events surrounding his fight with Toby, Jim Lawton selected the ones he thought most important and wrote this draft:

```
                  Fun Anger

     The lunch room was filled with that same dull roar
it's always filled with on a typical school day. It
seemed as if today's lunch would be the same old boring
"stuff" for both me and my close circle of friends who
totaled about 12 on this day.
     But then, suddenly, a hush fell on part of the
room. And before I could turn to see what was happen-
ing, a large, juicy meatball grazed the back of my
head. Before even brushing off my hair, I sprang to my
feet only to see two bodies streaking from the room.
     At this point, I was besieged with anger as well
as disgrace. I had to achieve revenge to save my name.
```

Applications

Storming in the direction the meatball came from, I heard the squeaks of little freshman voices as they shouted, "Toby did it! Toby did it!"

Furiously I raced around the school until I had found Toby hiding by his locker. By this time about 10 people were following me, egging me on. Confronting Toby, I asked him if he threw the meatball. He denied it, but I could tell he was lying. That was about the worst thing he could have done because I hate liars. But I didn't act immediately, partly out of fear of expulsion, and partly out of fear of Toby, the biggest freshman in the school.

However, my friends decided something must be done that lunch hour. We juniors couldn't let freshmen push us around. So I stealthily kiped some catsup from the food service and proceeded to hunt for Toby. He spotted me though, and the chase was on. But just as suddenly as it had started, it ended as Principal John Gorow rounded the corner. Revenge would not be mine until <u>after</u> school.

Huddling my friends around like a frenzied possy, I cleverly plotted a way to intercept Toby before he could reach his school bus. My anger now gone, I excitedly explained the procedure for the first froshing in two years at Gig Harbor High School.

And as the last bell rang the whole ordeal became a game, as we systematically chased Toby down, tackled him, tossed him into the back of a pick-up truck and escorted him down to the harbor docks. There, with compassion, Toby was given and chose the option to jump into the cool March water rather than be thrown.

Retribution had been achieved. Heading back up to school with a shivering Toby, I lectured to him on the virtues of honesty. And as I sat there with my gleeful friends I suddenly realized that there is such a thing as fun anger.

EXERCISE

Using the ideas generated by writing about your memories of a time when you were very frightened, write a draft recounting this experience. You may want to explore the relationship between real and imagined fears, and you may want to consider elements of fascination and thrill that accompanied this event.

Summary

During the early stages of writing about events, the following procedures can be useful:

- If you are writing about an event you have experienced, use a physical object, a drawing, or anything else that help you retrieve information from memory.
- Make a memory chain or write an account of what you recall.
- If you are writing about events you did not experience, collect information from books and articles.
- Select from the items you have collected.
- Write a draft using selected items.

Writing to Show Learning

Transforming a draft into a finished piece of writing requires several steps. These include reconsidering the assignment, thinking about the audience for whom you are writing, identifying and emphasizing your thesis, improving organization, and editing.

Reconsider the Assignment

When Jim Lawton looked again at the assignment: "Describe and narrate an event that you reacted to in a negative way—with, for example, disapproval, anger, or disbelief," he realized that he should show his feelings more clearly in a revised version of "Fun Anger." He made notes in places where he could add more details about how he felt as the incident with Toby unfolded.

After you have written in response to any assignment, going back for a second reading will almost always help you to re-see and revise your draft. You will be able to look at your draft in light of what the assignment calls for, noting the places where you need to add or delete or make changes.

EXERCISE

Return to your draft about a time when you felt very afraid. Consider this draft in light of the original assignment, noting places where you will need to add, delete or change in order to fulfill the requirements of the assignment.

Consider Audience

As he thought about his audience, Jim realized that individuals who read his account would know nothing about Gig Harbor High School and its traditions, about the details of the encounter with Toby, or about him and his friends. As he thought about how to describe the event, he realized that putting it in the third person would make it easier to talk about himself, so he decided to shift all the "I" statements to language about "Jim."

Applications

When he read his draft to his writing group, members raised several questions. They wanted to know why he felt angry and disgraced when the meatball hit him. They asked how Toby looked when Jim found him hiding by his locker. And they said they would like better descriptions of the school along with Jim and the others included in the account. This combination of attempting to put himself in the place of his audience and receiving comments from the audience of his writing group gave Jim several useful ideas about how to revise his "Fun Anger" draft.

As Jim's experience demonstrates, considering your audience can take several forms. You can read your own draft and try to imagine what a reader unfamiliar with your situation would need to know, or you can solicit responses from your peers, or you might have a conference with your instructor. Whatever form it takes, considering your audience will enable you to write more effective accounts of events.

EXERCISE

1. Look at your "fear" draft from the perspective of an audience, and determine what your readers will need to know in order to understand the event you describe.
2. Ask someone in your class to read and respond to your draft or read it in a writing group.

IDENTIFY YOUR THESIS

Looking at the title "Fun Anger" and rereading the whole piece made Jim realize that he intended to show how an incident that at first made him angry could lead to feelings of pleasure. Even though he had been furious when the meatball first struck, the subsequent actions he and his friends took led him to see the event more positively. Jim had, in other words, developed the thesis that an event that originally inspires anger can lead to feelings of pleasure. He responded to the requirements of the assignment by describing the event and his emotions, but he made the assignment his own by developing the progression from anger to pleasure. Once he had identified this thesis, Jim knew that he needed to give it greater emphasis in his final draft. He wanted to show his readers how he made the transition from feeling angry to feeling pleased about the situation.

As you reread drafts of your own accounts of events, try to identify the thesis in your draft. It needn't be expressed in a single sentence, but you should be able to explain the central idea of the piece in a sentence. Identifying the thesis of your draft enables you to see how you have transformed the general subject of an assignment into *your* subject.

Reporting Events

EXERCISE

Ask someone in your class to read your "fear" draft and write its thesis in a sentence. Compare this thesis with what you would have written.

Check Organization

Writing that recounts events often follow chronology, tracing the pattern of incidents as they occurred. Jim's draft followed this model, and as he reread it, he saw no reason to change it significantly. He thought it worked well to begin with the lunchroom scene before the meatball was thrown and follow the events in order until he and his friends had "froshed" Toby.

In some accounts of events straight chronology may not be the best pattern. Return to the Barbara Tuchman selection and notice how she shifts in and out of chronology. Even though she moves through time, she pauses to move from one area of Europe to another, to fill in details of documentation. Similarly, Frank Conroy's "Savages" draws upon past events to narrate the trial, and the organization is not entirely chronological.

In checking the organization of accounts of events, you can decide what organizational pattern works best for the material you are using. You may decide to begin with the last thing that happened or the most important or the most unusual, but you will need to give your readers some organizational pattern to follow.

EXERCISE

Identify the organizational pattern of your "fear" draft and then consider what would happen if you shifted that order, beginning, say, with the final event rather than leading up to it.

Evaluate Coherence and Cohesion

The word *organization* refers to the overall plan of a piece of writing, whether that plan is based on chronology or order of importance. The words *coherence* and *cohesion* describe organization in more local terms. Coherence enables a reader to "make sense" of writing, to see how one part connects with another. Cohesion helps parts of writing (often individual words or phrases) stick together.

One of the places where his writing group raised questions about "Fun Anger" was the part where Jim chases Toby to his locker, decides not to take retribution, and then joins his friends to hunt for Toby. Several people commented that they had difficulty following the action at this point, and Jim realized that he needed to work on the coherence of this section. Similarly,

Applications

writing group questions about why he felt angry and disgraced made Jim realize that he hadn't created a clear link between the bodies streaking from the room and his subsequent feeling. He knew he needed to work on cohesion here.

Responses of confusion from other readers provide one of the best indications of where you need to work on coherence and cohesion in your drafts. Because you know the events well, you can fill in all the details that might not be clear to someone who did not participate in what you are narrating, so their questions can tell you where to begin working on coherence and cohesion.

EXERCISE

Mark the places where another reader has questions about your draft and determine how you can make these parts more coherent and cohesive.

Editing

When you are satisfied with the general shape of your writing, comfortable that it achieves its purposes and addresses its audience effectively, it is time to look at details such as usage, mechanics, spelling, and punctuation. To be sure, you may correct some errors as you write drafts, but the final version should be a close to perfect as you can make it. This means careful proofreading.

After he had reconsidered his draft, Jim wrote the following revision of "Fun Anger." As you can see, he changed the title to make his thesis even more clear, and his additions, deletions and changes responded to what he had learned through considering the assignment, audience needs, the thesis, organization, coherence and cohesion, and through editing.

```
                    Revenge Can Be Sweet

     The lunch room was filled with that same dull roar
it's always filled with on a typical school day. The
students were spattered about the large area in their
usual spots, their insecurities normally forcing about
ten or so students to sit around a circular table
designed for four. Of course the crowding was the
worst in the frosh area where it wasn't uncommon for
20-25 of these underclassmen to cling together.
     For Jim Lawton, sitting at one of the tables unof-
ficially designated for upperclassmen, it seemed as if
today's lunch would be the same old boring "stuff" for
both him and his close circle of friends, who totaled
about twelve on this day. Talk of girl friends, sports,
```

the "incompetent" school administration, and the woes of assignments past were again being tossed from neighbor to neighbor.

But then, quite suddenly, a hush fell upon the room, much like the quiet that accompanies a snowfall, and Jim's day took on an entirely new look, as a large, juicy meatball came hurtling across the room from the freshman table and proceeded to graze the back of Jim's head.

Jim, before even brushing the residue of meatball from his hair, sprang to his feet in a fit of rage, only to see two bodies streaking from the room. Storming in the direction the meatball came from, Jim heard the squeaks of little freshmen voices as they shouted "Toby did it! Toby did it!"

Humiliated in front of what seemed like the whole school, Jim was furious and felt he had to gain retribution, especially because he was a very visible and respected member of the student body. One of the top students in his class and three-sport athlete, Jim was well-liked by almost everybody. He certainly wasn't going to be disgraced by a freshman. The fact that the meatball was intended for a freshman at a nearby table mattered little to him at this point.

So Jim angrily raced around the school until he found Toby hiding near his locker. By this time, about ten blood-thirsty delinquents were following him, egging him on, hoping for a fight. Confronting Toby, Jim asked him if he threw the meatball. Trembling, Toby denied it, and all present knew he was lying. Toby, sweating profusely, was unsure of what was next to come. Even Jim himself was unsure of what to do, partly out of fear of expulsion and partly out of fear of Toby, the biggest freshman at Gig Harbor High. He stood about six foot one and weighed about 190 pounds.

In addition, Toby was a troubled student, followed by rumors of drug use, dogged by bad grades and constantly struggling to gain acceptance by his peers. At this time, it seemed inevitable that with a few years growth, he would certainly blossom into a full grown bully.

Though Jim may have been confused as to how to react, his friends, a conglomerate of juniors from nearly all walks of life, were not. And in a few short moments they had him kiping catsup from the food service and chasing Toby throughout the school.

Applications

    The chase was intense, but short, and just as Jim caught Toby and was about to douse him over the head with catsup, Principal John Gorow intervened. Intending to handle the meatball incident with a note to Toby's parents, Mr. Gorow told Jim to forget about the whole thing.

    Now, it is important to note that in this day and age at Gig Harbor High, there was a general consensus among upperclassmen, and some underclassmen for that matter, that the freshmen in the school were getting extremely uppity. The common theory among Jim's friends was that the "elders" of the school were being too soft on the "youngsters." At this point, it was becoming quite apparent to set an example for all frosh. And Jim was just the man for the job. His peers were counting on him.

    Now realizing this, and the significance of his task, Jim was no longer feeling anger and humiliation, but rather joy and heroism instead. Revenge would be his after school.

    Huddling his friends around him like a frenzied posse, Jim cleverly plotted a way to intercept Toby before he could reach his school bus. His anger now gone, Jim excitedly explained the procedure for the first froshing in two years at Gig Harbor High.

    Meanwhile, Toby was agonizing through the final periods of the day, sensing all the while his impending doom. He was experiencing emotions not altogether new to him: fear, hatred, and rejection.

    And as the last bell rang the whole ordeal became a game of cat and mouse, as the posse of juniors systematically chased Toby down, tackled him, tossed him into the back of a pick-up truck, and escorted him down to the harbor dock. There, with compassion, they gave Toby the option of jumping into the cool March water or being thrown in.

    Gingerly, Toby approached the end of the dock, fully clothed. There was silence as Toby glanced back at the mob, not unlike a martyr looks at his crucifiers. Then, without a sound, he leaped high into the air and made an enormous splash. As he entered the water, shouts of joy burst from Jim and his friends. Because all the guys were in high spirits, they helped Toby from the water and gave him a ride back up to the school.

    Ironically, this event turned out well for all

parties involved. By being froshed, Toby gained the
notoriety among his peers that he had always longed
for, and the respect of upperclassmen for not telling
the principal. Meanwhile, Jim and his buddies felt
vindicated as well as extremely proud of their great
accomplishment.

E X E R C I S E

1. List the changes you see between this version and the first draft, "Fun Anger."
2. Write a revision of your "fear" draft, incorporating as many different kinds of changes as Jim has.

The final stage in producing a piece of writing is editing. In drafting you probably corrected some errors of spelling, usage, mechanics, or punctuation, but you may have ignored others because you were concentrating on different aspects of composing. Jim, as you may have noticed, misspelled "posse" in his first draft, but he corrected it in the final version.

Now is the time to proofread your paper carefully in order to find and correct all errors. If you have any questions about editing and proofreading, refer to the Handbook at the back of this book.

Copyright © E. A. Heiniger, The National Audubon Society Collection/Photo Researchers, Inc.

Chapter Six

Supporting Assertions

REPORTING events occurs naturally in many conversations, so it is relatively easy to shift such accounts into writing. When it comes to supporting assertions, however, the situation is different. If you listen to conversations you will hear people make claims without providing any support for them. Exchanges often sound like this:

Speaker 1: What is this new album?
Speaker 2: It's the latest by Sique Sique Sputnik.
Speaker 1: Is Sique Sique Sputnik a good group?
Speaker 2: Yes, they're awesome.
Speaker 1: I'll have to get that album.

Speaker 2 is not asked to offer any evidence to support the statement about Sique Sique Sputnik, and Speaker 1 seems completely ready to accept Speaker 2's assertion. The term "awesome" is not defined nor is there any comparison between this and any other group of musicians.

One form of "conversation" heard frequently in this country is the television talk show. Guests on these shows are asked to state opinions on a variety of topics, but it is rare for them to offer a careful justification for what they say. You might try listening to a talk show and noting how seldom substantial support for a position is given.

One characteristic of academic audiences is an insistence on support for generalizations. Your instructors will not be satisfied with statements such as "*The Great Gatsby* is a better book than *For Whom the Bell Tolls*." Instructors expect an assertion like this to be followed by an explanation of what criteria are being used, detailed comparisons of features in the two books, and examples that illustrate points being made.

Applications

Getting Ready to Support Assertions

Assertions should be followed by evidence that supports the claim being made. An analogy with courtroom assertions may make this point more clear. It is not sufficient for a defense attorney to state "My client did not commit the murder." The attorney must provide testimony by witnesses or experts in a given field, along with tangible evidence such as documents, blood samples, or weapons. Similarly assertions in college writing require the support of evidence. This evidence may take the form of *definitions, examples,* or *illustrations,* but it must be present for statements to be taken seriously.

DEFINITION

To define is to limit or set boundaries, to point to characteristics that distinguish this from that. If you make a statement such as "Fat people are better than thin people," you need to provide a definition of what you mean by "better." This bit of conversation illustrates the importance of definitions. One individual began a conversation by saying "Capitalization is driving me crazy." The second person, hearing this without introduction or guiding context had no idea whether the speaker was referring to raising money (as in the capitalization of assets) or using upper-case letters (as in capitalizing words). After an exchange of question and response, the second person learned that the speaker meant the latter, and then the two could continue talking. You have undoubtedly had similar experiences of having conversations come to a near standstill to define terms.

Readers, of course, do not have an opportunity to ask writers what a particular word means, so writers need to take special care to define their terms. An assertion based on an undefined term cannot be convincing. Consider, for example, this statement: "I dislike the book because the author insists on male superiority." If the author does not define "male superiority" what follows will have little effect. Readers will continue to wonder whether the author defines superiority in physical, intellectual, or political terms.

The following selection illustrates how a writer use definition to support an assertion. Suzanne Britt Jordan, a newspaper columnist, begins with the assertion that thin people need watching, and, although she never specifies an exact height-to-weight ratio for thin people, she provides evidence for this claim by defining thin people in contrast to fat ones. As you read, try to identify the different methods Jordan uses to define thin people and see how these forms of definition provide support for her assertion.

That Lean and Hungry Look

Suzanne Britt Jordan

Caesar was right. Thin people need watching. I've been watching them for most of my adult life, and I don't like what I see. When these narrow fellows spring at me, I quiver to my toes. Thin people come in all personalities, most of them menacing. You've got your "together" thin person, your mechanical thin person, your condescending thin person, your tsk-tsk thin person, your efficiency-expert thin person. All of them are dangerous.

Supporting Assertions

In the first place, thin people aren't fun. They don't know how to goof off, at least in the best, fat sense of the word. They've always got to be adoing. Give them a coffee break, and they'll jog around the block. Supply them with a quiet evening at home, and they'll fix the screen door and lick S&H green stamps. They say things like "there aren't enough hours in the day." Fat people never say that. Fat people think the day is too damn long already.

[*Notice how Jordan begins paragraphs with an assertion about thin people and moves to a contrasting statement about fat people.*]

Thin people make me tired. They've got speedy little metabolisms that cause them to bustle briskly. They're forever rubbing their bony hands together and eyeing new problems to "tackle." I like to surround myself with sluggish, inert, easygoing fat people, the kind who believe that if you clean it up today, it'll just get dirty again tomorrow.

Some people say the business about the jolly fat person is a myth, that all of us chubbies are neurotic, sick, sad people. I disagree. Fat people may not be chortling all day long, but they're a hell of lot *nicer* than the wizened and shriveled. Thin people turn surly, mean, and hard at a young age because they never learn the value of a hot-fudge sundae for easing tension. Thin people don't like gooey soft things because they themselves are neither gooey nor soft. They are crunchy and dull, like carrots. They go straight to the heart of the matter while fat people let things stay all blurry and hazy and vague, the way things actually are. Thin people want to face the truth. Fat people know there is no truth. One of my thin friends is always staring at complex unsolvable problems and saying, "The key thing is. . . ." Fat people never say that. They know there isn't any such thing as the key thing about anything.

Thin people believe in logic. Fat people see all sides. The sides fat people see are rounded blobs, usually gray, always nebulous and truly not worth worrying about. But the thin person persists. "If you consume more calories than you burn," says one of my thin friends, "you will gain weight. It's that simple." Fat people always grin when they hear statements like that. They know better.

Fat people realize that life is illogical and unfair. They know very that God is not in heaven and all is not right with the world. If God was up there, fat people could have two doughnuts and a big orange drink anytime they wanted it.

Thin people have a long list of logical things they are always spouting off to me. They hold up one finger at a time as they reel off these things, so I won't lose track. They speak slowly as if to a young child. The list is long and full of holes. It contains tidbits like "get a grip on yourself," "cigarettes kill," "cholesterol clogs," "fit as a fiddle," "ducks in a row," "organize," and "sound fiscsal management." Phrases like that.

They think these 2,000-point plans lead to happiness. Fat people know happiness is elusive at best and even if they could get the kind thin people talk about, they wouldn't want it. Wisely, fat people see that such programs are too dull, too hard, too off the mark. They are never better than a whole cheesecake.

[*Jordon shifts fat people to the beginning of the paragraph as she introduces an anecdote.*]

Applications

Fat people know all about the mystery of life. They are the ones acquainted with the night, with luck, with fate, with playing it by ear. One thin person I know once suggested that we arrange all the parts of a jigsaw puzzle into groups according to size, shape, and color. He figured this would cut the time needed to complete the puzzle by at least 50 percent. I said I wouldn't do it. One, I like to muddle through. Two, what good would it do to finish early? Three, the jigsaw puzzle isn't the important thing. The important thing is the fun of four people (one thin person included) sitting around a card table, working a jigsaw puzzle. My thing friend had no use for my list. Instead of joining us, he went outside and mulched the boxwoods. The three remaining fat people finished the puzzle and made chocolate, double-fudged brownies to celebrate.

The main problem with thin people is they oppress. Their good intentions, bony torsos, tight ships, neat corners, cerebral machinations, and pat solutions loom like dark clouds over the loose, comfortable, spread-out, soft world of the fat. Long after fat people have removed their coats and shoes and put their feet up on the coffee table, thin people are still sitting on the edge of the sofa, looking neat as a pin, discussing rutabagas. Fat people are heavily into fits of laughter, slapping their thighs and whooping it up, while thin people are still politely waiting for the punch line.

Thin people are downers. They like math and morality and reasoned evaluation of the limitations of human beings. They have their skinny little acts together. They expound, prognose, probe, and prick.

[*Jordan piles alliteration with cliche to create her concluding affirmation of fat people.*]

Fat people are convivial. They will like you even if you're irregular and have acne. They will come up with a good reason why you never wrote the great American novel. They will cry in your beer with you. They will put your name in the pot. They will let you off the hook. Fat people will gab, giggle, guffaw, gallumph, gyrate, and gossip. They are generous, giving, and gallant. They are gluttonous and goodly and great. What you want when you're down is soft and jiggly, not muscled and stable. Fat people know this. Fat people have plenty of room. Fat people will take you in.

As you return for a second reading of this selection, try to answer the following questions:

1. What effect does Jordan's continuing reference to food have on the definition she offers?
2. What characteristics of thin people Jordan provide by contrasting them with fat people?
3. When Jordan asserts "The main problems with thin people is they oppress," what definitions does she offer in support of her statement?
4. What does the final line contribute to Jordan's definition of thin people?

Throughout this selection Jordan employs several different strategies of defining. She looks at *sources,* at how thin people come to exist ("If you consume more calories than you burn . . . you will gain weight"); she explains

Supporting Assertions

how thin people *function* by explaining what they know, say, and do; she *contrasts* them with fat people; she draws *analogies* ("they are crunchy and dull, like carrots"); she *analyzes* types of thin people ("mechanical . . . condescending . . . tsk-tsk . . . efficiency expert"); she offers many *examples* of thin people's behavior; and she offers *synonyms* for thin people ("narrow fellows," "bony torsos"). When you write to support assertions, you will find many of these strategies useful.

Among the available methods for defining terms are these:

Etymology or looking at the source of the word or concept. Applied to a word such as *leader,* an etymological definition would be: "The word *lead* comes from the Anglo-Saxon *laedan* or *lithan* meaning 'to travel or go,' and so a leader can be described as one who determines a way of traveling or going."

Function or explaining what the person or object does, as in "A leader directs the course of activities."

Synonyms, or words that mean approximately the same thing, as in "Leadership means guiding groups or showing people how to proceed."

Analysis, or identifying distinctive features, as in "A leader is a person who directs the activities of others."

Comparison or *contrast* or *analogy,* as in "A leader flies at the point of the wedge, taking the full force of the wind."

Example or demonstration of the term, as in "Ralph became a leader for the littleuns in *Lord of the Flies,* and they came when he blew the conch because he was big enough to be a link with the adult world of authority."

ILLUSTRATION

Definitions can do a great deal to provide support for assertions, but illustrations are also useful. The old cliche tells us that a picture is worth a thousand words, and experience confirms the truth of this statement. A picture has two dimensions and represents the world more concretely than words can as they follow in one line after another. If both words and picture appear on the same page, our eyes will usually be drawn first to the picture. To see how pictures convey meaning, look at a publication that uses pictures and one that does not. You might, for example, compare a recent issue of *Time* magazine with a "Talk of the Town" section of *The New Yorker*.

In writing you can create pictures with words; you can illustrate. I use the word *illustration* here to mean the verbal example or anecdote that makes abstract language come alive. An illustration provides a brief account of a specific instance, one that makes an abstract point easier to understand. Jordan includes an illustration to reinforce her point about thin people. Her account of the four people doing a jigsaw puzzle illustrates the difference between thin and fat people.

To see how a writer can support an assertion with illustrations, read the following selection by Donald Hall. Hall, a poet who lives in new Hampshire, begins with the assertion that New England has one thousand seasons, and

Applications

the remainder of his essay provides evidence to support that claim. As you read, watch for illustrations that support Hall's claim for New England seasons.

Land of One Thousand Seasons

Donald Hall

New York has people, the Northwest damp, Iowa soybeans, Texas money, and new England seasons. Convention speaks of four, the observant New Englander numbers at least a thousand, and on a good day our spendthrift climate runs through seven or eight. Robert Frost lived his first ten years in mono-seasonal California; maybe that's why he became the laureate of weatherly mutability. "You know how it is," he wrote in "Two Tramps in Mud Time," with an April day/When the sun is out and the *wind is still,*/You're one month on in the middle of May." Then with sudden wind and cloud, "You're two months back in the middle of March."

October may be more so. When we wake we stoke the Glenwood and scrape ice off the pickup's windshield; at noon we take lunch sitting on the porch in T-shirts; the spot of rain at teatime is cold enough to send us checking the salt in the grainshed; but sunset blooms a soft rose in the west, promising Indian summer, which we remember with chagrin when we wake at midnight to the first snowfall.

However we number them, Spring is the least of our seasons. It begins with the glorious disaster of winter's melt, periodic in March, interrupted by blizzards, continuing through April as rivers roll down hillsides where no rivers were—gullying tunnels under snowdrifts, hollowing gray scrap bulwarks as rag-and-tatter as snow in Manhattan. When snow goes, mud takes over. For a week or two we struggle in mud as we never struggled in snow. Transmissions bust, the pond road is travel-at-your-own-risk, the bridge is out, and Fred keeps revving up the tractor to haul flatlanders out of the ditch the way Fred's grandfather Fred did with his oxen.

When mud goes dry, leaving stiff ridges and warps for bumping over, we do not sigh in relief, for if we sigh we inhale blackflies. We wish the mud back; it does not sting. Now snowdrops fly their small flags in our gardens, now daffodils rise in tentative glory—always, every year, the bravest rewarded with cupfuls of snow, in *Return of the Son of Winter*, rerun on every channel—but we do not wander happily on the daffodil hillside. We express our joy from behind windows, even storm windows, looking past the last garbage snow to the sun's blossoming hill, unless we are careless of skin and rapturous of bite and scratch.

And when the blackflies go, perhaps the mosquitoes have eaten them.

But even the least of seasons is beautiful. As we drive to the store, or garden protected by thick socks and a beekeeper's mask, we swim under the frail green of beginning leaves. There is nothing so tender as new green, smoke of red and yellow buds along with pale green smoke, loosening at the branch-ends of trees released from the cold hold of winter. Whole hillsides overnight smoulder up this tenderness, leaves unfolding daily and darkening week by week toward the vigorous black-green of summer's oak and maple. Now we walk, our hands slapping the air as if we bargained for a thousand rugs in a thousand Turkish markets, and inspect the winter's waste by pond and

Supporting Assertions

mountainside: what popples the beaver took, what birches we lost February's ice storm.

[*Notice Hall's use of analogy in the following section.*]

If Spring is least, it is also shortest. There are those who claim it occupies only the month of May. (Some few insist that spring occurs on May 17th, ten A.M. to two-thirty P.M.) But unless we confront a literalist of the calendar, there can be no controversy over the date of Summer's beginning. The rest of us plant our gardens, except for the peas we scatter on snow; after the full moon closest to Memorial Day—but the summer people seed themselves on Memorial Day itself. All summer, as corn inches up or doesn't, as the zucchini population of New Hampshire multiplies like Nashua, as green tomatoes wax and decide with heroic stubborness to remain forever green, the growth of summer people outdoes every other crop: Through drought and deluge, unseasonable cold or Bostonian mug and swelter, they pop from the cracked earth of June by the hundred-thousand; they spread in July greenly up, out, and over the rural dirt of New England; they take into themselves, abundancies of sun and water; they spread, thrive, fatten, elongate, swell, rippen: only, on Labor Day, afflicted suddenly by three hundred degrees of school-frost; work-frost, and duty-frost, instantly to wither, blacken, die, and vanish.

On their sudden, seasonal, and predictable disappearance—we hear of them miraculously altered, no longer tanned in the flesh but brown-suited in worsted as in Worcester, and felt-hatted in the suburbs of the ordinary life—we sigh without inhaling a single insect, enjoy the huge dark end-of-summer leaves, tidy our spent gardens, and hunker down for the best of times. The red branch on the green tree starts it off, one eruption marching to a different drummer. Then whole bogs blaze with swamp maples, dear deep reds followed by the great vulgar chorus of bellowing, billowing yellows, reds, russets, and rusts. Birch, maple, rare elm, oak, beech, ash, each in its own time and with its own pitch and tone swells the outlandish chorus. It is the London Philharmonic tripling up with orchestras from Bogota and Kuala Lumpur, Spike Jones conducting, and each shade and position contributes another violin, oboe, or triangle to the gorgeous cacophony of Autumn.

Always the persistent evergreen supplies continue. As Autumn endures and the leaves fall, the silvery sheen of empty trunks and branches becomes an increasing theme. Everywhere we walk we gaze at yellow leaves against unpainted barns, towering enormous flame-fountains beside white houses, varicolored Kearsarge altering each day, and through the day, by variety of light. Best of all, we love the hills of middle distance, with color-patches distinct when we focus on them; when we refocus on the whole hill, its colors contract to a single insane tweed of pinks, oranges, reds, russets, and silvers. It is dangerous to drive; who can look at the road?

[*Watch the transition from fall to winter.*]

After the sober and noble palette of late October and November, analytic cubism with its rectangles of granite and released stone walls, New England's seasonal journey retracts to the oneness of Winter, from outrageous multiplicity to white uniformity. Usually it begins at night, the black sky flaking full with whiteness, covering brown hayfield and granite hill, boulder, road, and barn

Applications

with the soft silence of its frigidity. We gather inside around the noisy Glenwood; we gather ourselves inside ourselves for the three months of our annual descent, internal Persephones of the personal underworld. On the full moon's Winter night, pewtery light reflects upward from snow to flicker against tin ceilings, ghost light.

[*See how Hall returns to his original assertion.*]

Of the one thousand seasons, Winter by actual count provides two hundred and twenty-seven. Of course, sixty-eight percent of Winter's seasons cause pain. This pain's bright side is our complaining and bragging: Every house wears two thermometers, the low one for Winter and the high one for Summer. And Winter is ours, although winter people wearing petro-chemical-dollar uniforms brighten white slopes. This long Winter gives us our identity: Mixed and intense, beauty and pain together, interrupted only by January's thaw with its anticipatory melt—Miami invading from the South—it is the name of our place. We must admit: Spring is annoying, Summer is not ours. Autumn is best—and Winter is New England's truest weather.

Now that you have an overview of Hall's essay, return for a second reading, and answer the following questions:

1. Hall includes references that may be unfamiliar. What does "multiplies like Nashua (a city in southern New Hampshire) mean? What image is created by "the London Philharmonic tripling up with orchestras from Bogota and Kuala Lumpur, Spike Jones conducting"? What is a Glenwood? Who is Persephone? What do these references contribute to Hall's selection?
2. Which of Hall's illustrations conveys the annoying quality of spring for you? Why?
3. Are you convinced that fall is the best season? Why?
4. Why is winter New England's truest weather?

Hall follows the chronology of the four seasons, illustrating each as he goes. Several factors contribute to the effectiveness of his illustrations. He uses language that is both *vivid* and *economical*. Reread, for example, his description of autumn colors. Hall chooses illustrations with which he is very *familiar*. His description of Fred conveys the impression that Hall has known this tractor driver for a long time; his discussion of garden vegetables shows that he knows gardening. Hall's illustrations contain *specific* details that add to their effectiveness. References to local landmarks such as Mount Kearsage, and place names such as Nashua, Boston, and Manhattan orient the reader to Hall's perspective. The naming of specific flowers and trees and of particular holidays such as Labor Day likewise make the illustrations in this selection work.

Writing to Learn

The earliest stages of writing to support an assertion usually focus on the nature of the assertion. Sometimes the assertion will be provided by an assignment, and your task consists of providing support for the given statement.

Supporting Assertions

Here, for example, is a writing assignment from an economics class:

> As a general rule, the elasticity of supply is greater in the long run than in the short run. Construct examples of situation in which supply might be virtually zero in the long run and almost infinite in the short run.

As you can see, the assertion (that supply is minimal in the long run and infinite in the short run) is provided by the assignment, and the student's task is to provide evidence that will support this claim. The following assignment from a literature class operates similarly:

> In what ways are Mark Twain's *Huckleberry Finn* and William Howell's *The Rise of Silas Lapham* specifically romantic works?

The assertion (that these two books are specifically romantic works) is built into the assignment, and the writer's task is to offer support for this claim.

EXERCISE

Consider the two assigments just quoted. Even if you know little about either subject, you should be able to identify terms that will require definition in writing to support the assertions given. What are these terms?

Other assignments, however, will leave the identification of an assertion to you. Here, for example is an assignment that asks the writer to decide on the central point:

Read a newspaper published on the day of your birth. Decide what subject within that newpaper can attract your interest in the sense of making an assertion such as the following:

> It Was the Best of Times
> It Was the Worst of Times
> Great Oaks from Little Acorns Grow
> The Way It Really Was

Your task in this paper is to support an assertion *not* based on your firsthand knowledge. In other words, you are being asked to acquaint yourself with a body of knowledge and transform it into a statement you can support.

 EXERCISE

Follow the procedure described in the assignment just quoted and develop an assertion that you might support in writing.

DEFINITION

Like most assignments that ask you to support an assertion, this one requires a definition of terms. If you are to assert that a certain period was the "best of times," you need to be able to define what you mean by "best." Definition is especially important when you use abstract terms such as "freedom" or "wickedness" or "truth," but it helps with all writing.

Many college writing assignments assume that a definition will be included even if one is not specifically requested, and so it is one of the writer's tasks to decide whether a definition is necessary. For example, here is a question from a political science class:

> Golding seems particularly preoccupied with the qualities that are necessary for effective political leadership. Evaluate Ralph's strengths and weaknesses as a political leader on the basis of what Golding writes about Ralph's thoughts and actions. Discuss the leadership capabilities of figures in the novel other than the protagonist.

This question is based on William Golding's *Lord of the Flies,* a novel that recounts the experiences of a group of English schoolboys on a tropical island during an atomic war. The plane in which the boys were traveling had been shot down and the pilot killed, and so the boys, ranging in age from six to twelve, were isolated from adults and free to make their own rules. Three boys, Ralph, Jack, and Piggy, who were among the older boys on the island, took leadership roles as the boys established themselves.

A satisfactory answer to this question would have to define several terms, including "effective political leadership," "leadership capabilities," and "strengths and weaknesses." Of course, merely a definition of these terms is not a complete response to this assignment, but it is an important part of it. As stated earlier, strategies of definition include *etymology, function, synonym, analysis, comparison/contrast/analogy,* and *example.*

Decisions about which method of definition to use depend on the direction of the writing. For example, a writer who begins with an examination of Ralph's thoughts and actions might find it useful to use example, analysis or analogy; whereas one who begins with the issue of effective political leadership may want to use a functional or synonym definition. For example, the following is the first paragraph of one student's response to the Golding question:

```
     Effective leadership can be defined as the ability
to keep a system together and functioning. Effective
leadership varies according to circumstances, and
someone who is a good leader under one set of cir-
cumstances may be a terrible leader in another situa-
tion. The situation we will look at is a group of
young boys stranded on an island.
```

As you can see, this student chose a functional approach to explain what leaders do (keep a system together and functioning). His definition of "effective leadership" is likewise a functional one that describes the difference in perfor-

Supporting Assertions

mance of people. Another student, one who began by considering Ralph's thoughts and actions, composed this introductory paragraph:

    Ralph has many of the qualities necessary to effec-
tive political leadership. He speaks convincingly when
he calls the boys together for meetings, and he demonstrates rationality and responsibility in his attempts
to keep a signal fire going so rescue planes can find
the boys. However, he has weaknesses that undercut
these strengths. The pressures of his situation make
him lose track of his thoughts, and he forgets in
front of the whole group why they are supposed to
build a fire.

This definition relies on examples. The writer defines Ralph as having the qualities necessary for leadership and then provides instances when Ralph exhibited these qualities. As you examine these two paragraphs, you can see that neither approach is more valid than the other, but in each case the writer chose a method of definition that worked for the general direction of the paper. Most writing tasks suggest possible methods for definition, but the final decision rests with the writer.

Frequently the context of writing can help the writer decide on a method and, more importantly, on whether a definition is even required. Clearly, no writer can define every term used, and so another aspect of using definitions is deciding when they are required. For example, the political science question on *Lord of the Flies* requires a definition of "effective political leadership" because this is a course in which students are expected to demonstrate their mastery of such terms. But if a speech writer for a politician were using "effective political leadership," no definition would be expected because it would be assumed that audiences for political speeches would not need such definitions. That same political audience, however, would need a definition of "protagonist" because knowledge of this literary term could not be assumed for a political audience. Deciding which terms should be defined is a complex process, but considering audience and context can make it easier.

EXERCISE

This writing assignment comes from an anthropology class:

> Edith Wharton's *The Age of Innocence* and Mark Twain's *Tom Sawyer* deal at great length with the theme of socialization in the American Life of the Nineteenth Century. Analyze a character of your choice from each novel, focusing on how he or she reaches a "compromise" with society.

Applications

1. Identify the terms in this question that will need to be defined.
2. Define one of these terms in at least three different ways.
3. Identify the terms that will not need to be defined because of the audience and context of writing.
4. Write a paragraph that sketches the way you might approach this question, and decide which kind of definition will be most appropriate. If you are uncertain about how to proceed, return to the question from *Lord of the Flies* and the following discussion.

If an assignment includes an abstract term, you may want to ask the following questions to enlarge your definition:

1. To what specific items, groups of items, events, or groups of events does the word or words connect, in your experience or imagination?
2. What characteristics must an item or event have before the name of the concept can apply to it?
3. How do the referents of that concept differ from those included with similar concepts (for example, *democracy* and *socialism*)?
4. How has the term been used by other writers? How have they implicitly defined it?
5. Does the word have "persuasive" value? Does the use of it in connection with another concept seem to praise or condemn the other concept?
6. Are you favorably disposed to all the things included in the concept? Why or why not?

A sociology assignment was phrased this way: "Write an essay in which you consider how people in our society confer prestige on occupations." A student writing in response to this assignment decided to begin by examining the term *prestige*. He scrawled his answers on the back of an old exam before he left for the library to begin looking for articles. Here is what he wrote:

1. TO WHAT ITEMS, EVENTS, OR GROUPS DOES THIS WORD CONNECT?
   Money, power, education; limousines, big houses, and people who follow you around to help you; privileges, special treatment, and feeling important.
2. WHAT CHARACTERISTICS MUST AN ITEM OR EVENT HAVE BEFORE THE CONCEPT CAN APPLY?
   Must be special, have class, not be ordinary.
3. HOW DO REFERENTS OF THE CONCEPTS DIFFER?
   Similar concepts (such as privilege) seem to mean the same thing--except maybe privilege seems less earned.
4. HOW HAS THIS ITEM BEEN USED BY WRITERS?
   Sociology books call prestige the power to

Supporting Assertions

> command esteem--here money doesn't seem as
> important as being thought highly of--people
> like professors and clergy who don't make much
> money are often highly esteemed.

5. DOES THE WORD HAVE PERSUASIVE VALUE?
   > When I hear something like "a prestigious club,"
   > it makes the club seem special; the word <u>prestige</u>
   > seems to praise the club.

6. ARE YOU FAVORABLY DISPOSED TO ALL THINGS INCLUDED IN THE CONCEPT?
   > It is good to feel special, to have people
   > respect you for what you do, and I like that
   > part of it. But it feels exclusive, too. After
   > all, not everyone can have a job with prestige.

As the student wrote his answers to these questions, he realized that his concept of prestige was tied to money and the things it can buy. But he realized that esteem is not always a function of money and that he needed to give more thought to his understanding of the term *prestige*.

The responses to this and the other sets of questions are by no means exhaustive or exemplary. They simply represent how students are able to use questions to develop definitions. Given the same topics and questions, you could undoubtedly come up with completely different answers.

Monica Caoili began the "day of your birth" assignment in the library, reading newspapers from her birthday in 1967. She became interested in articles about higher education and decided to write about college education at that time. The assertion she developed was: 1967—The Time for a College Education. Newspaper articles from 1967 gave her a general sense of the times, of the Vietnam War, of protest movements, and other social forces that affected college students during that period. She found a university catalog from 1967 and one from the current year and noted differences in fees, GPA requirements for various colleges, and course requirements. She interviewed an administrator who had worked in the College of Engineering since the mid 1960s and learned about changes in admissions patterns.

As she collected this information, Monica realized that it provided her with several definitions of "best." She could define it in economic terms by claiming that the 1960s made college more affordable to a greater number of students. She could define it in terms of accessibility because none of the professional schools such as business and engineering had admission quotas. She had a number of statistics and facts, but she did not feel they were adequate by themselves. Monica knew she needed illustrations to make the facts of her definition come alive.

ILLUSTRATION

Although it does not specify them directly, the "day of your birth" assignment, requires illustrations as well as definitions. Some college writing assignments

Applications

ask explicitly for illustrations, with admonitions such as "Support your responses with clear illustrations from the book." Even when instructors do not directly request illustrations, support of assertions requires illustrations because it is nearly impossible to provide justification for a claim without them. The following, for instance, is an excerpt from an essay written to support the statement that William Faulkner integrates theme and setting in *A Rose for Emily*:

> Miss Emily's status in the old order is revealed by some of the things around her. For example, only a lady of this society would buy her lover a monogrammed silver toilet set and go courting in a glittering yellow buggy with a matched team of bays. And only this kind of lady would have a studio in one of the downstairs rooms for giving china-painting lessons.

The statement about Emily's status in the old order is the central point of the paragraph, the "idea" that the writer is trying to convey, but the examples elaborate the idea by making it concrete and specific. The monogrammed silver toilet set, the glittering yellow buggy, and the china-painting studio "show" this idea in action. Aspiring novelists are often advised to "show, not tell," and I offer the same advice to all aspiring writers.

As is true for definitions, deciding which illustration to use (or whether to use any at all) depends on context and audience. The excerpt from the *Rose for Emily* paper uses illustrations from the text because that is the most effective way to explain the setting-theme relationship in a literature class. However, if the same text were read in a psychology class and the students were asked to discuss Emily's psychological state, it would be appropriate to draw illustrations from readings in psychology as well.

EXERCISE

The following is a writing assignment from a class in interpersonal communications:

> Explain in a three- to four-page paper your typical style of dealing with conflict, discussing how your self-concept has contributed to the development of this style. Illustrate your discussion by describing a conflict that you have been involved in or are often involved in. What role did perceptions play in the conflict? How did you respond? What was effective and not effective about your response? What areas would you improve?

1. Explain your usual style of dealing with conflict, but use no examples.
2. List examples that you might use to illustrate your style.
3. What examples might you use if you were describing the same conflict for a counselor helping you reduce the stress and conflict in your life?

In responding to the exercise just given, you may have found yourself trying to create pictures with words, to capture a situation of conflict in language. Creating an effective illustration by capturing this or any situation requires the use of *vivid* language. Strong verbs contribute directly to vivid

Supporting Assertions

language. Return to Donald Hall's "Land of One Thousand Seasons" and look at the verbs he chooses "We *stoke* the Glenwood," "However we *number* them," "We *struggle* in mud," "Transmissions *bust*," "Now snowdrops *fly* their small flags." Continue on in Hall's essay, noting the verbs that create vivid pictures in your mind.

Another feature that contributes to the effectiveness of illustrations is drawing upon what you know well. As was noted earlier, much of the effect of Hall's essay derives from the fact that he illustrates his claims with places and incidents with which he is very *familiar*. Writers who offer advice often say that it is important to write from what one knows, and this is particularly true for illustrations. Someone else's anecdote will not work nearly as well as something you have experienced directly, and it is impossible to offer convincing illustrations from a novel you haven't read or a text you haven't studied. The following exercise demonstrates the importance of drawing illustrations from what one knows.

E X E R C I S E

1. Pretend that you are meeting a group of people for the first time and that each of you has been asked to introduce yourselves by listing three accomplishments that contribute to your identity. These can vary from being a National Merit scholar to winning a pie-baking contest. The twist is that one of the three must be a lie.
2. Write three paragraphs, two describing your actual accomplishments and one describing the thing you did not do.
3. Read aloud your three paragraphs, and ask your audience (it can be one person or several) to select the lie.

When the three paragraphs are read aloud you will probably be able to identify the lie in most cases. What this suggests is that when we write about something about which we know nothing, the tone of the writing changes in ways that we may not notice but that are often obvious to a reader.

One explanation for this change in tone may be that when we write about things we don't know well we cannot be *specific,* and specificity is essential to effective illustrations. The author of the paragraph on *A Rose for Emily* might have written: *Miss Emily's status in the old order is revealed by some of the things around her, by the expensive gifts and lavish style of courtship she enjoyed, and by the rooms in her house.* This version contains essentially the same ideas as the excerpt given earlier, but it is a much less effective illustration because it lacks the specifics of the original.

To see the difference between vague and specific language, consider the following pairs:

Vague: The city street was busy.
Specific: The city street was lined with cars, pedestrians dashed from one corner to the next, and store lights flashed in the background.

Applications

Vague: The people in my dorm are diverse.
Specific: The people in my dorm come from twelve different countries on four different continents.

Vague: The cake was delicious.
Specific: The cake started with a layer of chocolate on which was spread a layer of chocolate mousse with a strip of raspberry jam dividing the two, then came another layer of chocolate topped by a fudge frosting with shavings of white chocolate.

EXERCISE

Rewrite the following sentences to make them more specific.

1. The countryside is beautiful.
2. My vacation was very peaceful.
3. The little boy's room is very neat.
4. The crowd was enthusiastic.
5. Your dog is exhausted.

Monica knew that she needed to include vivid, familiar, and specific illustrations to support her generalization about college education in the 1960s, and she decided that additional interviews with campus administrators would provide the best source.

EXERCISE

Collect the information you need for definitions and illustrations to support a generalization that responds to the "day of your birth" assignment.

DEFINING AND ILLUSTRATING IN A DRAFT

Once she had interviewed more people, Monica Caoili wrote a draft in response to the "day of your birth" assignment.

```
       The 60s--A Time for a College Education

    A college education is invaluable, whether it's
sought to improve one's self, to compete in today's
job market, or both. The cost of a college education,
however, has skyrocketed and has forced potential
students to abandon any hopes of obtaining a degree.
Today, the tuition rate for a full-time resident at
the University of Washington is $535 per quarter. In
1967, a student of the same status paid a quarterly
tuition of only $115. The tuition rate has more than
```

quadrupled in the last 19 years. In 1967 the yearly expenses at the UW, including tuition, books and supplies, and room and board totaled approximately $1,255 as opposed to $4,810 today.

The college student of that era had another major advantage over the college student of today--considerably less competition. Today, the requirements and minimum GPA needed to be accepted into the different departments and schools at the UW vary. Engineering is a very popular course and therefore it is not easy to be accepted into the different departments. The Department of Mechanical Engineering, for example, turned away approximately three of every four applicants for entrance for Fall Quarter. The approximate GPA of those accepted were 3.4. Those turned away can only try again next time or settle for less.

Joyce Lumsden has been a program assistant in the Mechanical Engineering since 1966. "Until 1978," she remembers, "No applications were needed to enter any of the departments of engineering. No one was turned away." She stated that it was simply a matter of declaring a major and transferring students' files from the College of Arts and Sciences to the appropriate department. In 1978, the situation changed. In order to limit the number of students entering the School of Engineering, a quota was declared. The dean of the school then told each department how many students it could hold at any time.

In the School of Business, there was a similar situation. Today the field of business is attracting many students also. The minimum GPA for entrance for Fall Quarter was approximately 3.1. During the late 1960s anyone could get into the school of business. Jerry Shigaki was a student at the UW in the late 60s and graduated with a BA in business in 1968. "No applications were needed back then," he stated.

Students at the UW were very fortunate that it was not very difficult to get into most of the departments and schools at the UW. They were not as limited as many students are today due to a lower GPA. They could pursue the area of study of their choice.

It was not always easy to be a student during the late 1960s. The Vietnam War forced many people to face death and incredible loss. Despite this hardship, however, students were able to finish and earn their degrees. Sandra Kroupa is a librarian at Suzallo Li-

Applications

brary. She graduated with a degree in English in 1968 and was able to do it in four years. When asked about how the war affected the environment at the UW, she replied, "It was not easy. Many of us were against the war and the draft, but we did remember that there was a time to demonstrate and a time to study. Many of my peers ultimately obtained their degrees." The Vietnam War did have certain positive effects on the young people of the time. As Sandra Kroup stated, "Many of us went to school not only for an education and to improve ourselves but also to do something for the world." It was ideals such as this that helped motivate students.

Each decade has had its concerns and today it is the threat of nuclear war and the situations in Central America and the Middle East that loom above us all. During the late 1960s it was the Vietnam War that weighed heavily on people's minds. But it must not be forgotten that out of the 1960s many young people matured, were educated, and achieved their goal of obtaining a college education. In terms of the opportunity to receive a college education, it was the best of times.

EXERCISE

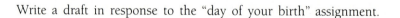

Write a draft in response to the "day of your birth" assignment.

SUMMARY

During the early stages of writing to support assertions the following can be useful:

- Develop a definition for your key terms drawing on sources, functions, contrasts, analogies, analysis, examples, and synonyms.
- Use questions such as those on page 152 to develop definitions for key concepts.
- Collect illustrations that are vivid, use material with which you are familiar, and employ specific language.

Writing to Show Learning

Transforming a draft into a finished piece of writing requires several steps. These include reconsidering the assignment, thinking about the audience for whom you are writing, identifying and emphasizing the thesis of the selection, revising, and editing.

Supporting Assertions

RECONSIDER THE ASSIGNMENT

Returning to the assignment after you have written a draft can enable you to see both the draft and your writing in a new light. You may discover aspects of the assignment that you didn't see the first time, and you may see places where you should add, delete, or change your draft. Or you may find that the draft addresses the assignment adequately.

When Monica returned to the "day of your birth" assignment, she reconfirmed her original impression that she was expected to make and support an assertion that grew out of reading newspapers from her birthdate in 1967. In rereading the assignment and her draft, she realized that she had not stayed with "the best of times" topic when she discussed the negative aspects of the Vietnam War, and she decided that ther conclusion should be changed to keep the emphasis on the 1960s as the best time for college education.

EXERCISE

Return to your "day of your birth" draft and consider it in light of the original assignment. Do you need to add, delete, or change substantial portions to fulfill the requirements of the assignment?

CONSIDER AUDIENCE

When Monica had finished her draft, her instructor handed out this form with instruction that pairs of students should read one another's drafts and evaluate them:

Student Evaluation

Your Name _____

1. Read the paper through once, without stopping to consider any particular feature of the paper.
2. Then address these questions, first by tentatively answering them based on your first reading, then by going back to the paper.
3. Answer, in as specific language as possible, the following questions.
    a. What seems to be the central assertion of the paper? Quote or summarize from the paper.
    b. What seems to be the strategy for supporting the assertion—definition, illustration and example etc.—and how do these strategies operate throughout the paper. Trace the "moves" of the support provided.
    c. How well does the paper work? If you approach it in as neutral a way as possible, do you find the assertion convincing? Try to define the strengths—and weaknesses—of this paper.

Applications

The student who evaluated Monica's paper felt that the central assertion about college education in the 1960s was clear and that she provided an adequate amount of support in the form of illustrations from documents and interviews. This student evaluator felt that the section on the Vietnam War did not really fit with the rest of the paper.

EXERCISE

Using the evaluation from above, respond to a classmate's paper on the "day of your birth" topic.

IDENTIFY YOUR THESIS

In a paper written to defend an assertion, the assertion will usually be the thesis. It may not be expressed in a single sentence, but it will be the central idea of the writing. As you reread your draft, watch for places where the writing drifts away from the central idea.

Monica knew that the title ("The 60s—A Time for a College Education") of her draft was a clear statement of her thesis, so she looked at the draft to see if she had supported it adequately. She felt that her illustrations were effective, but she realized that the discussion of the Vietnam War contributed nothing to her thesis.

CHECK ORGANIZATION

The chronology of "first this, then that" often serves to organize writing that recounts events, but there is no similarly obvious pattern for organizing papers that support assertions. If you return to Donald Hall's "Land of One Thousand Seasons," you will see that it follows the progression of the seasons, but Suzanne Britt Jordon's "That Lean and Hungry Look" follows a much less obvious pattern.

The initial claim that thin people are not fun is followed by explanations that they are mean and surly, and that they believe in logic. Next comes "The main problem with thin people is they oppress," and the conclusion emphasizes the contrast between thin people's emphasis on human limitation and fat people's acceptance of humanity. Throughout this progression Jordan expands her definition of thin people, providing support for her initial assertion that she doesn't like them and they are dangerous. The claims against thin people become more serious (the business of jogging and licking S & H Green Stamps progresses to reasoned evaluations of human limitation), and that progression provides an organizational structure.

In looking at her draft of "The 60s—Time for a College Education" Monica decided that her organizational plan was to move from financial advantages to academic ones, showing how both helped make the 1960s the best time to go to college. She decided this organization reflected the order of importance of the points she wanted to make.

Supporting Assertions

Organization according to *order of importance,* then, can be one way of structuring support for assertions. You can begin with the least important, as Jordan did, and move to the most important, or you can reverse the order. Another strategy is to follow the *structure of the topic,* like Hall's seasons, allowing that to create the organizational pattern. Still another alternative is to progress from *definition to illustration,* allowing the illustrations to help define what follows.

E X E R C I S E

Identify the organizational pattern of your "day of your birth" draft and decide whether this pattern should be changed in any way.

Evaluate Coherence and Cohesion

One of the most effective ways to evaluate your organizational plan is to check the coherence of your writing. Monica, with the help of a peer evaluator, found that the Vietnam War section did not "fit," did not cohere with the rest of her paper, and this illustrated an organizational problem at the same time that it showed a weakness in coherence. In writing to support assertions, the question of "fit" provides an excellent evaluator of coherence, just as "confusion" signals problems of coherence in writing that recounts events.

Issues of cohesion—within and between sentences—also deserve attention in writing that supports assertions. The student evaluator of Monica's draft raised a question about her use of "another" in the second paragraph, saying that it implied that a first advantage had been stated. This led Monica to rethink the relationship between the first and second paragraphs. She also noticed other places where cohesion between and within sentences could be improved.

Editing

Once she was certain that her draft addressed the assignment and its audience, that its thesis was clear, and that it was well organized, Monica was ready to edit her draft. She reread it as carefully as she could, watching for misspelled words, faults of usage, mechanics, and punctuation. Since much of the support for her assertions came from sources outside her experience, she was careful to document her sources. Here is her final version.

```
         The 60s--The Time for a College Education

    A college education is invaluable whether it's
sought to improve one's self, to compete in today's
job market, or both. Financially, the 1960s were an
ideal time to obtain a college education. Costs have
```

Applications

skyrocketed since that time, forcing potential students to abandon any hopes of obtaining a degree. Today the tuition rate for a full-time resident at the University of Washington is $535 per quarter. In 1967, a student of the same status paid a quarterly tuition of only $115 (<u>University of Washington Bulletin</u> 1967-69 General Catalog Issue, January, 1967). The tuition rate has more than quadrupled in the last nineteen years. While the purchasing power of the dollar has decreased by an even faster rate (<u>Survey of Current Business</u>, August, 1968, U.S. Dept of Commerce). In 1967, the yearly expenses at the UW, including tuition, books and supplies, and room and board (living off-campus) totaled approximately $1,255 as opposed to $4,810 today.

The college student of the late 1960s had an advantage even greater than the financial one--considerably less academic competition than today's college students face. Today the requirements and minimum grade point averages needed to be accepted into the different departments and schools at the UW vary. Engineering is a very popular program, and it is not easy to be accepted into its different departments. The Department of Mechanical Engineers, for example, turned away approximately three of every four applicants for entrance for fall quarter, 1986. The approximate grade point averages of those accepted was 3.4. Those turned away can only try again next time or compromise their initial goals for a discipline in which they can be accepted.

Joyce Lumsden has been a program assistant in the Mechanical Engineering office since 1966. "Until 1978," she recalls, "no applications were needed to enter any of the departments of engineering. In fact, no one who applied was turned away." She further stated that it was simply a matter of the student declaring a major and then transferring the student's files from the College of Arts and Sciences to the appropriate department. In 1978, the situation changed. In order to limit the number of students entering the School of Engineering, a quota was declared. The dean of the school then told each department how many students it could enroll at any time.

In the School of Business there was a similar situation. Today, the field of business is attracting many students also. The minimum GPA for entrance for

Supporting Assertions

fall quarter, 1986, was approximately a 3.1 GPA. Jerry Shogaki was a student at the UW during the late 1960s and graduated with a Bachelor's Degree in Business in 1968. He stated that the minimum GPA to get in, back then, was very low--approximately a 2.00. Students at the UW were very fortunate, indeed, that it was not difficult to get into most of the departments and schools at the UW. They were not limited as many students are today due to a lower GPA. They could pursue the area of study of their choice.

Some people argue that it was not easy to be a college student during the late 1960s because the Vietnam War forced students to face death and incredible loss. Students were, however, able to earn their degrees despite the war. Sandra Kroupa is a librarian at Suzallo who graduated with a degree in English in 1968 and was able to do it in four years. When asked about how the war affected the environment at the UW, she replied, "It was not easy. Many of us were against the war and the draft, but we did remember that there was a time to demonstrate and a time to study. Many of my peers ultimately obtained their degrees." And the Vietnam War had positive effects on students of the late 1960s. As Sandra Kroupa stated, "Many of us went to school not only for an education and to improve ourselves, but also to do something for the world." Ideals such as these helped motivate students.

The Vietnam War weighed on many students' minds during the 1960s, just as the threat of nuclear was and the situations in the Middle East and in Central America loom above us today. But it must not be forgotten that in the 1960s many young people matured, were educated, and achieved their goals of obtaining a college education. In terms of the opportunity for a college education, it was the best of times.

EXERCISE

1. List the changes you see between this version and the first draft.
2. Write a revision of your "day of your birth" draft, incorporating as many different kinds of changes as you think appropriate.

Copyright © Charles Ott, The National Audubon Society Collection/Photo Researchers, Inc.

Chapter Seven

Analyzing Information

ANALYSIS occurs frequently in your everyday life. If you commute to school you analyze traffic patterns or crowds of passengers, making decisions about where to enter and exit, how to negotiate your way. When you attend a football game or a movie you analyze the action, identifying a winning play or a climactic moment, observing the movements of individual players or actors. Even young children analyze their world. A four-year-old who visited his older sister's tumbling class made these observations as he watched the leotard-clad girls straddle, roll, and jump: "Some girls have socks, and some have bare feet. The good thing about socks is they keep your feet warm, and the bad thing is they make you slip on the floor. The good thing about bare feet is you won't slip, and the bad thing is you get cold feet." By dividing the large group into people with and without socks, Sam developed a new understanding of what it means to wear socks while doing gymnastics.

The informal analysis of your everyday life helps you understand your world because in analyzing you divide complex entities—whether groups of people, highway traffic, sports events, movies, or a tumbling class—into elements you can manage. The process of dividing enables you to see underlying principles. Similarly, analyzing in writing makes it possible for you to learn more about your subject. Many college writing assignments will ask you to analyze. Here, for example, is an assignment from a communications class:

> Locate on television a thirty- to sixty-second institutional spot commercial. It should be one produced by a major "Fortune 500" corporation. Note that companies such as General Motors, General Electric, oil companies (Chevron, Amoco, Shell, Exxon), and computer and business machine manufacturers (Xerox, IBM, Honeywell) are producing such commercials. They tend to cluster

Applications

around news and public affairs programs, especially the 6:00 PM and 11:00 PM newscasts (network and local), and during prime-time news specials.

Write an analysis of the ad. To do this, identify the subject matter it discusses—a case study of some corporation's success, some technological feat, its overall importance as an industry, criticism a company is trying to live down, whatever. Consider the use of visual and aural (music and the like) effects used. What do you think the sponsor was really trying to accomplish?

As you can see, this assignment requires that one separate the sponsor's purpose from the advertisement's visual and aural effects, and from its subject matter. It requires, in other words, analysis.

Getting Ready to Analyze Information

Whether the writing task calls for analyzing the components of a television advertisement, a theory of economics, or a poem, you begin by collecting information about the subject. As the television advertisement example illustrates, a single subject has many dimensions, and *metaphor* provides one way of generating ideas about these dimensions. Once ideas are generated, separation according to *categories, parts and wholes,* and *similarities and differences* aids the ongoing process of analysis.

METAPHOR

To think metaphorically is to try seeing one thing in terms of another, and this process generates new ideas. It may be easiest to begin by considering how metaphor works in everyday life.

Consider a statement such as "This course is a piece of cake." I have heard many students say something like this when they want to convey the idea that a course is easy, does not require a great deal of work, and will probably yield a good grade. On the surface, cakes and courses do not have much in common, but metaphorical thinking enables one to look at a cake's attributes of sweetness and softness and make connections between it and an easy course.

Here is another statement you have probably heard many times: "Our relationship is on the rocks." When you hear this, you probably assume that the speaker is part of a relationship that is disintegrating, that a separation and perhaps the complete end of the relationship lie ahead. Here the metaphor has two parts because it suggests that a relationship is like a boat, and boats tend to break apart when they hit rocks. This double set of connections—the relationship of boat and rocks to breaking up—conveys the idea. The difference between saying "My partner and I are going to break up" and "Our relationship is on the rocks" or "This is an easy course" and "This course is a piece of cake" derives from metaphorical thinking.

You can probably think of dozens of metaphors that you or others have recently used in conversations, such as

Analyzing Information

He has a new *set of wheels*.
She is *going to pieces*.
I've been studying all day, and I'm *running out of steam*.
My backhand is *a little rusty*.
He is the *low man on the totem pole*.

EXERCISE

1. Read the preceding five statements, and for each identify the two seemingly dissimilar ideas brought together by the metaphor.
2. List five other metaphors you have heard recently.
3. For each metaphor on your list, identify the two ideas that it unites.

You will probably have very little difficulty thinking of metaphors because you hear so many every day. The fact that they occur frequently suggests that they are not original, that they are "dead metaphors" and would be viewed as trite or clichéd in writing. The value of common metaphors lies not in what they can add to writing but what they can add to thinking, because looking at how two things resemble each other will broaden your understanding of both.

Consider, for example, how the extended metaphor in the following poem contributes to your understanding of fog.

Fog

The fog comes
on little cat feet.

It sits looking
over harbor and city
on silent haunches
and then moves on.
—Carl Sandberg

CATEGORIES

Metaphorical thinking fosters the generation of ideas about a subject, but analysis requires a shaping of these ideas. *Categories* offer one strategy for ordering ideas in analysis.

You may be familiar with a game called *Categories,* in which the object is to fill in a chart with names. Each player names one category, and a word is chosen to designate the first letter for each name in the category. All the players have the same amount of time to supply a name for every slot in each category, and the one who fills in the greatest number of unique names wins (unique means not used by any other players.) A completed chart looks like this:

167

Applications

	State Capitals	Baseball Players	British Authors	Popular Musicians	Minerals
P	Pierre	Jim Palmer	Barbara Pym	Elvis Presley	platinum
A	Augusta	Hank Aaron	Jane Austen	Paul Anka	aluminum
T	Topeka	Bobby Thomson	William Thackery	Billy Taylor	tin
C	Columbus	Ty Cobb	Samuel Coleridge	Johnny Cash	copper
H	Helena	Roger Hornsby	Thomas Hardy	Engelbert Humperdink	halite

As you can see, playing this game requires the ability to organize information into categories, and this same ability contributes to expository writing. To categorize is to divide into classes or groups, which means including some things (names of baseball players, for example) and excluding others (names of basketball players).

Writing tasks often include implicit or explicit requirements for categorizing. For example, an assignment that asks for a comparison assumes that the writer will create categories that can be compared. The categories usually include several items, and the categories provide a way of organizing what would otherwise seem like random bits of information. Categories are essential to explanation because they offer ways of organizing ideas.

Among the methods for categorizing are dividing according to similarities and differences and dividing into parts and wholes. The game of Categories exhibits both types of divisions. The words listed under categories such as rock musicians or British authors are wholes or groups into which individual names fit or of which they become parts. Similarly, the categories are similar in encompassing many individual items but are different in nature (rock musicians contrast with metals), and the items in a given category likewise have similarities and differences. They are similar because they fit into a single category, but they differ because they start with different letters and represent different parts. By categorizing or dividing information according to similarities and differences and parts and wholes, you can learn more about it, even as you clarify it for others.

Parts and Wholes. Categorizing by dividing into parts and wholes means creating large classifications into which smaller units fit. For example, the political science question on Golding establishes "effective political leadership" as the whole under consideration, and Ralph's strengths and weaknesses are parts in this whole. Or consider a cookie: This whole is composed of proportionate amounts of flour, sugar, eggs, butter, and seasoning that combine to form a food that few of us would refuse. Or consider a musical group, whether a symphony orchestra or a rock group. The parts are individual instruments, some wooden with strings, some metal tubes with keys to press, and some hollow shells covered with stretched skin, that unite to make the whole musical group produce sounds impossible for individual instruments.

The interesting thing about parts and wholes is that they so often change

Analyzing Information

places with one another. For example, gingersnaps, macaroons, and vanilla wafers are all parts of the whole we call cookies, but cookies in turn are part of the whole we call baked goods, and baked goods are part of the whole we call food. Likewise, atomic properties are part of the whole we call chemistry, but chemistry is part of the whole we call geology, and geology is part of the whole we call physical sciences. You might think about how musical instruments and musical groups fall into successive parts and wholes.

The combination of parts implies a dynamic process. Chemical reactions combine the ingredients of cookies into an edible whole, and the interaction of sound waves creates the music produced by an orchestra or a rock group. Even abstract qualities join actively; Jack and Ralph each act in ways that identify them as leaders, and these lumped together can be described as contrasting styles or qualities that define the political organization of the island. An important aspect of thinking about parts and wholes, then, is to consider the forces that unite them.

The following essay by John Updike, for example, illustrates how the question of friendship is a whole that can be subdivided into types of friends and into stages of friendship. As you read it, notice how Updike divides his friends into types. How does he make each one distinctive and still keep the commonality of friendship with all of them?

Three Boys

John Updike

A, B, and C, I'll say, in case they care. A lived next door; he *loomed* next door, rather. He seemed immense—a great wallowing fatso stuffed with possessions; he was the son of a full-fashioned knitter. He seemed to have a beer-belly; after several generations beer-bellies may become congenital. Also his face had no features. It was just a blank ball on his shoulders. He used to call me "Ostrich," after Disney's Ollie Ostrich. My neck was not very long; the name seemed horribly unfair; it was its injustice that made me cry. But nothing I could say, or scream, would make him stop, and I still, now and then—in reading, say, a book review by one of the apple-cheeked savants of the quarterlies or one of the pious gremlins who manufacture puns for *Time*—get the old sensations: my ears close up, my eyes go warm, my chest feels thin as an eggshell, my voice churns silently in my stomach. From A I received my first impression of the smug, chinkless, irresistible *power* of stupidity; it is the most powerful force on earth. It says "Ostrich" often enough, and the universe crumbles.

A was more than a boy, he was a force-field that could manifest itself in many forms, that could take the wiry, disconsolate shape of wide-mouthed, tiny-eared boys who would now and then beat me up on the way back from school. I did not greatly mind being beaten up, though I resisted it. For one thing, it firmly involved me, at least during the beating, with the circumambient humanity that so often seemed evasive. Also, the boys who applied the beating were misfits, periodic flunkers, who wore corduroy knickers with threadbare knees and men's shirts with the top button buttoned—this last an infallible

Applications

sign of deep poverty. So that I felt there was some justice, some condonable revenge, being applied with their fists to this little teacher's son. And then there was the delicious alarm of my mother and grandmother when I returned home bloody, bruised, and torn. My father took the attitude that it was making a boy of me, an attitude I dimly shared. He and I both were afraid of me becoming a sissy—he perhaps more afraid than I.

[*Updike weaves insights into his own nature into his account.*]

When I was eleven or so I met B. It was summer and I was down at the playground. He was pushing a little tank with moving rubber treads up and down the hills in the sandbox. It was a fine little toy, mottled with camouflage green; patriotic manufacturers produced throughout the war millions of such authentic miniatures which we maneuvered with authentic, if miniature, militance. Attracted by the toy, I spoke to him; though taller and a little older than I, he had my dull straight brown hair and a look of being also alone. We became fast friends. He lived just up the street—toward the poorhouse, the east part of the street, from which the little winds of tragedy blew. He had just moved from the Midwest, and his mother was a widow. Beside wage war, we did many things together. We played marbles for days at a time, until one of us had won the other's entire coffee-canful. With jigsaws we cut out of plywood animals copied from comic books. We made movies by tearing the pages from Big Little Books and coloring the drawings and pasting them in a strip, and winding them on toilet paper spools, and making a cardboard carton a theatre. We rigged up telephones, and racing wagons, and cities of the future, using orange crates and cigar boxes and peanut-butter jars and such potent debris. We loved Smokey Stover and were always saying "Foo." We had an intense spell of Monopoly. He called me "Uppy"—the only person who ever did. I remember once, knowing he was coming down that afternoon to my house to play Monopoly, in order to show my joy I set up the board elaborately, with the Chance and Community Chest cards fanned painstakingly, like spiral staircases. He came into the room, groaned, "Uppy, what are you doing?" and impatiently scrabbled the cards together in a sensible pile. The older we got, the more the year between us told, and the more my friendship embarrassed him. We fought. Once, to my horror, I heard myself taunting him with the fact that he had no father. The unmentionable, the unforgivable. I suppose we patched things up, children do, but the fabric had been torn. He had a long, pale, serious face, with buckteeth, and is probably an electronics engineer somewhere now, doing secret government work.

[*Notice the digression on friendship that introduces C.*]

So through B I first experienced the pattern of friendship. There are three stages. First, acquaintance: we are new to each other, make each other laugh in surprise, and demand nothing beyond politeness. The death of the one would startle the other, no more. It is a pleasant stage, a stable stage; on austere rations of exposure it can live a life-time, and the two parties to it always feel a slight gratification upon meeting, will feel vaguely confirmed in their human state. Then comes intimacy: now we laugh before two words of the joke are out of the other's mouth, because we know what he will say. Our two beings seem marvelously joined, from our toes to our heads, along tingling points of agreement; everything we venture is right, everything we put forth lodges in a corresponding socket in the frame of the other. The death of one would grieve the other. To be together is to enjoy a mounting excitement, a constant echo and amplification. It is an ecstatic and unstable stage, bound of its own agitation to tip into the third: revulsion. One or the other makes a misjudgment; presumes; puts forth that which does not meet agreement. Sometimes there is an explosion; more often the moment is swallowed in silence, and months pass before its nature dawns. Instead of dissolving, it grows. The mind, the throat, are clogged; forgiveness, forgetfulness, that have arrived so often, fail. Now everything jars and is distasteful. The betrayal, perhaps a tiny fraction in itself, has inverted the tingling column of agreement, made all pluses minuses. Everything about the other is hateful, despicable; yet he cannot be dismissed. We have confided in him too many minutes, too many words; he has those minutes and words as hostages, and his confidences are embedded in us where they cannot be scraped away, and even rivers of time cannot erode them completely, for there are indelible stains. Now—though the friends may continue to meet, and smile, as if they had never trespassed beyond acquaintance—the death of the one would please the other.

An unhappy pattern to which C is an exception. He was my friend before kindergarten, he is my friend still. I go to his home now, and he and his wife serve me and my wife with alcoholic drinks and slices of excellent cheese on crisp crackers, just as twenty years ago he served me with treats from his mother's refrigerator. He was a born host, and I a born guest. Also he was intelligent. If my childhood's brain, when I look back at it, seems a primitive mammal, a lemur or shrew, his brain was an angel whose visitation was widely hailed as wonderful. When in school he stood to recite, his cool rectangular forehead glowed. He tucked his right hand into his left armpit and with his left hand mechanically tapped a pencil against his thigh. His answers were always correct. He beat me at spelling bees and, in another sort of competition, when we both collected Big Little Books, he outbid me for my supreme find (in the attic of a third boy), the first Mickey Mouse. I can still see that book, I wanted it so badly, its paper tan with age and its drawings done in Disney's primitive style, when Mickey's black chest is naked like a child's and his eyes are two nicked oblongs. Losing it was perhaps a lucky blow; it helped wean me away from hope of ever having possessions.

[A new side of C appears in this concluding section.]

C was fearless. He deliberately set fields on fire. He engaged in rock-throwing duels with tough boys. One afternoon he persisted in playing quoits with me although—as the hospital discovered that night—his appendix was nearly bursting. He was enterprising. He peddled magazine subscriptions door-to-door; he mowed neighbors' lawns; he struck financial bargains with his father. He collected stamps so well his collection blossomed into a stamp company that filled his room with steel cabinets and mimeograph machinery. He collected money—every time I went over to his house he would get out a little tin box and count the money in it for me: $27.50 one week, $29.95 the next, $30.90 the next—all changed into new bills nicely folded together. It was a strange

Applications

ritual, whose meaning for me was: since he was doing it, I didn't have to. His money made me richer. We read Ellery Queen and played chess and invented board games and discussed infinity together. In later adolescence, he collected records. He liked the Goodman quintets but loved Fats Waller. Sitting there in that room so familiar to me, where the machinery of the Shilco Stamp Company still crowded the walls and for that matter the tin box of money might still be stashed, while my thin friend grunted softly along with that dead dark angel on "You're Not the Only Oyster in the Stew," I felt, in the best sense, patronized: the perfect guest of the perfect host. What made it perfect was that we had both spent our entire lives in Shillington.

To see the part-whole divisions in Updike's essay more clearly, return for a second reading and answer the following questions:

1. What significance do you attach to the activities associated with A, B, and C? Does it matter that Updike fights with A, makes things with B, and competes with C?
2. What is the effect of Updike's repeating the born/perfect host-born/perfect guest idea?
3. Consider the pattern of friendship Updike describes. What correlation do you see between this pattern and his experiences with A, B and C?
4. How does Updike's discussion of these three boys illuminate his concept of friendship?

SIMILARITIES AND DIFFERENCES

Recognizing Similarities and Differences. Parts and wholes provide one way of categorizing material, and thinking in terms of similarities and differences provides another. The grouping necessary to distinguish similarities and differences is central to the way we learn. Our explanations to ourselves and the world around us originate in the similarities and differences we note. Although much of the mystery of the human brain still eludes our understanding, we do know that learning proceeds by grouping information according to its similarities and differences. To illustrate this for yourself, try this exercise:

EXERCISE

Your task is to read the following list, cover it with your hand, and try to repeat as many of the words as you can remember:

difficulty
she
way
obstacle
whenever
a
encountered

the
around
girl
the
found

Now look at this arrangement of words:

Whenever she encountered difficulty, the girl found a way around the obstacle.

No doubt you found the second arrangement easier to recall because the words were arranged in a pattern similar to that of many other sentences you have read, and therefore you have a pattern in your brain that allows you to store the information much more efficiently, whereas you have read relatively few lists of unrelated words and have a much less well developed pattern for storing that information.

If you were given the task of memorizing the twelve words in some form other than a sentence, you might come up with several ways of grouping the words, such as making up an alphabetical arrangement:

a
around
difficulty
encountered
found
girl
obstacle
she
the
the
way
whenever

Or you might group the words according to their parts of speech:

Nouns	Articles	Verbs	Prepositions	Adverbs
girl	a	encountered	around	whenever
obstacle	the	found		
way				
difficulty				

Or you might arrange them according to whether they start with a vowel or a consonant, the number of syllables they contain, or some other system you devise. The point is that in each case you identify the words' similarities and differences according to some criteria.

Applications

Looking at information in terms of similarities and differences gives you a way to analyze it. The following essay by Susan Allen Toth illustrates how similarities and differences can structure a piece of analysis. As you read, notice the way she describes each of the men. How does she make each one seem different from the others?

Cinematypes

Susan Allen Toth

Aaron takes me only to art films. That's what I call them, anyway: strange movies with vague poetic images I don't always understand, long dreamy movies about a distant Technicolor past, even longer black-and-white movies about the general meaninglessness of life. We do not go unless at least one reputable critic has found the cinematography superb. We went to *The Devil's Eye,* and Aaron turned to me in the middle and said, "My God, this is *funny.*" I do not think he was pleased.

When Aaron and I go to the movies, we drive our cars separately and meet by the box office. Inside the theater he sits tentatively in his seat, ready to move if he can't see well, poised to leave if the film is disappointing. He leans away from me, careful not to touch the bare flesh of his arm against the bare flesh of mine. Sometimes he leans so far I am afraid he may be touching the woman on his other side. If the movie is very good, he leans forward, too, peering between the heads of the couple in front of us. The light from the screen bounces off his glasses; he gleams with intensity, sitting there on the edge of his seat, watching the screen. Once I tapped him on the arm so I could whisper a comment in his ear. He jumped.

After *Belle de Jour* Aaron said he wanted to ask me if he could stay overnight. "But I can't," he shook his head mournfully before I had a chance to answer, "because I know I never sleep well in strange beds." Then he apologized for asking. "It's just that after a film like that," he said, "I feel the need to assert myself."

[*Differences in types of films and conventions of behavior structure what follows.*]

Pete takes me only to movies that he thinks have redeeming social value. He doesn't call them "films." They tend to be about poverty, war, injustice, political corruption, struggling unions in the 1930s, and the military-industrial complex. Pete doesn't like propaganda movies, though, and he doesn't like to be too depressed, either. We stayed away from *The Sorrow and the Pity;* it would be, he said, just too much. Besides, he assured me, things are never that hopeless. So most of the movies we see are made in Hollywood. Because they are always topical, these movies offer what Pete calls "food for thought." When we saw *Coming Home,* Pete's jaw set so firmly with the first half-hour that I knew we would end up at Poppin' Fresh Pies afterward.

When Pete and I go to the movies, we take turns driving so no one owes anyone else anything. We leave the car far from the theater so we don't have to pay for a parking space. If it's raining or snowing, Pete offers to let me off at the door, but I can tell he'll feel better if I go with him while he finds a spot, so we share the walk too. Inside the theater Pete will hold my hand when I get scared if I ask him. He puts my hand firmly on his knee and covers it completely with his own hand. His knee never twitches. After a while, when the scary part is past, he loosens his hand slightly and I know that is a signal to take mine away. He sits companionably close, letting his jacket just touch my sweater, but he does not infringe. He thinks I ought to know he is there if I need him.

One night, after *The China Syndrome,* I asked Pete if he wouldn't like to stay for a second drink, even though it was past midnight. He thought a while about that, considering my offer from all possible angles, but finally he said no. Relationships today, he said, have a tendency to move too quickly.

[*Toth uses the same categories of types of films and conventions of behavior to analyze a third "type."*]

Sam likes movies that are entertaining. By that he means movies that Will Jones in the *Minneapolis Tribune* loved and either *Time* or *Newsweek* rather liked, also movies that do not have sappy love stories, are not musicals, do not have subtitles, and will not force him to think. He does not go to the movies to think. He liked *California Suite* and *The Seduction of Joe Tynan,* though the plots, he said, could have been zippier. He saw it all coming too far in advance, and that took the fun out. He doesn't like to know what is going to happen. "I just want my brain to be tickled," he says. It is very hard for me to pick out movies for Sam.

When Sam takes me to the movies, he pays for everything. He thinks that's what a man ought to do. But I buy my own popcorn, because he doesn't approve of it; the grease might smear his flannel slacks. Inside the theater, Sam makes himself comfortable. He takes off his jacket, puts one arm around me, and all during the movie he plays with my hand, stroking my palm, beating a small tattoo on my wrist. Although he watches the movie intently, his body operates on instinct. Once I inclined my head and kissed him lightly just behind his ear. He beat a faster tattoo on my wrist, quick and musical, but he didn't look away from the screen.

When Sam takes me home from the movies, he stands outside my door and kisses me long and hard. He would like to come in, he says regretfully, but his steady girlfriend in Duluth wouldn't like it. When the *Tribune* gives a movie four stars, he has to save it to see with her. Otherwise her feelings might be hurt.

[*Notice how Toth moves from the categories of films and behavior to conclude with her own criterion for movies.*]

I go to some movies by myself. On rainy Sunday afternoons I often sneak into a revival house or a college auditorium for old Technicolor musicals, *Kiss Me Kate, Seven Brides for Seven Brothers, Calamity Jane,* even once, *The Sound of Music.* Wearing saggy jeans so I can prop my feet on the seat in front, I sit toward the rear where no one can see me. I eat large handfuls of popcorn with double butter. Once the movie starts, I feel completely at home. Howard Keel and I are old friends; I grin back at him on the screen. I know the sound tracks by heart. Sometimes when I get really carried away I hum along with

Applications

Kathryn Grayson, remembering how I once thought I would fill out a formal like that. I am rather glad now I never did. Skirts whirl, feet tap, acrobatic young men perform impossible feats, and then the camera dissolves into a dream sequence I know I can comfortably follow. It is not, thank God, Bergman.

If I can't find an old musical, I settle for Hepburn and Tracy, vintage Grant or Gable, on adventurous days Claudette Colbert or James Stewart. Before I buy my ticket I make sure it will all end happily. If necessary, I ask the girl at the box office. I have never seen *Stella Dallas* or *Intermezzo*. Over the years I have developed other peccadilloes: I will, for example, see anything that is redeemed by Thelma Ritter. At the end of *Daddy Long Legs* I wait happily for the scene when Fred Clark, no longer angry, at last pours Thelma a convivial drink. They smile at each other, I smile at them, I feel they are smiling at me. In the movies I go to by myself, the men and women always like each other.

As you return for a second reading of "Cinematypes," note the way Toth handles similarities and differences and answer the following questions.

1. What, besides movies, do Aaron, Pete and Sam have in common?
2. How would you describe the differences between Aaron and Pete? Between Pete and Sam? Between Aaron and Sam?
3. What does the last line of Toth's essay contribute to your understanding of the whole piece?

Writing to Learn

The early stages of writing an analysis focus on generating material to be included in the analysis. Before Toth could analyze the types represented by Aaron, Pete, and Sam, she had to collect information about her experiences with each of them. Similarly, Updike's analysis of friendship did not emerge initially in its present form but evolved from recollections of his experiences with the persons represented by A, B, and C.

THINK METAPHORICALLY

As Updike and Toth demonstrate, *memory* can play a significant role in generating information for analysis. Remembering people and events, whether from childhood or the recent past, provides material that can be divided into comprehensible units of meaning. Metaphor can also be a very useful means for "having ideas" about a subject. By thinking metaphorically you can see new dimensions of a topic.

For example, a student was required to write a term paper in an atmospheric science class. The directions included instructions about the number of references to be included, the format for citing references, and this:

> Your paper should include a good meterological description of a weather or climate event. It does not need to be highly technical but should include background information.

Analyzing Information

The student decided to write about tornadoes and began collecting information. After she had exhausted library sources, she asked herself a series of metaphorical questions about tornadoes.

1. What disease would a tornado be? (mumps)
2. What would a tornado's coat of arms contain? (ball and chain)
3. How would you introduce the tornado as a guest on the Johnny Carson show? ("Someone who has swept parts of the country off its feet")
4. What musical instrument does the tornado play? (bells)
5. What are a tornado's favorite words? (thunder, rain, lightning)
6. What does a tornado really aspire to be? (a train)
7. What kind of junk food is the tornado? (Rocky Road candy bars)
8. What day of the year is the tornado? (May Day)
9. What song is the tornado? (Wagner's *Ride of the Valkyries*)
10. What is the tornado's favorite furniture? (dining room table)

As she looked at her responses to these questions, she realized that she was responding to tornadoes in a tactile way (a train reminded her of the tornado's sound as well as its capacity to run over everything in its path, and the ball and chain reminded her of the tremendous atmospheric pressure that precedes a tornado). She therefore decided that the physical aspects of tornadoes interested her most, and this led her to focus her paper on how people perceive tornadoes and how tornadoes affect people's lives. Although the whimsical answers to the metaphorical questions did not themselves contribute to her eventual paper, the process of answering them helped this student generate new ideas about tornadoes.

E X E R C I S E

Select an assignment from a class you are taking or have taken. It should require you to define and develop a topic. Think of a possible topic, and take one of its key words through the following metaphorical questions. For example, here is an assignment from a sociology class:

> State an interesting sociological question. Then gather information from the literature on it, including at least four articles from journals. Evaluate the information in terms of its adequacy in answering your question. Finally, draw a conclusion regarding the significance of what you have found. You might, for example, be interested in the criteria that people appear to use in conferring prestige on an occupation, or in the direction of change in the United States' birthrate, or in how priests have become committed to their social role.
>
> Your paper should be approximately five typewritten double-spaced pages, and it is due on March 12.

If you were responding to this sociology question, you might focus on the word *prestige* and apply the following questions to it:

Applications

1. The word is a boxer. What or whom is it fighting?
2. This word is as heavy (or light) as . . . ?
3. What would this word treat itself to when eating at a restaurant?
4. What kind of gift would this word be?
5. What political party would this word belong to?
6. What kind of a dance is this word?
7. Why would this word like you?
8. This word is a share of stock. On what exchange is it traded?
9. What motor vehicle is this word?
10. Where would this word be most comfortable in school?

Now list the new ideas you discovered about your topic. What are the best or the most helpful ones?

College writing that requires analysis takes many forms, but nearly all of them can be aided by metaphorical thinking. Here, for example, is an assignment that makes analysis central:

Find or purchase a magazine—or any periodical one would find at a newsstand, excepting newspapers—and consider it as a collection of texts whose common purpose is to reach a particular audience (or a relatively homogenous group of readers). Your task in this paper is to try to define that audience using the evidence you discover in the magazine. Try to construct a version of the magazine's audience using only the evidence of the text.

The first step in responding to this assignment is, of course, to gather information from the magazine itself. When he looked at the magazine *Meditation*, Adam Cooney made these notes:

```
            non profit, Intergroup of Planetary Oneness
                   quarterly, one year old

    Cover                              Layout
    colorful                           black & white
    faces                              photos
    optimistic

    Letters                Ads
    thank you              classes
                           crystals
                           color hydrotherapy

    Content
    love--helping one another
    Peter Caddy--Founder
    peace for the world
    you--breathing, bodysweeping, inner relaxation,
      walking
```

Analyzing Information

```
Poems
inspirational

Story
illustrations--love

Songs

Events
meditation program, services, classes
```

With this collection of information on the source and various texts of the magazine to guide him, Adam began thinking about the magazine in metaphorical terms by asking and answering these questions:

1. This magazine is a boxer. What/whom is it fighting?   *disunity*
2. What political party would this magazine belong to?   *the unity party*
3. What kind of dance is this magazine?   *waltz*
4. What would this magazine's coat of arms contain?   *dove, figure in yoga position*
5. What song is the magazine?   *Dona Nobis Pacem*

This process helped Adam see the magazine's texts more clearly and begin to visualize its audience.

CATEGORIES

Many college writing assignments assume, as does the magazine task, that analysis will employed, even if it is not mentioned specifically. One of the first steps in analyzing information is to divide it into small units or *categories* that can be considered individually. The magazine assignment suggests this by mentioning the "collection of texts" that comprise the periodical. Implicitly, if not explicitly, this assignment asks students to create descriptions of elements within the magazine. Adam's initial notes demonstrate how such descriptions can be generated.

As he looked at his notes, Adam realized that he could create some categories to organize the information he had collected. Here is his list:

```
Visual Effects
cover--colorful, optimistic faces
photographs--black and white, color
lay out

Advertisements
classes, events, services
crystals
color hydrotherapy
```

Applications

```
Content
articles--love, helping one another, peace for the
   world, breathing, bodysweeping, relaxation
poems/songs
fiction
```

By looking at his material in terms of the three categories of visual effects, advertisements, and content, Adam moved a step closer to understanding the audience of the magazine. He was able to see how the material contained in each of these categories contributed to the overall effect of *Meditation*.

E X E R C I S E

Following the directions of the magazine assignment, create categories for analyzing the elements of the periodical you select.

Using Parts and Wholes

In creating the three categories of visuals, advertisements, and content, Adam simultaneously looked at parts and wholes of *Meditation*. Individual articles about peace and love were part of the larger whole of "content," photographs were grouped with use of white space to form the whole of the category of "visual effects," and both the classified pages and ads appearing on pages with articles contributed to the whole of "advertisements." He recognized that the wholes of content, visual effects and advertisements were, in turn, part of the whole of *Meditation*.

Many college writing assignments assume that you will consider parts and wholes even though they do not explicitly ask for this consideration. For example, here is an essay exam question from a communications class:

> Select two major newspapers, and compare one aspect of them, perhaps their sports, arts, current events, or financial sections.

Although the assignment asks for comparison, it assumes that the writer will use several other strategies, including considering the several parts that comprise the chosen sections from each newspaper. In other words, the comparison will include attention to parts and wholes. One successful response to the assignment begins:

```
    The front page is the mask of the newspaper and
usually has an assemblage of articles accompanied by a
large picture of about three columns by six inches and
one or two smaller photos to engage the reader visu-
```

Analyzing Information

ally. The real substance of the paper lies beneath
this surface, but front pages have distinct attributes
that hint at the newspaper's true nature; layout, what
is said, and what is left unsaid all contribute to the
mask.

This selection illustrates how the dynamic relationship of parts and wholes can be described. The writer has selected the front page as the "one aspect" to consider in the newspapers being compared, and in this paragraph she enumerates some of the parts—layout, what is said, what is unsaid—that make up the front page. In addition, she coins the term *mask* to describe the dynamic relationship of all of the aspects of the front page and suggests that this mask changes as its components shift.

As she continues, the writer concentrates on parts and wholes:

Of the eight articles in this particular national
edition, there are two articles on international news
that continue inside, leading readers to more pages of
international news; two national articles; single articles on sports, education, Nobel Prize winners; a
local trial; and a news analysis.

By listing the articles that comprise the front page of the *New York Times*, the writer shows the parts that create one of the two wholes under discussion. A little later in the paper she lists the parts or articles on the front page of the *Seattle Times*:

The Seattle Times also had eight articles on the
front page, and two were devoted to Reagan's economic
policies. There were three other national news stories
on the front page, and the remaining three dealt with
local events. The local issues on the front page included a report on a female corpse; the theft of an
elderly woman's bicycle; and the navy submarine, Trident's, move to Kitsap County. Of these articles, the
Trident was the most accomplished. The history of
Trident was related to the reader, as were the economic
effects of the move, quotes from Washington's two
senators, and the article continued on the back page.

181

Applications

These paragraphs do not, of course, make up the total response to the communications assignment, but they demonstrate how the ability to focus on parts and wholes contributes to the comparison between the two newspapers. In addition, these paragraphs show how the parts and wholes shift places. The eight articles on the front page of the *Seattle Times* are parts of the whole called the front page, but the articles on the corpse, the theft, and the *Trident* comprise a whole called local articles.

E X E R C I S E

Select two television news programs, and compare one aspect of them, for instance, their coverage, their ordering of material, their features, or their use of visuals.

As you can see, this assignment has much in common with the one on newspapers. Answer the following questions, and then write a response:

1. How will you define the whole to which you address yourself in this question?
2. What are the parts of this whole?
3. How do these parts interact?

SIMILARITIES AND DIFFERENCES

In further thinking about his analysis of *Meditation,* Adam began to consider the ways it was similar to and different from other magazines. While he found articles on current events in other magazines, there were none in *Meditation*. Similarly, there were no analyses of sports or current fashion trends. Yet *Meditation* resembled other magazines in its layout, in its mixture of content and advertisements, and in its attempts to create visual appeal. In noting these differences and similarities, Adam understood more about the audience to which *Meditation* addresses itself.

Many writing tasks require you to group pieces of information according to similarities and differences. The communications assignment that asked for a comparison of two newspapers assumes that the students will recognize and group similarities as they look at the sections they have chosen. Here is part of one student's discussion of similarities and differences in the two front pages:

```
    The Seattle Times and the New York Times both
feature large photos on the front page of the October
14 edition of their paper; two photos for the Seattle
Times and three for the New York Times. Both had a
total of eight articles. The papers also had similar
banners with gothic print of the same letter size.
However, the similarities ended there.
```

Analyzing Information

>   The Seattle Times made wide use of the "white space" rule to attract attention. Atop its banner were two small photos pertaining to what was inside the paper, beckoning readers to take a peek. There was also a top-heaviness to the paper, with bold headlines on the top and headlines getting smaller toward the bottom of the page. The headlines were usually three columns wide and almost never bumped: The copy type was easy to read, and the articles had room to breathe.
>   In contrast, the New York Times had vertical lines separating the articles which were about a pica's length apart. Its type was small and the headlines were much more compact than the Seattle Times'. The headlines would collide if not for the lines.

In her discussion of layout, this student groups similarities of articles, photos, and typeface and then moves on to discuss the differences of spacing and arrangement. This grouping makes very clear the similarities and differences between the two front pages. Some college writing tasks focus almost exclusively on recognizing similarities and differences. Here, for example, is an assignment from a political science class:

>   Analyze the perception of a major world problem as reported in major newspapers in three different regions of the world, and map the frequency and extent of the column space used in these newspapers to cover international news events on the same day.

As you can see, the word *map* suggests acknowledging the similar and dissimilar features of news coverage in three areas of the world. A successful response to this assignment would include grouping the column spaces devoted to international news.

EXERCISE

The following assignment comes from a communications class:

>   Watch two hours of prime-time television programs in the coming week, and look for indications of stereotyping in their characters. Your task is to analyze, not criticize, the stereotyping. Notice how blacks, Asian Americans, and other ethnic minorities are treated, in comparison with whites, or whether they appear at all in the shows you watch. Are they minorities? What kinds of jobs do they have? What roles do they play? Are they main characters, heroes, villains, or minor characters? Are they in charge of their own lives, or do they need help from whites? Are they in the plot as tokens, or do they contribute meaningfully to the program? Notice how women are treated in

Applications

comparison with men. What kinds of jobs (or lack of jobs) do they have? Are they main or minor characters, heroines, or nice additions to the scenery? Are they in charge of their lives, or do they need help from men?

1. What similarities and differences does this assignment ask you to identify?
2. How can you group these similarities and differences?
3. Write a response to this assignment, listing the similarities and differences.

Having generated ideas by using metaphorical thinking and having considered categories, parts and wholes, and similarities and differences, Adam wrote the following draft in response to the magazine assignment.

```
               The Way It Should Be

    "By chance I got my hands on the Summer '86 Volume
of Meditation. How beautiful the articles are. . . .
Thank you again for this beautiful publication. At 66
years of age, I have finally found the 'Answer.'" This
letter, published in the Letters section of the Fall
'86 Volume of Meditation, reflects the tone and enthu-
siasm of the other letters from very satisfied readers.
    Meditation, a quarterly publication, is a rela-
tively new magazine, now completing its first year of
publication. It is published by the Intergroups for
Planetary Oneness, a nonprofit, tax-exempt organization
incorporated in the state of California. The cover of
the fall publication depicts young children eating.
One girl smiles. Another boy's face is covered, buried
in his bowl as he finishes the last of his meal. The
caption reads in red letters "Love is Feeding Every-
one." This feature article is very optimistic. In
fact, the entire magazine speaks of love, happiness,
and peace. The purpose of the magazine is "to explore
and promote meditation as a consciousness expanding
activity and to be a source of reference for meditation
activities and organizations."
    Readers turn to Meditation because it is different
when compared to many of the other magazines found in
news stands today. It contains neither the recent
developments in Lebanon, the score in last night's
World Series baseball game, nor the current fashion
```

trend. Meditation concentrates on helping people. Its articles include features about people who are sincerely happy telling about their experiences, how they achieved happiness, and what they are doing to help others.

Other articles are very informative and address the reader directly as "you." The articles inform readers on how they can live life to the fullest. Through meditation and relaxation, a deeper level of consciousness can be reached, resulting in better health, a better attitude, and a better sense of what life is all about. The articles show different methods for both the beginning and experienced meditators.

While many articles explain the methods of meditation, the ads show the different classes available in the area of meditation. Almost all the ads are related to meditation, including ads ranging from healing crystals to ads for classes with the headings "Come Help Transform the World!" and "Be in Charge." The ads certainly reach out to the person looking for help and advice. The advertisements are simple and clear. They are black and white and directly tell the reader that "We can help you."

By glancing through the classified ads and events section of the magazine, one notices that the magazine is directed at mainly readers in the state of California. Most of the classes offered are in the southern part of California. While the events section does show the dates and locations of lectures, study group meetings, and classes in Arizona, Colorado, and New York, these are very few. The majority are centered in Southern California.

Obviously, one doesn't pick up a copy of Meditation expecting to look at colorful pictures nor to be entertained. People who read Meditation are people looking for a better life and are serious enough to try different methods and attend classes and purchase books as its ads show. They are inspired by others who have already found happiness, and by the inspirational poems, stories and songs spread throughout the magazine.

These readers can include people ranging from the 40-year-old businessman struggling to support his family with a stressful and hectic job who looks for a way to relax to the experienced meditator whose life is dedicated to helping others who are in need and who

Applications

```
just wants to keep up on the upcoming events and meet-
ings in southern California. It can also include people
ranging from the well-to-do corporate president who
has achieved his goal of status and wonders "Is this
all there is?" to the elderly lady who has lived a
long life, watched her children grow and leave, and is
looking for the "Answer." Now, thanks to Meditation,
she has found it.
```

EXERCISE

Write a draft in response to the magazine assignment or some other writing task that requires analysis.

SUMMARY

During the early stages of writing to analyze information the following can be useful:

- Use metaphors to generate ideas and see your subject from a new perspective.
- Ask metaphorical questions such as those on page 177 to develop new metaphors.
- Group your ideas and information into categories.
- Divide categories or parts of categories into parts and wholes.
- Note similarities and differences between and among categories.

Writing to Show Learning

After completing his draft Adam knew he needed to transform it into a finished response to the magazine assignment, and his first project would be to return to the assignment itself. After that he would think about the audience for whom he was writing, reconsider aspects of analysis such as categories, parts and wholes, and similarities and differences. Then he would revise and edit the whole thing. Most writers go through similar processes as they turn drafts into polished writing.

RECONSIDER THE ASSIGNMENT

Once you have written a draft, you will see the original assignment differently. You may have new questions about what is expected, or you may understand key terms more completely. Returning to the assignment after you have completed a draft will help you get perspective on what you have written because the assignment suggests how someone else will look at your work.

Analyzing Information

When he had completed "The Way It Should Be," Adam returned to the magazine assignment. As he reread it, he realized that he needed to give more direct attention to the audience of *Meditation*. He needed to say more about the "homogeneous group of readers" to whom it was addressed. While it was important to include information about the magazine, he would include only data that indicated something about the audience. Accordingly, he decided to eliminate facts such as the name and location of the publisher.

EXERCISE

Reread the assignment for which you wrote your draft and consider what might be added or deleted to make it address the assignment more effectively.

CONSIDER AUDIENCE

When no audience is specified for a college writing assignment, you can assume that you should address the general reader who will have no special knowledge of your topic. Because you are writing for an academic audience, you can also assume that your readers will expect you to offer evidence to support your assertions, to present your case in an organized and coherent fashion, and to conform to the conventions of standard written English.

When Adam thought about the audience for "The Way It Should Be," he realized that most of his readers would not have seen *Meditation*, and he needed to show it and its audience as clearly as possible. As he thought about that, he realized that his title could be changed to reflect the magazine and its audience more directly. He decided to change the title to "Looking for the Answer in *Meditation*" because it captured the essence of the questions that most readers brought to the journal.

A classmate of Adam's read his draft and asked several questions including:

```
How does Meditation satisfy its audience?
Do we have enough information about the implied
  reader?
What is the effect of the interview style where
  people tell of their experiences with Meditation?
What are the implications of the fact that readers
  seem to be concentrated in southern California?
What on earth are healing crystals?
```

EXERCISE

Ask a classmate to read your draft and note the questions that emerge.

187

Applications

Reconsider Method of Analysis

In transforming a draft into a finished piece of analysis, consider how the method of analysis can be improved. Does the writing break the subject down into parts small enough to be understood? Should new categories be introduced? Are there other parts and wholes that can be included? What about additional similarities and differences?

As he thought about his analysis of *Meditation,* Adam decided that his original categories of visual appeal, content of articles, and advertisements were appropriate for his purposes. In addition, he decided to add a category of comparison with other magazines because it had emerged in his draft. He felt that looking at these four aspects of *Meditation* would provide the basis for describing its readers.

Check Organization

Your methods of analysis can create an organizational structure for your writing. If, for example, you develop categories, these may become the major sections of your paper. Or, if you consider a series of similarities and differences, you may want to organize your writing around these. Likewise, examination of the relationship between parts and wholes can help you organize your writing. As you look at drafts of analysis writing, consider which organizational plan will work best for you.

When Adam looked at his draft of "The Way It Should Be," he found that the letter from the 66-year-old woman created a kind of frame around the paper, and he decided that this was a good idea because it portrayed a reader of *Meditation* directly. The rest of the paper seemed to be organized around the categories of visual appeal, comparisons with other magazines, content of articles, and advertisements. He decided that the general structure was sound.

Evaluate Coherence and Cohesion

The places where things do not seem to "fit" usually indicate a problem in cohesion. These are the places where your readers will say "I don't understand" or "How do we get there from here?"

As he reread his draft, Adam realized that the section comparing *Meditation* with other magazines seemed out of place, and he remembered the question raised by his classmate. He decided that it should be shortened and included in the first paragraph because it provided more general information about readers. At the same time he realized that his description of the cover was inadequate because he had not explained its connection to the food program described in the feature article.

To deal with questions of cohesion examine the smaller units of analysis, those within and between sentences. Several of the questions raised by his classmate helped Adam see ways to improve the cohesion of his draft. The

Analyzing Information

question about the articles containing interviews led him to explain the effects of these interviews more fully, thereby creating better connections with the statements about addressing the reader and offering advice. The questions about southern California helped him see the need to add information about the importance of meditation in that part of the country, information that would create links between statements about geography and readership. And the question about healing crystals prompted him to explain these items in enough detail to connect them to the help offered by other advertisements.

EXERCISE

Construct a cloze test to check the cohesiveness of your draft. If you have questions about this procedure, see page 102.

Editing

Once he was certain that his draft addressed the assignment and its audience, that its method of analysis was sound, and that it was well organized, Adam began editing his draft. He reread it carefully watching for misspelled words, faults of usage, mechanics, and punctuation. He checked and found, for example, that the correct form is "newsstands." Here is his final version.

```
         Looking for the Answer in Meditation

      "By chance I got my hands on the Summer '86 Volume
of Meditation. How beautiful the articles are. . . .
Thank you again for this beautiful publication. At 66
years of age, I have finally found the "Answer." This
letter reflects the tone and enthusiasm of other let-
ters published in the Letters section of the Fall '86
volume of Meditation. These readers read Meditation
because it is different from many of the other
magazines found in newsstands today. It contains
neither the recent developments in Lebanon, the score
in last night's baseball game, nor today's fashion
trend.
      The cover of the fall publication depicts color
pictures of young children eating. A girl is smiling.
One boy's face is covered, buried in his bowl as he
finishes the last of his meal. The caption reads in
red letters "Love is Feeding Everyone." This feature
article is very optimistic, centered on goodwill. It
is about the LIFE Project--a delivery service to the
```

189

hungry in Los Angeles. The entire magazine, in fact, speaks of love, happiness, and peace.

The articles include features about people who feel truly content and at peace with the world. The articles are often in the form of interviews. People tell about how they achieved happiness and what they are doing now to help others. These interviews give the writing an oral quality, allowing readers to "hear" the words as they might at church. Other articles advise and address the reader directly by using the pronoun "you." They inform readers on how they can live life to the fullest. In today's world, life can be very busy, stressful, and painful. The articles explain that through meditation and relaxation, a deeper level of consciousness can be reached which will result in better health, a better attitude, and a better sense of what life is all about. The articles show different methods for both the beginning and experienced meditators.

While many articles explain the background and techniques of meditation, almost all of the advertisements are related to it as well. They range from advertisements of classes with the headings "You create your own reality" and "BE IN CHARGE" to those of Healing Crystals. Healing Crystals are usually advertised as natural quartz and as the name implies, one's health can benefit from them. Obviously, the advertisements reach out to the person looking for help and advice. They are simple and clear. While they do not overwhelm the magazine, they do attract attention. They are in black and white and tell the reader "We can help you!"

The advertisements in the classified section toward the end of the magazine are similar to those found throughout its pages. An interesting observation is that most of the classes, study group meetings, and lectures advertised in both the classified and events sections are located in southern California, the mecca of alternative lifestyles. While <u>Meditation</u> is circulated throughout the United States and Canada, a large proportion of its dedicated readers live in southern California, the area where the magazine is published.

Obviously, one doesn't pick up a copy of <u>Meditation</u> expecting to look at colorful pictures nor to be entertained. People who read <u>Meditation</u> want to improve themselves and/or are searching for a better approach

Analyzing Information

to life. They may have already found that approach--through meditation--and are only reading it to expand their knowledge. The readers are open-minded and are serious enough to try different methods, attend classes, and/or purchase books and other meditation accessories. They are inspired by those who have already found happiness and by the inspirational poems, stories, and songs found throughout the magazine.

The readers of Meditation can include people ranging from the forty-year-old businessman under constant pressure and stress who is looking for a way to relax to the experienced meditator who just wants to keep up-to-date on the upcoming meetings and events in southern California. They can also include the corporate president who has achieved his goal of wealth and status and is wondering "Is this all there is?" as well as the elderly lady who is looking for the "Answer." But now, thanks to Meditation, she has finally found it.

E X E R C I S E

1. Make a list of the ways "Finding the Answer in *Meditation*" differs from "The Way It Should Be."
2. Revise your own analysis incorporating several different kinds of changes.

Copyright © Georg Gerster, The National Audubon Society Collection/Photo Researchers, Inc.

Chapter Eight

Explaining Causes and Effects

The Universe

What
  is it about
      the universe
   about
us stretching out? We within our brains within it think
  we must unspin the laws that spin it. We think
      why because
          we think
    because.
    Because
         we think
         we think
      the universe
    about
   us
  But does it think,
  the universe?
Then what
  about?
  About
us? If not, must there be cause
     in the universe:
Must it have laws? And what
     if the universe
   is *not about*
  us? Then what?
What
 is it about
and what
  about
   us?
  —May Swenson

Applications

THE poet May Swenson wrote, "We think why because we think because," expressing a universal human preoccupation with trying to understand causal relationships. Causal relationships are in many ways the ultimate form of exposition, as the answer to why is always an explanation. From our earliest years we ask questions: "Why does the wind blow?" "Why does Grandma love me?" "Why do I have to go to bed?" This asking continues throughout our lives: Why do so many people want to go to college? Why do we have a winning football team? Why is the interest rate rising?

Of course there are limits to what cause-and-effect relationships can explain. As the second law of thermodynamics, the law of entropy, explains, randomness is part of the world's design. Many things in life defy the logic of cause-and-effect relationships. Yet despite important questions we cannot answer, we keep asking why because we think because.

Accepting the limitations of cause-and-effect relationships helps writers deal with the inevitable limits of individual knowledge. To acknowledge what we cannot know makes it easier to focus on what we can know. We can, for example, acknowledge that we do not know why the three laws of thermodynamics work and thus devote our attention to explaining how they do work.

Discussing causes and effects in exposition can proceed from two directions. You can begin with the causes and look at the effects, or you can begin with the effects and look at the causes. Take, for example, the issue of energy: you can look at diminishing supply as a cause that creates the effect of higher prices, or you can look at higher prices as an effect and seek causes such as diminishing supply.

Getting Ready to Write about Causes and Effects

When you are asked to write about causes and effects, you are usually presented with an effect—ranging from teenage suicide to changes in weather patterns to a chemical reaction—and asked to explain the causes. Accordingly, the first step is to generate ideas about possible causes for the effect you are considering. Alternatives for generating ideas include *chain outlines* and *questions about events or processes*. Once you have ideas about causes, you are ready to decide whether to structure your writing according to a *cause-effect pattern* (one that starts with a statement of a cause and then examines the effects) or an *effect-cause pattern* (one that begins by stating an effect and then moves into an exploration of its causes).

CHAIN OUTLINES

Most effects stem from multiple causes, and a visual representation can often help you see how these causes develop from one another and interact to create a single effect. A chain outline offers one way to represent causes visually,

Explaining Causes and Effects

and it works especially well when you know a subject well and simply need to recall details. Think of the chain outline as a tree with the effect at the base and the causes radiating out as branches. The structure will look like this:

```
cause                                           cause
           cause                    cause
                   cause
                            cause
                  EFFECT
```

Here is a chain outline made by Monica Caioli as she prepared to write about students who were forced to postpone their graduation from college.

```
    state revenues decreased        family income decreased
    university budget cut      private college unaffordable
                              university tuition increased
    faculty reduced
                               students must work while
                                     attending college
    course offerings reduced
                     difficult to schedule required courses
                        GRADUATION POSTPONED
```

Each of these words or phrases signified several concepts for Monica. "State revenues decreased," for example, reminded her of the declining timber industry in the state of Washington and its negative effects on the state economy. This, in turn, led to a series of cuts in the university budget because the state legislature was unable to tap additonal sources of funds such as an income tax. Although she was able to identify some conditions that contributed to graduation postponement, Monica eliminated student laziness and lack of preparation as causes. The chain outline enabled Monica to collect ideas that would help her write about what caused students to postpone their graduations.

QUESTIONS ABOUT EVENTS OR PROCESSES

If you know your subject less well and want to generate ideas or discover what additional information you need, you may find it more effective to ask yourself questions. Moving through a series of questions such as the ones that follow will probably give you more information than you need, but the process of answering them will help you see your subject more clearly.

Applications

1. Exactly what happened? (Tell the precise sequence. Who? What? When? How? Why? Who did what to whom? Why? What did what to what? How?)
2. What were the circumstances in which the event occurred?
3. How was the event like or unlike similar events?
4. What were its causes?
5. What were its consequences?
6. What, if anything, does it reveal or emphasize about some general condition?
7. Is it (in general) good or bad? By what standard? How do we arrive at that standard?
8. How do we know about it? What is the authority for our information? How reliable is that authority? How do we know it to be reliable (or unreliable)?
9. How might the event have been changed or avoided?
10. To what other events was it connected? How?

EXERCISE

Use the questions above to generate ideas about an event for which you would like to explore causes.

Cause-Effect Pattern

Once you have collected enough ideas to feel that you are ready to write about causes, you need to decide what general plan of organization you will follow. One option is to use a cause-effect pattern by beginning with the causes and proceeding to the effect. The following essay by Susan Allen Toth illustrates how writing can proceed from causes to effects. As she recounts her search for a scientist, Toth touches on a series of causes that led to her eventual divorce. Try to make a chain outline of the causes Toth identifies. How many can you find?

Science

Susan Allen Toth

When I left home at eighteen for college, graduate school, and I assumed, marriage, I hoped that I might find somewhere a man who could understand my passion for specifics. I didn't think of my search in quite that way, of course. I simply wanted to meet someone who could understand all the things I cared about, who knew what held them together, who could explain them to me. I thought what I needed was a scientist.

[*Toth's "need" for a scientist is the first cause introduced.*]

Explaining Causes and Effects

Finding the right sort of scientist turned out to be difficult. Friendly, giggly, and exuding a bright Iowa innocence, I was often asked to go out with someone's lonely brother or cousin, since I was sure to cheer them up. Many of these blind dates were engineers, who seemed to have more trouble finding girls than history or psych majors did. I could see why. They had trouble talking; though eager to answer questions, they never seemed able to think of any. They wore awkward bow ties and ill-fitting hairy jackets, and most of them had receding chins or twitches. Yet I knew that the ones who went to M.I.T. or Yale must be smart, or they wouldn't have been admitted. So I tried my best, but we never exchanged more than a few sentences about Science before my date would founder and stop. I learned to switch quickly to possible comparisons of Iowa with Massachusetts, or Amherst with Wesleyan, or the Dekes with the Theta Xis. I usually went home early.

My mistake, I finally decided, was in not sticking to the "pure" sciences, an adjective we all took for granted. Anything not directly useful, like chemistry, physics, or biology, was "pure"; anything "applied" was mechanical, dull, and somehow second-rate. I was sure they practiced "pure" Science at the Synchrotron. I envied Marcia Hayter across the hall, who was pinned to a premed chemistry, student named Tom. Once, when they had fixed me up with Tom's roommate, who was a lonely electrical engineer, we all four walked over to Tom's chem lab. I was entranced. The apparatus that covered several rows of long tables would have excited Snow White's stepmother. Test tubes bubbled, liquid coursed through curlicues of glass tubing into other test tubes, lights flashed and machinery hummed in unexpected places. At the end of the table a student in a white lab apron was bending over a particularly complicated set of intertwined tubes, which reminded me of the dizzying dreams I used to have of completing the most advanced construction in my Tinkertoy set. He was so engrossed in his manipulations that he didn't even notice us. I wished I knew who he was.

[*The distinction between pure and applied science establishes another cause.*]

When I finally fell in love, for what I thought was forever, I was disconcerted to find that the man I had chosen did not have a lab like that. He was a scientist, but not the "pure" kind. His first degree was, in fact, in engineering, though he told me that I could think of him as a sort of solid-state physicist if I liked. He did the same kind of stuff with atoms that they did, he said, and he was probably right. I asked him about his work at first, but he didn't usually like to talk about it, and I didn't really understand when he tried. So we went to lots of movies instead.

[*Another kind of cause has joined the list.*]

After we were married, Lawrence embarked on a long, complicated set of experiments. He did much of his work at home, with a slide rule, making pages of calculations which were transformed into hypothetical formulas to be carried out in his lab. He called it a lab, but it didn't seem like one to me. It was just a room filled with a few large, expensive instruments, boxes with dials that had to be kept at a difficult temperature under impossible conditions. He put pieces of metal into these boxes, made them very cold, and then

Applications

measured their conductivity. Nothing gurgled or whirred, no lights flashed, in fact nothing as far as I could see happened at all. This equipment kept breaking down, soundlessly, and then I wouldn't see Lawrence for days.

After a few months, Lawrence came home excited by an idea for an experiment he thought I could understand and even help him with. His adviser had suggested that he try to deduce something about the random diffusion of atoms by rolling some small steel balls in a pan of Jell-O, then letting them harden into whatever configurations they would. This seemed a sloppy way of conducting an important experiment, I thought, but Lawrence was already out the door on his way to buy three boxes of Jell-O. I had three cookie pans, and Lawrence thought we might as well fill them all. When he returned, I dutifully mixed all the red raspberry goo and ladled it carefully over the dozens of little balls now knocking about in my warped aluminum pans like berserk pinball machines. Lawrence, who had never even cooked an egg, wanted to put the pans in the oven. I argued that Jell-O wouldn't jell except in a refrigerator, but Lawrence insisted. If we left the pans alone long enough, he was sure the Jell-O would eventually coagulate. There wasn't enough room in the fridge anyway, he said, and he was right. I could never argue very long with Lawrence, because he was always so positive I was wrong that gradually I began to believe him. So I gave in about the Jell-O. Though I was the cook, I knew he was the scientist.

[*Still another set of causes appears here.*]

For three days I didn't bake anything in our oven. Several times a day I would open the door, peer at the sticky red mess that covered every shelf, and close the door again. Once I touched one of the little steel balls with my finger to see if it would move. It did. I wondered if I had altered an arrangement of atoms. Each night when Lawrence came home, he walked into the kitchen to see for himself. He never said anything as he stared at the experiment. The third night he grabbed one of the trays from the oven, stomped to the back door, and threw it open. From the window I could see him at the edge of the lot where the weeds grew thick and high, as he emptied the contents of the tray with one fling. Later that night I washed the pans, scrubbing hard where the Jell-O had dried in crusty blobs.

That was the last experiment Lawrence tried to do at home. Afterward, he spoke even less about his work than before, but I no longer minded. I had somehow lost interest, and I soon stopped asking to go along to his lab when he went there to check on his equipment. I even gave up trying to read *Scientific American* in the bathroom. We stayed married for eleven more years, but I sometimes think our Jell-O experiment was the beginning of the end.

[*The ultimate effort—of Toth's divorce—finally emerges.*]

Every fall, when students at the college where I teach begin to pour back on campus, and they sit inside my office to ask about their schedules, I feel an urge to sign up for courses myself. Something about my discussion of the merits of introductory anthropology versus beginning Latin, human geography or Latin-American history, stirs in me that same feeling of anticipation, of knowledge waiting just around the corner, that I used to have in Mrs. Gosselin's

Explaining Causes and Effects

eighth-grade science class. I briefly wonder whether I could audit a course in biology without taking the labs, or sit through all the lectures in "Physics for the Non-Physicist," or study vertebrates in zoology. But I never do.

Return for a second reading of "Science" and consider the following questions.

1. What does the distinction between "pure" and "applied" sciences contribute to Toth's examinat6ion of the cause of her divorce?
2. What, in your opinion, caused the Jell-O experiment to fail? (You will probably find a chain of causes rather than a single one.)
3. What causal connections do you see between the failed Jell-O experiment and Toth's divorce?

EFFECT-CAUSE PATTERN

An alternative to the cause-effect pattern is the effect-cause pattern of organization. Here, instead of beginning with the causes and working toward the effect, such as Toth's divorce, you can begin with the effect and work backward into the causes underlying it. The following essay by Carll Tucker illustrates this pattern as it moves from the fact of jogging to explaining why the author (and his contemporaries) choose to jog.

Fear of Dearth

Carll Tucker

I hate jogging. Every dawn, as I thud around New York City's Central Park reservoir, I am reminded of how much I hate it. It's so tedious. Some claim jogging is thought conducive; others insist the scenery relieves the monotony. For me, the pace is wrong for contemplation of either ideas or vistas. While jogging, all I can think about is jogging—or nothing. One advantage of jogging around a reservoir is that there's no dry shortcut home.

From the listless looks of some fellow trotters, I gather I am not alone in my unenthusiasm: Bill-paying, it seems, would be about as diverting. Nonetheless, we continue to jog; more, we continue to *choose* to jog. From a practically infinite array of opportunities, we select one that we don't enjoy and can't wait to have done with. Why?

[*Having established the effect of jogging, Tucker moves to causes.*]

For any trend, there are as many reasons as there are participants. This person runs to lower his blood pressure. That person runs to escape the telephone or a cranky spouse or a filthy household. Another person runs to avoid doing anything else, to dodge a decision about how to lead his life or a realization that his life is leading nowhere. Each of us has his carrot and stick. In my case, the stick is my slackening physical condition, which keeps me from beating opponents at tennis whom I overwhelmed two years ago. My carrot is to win.

Applications

[Tucker has explained his own cause and now moves on to others.]

Beyond these disparate reasons, however, lies a deeper cause. It is no accident that now, in the last third of the twentieth century, personal fitness and health have suddenly become a popular obsession. True, modern man likes to feel good, but that hardly distinguishes him from his predecessors.

With zany myopia, economists like to claim that the deeper cause of everything is economic. Delightfully, there seems no marketplace explanation for jogging. True, jogging is cheap, but then not jogging is cheaper. And the scant and skimpy equipment which jogging demands must make it a marketer's least favored form of recreation.

Some scout-masterish philosophers argue that the appeal of jogging and other body-maintenance programs is the discipline they afford. We live in a world in which individuals have fewer and fewer obligations. The work week has shrunk. Weekend worship is less compulsory. Technology gives us more free time. Satisfactorily filling free time requires imagination and effort. Freedom is a wide and risky river; it can drown the person who does not know how to swim across it. The more obligations one takes on, the more time one occupies, the less threat freedom poses. Jogging can become an instant obligation. For a portion of his day, the jogger is not his own man; he is obedient to a regimen he has accepted.

Theologists may take the argument one step further. It is our modern irreligion, our lack of confidence in any hereafter, that makes us anxious to stretch our mortal stay as long as possible. We run, as the saying goes, for our lives, hounded by the suspicion that these are the only lives we are likely to enjoy.

All of these theorists seem to me more or less right. As the growth of cults and charismatic religions and the resurgence of enthusiasm for the military draft suggest, we do crave commitment. And who can doubt, watching so many middle-aged and older persons torturing themselves in the name of fitness, that we are unreconciled to death, more so perhaps than any generation in modern memory?

[Notice how Tucker deals with causes emerging from commitment and avoidance of death to what he sees as the "real" cause.]

But I have a hunch there's a further explanation of our obsession with exercise. I suspect that what motivates us even more than a fear of death is a fear of dearth. Our era is the first to anticipate the eventual depletion of all natural resources. We see wilderness shrinking; rivers losing their capacity to sustain life; the air, even the stratosphere, being loaded with potentially deadly junk. We see the irreplaceable being squandered, and in the depths of our consciousness we are fearful that we are creating an uninhabitable world. We feel more or less helpless and yet, at the same time, desirous to protect what resources we can. We recycle soda bottles and restore old buildings and protect our nearest natural resource—our physical heath—in the almost superstitious hope that such small gestures will help save an earth that we are blighting. Jogging becomes a sort of penance for our sins of gluttony, greed, and waste. Like a hairshirt or a bed of nails, the more one hates it, the more virtuous it makes one feel.

That is why *we* jog. Why *I* jog is to win at tennis.

Explaining Causes and Effects

As you reread Tucker's essay, consider the following questions.

1. As you read from the beginning of the essay, how soon do you know what effect Tucker will discuss?
2. To what extent is improving his tennis game Tucker's real reason for jogging?
3. What is the effect of explanations of economists, philosophers, theologists?
4. How does jogging address the fear of dearth?

Writing to Learn

The first step in writing to learn about causes is recognizing that a discussion of cause and effect is called for. Many assignments do not mention cause and effect explicitly, even though that is what successful responses will include. Here, for example, is an assignment from a music appreciation class:

> Compare and contrast the different dramas embodied in the middle movements of Mozart's Piano concerto in G, K.543, and Beethoven's Piano Concerto in G, op. 58. Your paper should clarify the different functions of the two movements in the context of their respective concertos. Pay close attention to mode, meter, phrase structure, and the use of constructive devices. Other musical elements that might be considered as they bear on the drama include thematic material and instrumentation.

As you can see, cause and effect are not mentioned in this assignment, yet they have a central place in it because explaining the "different functions" of these two movements means explaining their effect, and the elements that students are admonished to consider (mode, meter etc.) are causes that produce this effect.

Sometimes, of course, cause and effect are mentioned explicitly in an assignment, as in this one from a composition class:

> This assignment is one of "causal analysis"—or the establishment of a hierarchy of causes that lead to the existence of a certain phenomenon. In more common terms, you should examine a condition in light of those factors or conditions that seem to you to have "caused" it.
>
> Take something in your life that, at first glance, may appear difficult to explain, or may simply be taken for granted. Your effort should be to "make sense" of this phenomenon *in terms of its causes*. The hierarchy of causes suggests that some causes are more "important" than others but that "contributing" causes play an important part also.
>
> Try thinking about the hierarchy of causes in two ways, arranged by your definition of their importance: a hierarchy by logic and a hierarchy by spatial/temporal distinctions. The first would explain, for example, the murder of a man in terms of the deadlines of the act; the second would examine the specific "network" of acts and conditions leading to the murder.

Applications

> Any causal analysis should also, by implicit or explicit means, reject certain phenomena as contributing to the condition under analysis. You are expected to make explicit refutations of those conditions that seem *possible* explanations but that you do *not* see as possible.

This assignment asks students to consider causes of whatever situation or event they choose. The directive to think about the hierarchy (or order of importance) of causes in terms of both logic and spatial/temporal distinctions implies that the students should not focus on a single set of causes but consider several different types. The final paragraph of the assignment directs students to anticipate and refute causes that they do not see as contributing to the effect under consideration.

Chain Outline

As is true for most writing, the early stages of writing about causes focus on generating ideas. Chain outlines provide a useful way of collecting ideas for writing about causes, particularly if your subject is a familiar one. In preparing to respond to the preceding composition assignment, Robert Johnson made the following chain outline about the drowning of his friend Steve. He followed the assignment's suggestion by looking at two kinds of causes, the logical ones and the spatial/temporal ones. For Robert, these divided themselves into human and environmental causes.

```
city council decision            strong river currents
                                 shifting river bottom
design of river park
                                 murky water
design inadequate
near fatal accidents
lack of public support
                                 DROWNING
not: poor swimming ability
     absense of a lifeguard
```

Making this chain outline helped Robert rehearse the series of events and circumstances that led to his friend's death. He recalled how the city council had decided to construct a riverfront park, how almost immediately there had been problems with the shifting river bottom because engineering designs failed to take the strong river currents into account. There had been several near fatalities, but the public was unwilling to allocate funds to make the park safe. In the process of creating his chain outline Robert was able to separate human and environmental factors and get a clearer idea of what caused his friend's death.

Explaining Causes and Effects

E X E R C I S E

Create a chain outline in preparation for writing about cause and effect.

QUESTIONS ABOUT EVENTS AND PROCESSES

When your subject is not one you have experienced personally, you may find that chain outlines are not adequate, and a series of questions will serve better to generate ideas. Here, for example, is an assignment from a history class:

> Your paper should analyze some topic taken from the history of Christianity—a figure, movement, event, or idea. It should be based on facts drawn from appropriate scholarly books or articles, but it should contain your own ideas. It should begin with a problem and develop a hypothesis about the problem. (Here a problem means a historical question such as "Why did *x* event occur?" or "How did *y* person come to act or believe in such-and-such a way?") Your paper should be fifteen hundred words long (five typewritten pages) and is due on Friday, October 10.

Although "analyze" is included in the assignment, successful completion of this task requires consideration of cause and effect.

A student in this class was interested in the Children's Crusade of 1212 and gathered information about it. Her initial intention was to deal with the question of why the Children's Crusade occurred. She began her exploration by answering the ten questions about events and processes. The actual piece of paper on which she wrote is too messy for reproduction here, because as she answered the questions she had second thoughts, wrote things in between the lines, and drew lines between things that seemed connected. But here is a slightly edited version of her answers:

```
1. WHAT HAPPENED?
   Children, many under twelve years old, from
   Germany and France gathered in 1212 to go to
   the Holy Land to liberate it from the Turks
   and their Muslim religion. The children, who
   traveled by foot, wanted to restore the holy
   land to Christian control. None of the children
   made it to the holy land. Many died along the
   way, and the remaining ones were kidnapped and
   sold as slaves.
2. WHAT WERE THE CIRCUMSTANCES?
   This crusade occurred after the Fourth Crusade
   (need to get dates of this). The crusades
   began because the Turks invaded Jerusalem
```

203

Applications

(when?) and prevented Christian pilgrims from visiting holy places. The pope (name?) preached that the knights from Europe should liberate Jerusalem, and the crusades began. I don't remember all the details for the first three crusades (have to check that), but the fourth one didn't get to the Holy Land at all. Instead it attacked Constantinople. (Why?) That led to the split between the Greek and Roman Christian churches. The Children's Crusade came next.

3. HOW WAS THE EVENT LIKE OR UNLIKE OTHER SIMILAR EVENTS?
   The Children's Crusade was like other crusades in that it intended to liberate the Holy Land, and like some of the other crusades, it was not successful. But it was different from all the others because the kids were so young, they had no money or equipment, and nearly all of them died.

4. WHAT WERE ITS CAUSES?
   Maybe one cause was that everyone was very religious back then and it wasn't unusual for crusades to get organized. (I need to know more about how the thing got started.)

5. WHAT WERE ITS CONSEQUENCES?
   I don't know much about the consequences of the Children's Crusade. It made people feel sad because so many children suffered and died, and maybe it made them feel guilty that kids had to do adults' work. (I need to find out about that.)

6. WHAT DOES IT REVEAL ABOUT A GENERAL CONDITION?
   The CC reveals that children are very influenced by what they hear. They must have heard stories of crusades or sermons about needing to free Jerusalem from the Turks, and they took it very seriously.

7. IS IT GOOD OR BAD?
   It was bad because of what happened to the children and because it didn't help anything. I guess my standard is that I don't like unnecessary suffering.

8. HOW DO WE KNOW ABOUT IT?
   I know about the CC because of what was in our book and what I heard in class. I need to look

Explaining Causes and Effects

           at articles and stuff to learn more. I guess everything I've collected so far is reliable.
9. HOW MIGHT HAVE IT BEEN CHANGED OR AVOIDED?
        The CC might have been avoided if things were explained to the children, so they knew how dangerous it was to go on a crusade. Or it might have had a better ending if adults had helped them instead of selling them as slaves.
10. TO WHAT OTHER EVENT IS IT CONNECTED?
        The CC is connected to all the crusades because that was what was going on then. Also, I think the CC might be connected to what happens in some countries today--places like Northern Ireland and El Salvador--where young children are involved in fighting for some cause.

As you can see, these questions prompted the student to ask additional questions, and she realized she needed more information before she could write the paper. She noted that writing the answers made her think of things she had not expected. For instance, connecting the Children's Crusade with contemporary events had not occurred to her until she started writing her answers. She began to think that if she could understand more about the young guerrilla forces in places like El Salvador and Northern Ireland, she would probably understand more about why the Children's Crusade took place. Northern Ireland seemed like a particularly good place to start because, as was true for the Crusades, the battle there centers on religious issues. Although she still has much work to do, answering these questions helped her generate an abundance of material.

Looking back over her answers and deciding which questions to pursue, she began the evaluation process. As she looked at her responses to the third question, for instance, she realized that she would probably never be able to know exactly why the children decided to join a crusade. It would be important to get more facts about who organized them and what else was going on in the world at the time, but she would probably never be able to understand their motivation. That made the comparison with contemporary children warriors seem helpful because she could look for information on why young Northern Irish children start throwing bombs and helping the Irish Republican Army.

The process of collecting and evaluating information helped this student realize the inadequacy of her original question, "Why did the Children's Crusade occur?" She knew she could not provide a satisfactory answer in five pages, but her questioning had led her to a new understanding of the issue. She decided that a better question would be, "Why did the adults of the time allow the Children's Crusade to occur?" By focusing on this more limited question, she could bring in many of the ideas that interested her.

Applications

EXERCISE

Answer the preceding ten questions with regard to freshman orientation at your college.

1. Which answers go in directions you will probably not follow?
2. Which answers helped you think of new things? Will you want to pursue them as you write? Why?

Develop Organizational Plan

Although you do not need to plan the entire structure of your essay before you begin a cause and effect draft, you do need to decide whether you will begin with effects and proceed to causes or the reverse. There is no right-wrong answer to the question of how to proceed. Both Toth and Tucker wrote effective essays even though they chose opposite ways of proceeding, and the following pair of excerpts demonstrates that more than one organizational plan can be used with the same material.

> By drinking alcohol you will become a better person, or at least that's what the ads say. All three of these ads (see attached) suggest that your life will be somehow better if you buy these alcoholic drinks.
> Drink the "Brandy of Napoleon," the "Vodka of the Czar," the whiskey that guarantees success. All three of these statements imply that drinking alcohol will make you successful. Each of these ads takes a different approach: the first uses the outdoors look and people climbing in the sun, anxious to get to the top so they can have a whiskey; the second emphasizes power by saying that the conqueror of most of Europe drank our brandy, shouldn't you? The third combines power and sensual pleasure. The czar of all Russia, a huge powerful man with a beautiful woman, a beautiful, dog, and a large house drinks this vodka; if you want to be like him, drink it too.

As you can see, the author begins with the effects of these advertisements—the idea that alcohol will make you better—and then moves to the causes—the appeals to success and glamour, that appear in the advertisements. This approach could be reversed so that the writing moves from effects to causes:

> Look at the gorgeous mountain scene with two attractive people climbing to the top where they can enjoy this whiskey. Or look at Napoleon, conqueror of most of Europe. He drinks this brandy. Here we have a wealthy czar who lives in mansion with a beautiful woman and a beautiful dog. He drinks this vodka. Wouldn't you like to be like one of these people? All of these ads say the same thing: Drinking alcohol will make you better.

Here the causes—the mountains scene, Napoleon the conqueror, and the wealthy czar—come at the beginning, and the effect—the idea that drinking

Explaining Causes and Effects

alcohol will make you better—comes at the end. Both approaches have advantages, and the decision about which to use depends on the context of writing as well as on the effect the writer wishes to create.

EXERCISE

Imagine that you have just now finished a paper that was due last week. You feel that you should attach a letter explaining why it is late. Write two versions of this letter. In the first, "This paper is a week late . . ." should be your first words, and in the second, they should be your last words.

After he had developed his chain outline, Robert decided to follow an organizational plan of cause-effect and wrote the following draft.

The Redesigning of a Deathtrap

The idea began with several good intentions. The city decided to remake Waterfront Park as part of a public service project. A new beach area was landscaped and a dock was extended with a larger boat ramp. Waterfront Park was finally refinished in 1975. Following the opening, several articles began to appear on how such a good job was done on the park and the dock. Sunbathers, boaters, and swimmers now had a place to go to enjoy themselves.

After one year of use, a problem began to emerge. The dangerous currents of the Columbia River soon began to dig out a deep hole just off the beach. What the engineers who designed the beach forgot was that the river bottom is constantly changing. The new drop-off was undetectable until someone stepped off the edge of it. It would suddenly go from three feet of water to twelve feet. Along with this drop-off was a swift undercurrent that sucked everything down deep and held it underwater and pushed the water toward pilings downstream. A peaceful swimming hole was turned into a deathtrap.

Several close swimming accidents soon accompanied this development. A few people began to write in the local paper. One article called "What's Wrong with Waterfront Park" depicted one swimmer's close call. Evidently she was a strong swimmer, but she did not see the drop-off because of the murky water. When she tried to stand up in what she thought was shallow water, her legs were soon pulled down by the current. It was only through her strong swimming capabilities that she was able to make it to shore. Her main point was that an average swimmer would not have been able to escape the currents. Like many of the problems of today, the city government didn't do anything to fix the drop-off. According to city officials, since there had not been any fatalities and only a few minor close calls, there wasn't any serious danger. The issue soon died out due to lack of public interest.

August 28, 1976, the day that was going to force this issue out into the open, began on a good note. The sun was out and my family decided to join the Anderson family at Waterfront Park for the day. We had always been good friends, and Steve and Walt were two of my best friends. The day was perfect for swimming with the temperature in the upper nineties. When we reached the park, we quickly ran across the blistering hot sand. All day long we had lots of fun playing with frisbees and paddling around in inner-tubes in the water. When the day was finally winding down, I suggested to Steve that we paddle to shore and get ready to leave. He agreed, and we started in to shore with Steve behind me. That was the last time anyone saw Steve. When I got to shore and turned around, all I could see was Steve's tube floating away. Several people who were excellent swimmers dove in the water to find him, but they did not have any luck. They also discovered a deep hole with a very strong undercurrent that almost pulled them under.

The Coast Guard finally found Steve's body the next day in some wood pilings just forty feet downstream from where Steve went underwater. They estimated that Steve must have slipped off his tube, got caught in the current, and been pushed down into the pilings. A person might think that since Steve was not a good swimmer was why he drowned, but the Coast Guard said that even a good swimmer once caught in the current could not escape, and that the force of hitting the pilings would have knocked anyone out. The lack of a lifeguard did not even contribute to his death because the Coast Guard estimated that it probably happened in just a few seconds. The murky water would have made it impossible for a lifeguard to find him. What it finally came down to was that the bad design of the engineers

Explaining Causes and Effects

created a dangerous spot that killed one of my best friends. They should have considered the current and removed the pilings.

A few weeks after this day, city officials decided to fill in the hole and build a gradually sloped bottom. City workers now continually check the bottom and fill in any holes that start to form to make sure that no one else drowns. There were many reasons for officials to do this because there were several close swimming accidents. There were also reports on the park detailing the possible dangers. The lack of public interest also delayed the renewal, but there was some support to pressure officials into fixing the park but just not enough. It wasn't until there was a death that officials got off their bureaucratic butts and fixed the park. This is a very bad excuse to me to do what is right especially when it was the death of one of my best friends.

EXERCISE

Write a draft that considers causes.

SUMMARY

During the early stages of writing about causes the following can be useful:

- Create chain outlines linking different types of causes to effects.
- Answer questions such as those on page 196 about events or processes.
- Decide on the overall organizational pattern for your writing—either effect-cause or cause-effect.

Writing to Show Learning

When he had completed his draft, Robert realized that it needed further work. He still felt angry when he thought about Steve's needless death, and he knew that some of that anger was distracting him from exploring and explaining causes fully. He also thought there was probably too much repetition toward the end of the essay. To get a new perspective on his work, he decided to return to the original assignment.

RECONSIDER ASSIGNMENT

Once you have completed a draft, the original assignment will look different. You may have new questions or you may understand it differently. The process

Applications

of returning to the assignment will give you some distance from what you have written because the assignment suggests how someone else will look at your work.

When he looked at the assignment again, Robert realized that he was expected to suggest the relative importance of causes, to create a hierarchy. He also recalled, especially when he looked at his chain outline, that he needed to distinguish between the logical and spatial/temporal causes or what for him had become human and environmental causes. Robert decided that he should probably revise his draft to reflect these causes more explicitly.

EXERCISE

Reconsider an assignment for cause and effect writing and decide how you might change your draft.

Consider Audience

Many college writing assignments fail to specify an audience, but you can always assume that your audience does not know what and how you think, so trying to put yourself in the place of someone else is always a good way to consider your readers. Try to imagine how someone who does not know you would read what you have written.

To help students see how an audience might respond to their work, Robert's instructor asked pairs of students to read and critique one another's drafts and answer the following questions:

1. Pinpoint the phenomenon or fact or existing state that the writer intends to analyze. Is this phenomenon clearly defined? Do you share a knowledge of this phenomenon—or do you consider it unique to the writer's experience?
2. Try to list at least a majority of the causes the writer has chosen to name in his analysis—more if you have the space.
3. This is similar to 2, but this time, simply narrate, as clearly as possible, the chain of events and conditions contained in the paper, concluding with the existing phenomenon.
4. Evaluate the causal analysis, the basic question being: do you understand—how well do you understand—why something came into being (or why something happened)?

Here is how one of Robert's classmates responded to his draft:

1. Pinpoint the phenomenon or fact or existing state that the writer intends to analyze. Is this phenomenon clearly defined? Do you share a knowledge of this phenomen—or do you consider it unique to the writer's experience?

Explaining Causes and Effects

> It is very ambiguous as to what effect you are trying to show cause to. Is it the events that led to fixing the bottom of the swimming area, or the death of Steve that is being analyzed? Your real effect needs to be clearer.

2. Try to list at least a majority of the causes the writer has chosen to name in his analysis—more if you have the space.

> A list of causes might be the construction of the park, the planning that went into the construction of the park, the current and the lack of public or official concern.

3. This is similar to 2, but this time, simply narrate, as clearly as possible, the chain of events and conditions contained in the paper, concluding with the existing phenomenon.

> The park was changed, and then the current started to erode the bottom resulting in a dangerous current which culminated in the death of Steve.

4. Evaluate the causal analysis, the basic question being: Do you understand—how well do you understand—why something came into being (or why something happened)?

> Yes, it is clear that the failure of the design engineers to consider all possibilities resulted in the death of Steve.

When he received this response sheet, Robert realized that he needed to make clear that Steve's death was the issue he was examining and that the causes considered in the paper should all focus on this event.

CHECK ORGANIZATION

The central question in checking the organization of writing that considers causes is whether you wish to move from causes to effect or from effect to

Applications

causes. Both organizational plans work well, and you simply need to decide which will serve your purposes better.

As he considered his draft, Robert decided that he needed to reorganize it to make Steve's death more central. In addition to changing his title to "The Death of a Friend," he decided to restructure his writing to put Steve's death at the beginning and then look at causes such as the city's failure to fix the bottom of the swimming area.

Evaluate Coherence and Cohesion

Coherence plays an especially important part in writing that considers causes. It can make the relationship between effects and causes clear so that readers are able to discern your point. When readers have difficulty distinguishing the causes and effects in your writing, you probably need to work on coherence.

When his classmate said that he didn't know whether it was fixing the swimming area or Steve's death that was being analyzed, Robert knew he had to improve the coherence of his draft. In addition to changing the title and the organizational pattern, he decided to work on a transition between recounting the events on the day Steve drowned and explaining the events that contributed to his death. In addition, he decided to use the idea of the family atmosphere of Waterfront Park to link the establishment of the park with problems it posed.

Cohesion within and between sentences also contributes to the effectiveness of writing that considers causes. In considering his draft, Robert realized that the connection between the statements that the river began to erode a deep hole just off the beach and that the engineers forgot about the constant changes of the river bottom needed to be tied more directly to the following statement about the drop off. He decided to add this sentence: "As time went by, this hole developed into a deep drop off."

EXERCISE

Mark the places where another reader has questions about your draft and determine how you can make these parts more coherent and cohesive.

Editing

After he had considered the audience and assignment for which he was writing, modified his organizational plan, and found ways to improve the coherence and cohesion of his draft, Robert edited it carefully, checking for misspelled words, faults of usage, mechanics, and punctuation. He decided that "close swimming accidents" was not an effective usage to express the idea that several people had nearly drowned, he added an apostrophe in "one swimmer's close call," and changed "that since Steve was not a good swimmer was why he

212

Explaining Causes and Effects

drowned" to "that Steve drowned because he was not a good swimmer." Here is Robert's final draft.

The Death of a Friend

August 28, 1976, the day that was going to scar me for life, began on a good note. The sun was out and my family decided to join the Anderson Family at Waterfront Park for the day. We had always been good friends, and Steve and Walt were two of my best friends. The day was perfect for swimming with the temperature in the upper nineties. When we reached the park, we quickly ran across the blistering hot sand. All day long we had lots of fun playing with frisbees and paddling around on inner-tubes in the water. When the day was finally winding down, I suggested to Steve that we paddle to shore and get ready to leave. He agreed, and we started in to shore with Steve behind me. That was the last time anyone saw Steve. When I got to shore and turned around, all I could see was Steve's tube floating away. Several people who were excellent swimmers dove in the water to find him, but they did not have any luck. They also discovered a deep hole with a very strong undercurrent that almost pulled them under.

The Coast Guard finally found Steve's body the next day in some wood pilings just forty feet downstream from where Steve went underwater. They estimated that Steve must have slipped off his tube, got caught in the current, and been pushed down into the pilings. A person might think that Steve drowned because he was not a good swimmer, but the Coast Guard said that even a good swimmer once caught in the current could not escape, and that the force of hitting the pilings would have knocked anyone out. The lack of a lifeguard did not even contribute to his death because the Coast Guard estimated that it probably happened in just a few seconds. The murky water would have made it impossible for a lifeguard to find him. The real set of causes was a chain of events, both environmental and human, that led to his death.

The idea began with several good intentions. The city decided to remake Waterfront Park as part of a public service project. A new beach was landscaped, a grass picnic area was laid out, and a dock was extended

Applications

with a larger boat ramp. Waterfront Park was finally refinished in 1975. Following the opening, several articles began to appear on how such a good job was done on the park and the dock. Sunbathers, boaters, and swimmers now had a place to go to enjoy themselves. The city had finally created an enjoyable family atmosphere for people to use.

This family atmosphere soon began to change. After one year of use, the park developed a problem. The dangerous swirling currents of the Columbia River soon began to gently erode a hole just off the beach. As time went by, this hole developed into a deep drop off. What the engineers who designed the beach forgot was that the river's bottom is constantly changing. The new drop off was undetectable until someone stepped off the edge of it. It would suddenly go from three feet of water to twelve feet. Along with this drop off was a powerful swift undercurrent that sucked everything down deep, held it underwater, and pushed the water along with everything else toward wood pilings downstream. A peaceful swimming hole was thus turned into a deathtrap. This effect was due to man-made and natural causes. The natural cause was simply the river and its powerful currents. The man-made cause was bad design by the engineers. They failed to consider the currents of the river and their effect on the bottom. The wood pilings downstream should have never been allowed to stay there. The engineers should have also continually checked the river's bottom. Human error led to more human error, which created a dangerous swimming hole.

This development was later followed by the biggest man-made cause of all, which was lack of public support to fix the problem. Several near drowning incidents began to be reported. A few people began to write in to the local paper. One article called "What's Wrong with Waterfront Park" depicted one swimmer's story of how she almost drowned. Evidently she was a strong swimmer, but she did not see the drop off because of the murky water. When she tried to stand up in what she thought was shallow water, her legs were soon pulled down by the current. It was only through her strong swimming capabilities that she was able to escape the currents. As it so often does with problems of today, the city government didn't do anything to

Explaining Causes and Effects

fix the drop-off. According to city officials, since there had not been any fatalities and only a few minor swimming problems, there wasn't any serious danger. However, turning your back on a problem does not make it go away. This was only the first part of man's apathy toward the problem. Lack of public interest was the second part. It is true that a few letters were written to the paper concerning the problem, but that is as far as it went. If the public had taken an active role in this problem, then city officials would have moved more quickly to solve it. The other causes did lead to Steve's death, but the public and city officials' apathetic views of the problem was the main cause. If they had tried to fix the problem, then he wouldn't have died.

EXERCISE

List the differences you see between the first and second versions of Robert's paper. In what ways is the second version more effective? Revise your own consideration of causes, incorporating as many changes as you think appropriate.

Copyright © Myron Wood, The National Audubon Society Collection/Photo Researchers, Inc.

Chapter Nine

Arguing Proposals

Supporting propositions resembles supporting assertions (see Chapter Six) because both require evidence that lends strength to a claim, but propositions differ from assertions. Assertions (such as "*Love Medicine* is a better book than *The Color Purple*") address what already is, while propositions (such as "Officers in the student government association should be given office space in the student union") speak to the future. Propositions emerge from a writer's desire to change something. They propose a course of action or consideration of an idea.

Supporting propositions involves a transaction between writer and reader. Usually writers begin by identifying a problem, offering a solution in the form of a proposition, and then they argue in favor of that proposition. To be effective, support for a proposition must include a careful and detailed explanation of the problem, including an exploration of its sources and history. All the terms used in the proposition or solution should be fully defined so the reader can understand exactly what is being proposed, and the argument in favor of the proposition should offer a reasoned explanation of the benefits of the proposition at the same time that it anticipates any questions or counter-arguments the reader may have.

Opportunities for supporting propositions occur both within and beyond college classes. You may receive assignments that ask you to write in support of a proposal. Here is one from a political science class:

> Write an essay in which you argue that it is imperative that the United States increase its support of the World Bank.

The following assignment comes from an ecology class:

> Write in support of the following statement: Federal regulations for construction of nuclear power plants need to be made more stringent.

Applications

Here again, the assignment includes the problem to be addressed (inadequate Federal regulations), and the writer's task is to explain why current regulations are inadequate, to outline what changes might make these regulations more effective, and to provide convincing support for the proposed changes.

Writing in support of propositions also occurs frequently outside the classroom. A group of students, for example, became concerned because there was no campus writing center where they could go to receive help with their assignments. They decided that a writing center should be established, and they wrote a proposal to the student government association supporting the proposition that a writing center be established and supported by the association. They argued that it was necessary because so many students were having difficulty with writing. They pointed out that professors were complaining about the quality of written work they received and that many other colleges and universities were providing writing centers for their students. They claimed that it would be cost-effective because it could use peer tutors, that some of the space already allocated to the student government association could be used for the center, and that establishing such a center fit exactly the mandate of the new office of academic affairs within the association.

You may have had similar opportunities to write in support of propositions. Perhaps you have joined other students to request that graduation requirements be changed, to ask that the staff of the student placement office be expanded, or to propose a change in dormitory policy. Alternatively, perhaps you have written in support of a proposition to change something in your work or living situation. You may have thought of a more efficient way of accomplishing some task, a way to increase the funds available for student loans, or a more effective way of allocating parking spaces in your apartment building, and you may have written in support of your proposition.

Both within and beyond the classroom, writing in support of propositions requires a plan of action, a detailed explanation of what should be done. This plan of action should be accompanied by information that supports the plan and by careful attention to the audience, anticipating possible objections.

Getting Ready to Support Propositions

The first step in writing to support propositions is to develop the problem at issue. When the writing task specifies the problem by telling you to write in support of tighter regulations for nuclear plants or increased support for the World Bank, the problem will require less development than if you begin by knowing that you want to say something about a writing center. Asking the five *"W"* questions—who, what, when, where, and why—about the issue can help you develop it.

Effective support of a proposition requires presentation of information about the issue. On some occasions you may have all the information you need to write convincingly, but more frequently you will find that you need to *collect* additional information. You may need to interview people, look at documents, or read books and articles about your topic. The information you collect should help you explain your proposition in detail.

Arguing Proposals

The essay that follows illustrates the importance of collecting information to make an effective proposition. As you read, notice the various sources of information David Brewster mentions as he proposes ways of measuring the effectiveness of Seattle's public schools. How many different sources do you find?

Reversing the Downward Drift of American Education
David Brewster

One of the saddest indications of the irrelevance of liberalism in these times is its almost complete bankruptcy of ideas about education. American education, one of the bedrocks of our democracy, is in terrible need of reform and rethinking. What do the liberals propose? Spend more money on it. Period.

In fact, Americans already do spend lots more money than anyone else: about twice the percapita public expenditures than in Europe, for instance. In the past 20 years, outlays for K-12 public education have increased sixfold, even while enrollments have dropped. Average classroom size has fallen from 25.6 students in 1962 to 18.9 today. Meanwhile, performance has plummeted. Spending more is clearly not the answer, without basic reforms.

The answer, instead, is to find out what works in public schools and then have the political guts to reshape education to those goals. Seattle Superintendent Donald Steele, having shaken up his staff and generally served notice of a desire to get beyond merely integrating urban schools as the sum and substance of educational reform, seems bent on just such a course. I for one hope the city will let him get somewhere with such a daring approach.

[*Brewster has identified his version of the problem with American education.*]

Raising the question of "what works?" in public schools has for years been declared bad form. Teachers are to be allowed to do their own thing in the classroom, free from bothersome questions about whether this pays off. Tests, grades, and standard curricula are accordingly downplayed: they lead to sterility, uniformity, "teaching to test scores," and rewarding of drones. Besides, there are more important things to impart in school than basic skills: cultural pride, creativity, social skills, and the other items from the relevance smorgasbord. Asking "what works?" is a fancy way of imposing the dreaded white-middle-class value system on a diverse ethnic country. It's almost as bad as assigning homework.

Well, the question cannot be put off much longer, and the researchers are efficiently answering it once again. The major source of answers is James S. Coleman's study *High School Achievement* (1981), which confirmed what common sense long knew. Schools that give more homework, put a greater emphasis on academic subjects (like science and foreign language), maintain better discipline, discourage absenteeism, foster shared sets of values within the building, and generally demand more of the students, do better than those that don't. Private schools, including Catholic schools, generally follow these guidelines and so—despite teacher pay of about $5,000 a year less than public teachers get, larger classroom loads, and generally fewer support facilities—these schools turn out better-performing students, even when differences in family background are taken into account. Likewise, public schools that follow the formula of demanding more turn out better achievers, too. Contrary to the expectations of liberals, private schools usually narrow the achievement gap between white and minority students by focusing on these approaches, while in public schools the gap widens as the years—and the confusing stress on "relevance"—go by.

What underlies this willingness to study what works in the classroom, in a measurable way, is a desire to return to more formal classrooms, away from the open-classroom concept that enjoyed a vogue in the 1960s and '70s. Many studies in the Western countries have been made on this topic. Summarizing them, Barbara Lerner writes in the Fall, 1982, issue of *The Public Interest*: "Again and again, they found that contemporary students in open classrooms made less intellectual progress on average than their more formally instructed peers, and emerged with no compensating gains in creativity or freedom from anxiety."

One of the interesting sidelights of these studies, incidentally, is the discovery that female students in particular have trouble in less structured classrooms. This may help explain the curious fact that female scores in the SAT verbal tests, which consistently beat male scores in the area for years, have since 1972 lagged behind male scores. (SAT scores, incidentally, have dropped from a steady plateau of 475 in verbal and 498 in math-reasoning in the 1950s and early '60s to the current levels of 427 and 467, respectively.)

Data supporting Brewster's proposition appears in both verbal and numerical form.

But to know what works in the classroom is a long way from being able to change policies accordingly. Few school systems would even try, but Seattle is about to make a stab at it. Next month, Superintendent Steele will release the first detailed studies of how Seattle students are performing, school by school, class by class, adjusting for socioeconomic origins. Reports like these, long considered too hot a potato for release to the public, are the first step toward making classrooms and teachers measurably effective once more.

Such reports will be dynamite, which is why teachers have resisted them. Suppose a parent can discover that a certain school in West Seattle does a demonstrably better job with children from disadvantaged homes than a similar school in Wallingford? Can they not then reasonably demand some changes in Wallingford? May not the principal there be put on the spot? Might not the West Seattle principal get a promotion and some more money to spend on new programs? May not a few poor teachers in Wallingford be put on probation? Many overdue administrative steps will be possible, once the data are there to justify them.

Naturally, the entrenched educational bureaucracy will fight such accountability, aided by the liberal mindset that long ago married middle-class guilt with John Dewey's educational dreams. But the return to a more formal, more measurable, more truly helpful educational style is probably going to prevail in the long run. The disadvantaged classes have woken up. Parents who used to think an eventual escape to private schools would enable them to ignore the decline of public schools have run into cost barriers. And the decline of America's economy is increasingly being traced to the long erosion of our schools—not from shortages of money but from shortages of political will power to make them work again.

Arguing Proposals

[*Notice how Brewster anticipates objections to his proposition.*]

The Lerner article cited above, for instance, examines how American students compare with their peers in the rest of the world. She analyzed results from tests given in math, reading, vocabulary, sciences, literature, civics, and foreign-language facility. U.S. students do quite poorly, even allowing for the fact that we retain more poor students in high school than most other countries. We are almost always near the bottom of the list among developed countries, never coming in first. Students from Iran and Chile at age 18 outperform U.S. students in vocabulary, and Thai 18-year-olds in science are closer to U.S. standards than U.S. students are to any developed country. It is a devastating indictment of American education, which is far better funded than any country's and yet performs in a thoroughly mediocre fashion on the international scale.

[*Now Brewster explores another dimension of the causes of the problem before moving on to a final statement about his proposition.*]

There are many other reasons for public education's betrayal of the public, besides the exaggerated hopes of open classrooms, relevance, and unmonitored instruction. One cause, often overlooked, is the very success of feminism. "A quarter of a century ago," notes Phil Keisling in *The New Republic* (November 1), "widespread sexism gave intelligent, motivated women access to few professions other than teaching; today, those same women are pursuing careers in law; medicine, and business. Unfortunately what is long-overdue equity for women is also our children's loss." Teachers (only in public schools, however) must endure numbing programs in teacher-education, which further dissuade bright students from becoming teachers; bad teachers are fired about as often as presidents are impeached; the NEA opposes salary differentials, which would help attract science and math teachers, now in critically short supply; the Democratic Party has become a captive of the NEA, a ferocious special-interest group; and the struggle to integrate American schools has consumed so much money and political capital as to make further educational reform almost impossible.

Given all this, the best way I can see to cut through all the educational mumbo-jumbo and all the accountability run-arounds is by instituting measures of effectiveness. Is a given school doing as well with its children—advantaged and poor—as can be expected? If not, what is the school going to do about it? And if it fails to do better, why not put the principal and the staff on notice?

Of course, there will be problems and abuses with measuring effectiveness. But nothing compared with the current slide to non-schooling. The whole city ought to be glad that we have a superintendent feisty and enlightened enough to want to take this bull by the horns.

Return for a second reading of Brewster's essay, paying particular attention to the types of information he includes to support his proposition.

1. State Brewster's proposition in one sentence.
2. What does Brewster's use of statistics contribute to the effectiveness of his proposal?
3. List at least five sources of information to which Brewster refers.
4. To what audience does Brewster address himself?

Applications

Once you have collected enough information to provide a detailed explanation of your proposition, you can *state your proposition* and *define the proposition's terms* so a reader will know what you mean. You will also need to ascertain that your explanation about the proposition includes sufficient information about the causes and effects of the issue you discuss.

In making an argument in support of your proposition, you will need to *avoid fallacies* and present your case in a manner that will convince the audience. This means anticipating your readers' needs as well as discerning the arguments that will be most convincing to them. This does not always mean being entirely serious, as the following essay by Judy Syfers illustrates. As you read, notice the kind of evidence Syfers uses to support the proposition that she should have a wife.

I Want a Wife

Judy Syfers

I belong to that classification of people known as wives. I am A Wife. And, not altogether incidentally, I am a mother.

Not too long ago a male friend of mine appeared on the scene fresh from a recent divorce. He had one child, who is, of course, with his ex-wife. He is looking for another wife. As I thought about him while I was ironing one evening, it suddenly occurred to me that I, too, would like to have a wife. Why do I want a wife?

[*Having introduced her proposition, Syfers moves on to explain it.*]

I would like to go back to school so that I can become economically independent, support myself; and, if need be, support those dependent upon me. I want a wife who will work and send me to school. And while I am going to school I want a wife to take care of my children. I want a wife to keep track of the children's doctor and dentist appointments. And to keep track of mine, too. I want a wife to make sure my children eat properly and are kept clean. I want a wife who will wash the children's clothes and keep them mended. I want a wife who is a good nurturant attendant to my children, who arranges for their schooling, makes sure that they have an adequate social life with their peers, takes them to the park, the zoo, etc. I want a wife who takes care of the children when they are sick, a wife who arranges to be around when the children need special care, because, of course, I cannot miss classes at school. My wife must arrange to lose time at work and not lose the job. It may mean a small cut in my wife's income from time to time, but I guess I can tolerate that. Needless to say, my wife will arrange and pay for the care of the children while my wife is working.

I want a wife who will take care of *my* physical needs. I want a wife who will keep my house clean. A wife who will pick up after my children, a wife who will pick up after me. I want a wife who will keep my clothes clean, ironed, mended, replaced when need be, and who will see to it that my personal things ar kept in their proper place so that I can find what I need the minute I need it. I want a wife who cooks the meals, a wife who is a good cook. I want a wife who will plan the menus, do the necessary grocery shopping, prepare the meals, serve them pleasantly, and then do the cleaning up while I do my studying. I want a wife who will care for me when I am sick and sympathize with my pain and loss of time from school. I want a wife to go along when our family takes a vacation so that someone can continue to care for me and my children when I need a rest and change of scene.

[*Notice now Syfers enumerates what wives do as she explains the sources of her proposition.*]

I want a wife who will not bother me with rambling complaints about a wife's duties. But I want a wife who will listen to me when I feel the need to explain a rather difficult point I have come across in my course of studies. And I want a wife who will type my papers for me when I have written them.

I want a wife who will take care of the details of my social life. When my wife and I are invited out by my friends, I want a wife who will take care of the babysitting arrangements. When I meet people at school that I like and want to entertain, I want a wife who will have the house clean, will prepare a special meal, serve it to me and my friends, and not interrupt when I talk about things that interest me and my friends. I want a wife who will have arranged that the children are fed and ready for bed before my guests arrive so that the children do not bother us. I want a wife who takes care of the needs of my guests so that they feel comfortable, who makes sure that they have an ashtray, that they are passed the hors d'oeuvres, that they are offered a second helping of the food, that their wine glasses are replenished when necessary, that their coffee is served to them as they like it. And I want a wife who knows that sometimes I need a night out by myself.

[*Notice the escalation of expectations assigned to wife and how these build to the final question of the propositon.*]

I want a wife who is sensitive to my sexual needs, a wife who makes love passionately and eagerly when I feel like it, a wife who makes sure that I am satisfied. And, of course, I want a wife who will not demand sexual attention when I am not in the mood for it. I want a wife who assumes the complete responsibility for birth control, because I do not want more children. I want a wife who will remain sexually faithful to me so that I do not have to clutter up my intellectual life with jealousies. And I want a wife who understands that my sexual needs may entail more than strict adherence to monogamy. I must, after all, be able to relate to people as fully as possible.

If, by chance, I find another person more suitable as a wife than the wife I already have, I want the liberty to replace my present wife with another one. Naturally, I will expect a fresh new life; my wife will take the children and be solely responsible for them so that I am left free.

When I am through with school and have a job, I want my wife to quit working and remain at home so that my wife can more fully and completely take care of a wife's duties.

My God, who wouldn't want a wife?

As you return for a second reading of Syfers's essay, consider the following questions:

Applications

1. What assumptions does Syfers make about her readers' knowledge of wives? How do these assumptions contribute to the effectiveness of her proposal?
2. Compose a one sentence response to Syfers's question "Why do I want a wife?" that summarizes her proposition.
3. What causes can you see for Syfers's proposal? What effect does it have?
4. Consider the arrangement of the information Syfers presents about the wife she would like. What, for example, would happen if the paragraph about sexual needs came first?

Writing to Learn

In the early stages of writing to support propositions, looking at the issue under discussion will take prominence. Before you can provide a convincing case for a proposition you need to develop it. One way to develop a proposition is to ask questions about the issue you are writing about.

Ask Five "W" Questions

The five "W" questions—who, what, when, where, and why—are always asked by journalists as they prepare news stories, and they can also be helpful in developing an issue. Each question concentrates on a different dimension of a situation, and when all five of them are directed toward a single issue, considerable development is possible.

In general these five "W" questions work well with events or situations (which is not surprising, given their journalistic origins), but they work less well with questions about a single physical item. Information for the question about support for the World Bank or regulation of the nuclear industry could be generated by using these questions, but they would be less effective for responding to a question about a raindrop's shape.

Who

"It doesn't matter what you know; who you know is what counts." "Who did it?" Our language is full of sayings that underscore the importance of considering the person or agent behind events and issues. Asking "who" about a topic pushes you to think about the giver and receiver of action or event. "Who" asks for more than the name of an individual: a thorough answer to the question tells us something about the individual's values, background, and role. Asking in a Shakespeare class "Who is Iago?" generates background information about Iago's previous experiences, his relationship to the other characters, and the motivations behind his actions.

Asking "who" can help you develop a proposition in response to an assignment. Here, for example, is an assignment that asks writers to develop and support a proposition:

Arguing Proposals

In this paper you should present a proposition to another individual. The presentation should have three parts: a description or discussion of a problem; an analysis of that problem's causes and effects; and a solution or solutions that you believe should be implemented (or supported) by the individual addressed.

The addressee should be someone you know either personally or by reputation. In other words, your audience is singular and reachable. To address this paper to that individual can lead to more than completing an assignment. Your writing can have wide-ranging consequences if you can actually insert this text into a wider sphere, such as politics, with the intention of effecting change.

Patrick Johnson began this assignment by thinking about the "who" question, in this case to whom he should address his proposition. He liked the idea of writing to effect change and decided that he would have the best chance of doing this if he wrote to someone in the political arena. Then he began to consider which politician would be most likely to respond and have the capacity to effect change. He decided that someone who represented him would be responsive, that a national rather than a local or regional representative would have more effect, and that a congressional representative would be more concerned with the local constituency than a senator. Accordingly, he decided to address Representative Mike Lowry.

WHAT

Details about events and issues answer the "what" question. "What is it?" we ask, and the answer, whether about an object or a situation, supplies all the essential information. In its simplest terms, "what" supplies a definition, but it is a substantive definition. When the question "What constitutes adequate support for the World Bank?" is posed, one answer is a dollar amount. However, a complete answer to the what question would supply considerable detail about the shape and context of that support.

Patrick decided to focus on this issue of drug abuse because he had a number of friends whose lives had been negatively influenced by drugs. He decided that what he meant by drug abuse was use of illegal drugs that led to deaths and hospitalizations, problems with school and families, and many other social problems. As he defined drug abuse, Patrick realized that he needed to gather additional information in order to define drug abuse more precisely. He would need statistics and examples of what he meant by abuse.

WHEN

Complete answers to the "when" question provide much more than just chronological time. "When" asks for time in relation to other times; it seeks to establish connections between events. "The Children's Crusade occured in 1212" answers the chronological "when" question, but a more complete answer

Applications

explains that this crusade followed the disastrous Fourth Crusade, which split the Roman and Byzantine churches.

In answering the when question in relation to the issue of drug abuse, Patrick decided that he would concentrate on the present, but he realized that comparisons with other time periods would be necessary to convince his reader that drug abuse was increasing. In addition, he knew that he would have to place the issue of drug abuse in the context of contemporary culture, considering such things as media, law enforcement, and educational programs.

WHERE

"Where" asks for more than physical location, although that is important. The larger dimensions of "where" include context and surroundings. "The food bank is located at 201 First Avenue" provides the location, but details such as "in a neighborhood of bars, cheap hotels, and pawn shops" or "where unshaven men sitting on park benches hold brown paper bags between gnarled hands" create an environment.

As he thought about "where" in relation to drug abuse, Patrick had two reflections. One led him to look at where in the culture drug abuse occurs; he knew he would need to look at different populations such as teenagers and middle-aged citizens and at different economic groups. The second reflection led him to realize that drug abuse has international as well as national dimensions since so much of the drug supply is imported from other countries.

WHY

This most popular and difficult question—"why?"—probes causes, motives, and forces. "Why will San Francisco disappear into the ocean some day?" we ask, and the answer includes a long catalogue of geological information. This life does not provide answers to ultimate causes, but there is a great deal to be said in response to a "why" question.

Considering the "why" of drug abuse led Patrick back to some of the ideas he had generated in response to earlier questions. In particular, he decided that it would be important to address the question of why drug abuse has increased so dramatically in recent years (which took him back to the "when" question), why some populations are more affected than others, and why such large quantities of illegal drugs get through the borders of this country (both of which took him to "where").

EXERCISE

Use the five "W" questions to develop an issue on which you can support a proposition.

Arguing Proposals

COLLECT EVIDENCE

To provide evidence is to "support your opinions," to "give examples" to help your reader understand why you are supporting a given proposition. In order to be convincing, your evidence must be reliable, adequate, and verifiable. The first step toward evaluating the quality of evidence is to be aware of the types of evidence available to writers. These include:

Statistics. Numbers can often be convincing, particularly when they are combined to show a trend, as statistics do. To say that 80 percent of the population supports handgun control is much more convincing than to say that many people support handgun control. Conducting public opinion polls, which provide statistical evidence about people's views on a political candidate or a brand of cheese, is a thriving industry in this country. The statistical evidence derived from polls convinces many people: Think of the advertisements of election predictions that use statistical evidence.

However, when you use statistics in your writing, you will need to be careful about your sources and how you use the statistics. Statistics provided by political candidates or corporations interested in selling products are not as reliable as those collected by independent firms, such as Harris or Gallup, or by university-based research groups. In particular, you should avoid using vague statistics such as "a large percentage" and unspecified sources such as "researchers have found" or "studies show." It is a common saying that statistics can be used to prove anything, and as a writer you must ascertain that the statistics you use are reliable.

Personal Testimony. Religious leaders have long known that personal testimony can be convincing, but personal testimony is not their exclusive province. The sincere young woman in an advertisement relies on the convincing force of personal testimony as she claims that a certain shampoo or cosmetic has changed her life for the better. You can probably think of a number of times when you made a decision because of the personal testimony of someone you knew. Perhaps your decision of which college to attend was based in part on the personal testimony of a loyal student or a member of the alumni.

When you are writing in support of a proposition, personal testimony can often be convincing. Your own experiences can provide material for personal testimony, and you can also call on the experiences of others. As with reports, you will want to consider the sources of the testimony, but the personal message can be very powerful.

Factual Reference. "Facts," said the tyrannical teacher Gradgrind in Charles Dickens's *Hard Times*, and he tried to beat facts into his students. Today much educational energy is still spent on acquiring facts. Perhaps it is because they are so convincing; there is, as we have already seen, no way to argue with a fact. Statements such as "Bismark is the capital of North Dakota," cannot be refuted. Of course, for facts to be convincing, they must be accurate, and the

227

Applications

person who claims that Fargo is the capital of North Dakota will have difficulty convincing the reader of other statements that appear in the paper. But as long as they are accurate, factual references can do much to strengthen a proposition.

Appeal to Authority. Authority comes in a variety of forms, ranging from a police officer's authority of position to a scientist's authority of expertise. The race car driver who endorses a motor oil will usually be more convincing than a violinist would be, because the race car driver is seen as someone who has expertise in car mechanics.

A major portion of your evidence will probably come from authorities of one sort or another. When you quote "experts" whose articles and books you have read, you are citing authority, and when you refer to the opinions of someone who has a professional reputation in a given field, you are likewise citing authority. But you will often find that authorities in the same field do not agree with one another, and part of your task will be to decide which source of authority helps advance your argument.

Knowing the kinds of evidence available to you makes it easier to decide which forms are appropriate for a given assignment. The process of sifting through various kinds of evidence and deciding on those best suited for a particular argument can help you learn a given subject. For example, distinguishing among authoritative statements by professional chemists and citing facts gleaned from empirical research can help you understand chemistry more fully.

Patrick read a number of articles, taking notes on each, to collect evidence for his discussion of drug abuse. He found statistics on the amount of money spent on drugs, the number of drug-related deaths, and business losses attributable to workers' drug use. He found personal testimony in the form of statements by James Mills, author of a book on drug abuse. Patrick's collection of facts included information on the countries from which drugs are smuggled, sentencing of drug offenders, and drug education programs. He found quotations from an administrator with the Drug Enforcement Agency that would provide him with an appeal to authority.

E X E R C I S E

Collect evidence that you can use to support a proposition.

STATE YOUR PROPOSITION

A proposition is not a statement of fact; it proposes something with which your reader could disagree. The following sentences, for example, do not contain propositions:

Ulysses S. Grant was the eighteenth president of the United States.

Arguing Proposals

> Marie Curie received the 1911 Nobel Prize in chemistry for her work on radium.
>
> The fire caused $100,000 worth of damage to the house.

Now considered these revised sentences:

> Ulysses S. Grant should be designated the worst president of the United States.
>
> Marie Curie deserves special recognition for receiving the 1911 Nobel Prize in chemistry for her work on radium.
>
> The tragic fire caused $100,000 worth of damage to the house, and we plan to establish a fund to aid its residents.

In each case, changing or adding a few words changes a statement of fact into a proposition. Maybe Grant was the worst president and maybe he was not. Perhaps Curie deserves special recognition for her Nobel Prize and perhaps she does not. By whose definition was the fire tragic, and is it a good idea to raise funds for those who lived in the house? As you develop writing that supports a proposition, be sure you can make a statement that expresses the proposal you intend to support.

EXERCISE

Sometimes assignments indicate the proposition to be supported. For each of the following indicate the proposition writers are expected to support.

1. It is often charged that Marxism in practice has failed to deliver on what it promises in theory. To what extent can the same charge be made against liberal democratic ideology?
2. Why is falsification of a scientific hypothesis inconclusive?
3. This painting was completed in the period commonly referred to as *postimpressionism*. Write an essay in which you analyze the features that identify the artist of this painting as a postimpressionist.

Although he knew that he wanted to write about drug abuse, Patrick had not yet developed a proposition to support. As he thought about the issue, he decided that he wanted to focus on two issues—legislation to limit the flow of illegal drugs from foreign countries and drug education programs. His proposition was that his congressional representative should work to support both because drug abuse is a great national problem.

DEFINE THE TERMS OF YOUR PROPOSITION

As you no doubt know by now, what is perfectly clear to you may be a complete mystery to someone else, and this is particularly true with propositions for arguments. One way to enhance the clarity of your propositions is

Applications

to be sure the terms you use are adequately defined. (Use the same kind of definition as discussed in Chapter Six.) For example, an argument that begins "In *Moby Dick*, Herman Melville explores the conflict between fate and free will" uses two terms, *fate* and *free will,* which have a number of meanings. For this to be a convincing argument, the writer must precisely define these terms. It is not necessary that the writer's definitions be in the proposition itself, but they should follow closely after the initial statement so that the rest of the argument will be informed by the definitions.

As I said earlier, the proposition becomes the subject of an argument, and defining vague words in the proposition can become part of the argument itself. The important thing is to recognize the need for such definition. Just because you know exactly what *you* mean by free will or democracy or justice does not mean that your reader will have any idea. If vague words in the proposition remain undefined, your argument will be weakened.

EXERCISE

Each of the following propositions contains vague words that need to be defined. Identify them, and outline ways of defining them.

1. Many economic investments are concerned with the immediate future.
2. The contemporary forester is faced with meeting the social demands of the present while setting the stage for the demands of the future.
3. The Chinese have this practice, *bi-sun* that one would think ridiculous if one did not understand the reason behind it.
4. A revolution is caused by the misery of the people.
5. In his island world, Prospero is a good man.

Clarity Through Context. Often the clarity of a proposition can be enhanced by defining the words in it, as the preceding examples illustrate. Sometimes, however, a proposition can be clarified by explaining its history, by giving it a context. As a reader, you already know the importance of context. When you scan the newspaper, you see many examples of context in reports. Lines such as "Smith, the accused slayer of the Hearst heiress" or "Chad, the landlocked African Country ravaged by drought" or "Harvey, who ran unsuccessfully for sheriff in 1984" provide background information for news stories. Propositions require a more extensive context than do subjects of newspaper articles, but the principle is the same. By supplying context, you enable your readers to make sense of your argument.

For example, if your proposition is that the length of the terms at your school be changed, you might need to provide background information on how the terms came to be their present length, explore the rationale behind this decision, or include information about the length of terms at schools similar to yours. By including such information, you will make it easier for your readers to understand your proposition.

Arguing Proposals

In thinking about his proposition to his congressional representative, Patrick decided that he would have to define several of its terms. Specifically, "drug abuse," "great national problem" and "drug education programs" would need to be defined.

SPECIFY CAUSES

In writing to support propositions it is easy to overlook underlying causes. Usually the situation that prompts a proposition has some identifiable causes, and effective propositions will explore these. To see the difference between a proposition that includes consideration of cause and one that does not, look at these two sentences:

> Professor Smith is a tough grader, and enrollment in her classes is generally quite low.
>
> Because Professor Smith is a tough grader, enrollment in her classes is generally quite low.

The first sentence puts two pieces of information next to one another but fails to show their causal relationship. The two facts might be mere coincidence. But the second sentence makes it clear that the first fact causes the second, and in the process it also transforms two statements into the proposition that tough grading leads to low enrollment. This simple example illustrates the importance of exploring causes in supporting propositions.

The following excerpt from a student's paper shows how failure to specify causes weakens propositions.

```
     In nearly half the conversations I've had in the
last couple of weeks, the word apathy has come up
repeatedly. Apathy disturbs me greatly and I consider
it is a dangerous threat to our campus as well as to
the democratic freedom in this country.
```

The missing element here is a statement about the cause, low voter turnout, that links the two statements. By inserting a sentence such as "In the recent student government election, only 325 out of 15,000 students voted, which makes it easy to see why the word *apathy* is getting such active use" the author could reveal the causal connection between these two sentences, thereby creating a more convincing proposition.

As he thought about writing on drug abuse, Patrick realized that he would need to make the causal connections between illegal drug imports and drug abuse clear. In addition, he would need to show how drug education programs could cause a reduction in drug abuse.

Applications

EXERCISE

Read the following excerpts and then write a sentence for each that will make the causal connections more clear.

1. At the present time, safety regulations for nuclear power plants are under constant upgrading. When a firm draws up its plans, it knows that they will have to be changed many times, due to new regulations, by the time the plant is completed.
2. The weapons the Soviet Union possesses are of poor quality and are operated by ill-equipped crews. So if the United States budget were cut by 50 percent, nothing would happen.

After thinking about all these aspects of his topic, Patrick wrote the following draft.

From: Patrick S. Johnson, University of Washington Student

To: Mike Lowry, Washington Congressman

Re: Problems and Solutions of Drug Abuse in the United States

The abuse of illegal drugs by people of all ages and social classes is one of this country's greatest problems. "It is a plague that is controlling the minds and bodies of children and adults alike" (Reagan, p. 2). I feel that it is time for this country to take steps in controlling this growing problem.

In 1985 alone Americans spent $30 billion on illegal drugs, more than they spend for housing or clothes in a year (U.S. News, p. 19). The booming drug market no longer serves only poor junkies and adolescent pot smokers; during the last decade drug use has become increasingly fashionable among the well-to-do. The "drug problem" now means affluent lawyers, doctors, and investment bankers serving cocaine at parties, offering it in clubs, even taking a snort or two before an important business meeting. These new customs are resulting in more money and more encouragement for the dealers (Danner, p. 30).

But for the rest of us the growing problem of drug abuse in this country has produced nothing encouraging whatsoever, but rather a relentless list of astonishing results. The most dramatic and terrifying is death.

232

Arguing Proposals

Figures show that "deaths caused by cocaine abuse are up over 300 percent since 1980" (Lipshy, p. 479). Deaths and hospitalizations from other illegal drugs such as methaphetamine, an illegally manufactured drug sold on the black market, are also up. "Last year methaphetamine-related hospital emergencies rose 20 percent" (U.S. News p. 323). The death and hospitalization rates for many other drugs are also rising as a result of the current drug epidemic (Lawn, p. 323).

Another effect of the growing drug problem in the U.S. that employers in particular, are concerned about is money. Drug users cost companies about $47 billion a year. It adds up through lost efficiency, lost productivity, accidents on the job, claims for workers compensation, medical expenses, absenteeism, and crime costs due to drug use. "A drug user will steal from his employer and deal drugs to other employees. Thus the drug user has now made the work environment a convenient place to use drugs and sell them as a source of funds to support his habit" (Lawn p. 323).

Another result of the growing drug problem is the adverse effects on the daily lives of teenage drug users. In his speech, Lawn also mentioned a study conducted by the Cocaine Hotline, which receives an average of 1200 calls a day. This study shows that cocaine abuse causes many teenagers to have problems with school, with their families, and with their friends. It states that out of the teenagers that call, 71 percent admit to a drop in grades, 39 percent begin to steal from their families and friends, and 89 percent admit that problems with their parents were attributable to cocaine abuse. It also states that over 37 percent of the teenage callers believe that suicide is their only escape from their condition, and 9 percent of them had already tried to kill themselves. Drug related accidents, suicide and killings are taking the lives of many teenagers today. And while the average life expectancy has improved for almost all age groups, it has declined for teenagers. Drug abuse is largely responsible for this.

However, teenagers aren't the only drug abusers in our society. The implications of cocaine use for adults are just as staggering. The hotline's research has shown us that of the adults that call, 42 percent have lost all monetary assets, 45 percent have stolen from their employers or families, and over 70 percent say

Applications

that cocaine is more important than their families or friends (Lawn, p. 323). These studies show how the effects of the current drug abuse problem are impacting the daily lives of millions of people in this country who are abusing cocaine and other drugs.

As you can see from the facts and opinions I have stated thus far, I consider drug abuse to be one of the major problems facing the country right now. But I also feel that there are definite steps that this nation can take to attack this problem. The government and communities of our country must work together to find a solution and put it into action in order to solve the growing problem of drug abuse.

The solution to such an enormous problem as drug abuse in the U.S. is not singular. It has many parts and steps which attack the problem from several different angles. Some of the solutions can be found by looking at the causes of the problem. If we can eliminate or reduce some of the causes then the problem will also be reduced.

Two major causes of the drug epidemic are availability and low price. Recently the demand has been so high that smugglers have been flooding the U.S. market with illegal drugs, especially cocaine. The producers are responding to the demand also. In Bolivia, the production of coca, the source of cocaine, increased 78 percent in four years. Between 1982 and 1985, world opium production was up 50 percent, coca was up 40 percent, and marajuana was up 20 percent. A lot of this ends up in the United States which is the principle victim for smugglers.

In order to stop these two causes several steps need to be taken. First, to decrease the availability, we need to use political and diplomatic muscle to get the drug producing countries to eradicate their coca fields and other drug facilities. Second, we need to make more effective use of the military in patrolling our coasts and borders.

The drug producing countries are Colombia, Bolivia, Peru, and Mexico. Colombia provides 80 percent of the world's cocaine, and Bolivia and Peru produce 95 percent of the world's coca. Mexico is our major source of marijuana and heroin (U.S. News p. 19). By forcing these countries, through political and economic sanctions, to reduce their drug production, and by improving our border patrols, we can seriously reduce the

Arguing Proposals

flow of illegal drugs into this country. Subsequently the supply would drop below demand and prices would go up, forcing and encouraging people to stop using the drugs (Danner, p. 49).

The best way to fight drug abuse within this country is to educate people about the evils and dangers of drugs. Right now the system for educating our population about drug abuse is lacking. Some people don't even realize that marajuana and cocaine are harmful. We have to find more effective ways of teaching young people not to use drugs to solve their problems. By doing this we can prevent many people from turning to drugs when trying to deal with problems in life. For people that have already turned to drugs the objective is to get them to stop. One reason that people are currently using drugs is that the pleasure that they receive is greater than the risk of getting caught. It is easy to get away with so they continue their drug abuse.

By putting solutions such as improving education and decreasing availability into action, I am convinced that the drug problem in America can be greatly reduced. I feel that there are two main things that you could do. First, by advocating such solutions in Congress more action will take place against the countries that are producing illegal drugs. As James Mills said these countries are assaulting us with drugs. They have done way more damage to our citizens than Libya's terrorism ever did. Secondly, I believe that by using your influence in our local communities you can encourage the foundation of programs to educate people about drugs and change our society's attitude toward drug abuse. Such actions will certainly reduce drug abuse in our community and in our nation as a whole.

Thank you very much for your time.

EXERCISE

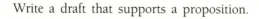

Write a draft that supports a proposition.

SUMMARY

In the early stages of writing to support a proposition, the following can be helpful:

Applications

- Ask the five "W" questions about your general area of interest.
- Collect evidence.
- State your proposition.
- Define the terms of your proposition.
- Specify the causes of the situation or issue you address.

Writing to Show Learning

When he had finished the draft of his letter Patrick realized that he needed to revise it before he could send it to Congressman Lowry. He knew he should include more documentation for some of the claims he made, and he wanted to make his claims even more convincing. As a first step he returned to the original assignment.

RECONSIDER THE ASSIGNMENT

When you have completed a draft, the assignment to which it is addressed will look different. You may have new questions about what is expected or you may understand the terms of the assignment differently. Returning to the assignment will give you an objective perspective on your draft at the same time that it helps you generate ideas for additions.

When Patrick reread the assignment for which he was writing on drug abuse, he found himself paying special attention to the three parts specified—the description of the problem, the analysis of the problem's causes and effects, and the proposed solution. He realized that the basic structure of his draft followed this progression, and he decided to strengthen this structure in his revision.

In rereading the portion of the assignment dealing with the addressee, Patrick reaffirmed his original feeling that writing to his congressional representative would give him the best opportunity for actually effecting change. He decided that Lowry had the kind of political clout that could guide legislation through the political process, and he felt that drug abuse was an issue with which Lowry would have sympathy.

CONSIDER AUDIENCE

As the first part of this chapter explained, some college writing assignments will ask you to write in support of a proposition without specifying a particular audience. In these cases the usual academic concerns with stating your position clearly, offering evidence, and observing the conventions of standard written English will guide your consideration of audience.

When you write to a specific audience, however, you will frequently have personal acquaintance with this group or individual. If you write to college administrators, your employer, or a local government group, you will probably know some of your readers. Even if you do not know individuals personally, you will undoubtedly know a good deal about them. Information about their

Arguing Proposals

positions on issues, voting records, priorities, and, even, special interests will be available to you.

Asking questions about your readers will help you address them more effectively. These questions can be a good beginning for addressing your audience:

1. What values does this audience hold?
2. What does my audience know about this topic?
3. Does my audience have any strong opinions about this topic?
4. What effect do I want to have on my audience?

Patrick considered the audience for his drug abuse proposition from the perspective of these questions. As he thought about the values held by Mike Lowry, he recalled that he is a liberal democrat with a strong voting record in support of social programs. This voting record indicates a high value for legislation designed to improve the quality of people's lives. Patrick did not have any information about Lowry's knowledge on the specific issue of drug abuse, but he assumed that the attention given it by the administration and by the media would ensure that Lowry had a fair amount of information.

Patrick was certain that Lowry would be, in general terms, opposed to drug abuse and would be in favor of reducing or eliminating it. But he didn't know what opinions Lowry had about drug education programs or efforts to limit the smuggling of illegal drugs into this country. Patrick did know exactly what effect he wanted to have on Lowry, however. He wanted to persuade Lowry to initiate or support legislation that would establish more effective local drug education programs and eliminate or reduce illegal drug traffic across national borders.

EXERCISE

Use the four questions about audience to reconsider the audience for your proposition.

AVOID FALLACIES

One way to anticipate audience objection to your propositions is to avoid mistakes in argument. You have probably heard statements such as "That's a red herring," or "Don't use an *ad hominem* argument with me." These and other similar terms refer to the fallacies or mistakes one can make in supporting a proposition. Among the fallacies to avoid are the following.

Arguing Against the Person. Appealing to your audience's emotions is part of supporting a proposition, but this can be extended to fallacy when you shift ground and argue against the person. The Latin *ad hominem* refers to an argument that focuses on a person rather than concentrating on the issue under discussion. You have probably heard or participated in arguments in which this mistake occurred. For example, imagine the teenager trying to persuade his parents that he should be allowed to use the family car on Friday night, even though his parents have grounded him for not returning the car on time on the preceding Friday. Instead of dealing with the question of responsibility, the teenager might turn on his parents with an accusation such as "You're always so mean to me. I don't think you love me at all." This argues against the parents, not the car issue. Or you may have heard a politician argue against a bill by attacking its supporter: "Senator Polk is behind this legislation; there isn't anyone more against human rights than he is. If Polk is for the bill, I'm against it."

This fallacy can appear when you write to support propositions. For example, a student who was asked to argue for a particular reading of Shakespeare's *Hamlet* wrote: "We all know that Shakespeare didn't really write most of the plays attributed to him. He stole from his contemporary Marlowe and others whose names we don't know." But these statements do nothing to advance the argument about the play because they introduce an *ad hominem* fallacy.

Arguing a False Cause. The Latin words *post hoc, ergo propter hoc* translate as "after this, therefore, on account of this" and refer to an argument that assigns false causes. This is the mistake of assuming when one thing happens and then a second thing happens that the first caused the second. For example, suppose that epidemiologists are working to discover the cause of Reyes syndrome, an often-fatal disease that afflicts youngsters between the ages of five and fifteen. In examining the data on recent victims, they discover that all drank milk every day. To argue that milk causes Reyes syndrome would be arguing a false cause, unless more substantial evidence against milk appeared.

Confusing correlation with causation is another way to describe this fallacy. Correlation means that two things co-occur, but causation means that one results in the other. For examples of this fallacy, return to the section entitled "Specifying Causes," because a common form of this fault is to put two pieces of information next to each other without indicating their relationship.

Confusing the Issue. The term *red herring* is often used to describe mistakes in an argument that bring an unrelated issue into the discussion, thereby diverting attention from the central question. Often the unrelated issue arouses emotion. For example, a politician who is being publicly accused of involvement in underworld gambling may respond: "The media, as you know, frequently engage in personal attacks in an effort to discredit public figures. I think we should take action against the media before they become so powerful that they begin to run this country." This response says nothing about what the person has or has not done with underworld gambling and tries to argue for the politician's innocence by directing the audience's attention to the media.

A sentence such as "The book I needed was checked out of the library" illustrates this fallacy. Such statements have no bearing on the actual question under consideration, and they merely confuse the issue.

Arguing Proposals

Begging the Question. To beg the question is to avoid making any argument and simply to restate the original position in slightly different words. Advertisers frequently use this strategy to promote their products. For example, an ad will claim that a given product is "new and improved" but offer no explanation of what "new and improved" means, no evidence of the ways in which the product is new or improved. Instead, the ad will go on to say that the product is "better than ever," which merely restates the first statement.

An underdeveloped argument often begs the question. This means stating the issues and then restating them as a kind of conclusion but insert no reasoning or presentation of evidence between the proposition and the conclusion. For example, the sentence "Guards cannot be denied because these guards are essential to campus life" does not include any reasoning or evidence. This kind of premature closure of argument begs the question just as much as the empty claims of advertising do.

Appealing to Emotion. Appealing to emotion substitutes emotion for evidence and tries to persuade through feelings rather than reason. Examples of this kind of fallacy appear regularly in magazine advertisements urging you to "adopt" a child from a third world country. Pictures of attractive but sad-eyed and poorly clad children feature prominently in these ads, and they claim that by sending a specified sum of money each month you can brighten this child's life by adopting him or her. Authors of these ads play upon readers' emotions of charity, pity, and love of children to convince them of the proposition that sending checks is the same as adopting a child.

Appealing to False Authority. The mistake in appealing to false authority is to give credit where it is not due. Think, for example, of the former baseball player who advertises coffee or the ex-football player who advertises rental cars. Neither of them has special expertise in coffee or cars, and the advertisements make an appeal to false authority by making it appear as if success in sports bears a relationship to a discerning taste or a discriminating business sense.

As Patrick read his draft he found some fallacies in his support of propositions. He reread the claim that increased prices resulting from decreasing the flow of illegal drugs into the country would cause decreased drug use and decided that it was arguing a false cause. It was false because he could not demonstrate that higher prices would lead to decreased drug use. Similarly, in rereading Mills's claim that countries producing illegal drugs have done more harm than Libya's terrorism he decided that this was a fallacy of emotional appeal. By equating drug producers with terrorists, Mills was playing on his audience's fear of terrorism.

CHECK ORGANIZATION

Specifics of issue, context and audience will shape the precise nature of an organizational plan for writing that supports propositions, but in general the

Applications

structure will follow a plan of presenting the problem or issue to be discussed, exploring the sources of or evidence about the problem or issue, and proposing a way of looking at the issue or solving the problem. While it is possible to begin with the solution or perspective, it is usually more effective to begin with the nature of the issue or problem and work toward the solution or conclusion. The shape of this plan can be visualized this way:

> present problem/issue
> explore sources/evidence
> propose solution/perspective

As Patrick noticed when he reread his assignment, the three suggested parts—describe the problem, analyze the problem's causes and effects, and offer a solution to be implemented by the individual addressed—provided an organizational plan for his writing. His draft followed this general plan, and he decided that it was the best way to respond to the assignment.

EXERCISE

Use the structure outlined above to evaluate the organizational plan of your draft.

Evaluate Coherence and Cohesion

Writing an effective proposition requires coherence. If the parts of the proposition do not work together, it cannot be convincing to a reader. The statement about the issue or problem should lead smoothly into an exploration of the sources/evidence, and this, in turn, should lead to the proposed solution/perspective. In rereading your draft watch for transitions between the parts and pay special attention to areas that raise questions for classmates who read your draft.

As he reread his draft, Patrick realized that there were several places where he could improve the coherence of his writing. The transition between the first and second paragraphs struck him as awkward, and he noticed several places where he needed to add quotations from his reading to make his explanations more fully developed and comprehensible. In addition, he knew that he needed to make better preparation for the concluding paragraph by introducing the idea of an education program sooner and more thoroughly. He saw that the causes and solutions became confused toward the end. At one point he identified the two causes as availability and low price and suggested solutions for them, but later he identified lack of drug education as a problem and urged Congressman Lowry to support improved drug education as well as trying to restrict availability.

Patrick noticed a special problem of cohesion as a result of quoting sources to support his propositions. He found that he had to reword several sections to make a smoother connection between the language of quotations and his

Arguing Proposals

own statements about drug abuse. This can be a problem in writing to support any proposition. Cohesion can suffer if special care is not taken to weave quotations into the text.

EXERCISE

Look at all the places where you have quoted sources in your draft and see where you can improve cohesion between these and the rest of your text.

Editing

After he had considered the audience and assignment for which he was writing, reconsidered his organizational plan and identified places where he could improve the coherence and cohesion of his draft, Patrick edited it carefully, checking for misspelled words, faults of usage, mechanics and punctuation. Among other things, he found that he had misspelled "marijuana" in his draft. He checked on the proper way to address a congressional representative and asked his instructor about how to document his sources of information. Here is Patrick's final draft:

```
To: The Honorable Mike Lowry, Representative in
Congress

From: Patrick S. Johnson, University of Washington
Student

Re: Drug Abuse in the United States

Dear Representative Lowry:

     The abuse of illegal drugs by people of all ages
and social classes is one of this country's greatest
problems. "It is a plague that is controlling the
minds and bodies of children and adults alike" (Reagan,
p. 2). I feel that it is time for this country to take
steps in controlling this growing problem.
     A closer look at the problem shows that in the
past few years drug abuse has increased to epidemic
proportions. Some experts estimate that there are five
to ten times as many cocaine users today as there were
a decade ago (Danner, p. 41). Currently, there are
about 20 million regular marijuana users in the United
States and about five percent of our high school
seniors are smoking marijuana daily. As for heroin,
there are one-half million addicts in our country,
```

241

Applications

many of whom resort to a life of crime in order to support their addictions (Lawn, p. 323).

The smugglers and dealers are ecstatic about these increasing numbers. In 1985 alone, Americans spent $30 billion on illegal drugs, more than they spent on food, housing, or clothing (U.S. News & World Report, Aug. 25, 1986, p. 19). Mark D. Danner, senior editor of Harper's magazine, recently wrote in an article on drug abuse, "The booming drug market no longer serves only poor junkies and adolescent pot smokers; during the last decade drug use has become increasingly fashionable among the well-to-do. The 'drug problem' now means affluent lawyers, doctors, and investment bankers . . ." serving cocaine at parties, or offering it at clubs, or even taking a snort or two before an important business meeting. These new customers are producing more business and more encouragement for the dealers (Danner, p. 39).

But for the rest of us, the growing problem of drug abuse in this country has produced nothing encouraging whatsoever, but rather, an astonishing list of dreadful results. The most dramatic and terrifying result is death. More of our citizens are dying from drug overdoses every day. Figures show that death caused by cocaine abuse are up over three hundred percent since 1980 (Lipshy, p. 479). John C. Lawn, Administrator from the Drug Enforcement Administration, cited in a recent speech on drugs in America, asserted that deaths and hospitalizations from abusing other illegal drugs such as methaphetamine, an illegally manufactured drug sold on the black market, are also up. "Last year, methaphetamine-related hospital emergencies rose twenty percent." The death and hospitalization rates from many other drugs are also rising as a result of the current drug epidemic (Lawn, p. 323).

Another effect of the growing drug problem in the United States, that employers, in particular, are concerned about, is the cost of drug abuse to businesses. John C. Lawn noted that drug users cost United States companies about $47 billion a year. It adds up through lost efficiency, lost productivity, accidents on the job, claims for workers' compensation, medical expenses, absenteeism, and crime costs due to drug use." A drug user will steal from his employer and deal drugs to other employees. Thus, the drug user has now made the work environment a convenient place to use drugs and sell them as a source of funds to support his habit (Laws p. 323).

Another result of the growing drug problem is the adverse effects on the daily lives of teenage drug users. In his speech, Lawn also mentioned a study recently conducted by the Cocaine Hotline. The hot-line receives an average of 1200 calls a day from people who are addicted to cocaine and need help. The study has shown that cocaine abuse causes many teenagers to have problems with school, their families, and their friends. It states that out of the teenagers that call, seventy-one percent admit to a drop in grades due to the use of cocaine, thirty-nine percent begin to steal from their families and friends, and eighty-nine percent admit that problems with their parents are attributable to cocaine abuse. It also states that over thirty-seven percent of the teenage callers believe that suicide is their only escape from their addiction, and nine percent of them have already tried to kill themselves. Drug-related accidents, suicides, and killings are taking the lives of many teenagers today. And while the average life expectancy has improved for almost all age groups, it has declined for teenagers. Drug abuse is largely responsible for this.

However, teenagers are not the only drug abusers in our society. The implications of cocaine use for adults are just as staggering. The hot-line's research has shown us that out of the adults that call, forty-two percent have lost all monetary assets, and over seventy percent say that cocaine is more important than their families and friends (Lawn, p. 323). These studies show how the current drug abuse problems are affecting the daily lives of millions of people in this country who are abusing cocaine and other drugs.

As you can see from the facts and opinions I have stated thus far, I consider drug abuse to be one of the major problems facing the country right now. But I also feel that there are definite steps that this nation can take to attack this problem. The government and communities of our country must work together to find a solution and put it into action in order to solve the growing problem of drug abuse.

The solution to such an enormous problem as drug abuse in the United States is not singular. It has many parts and steps which attack the problem from

Applications

several different angles. The steps involved in this solution fall into two main categories: attacking the supply and reducing the demand. By working to achieve these goals, we can seriously reduce the drug problem in the United States.

The increasing supply of illegal drugs reaching the users on our streets has been a major factor in producing the current epidemic. Recently, the demand has been so high that smugglers have been flooding the U.S. market with illegal drugs, especially cocaine. There is so much cocaine pouring into the country right now that the price has actually gone down (Danner, p. 41). The producers are responding to the demand also. In an interview with <u>U.S. News and World Report,</u> James Mills, author of <u>The Panic in Needle Park,</u> said, "In Bolivia between 1982 and 1985, opium production was up fifty percent, coca was up forty percent, and marijuana was up twenty percent." A lot of this ends up in the United States, which is the principle victim for smugglers.

Colombia, Bolivia, Peru, and Mexico supply the U.S. with the majority of its illegal drugs. Currently, Colombia provides eighty percent of the world's cocaine (<u>U.S. News and World Report,</u> p. 19). At a meeting of several drug experts covered by <u>Harper's</u> magazine, Rudolph W. Giuliani, the U.S. Attorney for the Southern District of New York, pointed out that by forcing these countries through political and economic sanctions to reduce their drug production, and by improving our border patrols, we can seriously reduce the flow of drugs into this country.

In attacking the supply further, we can take steps within our own country to deter the circulation of illegal drugs. We can do this by increasing police forces and drug related arrests, and by imposing stricter punishments on the offenders. On this issue, Rudolph Giuliani states, "The message must be clear: if you deal drugs you go to prison." Today, drug dealers in large cities know that if they get arrested, they will probably not go to prison. "In New York City last year, only one out of nine people arrested for selling drugs was imprisoned." Right now, the punishments are not harsh enough and the risks are not great enough to deter the pushers from dealing illegal drugs (Danner, p. 49). With an increase in law enforcement against drug offenders, stepped up border patrol, and

Arguing Proposals

major political and economic sanctions against the drug producing countries, the supply of illegal drugs will decrease substantially. This is a major part of the solution of the current drug epidemic.

Putting these solutions into action will definitely help to solve the drug problem, but the best way of stopping the flow of illegal drugs into the United States is by stopping the demand. With little or no demand, the producers, smugglers, and pushers will be out of jobs and the supply will immediately dry up. I firmly believe that this would be the most successful means of stopping the drug problem.

In order to do this, our government and communities need to work together to inform our citizens of the evils of drug abuse and show them that abusing drugs is not acceptable. We have to get our society to change its tolerant attitude toward drug abuse. During the past few years, that attitude has been slowly changing; parents will no longer accept as inevitable that their children will use illegal drugs (Danner, p. 49).

But, unfortunately, many of the drug abusers today are children. In his speech John C. Lawn stated that the high school graduating class of 1986 will have spent 11,000 hours in the classroom and 16,000 hours in front of a television set. This figure shows how much of an influence television can have on a child. But what kind of influence is this? Well, if you watch television, "you will see that one out of six commercials tells you and me and your youngsters that if you are not feeling well, there is a substance that will make you feel better. . . ." Our children learn from the time they are infants, that in order to feel better they must put something into their systems. The result of this fact is that our children's minds are being infiltrated with the idea that substance abuse is acceptable in our society (Lawns, sps. 323).

At the meeting about drug abuse covered by Harper's magazine, Rudolph Giuliani said that the best way to fight this is to educate people about the evils and dangers of drugs. Right now, the system for educating our population about drug abuse is lacking. Giuliani said that some people do not even realize that marijuana and cocaine abuse are harmful. "We have to devise more effective ways of teaching young people not to use drugs . . . " to solve their problems. We need to teach them not to use drugs at all! (Danner, p. 49).

Applications

For many years now, our schools have been teaching children both good and bad aspects of illegal drugs in hopes they will choose not to use them. I strongly believe that in order to stop people from abusing drugs we need to throw away this idea of allowing each person to make an independent analysis and then decide whether or not illegal drugs are the thing for him. It cannot be viewed as a privilege for an individual to use illegal drugs and drag others down the road to a life of crime and addiction. "It's nothing short of ridiculous to devote so many of our resources to cutting off the supply of drugs and at the same time carry on with a soft, compassionate approach at the demand end." So in order to make drug abuse education work, we need to tell people that drug abuse is bad. There is no need for pro-and-con debate. Drugs can destroy the mind and kill the body (Lawrence, p. 649).

To get this message across to society, our communities and government need to work together. Local communities should help schools fight drugs by providing them with the expertise and financial resources of community groups and organizations. They should also involve local law-enforcement agencies in all aspects of drug prevention: assessment, enforcement, and education.

The government needs to work with the communities by supporting their efforts through financial aid and through the foundation of its own drug abuse prevention agencies. Likewise, the communities need to support the government by advocating its policies regarding the attack on the supply side of the problem (Werner, p. 19).

By working together to put solutions, such as improving prevention efforts and decreasing supply, into action, I am convinced that the drug problem in America can be greatly reduced. I feel that there are two main things that you can do to improve our current situation. First, by advocating these solutions in Congress, more action will be taken both at home, in deterring the dealers from selling illegal drugs, and abroad, against the countries that are producing illegal drugs. James Mills, in his interview with <u>U.S. News & World Report,</u> pointed out that these countries are killing our people. These countries are assaulting us with drugs and we need to stop them now (<u>U.S. News & World Report,</u> p. 19). Secondly, I believe that by using your influence in our local communities you can encourage the foundation of programs that will teach people about the evils of drug abuse. We need to change society's tolerant attitude toward drug abuse and the best way to achieve this is through education. Such actions will certainly reduce drug abuse in our own communities and in our nation as a whole.

Thank you very much for your time.

Bibliography

Danner, Mark D. "What Is Our Drug Problem?" *Harper's* Dec. 1985, pp. 39-51.

Lawn, John C. "Drugs in America," *Vital Speeches of the Day*, March 15, 1986, pp. 322-326.

Lawrence, Malcom. "Drug Abuse Prevention," *Vital Speeches of the Day*, Aug. 15, 1986, pp. 648-651.

Lipshy, Bruce A. "The Important Role of Business in Our Teenage Crisis," *Vital Speeches of the Day*, May 15, 1986, pp. 478-480.

Reagan, Nancy. "The Drug Abuse Epidemic," *American Education*, Oct. 1984, pp. 2-3.

U.S. News & World Report. "Stop Drugs at the Source," Aug. 25, 1986, p. 19.

Werner, Leslie M. "U.S. Issues Guide Urging Schools to 'Get Tough,'" *The New York Times*, Aug. 12, 1986, sec. A, p. 19.

EXERCISE

1. List the differences you see between the first and second versions of Patrick's paper.
2. Revise your own proposition, incorporating changes that will make it as convincing as possible.

Copyright © Alexander Lowry, The National Audubon Society Collection/Photo Researchers, Inc.

PART THREE

THE STRUCTURE OF WRITING

Copyright © Joe Munroe, The National Audubon Society Collection/Photo Researchers, Inc.

Chapter Ten

Paragraphs

Although they appear in all contemporary texts, paragraphs are a relatively recent form. Manuscripts from several hundred years ago do not observe paragraph breaks. The first indication of a paragraph came in the ¶ inserted in the margins of a text by printers. These marks, designed to make reading easier, led to the practice of indenting, and many contemporary manuscripts observe this form of paragraphing. As you may have observed, however, some writers indicate paragraph breaks with extra lines of space between paragraphs. For an example of this form, turn to the section on business letters on page 409.

For contemporary writers, paragraphs are building blocks of prose. The sentences that comprise a paragraph work to create multiple effects. For the reader the paragraph signals a break, an opportunity to stop briefly and absorb what has gone before. For the writer, the paragraph provides a place to develop an idea, to elaborate upon a statement. Effective use of paragraphs enables writers to call attention to ideas they wish to highlight, to separate one point from another, to structure the reader's experience with the written text.

Deciding Where Paragraphs Begin and End

The issues writers face in shaping paragraphs are similar to those for longer selections of writing: purpose, organization, cohesion, and style. Paragraphs are miniature versions of longer selections of writing; they introduce an idea and develop it through a variety of strategies. Just as a longer piece of writing reaches a conclusion, so a paragraph draws to an end and another begins. One of the issues you will face in paragraphing is deciding where one paragraph should end and another should begin.

There is no handy list of rules for making this decision. It is true that most paragraphs contain at least three or four sentences, and few extend beyond a dozen, but there is no "ideal" length. Your decisions about where to insert

The Structure of Writing

paragraph breaks will depend upon the type of writing you are doing (newspapers, for example, use much shorter paragraphs than do most college essays); the issues you wish to highlight (readers will give greater attention to the first sentence of a paragraph than one in the middle); and your personal style (individual writers' sense of rhythm can manifest itself in paragraphing). The following exercise illustrates how different individuals can paragraph the same prose in various ways.

EXERCISE

Read the following twenty-five sentences from which all the paragraph indentations have been eliminated. Decide where each paragraph should begin, and indicate your choice by listing the number of the sentence that should be indented. After you have made your decisions, compare them with those of others who have done this exercise.

Agriculture is one part of the biological revolution; the domestication and harnessing of village animals is the other.(1) The sequence of domestication is orderly.(2) First comes the dog, perhaps even before 10,000 B.C.(3) Then come food animals, beginning with goats and sheep.(4) And then come draught animals such as the onager, a kind of wild ass.(5) The animals add a surplus much larger than they consume.(6) But that is true only so long as the animals remain modestly in their proper station, as servants of agriculture.(7) It is unexpected that the domestic animal should turn out exactly to contain within itself, from then on, the threat to the surplus of grain by which the settled community lives and survives.(8) Most unexpected, because after all it is the ox, the ass, as a draught animal that has helped to create this surplus.(9) (The Old Testament carefully urges that they be treated well; for instance, it forbids the farmer to yoke an ox and ass to the plough together, since they work in different ways.(10) But round about five thousand years ago, a new draught animal appears—the horse.(11) And that is out of all proportion faster, stronger, more dominant than any previous animal.(12) And from now on that became the threat to the village surplus.(13) The horse had begun by drawing wheeled carts, like the ox—but rather grander, drawing chariots in the processions of kings.(14) And then, somewhere around 2000 B.C., men discovered how to ride it.(15) The idea must have been as startling in its day as the invention of the flying machine.(16) For one thing, it required a bigger, stronger horse—the horse was originally quite a small animal and, like the llama of South America, could not carry a man for long.(17) Riding as a serious use for the horse therefore begins in the nomad tribes that bred horses.(18) They were men out of Central Asia, Persia, Afghanistan and beyond; in the West they were simply called Scythians, as a collective name for a new and frightening creature, a phenomenon of nature.(19) For the rider visibly is more than a man: he is head-high above others, and he moves with bewildering power so that he bestrides the living world.(20) When the plants and the animals of the village had been tamed for human use, mounting the horse was a more than human gesture, the symbolic art of dominance over the total creation.(21) We know that this is so from the awe and fear that the horse created again in historical times, when the mounted Spaniards overwhelmed the armies of Peru (who

Paragraphs

had never seen a horse) in 1532.(22) So, long before, the Scythians were a terror that swept over the countries that did not know the technique of riding.(23) The Greeks when they saw the Scythian riders believed the horse and the rider to be one; that is how they invented the legend of the Centaur.(24) Indeed, that other half human hybrid of the Greek imagination, the satyr, was originally not part goat but part horse; so deep was the unease that the rushing creature from the East evoked.(25)

—Jacob Bronowski, *The Ascent of Man*

IDENTIFY IMPORTANT PARTS

As you compare your decisions with those of others, you will probably find that you do not agree entirely about where the paragraphs should begin. As you and your classmates explain your choices, you will probably find that you agree on a central principle of paragraphing—paragraph indentations should highlight important ideas.

 This principle, the same one that guided early printers as they inserted ⁋ marks in the margins of texts, seems straightforward enough. The problem lies in agreeing on what constitutes the important parts. At least three factors will help your decision:

1. *The content of the prose.* "Content" here refers to the level of difficulty and the shifts in topic within the selection.
2. *The author's intentions.* "Intentions" refer to the purposes for writing and the effects desired.
3. *Audience.* The audience's knowledge, opinions, and values all contribute to decisions about paragraphing.

To see how these three factors contribute to paragraphing, consider these two versions of a discussion of thermodynamics:

I. Thermodynamics is the science of heat and temperature and, in particular, of the laws governing the conversion of heat into mechanical, electrical, or other macroscopic forms of energy. It is a central branch of science with important applications in chemistry and other physical sciences, in biology, and in engineering. Thermodynamics is a macroscopic theory, concerning quantities such as pressure, temperature, or volume. It is both the strength and weakness of thermodynamics that the relationships based upon it are completely independent of any microscopic explanation of physical phenomena. The *strength* is that thermodynamics relationships are not affected by the changes in microscopic explanations that continue to occur as the theories of atomic and molecular interactions and structure are modified and improved. On the contrary, the conclusions of atomic and molecular theories *must not* contradict those of thermodynamics, so that thermodynamics can be used as a guide or as a touchstone in the development of microscopic theories. Much of thermodynamics was, in fact, developed at a time when many scientists did not believe in atoms and molecules, long before detailed atomic theories were available. The *weakness* of thermodynamics is that it does not provide the deep insight into chemical and physical phenomena that is afforded by microscopic models and theories. Although thermodynamics is a completely self-contained macroscopic theory, it is nevertheless possible to find a microscopic interpretation of it in what is called statistical mechanics, which provides considerable insight and is of great value for a full understanding of thermodynamics. On the other hand, to understand statistical mechanics a great deal of mathematics is required, whereas the more simple aspects of calculus suffice for thermodynamics. Several postulates, referred to as *laws*, are basic to thermodynamics. Although these laws are consistent with the results of all known experiments, this great mass of observational material serves only as support, not as proof. The "laws" of thermodynamics are postulates, or axioms, as are all "laws" of nature. An important characteristic of thermodynamics is that it permits the derivation of *relationships* among various laws, even though those laws themselves are not a consequence of thermodynamics. For example, if Raoult's law of vapor-pressure lowering is assumed, other colligative properties of a solution, such as the osmotic pressure law, can be derived. Neither Raoult's law nor the osmotic law, however, is an individual consequence of thermodynamics. One or the other must be accepted on the basis of experiment or derived from a detailed molecular theory of solutions. As we shall see in the following chapter, it is possible to give thermodynamic criteria for the direction in which a chemical reaction is likely to proceed. However, it is only in this sense that thermodynamics is concerned with time—in the sense of the direction of the flow of time, or what has been called "time's arrow." It is not possible to establish by thermodynamics how rapidly a reaction proceeds toward equilibrium. In favorable cases this may be established by detailed molecular theories, but in general each reaction must be investigated experimentally (Chap. 20). Thermodynamics might thus more properly be called thermostatics, but the term *thermodynamics*, coined in the early days of steam-engine theory, is somehow more enticing and is firmly entrenched.

II. Thermodynamics is the science of heat and temperature and, in particular, of the laws governing the conversion of heat into mechanical, electrical, or other macroscopic forms of energy. It is a central branch of science with important applications in chemistry and other physical sciences, in biology, and in engineering.

Thermodynamics is a macroscopic theory, concerning quantities such as pressure, temperature, or volume. It is both the strength and weakness of thermodynamics that the relationships based upon it are completely independent of any microscopic explanation of physical phenomena. The *strength* is that thermodynamics relationships are not affected by the changes in microscopic explanations that continue to occur as the theories of atomic and molecular interactions and structure are modified and improved. On the contrary, the conclusions of atomic and molecular theories *must not* contradict those of thermodynamics, so that thermodynamics can be used as a guide or as a touchstone in the development of microscopic theories. Much of thermodynamics was, in fact, developed at a time when many scientists did not believe in atoms and molecules, long before detailed atomic theories were available.

The *weakness* of thermodynamics is that it does not provide the deep insight into chemical and physical phenomena that is afforded by microscopic models

Paragraphs

and theories. Although thermodynamics is a completely self-contained macroscopic theory, it is nevertheless possible to find a microscopic interpretation of it in what is called statistical mechanics, which provides considerable insight and is of great value for a full understanding of thermodynamics. On the other hand, to understand statistical mechanics a great deal of mathematics is required, whereas the more simple aspects of calculus suffice for thermodynamics.

Several postulates, referred to as *laws*, are basic to thermodynamics. Although these laws are consistent with the results of all known experiments, this great mass of observational material serves only as support, not as proof. The "laws" of thermodynamics are postulates, or axioms, as are all "laws" of nature.

An important characteristic of thermodynamics is that it permits the derivation of *relationships* among various laws, even though those laws themselves are not a consequence of thermodynamics. For example, if Raoult's law of vapor-pressure lowering is assumed, other colligative properties of a solution, such as the osmotic pressure law, can be derived. Neither Raoult's law nor the osmotic law, however, is an individual consequence of thermodynamics. One or the other must be accepted on the basis of experiment or derived from a detailed molecular theory of solutions.

As we shall see in the following chapter, it is possible to give thermodynamic criteria for the direction in which a chemical reaction is likely to proceed. However, it is only in this sense that thermodynamics is concerned with time—in the sense of the direction of the flow of time, or what has been called "time's arrow." It is not possible to establish by thermodynamics how rapidly a reaction proceeds toward equilibrium. In favorable cases this may be established by detailed molecular theories, but in general each reaction must be investigated experimentally (Chap. 20). Thermodynamics might thus more properly be called thermostatics, but the term *thermodynamics*, coined in the early days of steam-engine theory, is somehow more enticing and is firmly entrenched.

—Jung Waser, *Chem One*

For most readers this *content* is fairly difficult, and so the relative frequency of paragraphs makes the second version much easier to comprehend. In addition, the topics within the passage help determine where the paragraphs should begin. The progression of topics within this selection is introducing thermodynamics and connecting it to other disciplines, exploring the macroscopic and microscopic dimensions of thermodynamics, defining the "laws" of thermodynamics, explaining how thermodynamics influences other laws of science, and defining thermodynamics' relationship to time. Each paragraph in this selection explores a different aspect of thermodynamics, and the shift of topics determines where paragraphs occur.

A piece of writing cannot precisely reveal an author's intentions, but we can guess here that the writer wanted to introduce readers to a broad range of general issues surrounding thermodynamics with an eye to developing them later in the chapter. In addition, we can assume that the writer wished to make relatively complicated material accessible to the readers and to show the relationship between thermodynamics and other ideas previously discussed.

Thus the writer's intentions play a major part in determining the paragraphs.

The Structure of Writing

If the author of the thermodynamics selection had wanted to give more emphasis to the strengths of thermodynamics, he might have divided the second paragraph into two. The fact that the fourth and fifth paragraphs are separate suggests that the author wanted to highlight the distinction between the laws of thermodynamics and the relationship between these and other laws of science.

No matter what else they expect of paragraphs, readers always assume that paragraphs will provide a break in the prose. No doubt you had some difficulty reading selections in which the paragraph indentations were omitted. Just as you rely on the capital letters and end punctuation of sentences to signal their closure, so you count on paragraphs to end groups of sentences. This momentary break in the stream of language gives you an opportunity to absorb what you have read and to collect your thoughts before proceeding to the next complex of ideas. In the words of H. W. Fowler in *Modern English Usage*, "The purpose of the paragraph is to give the reader a rest."

Although all audiences share the view that paragraphs provide a rest, they vary in their other expectations. The audience's sophistication, for example, contributes to the determination of paragraph length. Children's books, for instance, usually have much shorter paragraphs than do books for adults, because children's reading experience does not prepare them for long sections of uninterrupted prose. Likewise, textbooks introducing new information to students usually have shorter paragraphs than do professional journals dealing with the same subject matter, because the students' inexperience with the subject matter makes it necessary for them to have more opportunities to stop and absorb the information.

The conventions of the written format also contribute to the audience's expectations about where paragraphs should appear. Newspapers usually have much shorter paragraphs than do articles in magazines, and there are many variations in standard paragraph length among different types of magazines.

EXERCISE

Collect samples of prose from at least three different types of publications. These could include novels, technical reports, children's books, newspapers, professional journals, advertisements, repair manuals, or any other type of prose that interests you. In each selection read at least three paragraphs, count the number of words in each, and determine the average. Compare the three averages.

After you have determined the average paragraph length for your three sections, reread all three to see how factors of content, author's intention, and audience influence the paragraph length in each.

Types of Paragraphs

All paragraphs need to be set off from one another, but not all paragraphs are exactly the same type. In addition to highlighting the important parts, paragraphs serve different functions within a piece of writing. These functions

Paragraphs

include introducing ideas to be developed within the piece that follows; making transitions from one issue to another; developing a topic; and concluding a piece of writing.

INTRODUCTORY PARAGRAPHS

An introductory paragraph orients readers to what will follow. It gives readers an overview so they know what to expect as they continue reading. Like first impressions made by people you meet, the introductory paragraph creates an initial impression—it indicates whether the writing that follows will be engaging or dull; it may even help readers decide whether to continue reading your prose or stop altogether.

The following introductory paragraph illustrates how both an overview and engagement of the reader can be effected:

> The life of Henry David Thoreau has been thoroughly explored for almost a century by critics and biographers, yet the mystery of this untraveled man who read travel literature has nowhere been better expressed than by his own old walking companion Ellery Channing, who once wrote: "I have never been able to understand what he meant by his life. Why was he so disappointed with everybody else? Why was he so interested in the river and the woods? . . . Something peculiar here I judge."
>
> —Loren Eisley, *The Starthrower*

This paragraph introduces the mystery of Thoreau, the mystery that will be the central question of this essay. Eisley summarizes studies of Thoreau and offers a glimpse of the person (an untraveled man who read travel literature) and then moves to the Channing quotation. This quotation ends the paragraph and at the same time suggests what is to come (something peculiar here I judge). Eisley's focus on the mystery of Thoreau captures the reader's attention at the same time that his movement from previous studies to Thoreau's unusual qualities to the Channing line suggest the territory to be covered in what follows.

Because they provide an overview and can shape a reader's attitude, introductory paragraphs are often difficult to write. You may find yourself chewing pencils, frowning, writing a few words, rereading what you have written, crumpling up pieces of paper and starting over in an attempt to write a "perfect" introductory paragraph. This can be a very frustrating and unproductive process if you try to write an introductory paragraph before you have written any other part of a paper. In particular, you may find it difficult to attend to this level of detail before the whole piece has taken shape. It is like trying to paint a house before the structure has been completed, trying to do too much too soon.

As you compose a first draft, you may begin with an introductory paragraph, but try not to worry about making it "perfect" the first time. After you have completed a draft and have moved toward revision's consideration of audience,

The Structure of Writing

purpose, organization, cohesion, and style, it is time to think about refining an introductory paragraph into a form that will give your readers a clear idea of what follows and will capture their interest and attention.

The two paragraphs that follow (both from Monico Caoli's essay that appears in Chapters 2 and 3) illustrate how revision after the first draft can improve introductory paragraphs:

> Costa Rica is a beautiful country. I have many pleasant memories of my stay there. I lived there for five months with a Costa Rican family as a foreign exchange student. I lived in Tibas, San Jose.

This paragraph does little to capture the reader's attention because it suggests so little about why the reader should be interested in Costa Rica or Monica's experiences there. Similarly the statement about being an exchange student does not give any indication of what aspects of that experience will be discussed in the following paragraph.

Here is a revised version of the same paragraph:

> San Jose, Costa Rica, is unlike the major cities of the United States in that it isn't nearly as developed, although it is the largest city as well as the capital city of Costa Rica. There are no towering skyscrapers, no subways, and little air pollution. The buses and taxis serve as the main means of transportation. The air is somewhat humid. Walking along the streets and passing through the parks, you inhale the aroma of fresh fruit and freshly baked bread until car exhaust and noise interrupt the peace as the city comes to life. Clusters of litter are scattered here and there along the sidewalks. The people are a sea of dark skin and black hair, except for the few mestizos (mixed) and foreigners sprinkled among them. A girl with blonde hair and blue eyes is a rare sight and a treat for the men. Accordingly, the men react with stares and smiles, sometimes going as far as reaching out to touch her.

As you can see, this version provides enough detail to engage the reader with the exotic qualities of Costa Rica. At the same time, the discussion of skin and hair color and the mention that men sometimes touch fair women prepare the reader for the narration that follows.

Paragraphs

TRANSITIONAL PARAGRAPHS

Even when an introductory paragraph has done a good job of forecasting the general topic of a piece of writing, there will often be small shifts of topic within the piece. These shifts can be accomplished with transitional paragraphs. The following is a transitional paragraph that appears later in Eisley's essay:

> In a studied paragraph Carl Jung, with no reference to Thoreau, perhaps pierced closest to Thoreau's purpose without ever revealing it. He says in his alchemical studies, "Medieval alchemy prepared the greatest attack on the divine order of the universe which mankind has ever dared. Alchemy is the dawn of the age of natural sciences, which, through the *daemonium* of the scientific spirit, drove nature and her forces into the service of mankind to a hitherto unheard of degree.... Technics and science have indeed conquered the world, but whether the soul has gained thereby is another matter.
> —Loren Eisley, *the Starthrower*

This paragraph moves the essay away from the question of Thoreau to the larger question of science's impact on humanity. The Jung quotation ends with the implicit question of how the human soul has been affected by science and technology. This question shifts the direction of the essay away from the details of Thoreau's life and motivations by introducing Jung; yet like most transitional paragraphs, it adds a new dimension to the central topic—Thoreau's unfinished business.

The need for transitional paragraphs is not always evident in writing a first draft. Because our minds lead us from one idea to another as we write, it is easy to forget that a reader's thinking may not follow exactly the same patterns. The process of revising often leads writers to recognize the need for a transitional paragraph. This kind of recognition led Jim Layton to insert a transitional paragraph in his essay (see page 139).

In the first draft Jim moved directly from a paragraph about being hit by the meatball to one describing how he caught Toby, the boy who threw it:

```
    At this point, I was besieged with anger as well
as disgrace. I had to achieve revenge to save my name.
Storming in the direction the meatball came from, I
heard the squeaks of little freshman voices as they
shouted, "Toby did it! Toby did it!"
    Furiously I raced around the school until I had
found Toby hiding by his locker. By this time about
10 people were following me. . . .
```

As he revised this draft, Jim realized that he needed to create a transition from the throwing incident to the moment he caught Toby, so he added this transitional paragraph (he also changed to the third person):

259

The Structure of Writing

> Humiliated in front of what seemed like the whole school, Jim was furious and felt he had to gain retribution, especially because he was a very visible and respected member of the student body. One of the top students in his class and three-sport athlete, Jim was well-liked by almost everybody. He certainly wasn't going to be disgraced by a freshman. The fact that the meatball was intended for a freshman at a nearby table mattered little to him at this point.

By adding this transitional paragraph, Jim made it easier for his readers to follow his account.

Topical Paragraphs

Although introductory and transitional paragraphs are essential for writers, they are much less numerous than topical ones. The majority of paragraphs develop ideas—they are topical. These workhorse paragraphs enable writers to convey ideas clearly and completely. The following topical paragraph, in which Eisley develops the idea introduced in the transitional paragraph illustrates:

> Thoreau was indeed a spiritual wanderer through the deserts of the modern world. Almost by instinct he rejected that beginning wave of industrialism which was later to so entrance his century. He also rejected the peace he had found on the shores of Walden Pond, the alternate glazing and reflection of that great natural eye which impartially received the seasons. It was, in the end, too great for his endurance, too timeless. He was a restless pacer of fields, a reader who, in spite of occasional invective directed against those who presumed to neglect their homes for far places, nevertheless was apt with allusions drawn from travel literature and quick to discern in man uncharted spaces.
> —Loren Eisley, *the Starthrower*

This paragraph builds on the Thoreau-science connection discussed in the preceding paragraph. In so doing, it develops the issue of Thoreau's "peculiarity" and simultaneously connects this trait to the issues raised in the Jung quotation. Notice, too, that the travel literature mentioned in the introductory paragraph is explained in more detail in this topical paragraph.

Revision of topical paragraphs gives attention to development—trying to make the ideas clear and detailed enough to give a full picture to readers. These two versions of the same paragraph from Adam Cooney's "The Way It Should Be" (see pages 184–185) demonstrate how development of topical paragraphs can make the reader's task easier. Here is a paragraph from Adam's first draft:

> Readers turn to <u>Meditation</u> because it is different when compared to many of the other magazines found in

Paragraphs

> newsstands today. It contains neither the recent developments in Lebanon, the score in last night's World Series baseball game, nor the current fashion trend. Meditation concentrates on helping people. Its articles include features about people who are sincerely happy telling about their experiences, how they achieved happiness, and what they are doing to help others.

The paragraph does a good job of detailing what the magazine does not contain, but the explanation of what it does contain remains vague and general. Terms like "helping people," "sincerely happy," and "help others," give readers little idea of what is actually in these articles.

In contrast, consider the following:

> The articles include features about people who feel truly content and at peace with the world. The articles are often in the form of interviews. People tell about how they achieved happiness and what they are doing now to help others. These interviews give the writing an oral quality, allowing readers to "hear" the words as they might at church. Other articles advise and address the reader directly by using the pronoun "you." They inform readers on how they can live life to the fullest. In today's world, life can be very busy, stressful, and painful. The articles explain that through meditation and relaxation, a deeper level of consciousness can be reached which will result in better health, a better attitude, and a better sense of what life is all about. The articles show different methods for both the beginning and experienced meditators.

By adding specific details about both the style and content of the articles in *Meditation*, Adam made it much easier for his readers to understand the nature of the magazine.

CONCLUDING PARAGRAPHS

As the name suggests, concluding paragraphs refer to what has gone before. This reference can take two forms—summarizing and evaluating—and frequently concluding paragraphs do both. In the process of summarizing a piece of writing, concluding paragraphs often comment upon it, thereby performing an evaluation. Eisley's concluding paragraph illustrates:

261

> We see, as artists, as scientists, each in his own way, through the inexorable lens we cannot alter. In a nature which Thoreau recognized as unfixed and lawless anything might happen. The artist's endeavor is to make it happen—the unlawful, the oncoming world, whether endurable or mad, but shaped, shaped always by the harsh angles of truth, the truth as glimpsed through the terrible crystal of genius. This is the one sure rule of that other civilization which we have come to know is greater than our own. Thoreau called it, from the first, "unfinished business," when he turned and walked away from his hut at Walden Pond.
>
> —Loren Eisley, *The Starthrower*

As you can see, Eisley summarizes Thoreau's "peculiar" qualities, explaining them as resulting from the "terrible crystal of genius." But he does not stop with a summary. He goes on to evaluate Thoreau in the larger context of artists and scientists, of the relationship of humans to nature, and, thereby, lends greater significance to the qualities he has identified.

If you have difficulty writing concluding paragraphs, it may be because you do not include the evaluative dimension in your thinking. Merely summarizing the main points of a paper does not produce effective conclusions. To see the difference evaluative thinking can make in concluding paragraphs, consider the following. Here is the conclusion to the first draft of Robert Johnson's "The Death of a Friend":

```
    A few weeks after this day, city officials decided
to fill in the hole and build a gradually sloped bot-
tom. City workers now continually check the bottom and
fill in any holes that start to form to make sure that
no one else drowns. There were many reasons for offi-
cials to do this because there were several close
swimming accidents. There were also reports on the
park detailing the possible dangers. The lack of public
interest also delayed the renewal, but there was some
support to pressure officials into fixing the park but
just not enough. It wasn't until there was a death
that officials got off their bureaucratic butts and
fixed the park. This is a very bad excuse to me to do
what is right especially when it was the death of one
of my best friends.
```

This paragraph summarizes some of the history of reports on the park's dangers, and reminds readers that lack of attention to these dangers led to the friend's death. It does not, however, offer much evaluative commentary on the situation. Here the last part of the revised version:

Paragraphs

> According to city officials, since there had not
> been any fatalities and only a few minor swimming
> problems, there wasn't any serious danger. However,
> turning your back on a problem does not make it go
> away. This was only the first part of man's apathy
> toward the problem. Lack of public interest was the
> second part. It is true that a few letters were written
> to the paper concerning the problem, but that is as
> far as it went. If the public had taken an active role
> in this problem, then city officials would have moved
> more quickly to solve it. The other causes did lead to
> Steve's death, but the public and city officials'
> apathetic views of the problem was the main cause. If
> they had tried to fix the problem, then he wouldn't
> have died.

This revision summarizes a number of events discussed earlier in the paper, but it goes beyond summary to evaluate by assigning blame.

Revising Paragraphs

The paragraphs you write will fall into these four categories—introductory, transitional, topical, and concluding. Just as strategies of development rarely operate in isolation from one another, so you will frequently write paragraphs that are a combination of these four categories. Many of your topical paragraphs will include introductory elements; your transitional paragraphs will contain conclusions; and so on. However, no matter what combinations your paragraphs use, the time to revise them is after you have written a draft and reread the whole.

REVISING FOR PURPOSE

When you are revising your own paragraphs the issue of intentions or purpose becomes central. Often, as Chapter 9 pointed out, you can discern more about your purpose by asking questions about a draft. The same applies to revising paragraphs because paragraphs are miniatures of longer pieces of writing. The process of asking these questions will help you discover how to plan your paragraphs.

1. What question does this paragraph try to answer?
2. What is the answer to this question? Respond by completing this sentence: "In this paragraph the writer (asserts) (maintains) (argues) that . . ."
3. What are the major reasons supporting this assertion? Respond by completing this sentence: "To support this statement, the author makes the following points . . ."

263

The Structure of Writing

4. What conclusions does the author draw? Respond by completing this sentence: "The author concludes..."

The same questions that can be asked about a whole draft can also be applied to paragraphs. For paragraphs, the answer to the first question has two parts. One is to describe the subject matter of the paragraph, much as you would describe the subject matter of a longer piece of writing. The second part is to explain the paragraph's function in the writing. Each of the four types of paragraphs, introductory, transitional, topical, and concluding, serves a different function. Knowing a paragraph's function as well as the questions it attempts to answer can make easier your response to the second question because you can interpret the question in light of how the paragraph fits into the whole piece. Usually a paragraph contains some reasons or points to support its major assertion, but because paragraphs are parts of larger wholes, these points may extend into the following paragraphs, and so it may not always be easy to answer the third question. This is particularly true of topical paragraphs, which are the most common in extended prose. Likewise, not all paragraphs come to a conclusion, as concluding paragraphs do, but the fourth question is valuable because all paragraphs provide a kind of closure, and this closure can often include a conclusion.

Here is the first draft of a paragraph in a physics paper:

```
                        Flight

    (1) I find it incredibly strange and amazing that
we, in almost one lifetime, have conquered the barrier
of powered flight, human-powered flight, jet-powered
flight, supersonic flight, and space flight. (2) How
lucky we are at this time to benefit from the recent
opening of a new frontier and to experience the advan-
tages of a highly sophisticated form of that discovery
in just eighty years. (3) Why was this accomplished
during our existence and not two hundred years ago or
in the future? (4) How much further are we to go and
how much faster? (5) At the rate we are improving our
knowledge and innovative capabilities, we should wit-
ness some very incredible things in aviation in the
very near future. (6) My study consists of the basic
principles of flight, answering the question "What
makes lift?" (7) This study also deals with the scien-
tists who made human flight possible and how they came
to their discoveries, and the differences between
their motives and their methods. (8) In particular, I
shall compare and contrast the styles and beliefs of
Leonardo da Vinci and the Wright brothers, three people
```

Paragraphs

who had a strong belief that man was due to conquer the sky.

The student who wrote this paragraph answered the questions about the general purpose of the paragraph this way:

1. This introductory paragraph answers questions about the subject of the paper. In particular, it tries to answer questions about principles of flight and about the convergence of history that made human flight possible.
2. The writer asserts that Leonardo da Vinci and the Wright brothers were important figures in the development of human flight and that their differing motives and methods contributed to understanding what makes lift. (The trouble is I'm trying to talk about principles of flight at the same time.)
3. To support this thesis, the author cites the rapid change that has occurred in the past eighty years. He also claims that the contrasting styles and beliefs of Leonardo and the Wright brothers contributed to conquering the sky. (Somehow the rapid changes do not seem to fit with what I'm saying about Leonardo and the Wright brothers.)
4. The author concludes that Leonardo and the Wright brothers contributed directly to the rapid developments in human flight. (But I'm not really saying that here.)

By answering these questions about the introductory paragraph, the author of this paper realized that he needed to shift his emphasis away from the issue of new frontiers and focus on the contrasting styles and beliefs of the three figures under investigation. In addition, he found that his study was not so much an examination of the principles of flight as it was an investigation of how the work of Leonardo and the Wright brothers contributed to making the principles of flight accessible to humans.

This student found, as many writers do, that his first draft paragraph was unsatisfactory from a reader's point of view because it did not make clear the questions it raised or answers it provided. By asking the four purpose questions about his paragraph, the student was able to begin to see the location of the difficulties in the paragraph. Then he was able to write this revision:

During the past eighty years humans have opened the frontier of flight. We have moved past the barrier

The Structure of Writing

of powered flight to human-powered flight, jet-powered flight, supersonic flight, and space flight. And we can look forward to some even more incredible aviation advances in the very near future. The work of three scientists helped make these advances possible. The three, Leonardo da Vinci and the two Wright brothers, had different motives and used different methods, but all made discoveries which helped humans understand the basic principles of flight. This study deals with scientists who made human flight possible and explains how they came to their discoveries.

EXERCISE

This paragraph appeared later in the first draft of "Flight." Apply the four purpose questions to it in order to suggest how it might be revised.

Leonardo da Vinci's view of science foreshadowed the critical/constructive methods of modern times. He proceeded step by step. Through his senses he experienced the world around him as a starting point, then he contemplated and reasoned about what would be more important than his senses because of biases he knew he had. Then he would compare these reasonings with laws or experiences that he already had, and set them up in logical sequence like a mathematical proposition and then finally he would test these laws by experiment. Leonardo's purpose for acquiring knowledge was that he wished to obtain the ability to produce creations of his own and answer previously unsolvable questions. He was opposed to philosophical systems founded solely on words.

Write a revision of this paragraph.

Revising for Organization

Deciding on the purpose of a paragraph can help you revise it, but this is not the only strategy for revising paragraphs. Another important factor is organization. Strategies of organization for whole papers apply equally well to paragraphs: Paragraphs can be organized around comparison, if-then plans, description, statement-response, and time order. If you return to the first draft

Paragraphs

of "Flight," you will see that several strategies of organization have been employed. The first sentence provides a statement and description by listing the many forms of flight that have been developed in recent years. The second sentence responds to the statement of the first sentence by commenting on our good fortune during the past eighty years. The next three compare the present with the past and the future. The "my study" sentence and the one following describe the contents of the paper, and the final sentence continues the description at a more concrete level, by specifying the nature of the study.

Although there is an organizational plan in this first draft, it needs revision because the author appears to move randomly from one organizational strategy to another. When you compare this first draft with the revised version of "Flight," you can see how revision of organization improves the paragraph. Here the first three sentences are organized around the time order of the history and future of aviation. The next sentence makes a statement about the scientists responsible for aviation, and the following sentence responds to this statement by providing details in the form of a comparison. The final sentence of the paragraph describes the issues raised in this paragraph and connects them to the paper that follows.

Although you can undoubtedly see that the revised paragraph is superior in organization, you may wonder how to revise the organization of your own paragraphs. You can begin by assessing the organization of the paragraphs in your drafts. One way to evaluate strategies of organization in paragraphs is to consider the management of old and new information within the paragraph. The old information is the "given," what the reader already knows, and the new is what the reader learns from continuing. To see the difference that the placement of old and new information can cause, return to the first draft of "Flight." The sixth sentence (My study consists . . .) introduces new information that has little relationship to what has gone before. Previous sentences have focused on the benefits of aviation development, and suddenly the principles of flight emerge in this sentence. The following sentence returns to a more historical approach to aviation but introduces new information on the scientists responsible for the development of aviation. The eighth and ninth sentences demonstrate that there are times when new information can precede old; it would be impossible to write without occasionally introducing new information. However, the information in these sentences builds on the old information of the sentences that discuss aviation history. In contrast, the new information of the seventh sentence moves in a completely different direction and illustrates how inappropriate new information can distract the reader.

EXERCISE

Revise the following paragraphs so that old information precedes new:

(1) In *My Antonia,* instead of doing everything that is expected of her, Antonia does what she feels like doing. (2) A poet once said, "If marriages are made in heaven, they should be happier." (3) Many twentieth-century writers

focus on that maxim. (4) Willa Cather's heroine has the same degree of freedom that men have, no more, no less. (5) Authors show how destructive literary roles can be when used in real life. (6) Feminist literature is on the rise.

(1) We know cave dwellers had some communication, although it may not have been vocal. (2) All human societies have some kind of communication software: alphabets, symbols. (3) It's only the more advanced, industrial and aesthetically developed societies where you find communication hardware such as television, the press, and radio. (4) We believe cave paintings tell stories of hunt, food, where to find places, and reproduction of animals. (5) Cave paintings dating back to 20,000 B.C. show deliberate efforts to communicate to neighbors and perhaps through time. (6) Pigments that last over twenty thousand years were used. (7) Paintings were done in caves where atmosphere wouldn't change them through erosion. (8) About 2500 B.C. the Egyptians developed papyrus, a paperlike substance made of reeds. (9) It was not until 3500 B.C. that useful symbols of communication appeared when the Mesopotamians and Egyptians used hieroglyphics for pictographic writing. (10) Papyrus replaced clay tablets.

(1) The Catholic monasteries in Europe became the sole source of learning. (2) They had a monopoly. (3) Gutenberg published the Bible. (4) The Chinese developed moveable type printing in A.D. 1200. (5) The type was of wooden blocks and were not very durable. (6) The first metal type used on nonoriental type was in A.D. 1445 when Johann Gutenberg developed a press for the Arabic alphabet. (7) The first works published were of a religious rather than scientific nature. (8) Four to five million books were published and distributed to common people.

Another issue to consider in organization of sentences within paragraphs is *emphasis through placement*. The first sentence in a paragraph receives special attention because the reader's eye, fresh from the rest of the indentation space, focuses on the new line with special intensity. Likewise, the final sentence of a paragraph provides closure, thereby attracting special attention from the reader. Accordingly, sentences that appear first or last in a paragraph receive special emphasis.

Reread the first and second drafts of "Flight" to see how they do or do not use sentence placement for emphasis. As you read the first sentence of the first draft, you will see that it introduces the idea of amazement which distracts readers from the point about recent progress. The remainder of the paragraph focuses on the causes of this progress, not the strangeness of it, and so words like *strange* and *amazing* seem out of place. The second version improves on this by focusing on the central topic of aviation progress during the past eighty years.

The final sentences of both drafts could be described as topic sentences because they provide the most complete statement of what the paragraphs are about. The second one improves on the first because it makes an even more concise statement of the paragraph's purpose and the paper as a whole. The topic sentence of any paragraph states the main point of the paragraph. Some-

Paragraphs

times the topic sentence appears at the beginning of a paragraph; sometimes, as in this case, it appears at the end; and sometimes a paragraph has no explicit topic sentence, even though the paragraph is clearly organized around a single idea.

EXERCISE

Read the following paragraph and note where placement could enhance emphasis. Then write a revision that uses placement for effective emphasis.

> At this point the Wright Brothers put modern technology to work. They recognized the unsolved problems as many-faceted ones and attacked them one by one. As they grew close to the answer they began to understand the physical properties involved. Once they understood these properties, their only task was to construct an aircraft to the specification required by these principles. The Wright brothers were very fortunate that at the time they were working on this venture modern technology enhanced their ability to carry out their tests and experiments. Construction was made easier because of tools like a gas-powered lathe and a wind tunnel to test the efficiency of wing shape. I look at the Wright brothers as the mechanics of flight, not the inventors. They pieced together the missing parts and combined them with the information from other sources.

REVISING FOR COHESION

Cohesion in paragraphs, like cohesion in larger sections of writing, refers to the capacity of writing to stick together. The devices that create cohesion in whole papers work equally well in paragraphs; cohesive ties of reference and conjunction along with substitution create links between and within sentences of paragraphs. As is true for longer passages, simply using cohesive ties does not create cohesion in paragraphs. To illustrate this statement, return to the first verison of "Flight." The "we should witness . . ." of the fifth sentence and the "my study . . ." of the sixth sentence do not cohere, even though both phrases contain personal pronouns. The shift from *we* to *my* signals a problem in this section, as do the general comments about aviation that move with no warning to the statement about the principles of flight. However, in the revised version of this "Flight" paragraph, this problem has been removed.

EXERCISE

To see reference at work, return to the revised version of "Flight," and list the pronouns and comparatives that unite the paragraphs.

You may recall that the forms of conjunction that aid cohesion include words that indicate addition, opposition, causation, and temporal relationships. Punctuation also signals conjunction, although false cohesion can be created

The Structure of Writing

with conjunction. For an example, reread "Flight," and note the forms of conjunction that appear there. The "also" that follows "this study" suggests a relationship between investigating the principles of lift and the scientists who made human flight possible, but the two ideas have no evident relationship to each other.

Another form of cohesion is created by substitution, in which one word takes the place of another. The following paragraph from "Flight" demonstrates how substitution operates:

```
    What Leonardo finally ended with was a promise to
make history by constructing a "great bird." His suc-
cess or failure cannot be graded because there were no
witnesses to the testing of his flying machine. The
future use of his notations by others was the real
test. The design of Otto Liliethal's one-man glider
was copied almost exactly from Leonardo's notebook
approximately four hundred years later. The German
glider pioneer was successful in over two thousand
flights down a hill; yet he was still not recognized
as a sky conquerer when he was killed in 1896.
```

The term "flying machine" is substituted for "great bird"; "notebook" is substituted for "notations"; "sky conquerer" is substituted for "glider pioneer"; and "four hundred years later" is substituted for "future use." This process of substitution allows the author to vary the language of the paragraph and at the same time ensure coherence. As is true with other cohesive devices, substitution does not always help writing stick together—for substitution to work, the terms must be clearly interchangeable. If they are not, the substitution will appear to introduce a new and unrelated idea.

EXERCISE

Read the following paragraph, and list all the substitutions that add to its coherence.

```
    Leonardo's fascination with flight went back to
his childhood. He once wrote in his notebook that he
must have been predestined to write about flight be-
cause of his earliest recollections of his life. He
dreamed that a large bird called Kite flew down to his
cradle and struck him several times with his tail.
Because of this dream, Leonardo had a fascination with
birds; in pity he often purchased the caged creatures
```

and set them free. Their flight was a continuous source
of inspiration to him. He loved to watch these winged
wonders soar and flap their wings.

This examination of cohesive ties in "Flight" shows that simply using words that signal cohesion will not result in coherent paragraphs. Cohesion depends on the paragraph's general plan and organization, the kinds of issues covered by asking the four purpose questions, and the strategies of arrangement used within the paragraph. When the general plan and arrangement of a paragraph are in order, cohesive ties can highlight the parts.

REVISING FOR STYLE

Paragraphs, like longer pieces of writing, have a characteristic style, which, as in longer selections of writing, results from many factors. Choices regarding purpose, arrangement, and coherence all contribute to style. Perhaps the best way to describe style in paragraphs is in terms of *texture*. As you have seen, there is no one best strategy for arrangement, and a combination of strategies is often used in a single paragraph. This combination of organizing according to if-then plans, description, comparison, response, and time order all contribute to texture in a paragraph. The lexical variety provided by cohesive ties that refer and connect within and between sentences also contribute to a paragraph's texture. Likewise, the level of formality, choices of diction, and levels of abstraction all add to the "feel" that we describe as texture. Just as it is important to maintain a consistent style throughout a whole piece of writing, so it is important to hold the style constant within paragraphs. The effect of a shifting style is evident in this paragraph:

        Leonardo utilized birds to study flight in nature.
He tickled his brain with the question of what happens
to air when a bird flaps its wings. This pondering led
to drawings of the parachute, aerial screw (precursor
to the modern-day helicopter), the hydrometer, and a
wind force and direction indicator. Leonardo had few
clues to go on except his hunches.

By shifting from language such as *utilized, pondering,* and *precursor* to *tickled his brain* and *hunches,* the author gives this paragraph a very uneven style. These abrupt shifts do not seem to be planned or conscious; rather, they seem accidental and careless. As a result, readers find themselves uncertain about the author's attitude toward the subject and the audience.

The Structure of Writing

EXERCISE

Try rewriting the preceding paragraph to give it a consistent style. Or revise a paragraph of your own that seems to have an uneven style.

Often it is easier to attend to issues of style at the paragraph level than for the whole essay. Such things as clichés, jargon, euphemisms, pretentious language, and connotations of words are usually easier to spot when you consider one paragraph at a time.

A mixture of abstract and concrete language improves the tone of a paragraph, and it can also contribute to its actual development. Some paragraphs move from a relatively abstract statement to a series of more concrete ones that support it, and others do the reverse. As is true with larger selections of writing, paragraphs benefit from a variety of levels of generality, ranging from the concrete to the abstract.

Consider the following:

> The principle of lift is a difference of pressure on two sides of the same surface. If the surface is a wing, the relative pressure on the bottom side of the wing must be great enough to push the weight of the wing and attached body upward. You can think of lift as a mechanical crane raising an aircraft by its wings with a harness. The force needed to produce this lift is the same no matter how you think of it, and it is equal to the mass of the aircraft times the vertical acceleration $F - MA$).

This paragraph begins with the relatively abstract statement about lift in terms of pressure and moves toward an increasingly concrete description of the principle, that is, from abstract to concrete descriptions of life. But this pattern could be reversed for an equally effective result.

> Think of an aircraft with a harness on its wings attached to a mechanical crane. As the crane moves upward, the aircraft rises in the air. The force (in this case the crane) that raises the aircraft is called lift. For the aircraft to lift, the pressure on the bottom side of the wing must be greater than on the top side. The principle of lift is a difference of pressure on two sides of the same surface.

Although the language has been changed slightly, this paragraph says essentially the same thing as the preceding one does, but its pattern of development is just the opposite. Here we begin with a very concrete statement and move toward the concluding abstract statement about lift.

EXERCISE

The following paragraph follows an abstract-to-concrete pattern of development. After reading it carefully, write a revision that moves from the concrete to the abstract.

Paragraphs

    The faster that air particles move over a surface, relative to other air velocities over the same body, the lower the pressure will be. This principle, discovered by Daniel Bernoulli over two hundred years ago explains the cambered shape of both natural and manufactured wings. As air approaches the wing, the leading edge severs the air and forces some of the air to travel over the wing and some to travel under it. Because the distance on the top of the wing is longer, an air particle must travel at a faster speed if it is to arrive at the trailing edge of the wing at the same time that an air particle from underneath does.

Briefly explain how a clear statement of purpose, organization, cohesive ties, and style are achieved in this paragraph.

    Grammar is a piano I play by ear, since I seem to have been out of school the year the rules were mentioned. All I know about grammar is its infinite power. To shift the structure of a sentence alters the meaning of that sentence, as definitely and inflexibly as the position of a camera alters the meaning of the object photographed. Many people know about camera-angles now, but not so many know about sentences. The arrangement of the words matters, and the arrangement you want can be found in the picture in your mind. The picture dictates the arrangement. The picture dictates whether this will be a sentence with or without clauses, a sentence that ends hard or a dying-fall sentence, long or short, active or passive. The picture tells you how to arrange the words and the arrangement of the words tells you, or tells me, what's going on in the picture.

    —Joan Didion, *The Writer on Her Work*

Copyright © Tony Ganba, The National Audubon Society Collection/Photo Researchers, Inc.

Chapter Eleven

Sentences

Perspective on Sentences

In an essay entitled "The Historian As Artist," Barbara Tuchman makes this claim about sentences:

> When it comes to language, nothing is more satisfying than to write a good sentence. It is not fun to write lumpishly, dully, in prose the reader must plod through like wet sand. But it is a pleasure to achieve, if one can, a clear running prose that is simple yet full of surprises. This does not just happen. It requires skill, hard work, a good ear, and continued practice, as much as it takes Heifetz to play the violin. The goals, as I have said, are clarity, interest, and aesthetic pleasure.
>
> —*Practicing History*

One of the premises of Tuchman's claim is that sentences are the fundamental unit in writing. Revising paragraphs and longer sections of writing is important, but ultimately the quality of your writing depends on your sentences. The strengths and weaknesses of your sentences will shape the quality of your writing generally, and so you will want to give serious attention to sentences as you revise. You may, at first, think it redundant to consider sentences in revising; after all, you write sentences in your first drafts. However, the "good" sentence that Tuchman describes rarely appears in the first draft. Usually it takes sentence revising to transform the lumpish language of a draft into the clear running prose of a finished product. This chapter suggests strategies for revising sentences, with Tuchman's three goals of clarity, interest, and aesthetic pleasure in mind. As is true for revision in general, sentence revision proceeds on several levels.

As Joan Didion suggested, it is possible to write well without knowing any grammatical terminology, and so I have kept technical language to a minimum in this chapter. If you do not want to be limited to playing the grammar piano by ear and/or if you see unfamiliar terms, you may wish to turn to Chapter

The Structure of Writing

15. But whether or not you use technical terminology, you probably have a good sense of "sentenceness." As a demonstration, consider the following:

   1. although the consequences have not yet been assessed.
   2. stop.
   3. having begun the process.
   4. the data are incomplete.

EXERCISE

Which of the preceding phrases are complete sentences? How do you know?

Combining Sentences

You probably identified the groups of words after numbers two and four as sentences in the preceding exercise. Even if you do not normally use terms such as subject and predicate, your instinctive sentence sense helps you identify groups of words that contain both. There are, of course, single word sentences such as "Stop," "Yes," and "Perhaps," but these occur only occasionally, and they contain an implied subject and predicate (You stop doing that; Yes I will; Perhaps it will rain.) In their more common form, sentences contain a subject and predicate, as in a group of words such as:

Subject *Predicate*
Dogs bite.

The predicate provides information about the subject, a noun or noun substitute. A complete predicate includes all complements or modifiers such as:

Subject   *Predicate*
Frank does not drink.

Subject   *Predicate*
The data are incomplete.

MODIFICATION

Sentences composed of subject and predicate alone can be effective occasionally, but too many of them lead to choppy reading. Combining sentences through modification can incorporate more information as it leads to smoother reading. Modification enables you to build sentences by adding to, limiting, or qualifying what they contain. In so doing, you can make your meanings more clear. One form of modification is to add adjectives to nouns, as in:

Mozarella is a cheese.
The cheese is Italian.

Sentences

These two sentences can be combined to form:

Mozarella is an Italian cheese.

EXERCISE

Combine the following pairs of sentences:

Computers represent a technology.
The technology is recent.

A woman sits on the front porch.
The woman is tired.

Similarly, verbs can be modified with adverbs through sentence combining.

The fire burned.
The burning was rapid.

These can be combined to:

The fire burned *rapidly*.

EXERCISE

Combine the following pairs of sentences:

The man ate.
The eating was ravenous.

Students waved their arms.
The waving was strenous.

These combinations are relatively simple, but adjective and adverb phrases can be used to create more complex combinations. Adjective and adverb phrases can modify both nouns and verbs. The following demonstrates a noun-adjective phrase combination.

New York is a city.
The city has 8 million residents.
The residents come from all over the world.

New York is a city with over 8 million residents from all parts of the world.

Similarly, adverb phrases can be added to verbs, as in this example:

The duck paddled.
The paddling was on Sylvan Lake.
The waters of Sylvan Lake were dark.
The waters of Sylvan Lake were smooth.

277

The Structure of Writing

The duck paddled *on the smooth dark waters of Sylvan Lake*.

When you combine sentences, the modification can appear anywhere in a sentence—at the beginning, in the middle, or at the end. And it can be used in more than one place. Wherever it appears, sentence modification answers readers' questions about the subject and predicate.

Running along the dusty road next to the car, the dog barked *furiously*.

Here modifiers tell *where* the dog was as well as *how* he barked.

Great teachers *like John Dewey and Louise Rosenblatt* change education significantly for the better.

EXERCISE

Combine the following groups of sentences by creating adjective and adverb phrases that modify the subject and predicate.

1. The teacher stands alone.
   The teacher stands in the center of the classroom.
   The teacher is harried.
   The teacher is surrounded by students.
   The students are clamoring.
   The students are clamoring for the teacher's attention.
2. Nebraska's horizon has many grain elevators.
   Many farms are located in the state.
   Some farms are owned by families.
   Some farms are owned by corporations.
   The land is generally flat.
   Nebraska produces corn and hay.

Combining other people's sentences through modification can help you learn new patterns for shaping sentences, but the real goal is to develop your own modifications.

EXERCISE

Build upon each of the following sentences by adding modification.

1. The waiter brought our coffee.
2. Skydiving can be dangerous.
3. John F. Kennedy was assassinated.
4. The subway stopped.
5. The students stood in the lobby.

Sentences

COORDINATION

When you coordinate your wardrobe, you combine different parts to make an outfit. Similarly, sentences can be combined through coordination to make a more inclusive whole. Similar elements—words, phrases, or clauses—can be joined into pairs or a series through coordination. Here is an example:

> Copying a text word-for-word is one form of plagiarism. Appropriating ideas is another.

These two sentences can be combined through coordination to:

> Copying a text word for word and appropriating ideas are both forms of plagiarism.

When you combine two independent clauses into a single sentence, the result is a *compound sentence,* as in the following example.

> Many of the onlookers covered their eyes as the plane crashed. The television crew kept running the cameras until it hit the ground.

These two sentences can be combined to:

> Many of the onlookers covered their eyes as the plane crashed, but the television crew kept running the cameras until it hit the ground.

In combining sentences through coordination, *parallel structure* must be maintained. This means putting all coordinate elements in the same form, as in:

> She liked to eat, to dance, and to spend her parents' money. The repetition of the "to" form gives this sentence parallel structure, but this version lacks it:

> She liked to eat, to dance, and spending her parents' money.

The combination of "to" forms with an "ing" form, as in "spending" breaks the parallel structure.

Parallel structure can take several forms. These include:

Parallel predicates: The kite *soared into the air, dipped as it hit an air pocket, twisted in the wind,* and *crashed to the ground.*

A series of nouns followed by a parallel series of adjectives: Automobile manufacturers produce *cars, jeeps and trucks* to suit every *aesthetic, mechanical, and physical* need of drivers.

A series of prepositional phrases: In sky gliding class we learned *to read wind patterns, to manipulate the rudder,* and *to land safely in an open field.*

A series of participial phrases: I could see her golden retriever *splashing into puddles, chasing ducks, and licking small children* as he loped across the park.

EXERCISE

Combine the following groups of sentences through coordination, being sure to maintain parallel structure.

The Structure of Writing

1. My parents taught me to keep promises. They also taught me money management.
2. She stood up from the table. Then she began picking up the plates and carrying them into the kitchen. At last she began to wash the dishes.
3. A great band played at last Saturday's party. Everyone was there. The food was delicious.
4. Now write a sentence of your own that combines a series of prepositional phrases.

Subordination

The word *subordinate* means of less importance, and combining sentences through subordination indicates to readers which parts of the sentence are more or less important. In some cases, combining sentences through subordination will create complex sentences consisting of an independent and dependent clause. The *independent clause* will contain the main or most important ideas, and the less important information will appear in the subordinate or *dependent clause*. The following examples illustrate how this type of sentence combining works:

He had spent the last of the family fortune.
His high living did not diminish significantly.

These two sentences can be combined by using the subordinating conjunction "although":

Dependent Clause   *Independent Clause*
Although he had spent the last of the family fortune, his high living did not diminish significantly.

Similarly, these sentences can be combined:

We left for the airport two hours early.
It was snowing hard.

Independent Clause   *Dependent Clause*
We left for the airport two hours early because it was snowing hard.

Subordinating conjunctions enable you to combine simple sentences into complex ones. The list of these conjunctions includes:

after	if
although	since
before	until
because	when

Sentence combining through subordination does not always create complex sentences. Sometimes it is more effective to embed one sentence as a phrase

Sentences

in another. This kind of subordination enables you to include much more information in one sentence. While simple sentences have their place, one measure of maturity in writing is the amount of information conveyed by a single sentence. Learning to combine several simple sentences through various patterns of subordination can lead, then, to more mature writing. Here is an example of how such combination can occur:

> Last week I took the train into the city.
> My sister went with me.
> We spent the day in the public library.
> We were looking for information on our family's geneology.
> We found records dating back to 1642.

> Last week my sister and I took the train into the city where we spent the day in the public library looking for family geneology information and found records dating back to 1642.

Notice that the single sentence contains 33 words, as opposed to the 38 words in the four short sentences, but more important than the economy of language is the density of the longer sentence. It feels more substantial because of the amount of information embedded in it and because words like "where" and "and" clarify relationships between the parts.

EXERCISE

Use subordination to combine the following groups of sentences.

1. We bought fresh fish at the market.
   I had been hungry for ling cod with dill sauce.
   The fish was tender and juicy.
2. Fog surrounded the airport.
   Flights were delayed or cancelled.
   People stood in long lines in front of the ticket counters.
   Ticket agents looked harassed and anxious.
3. Karl Stevens was elected president of the student body.
   He won by 205 votes.
   Only 38 percent of all students voted.
   Eighty percent of all fraternity and sorority members voted.
4. The hull of the boat is green and shiny.
   It resembles the body of a whale.
   It looks like it should be in Marineland.
   It is on the shore.
   It looks like it is about to dive under the water.

Revising Sentences

Like whole drafts and paragraphs, sentences need revising. Even after sentences have been combined through modification, coordination, and subordination, they can profit from further revision. Some of your revisions may include

The Structure of Writing

sentence combining, but choices about individual sentences will be guided by the larger effects you seek in writing.

Revising For Clarity

Clarity is the first goal in revising sentences. This seems a rather modest goal until you start thinking of all the ways that sentences can go awry and fail to say what you intend. The following excerpts from student papers illustrate some obstacles to clarity:

Dangling Modifiers

> As teachers we need to provide affirmation of students' language. By acknowledging the existence and supporting the use of black English, the children will retain their cultural and personal identity.

This sentence is confusing because it seems to say that the children should acknowledge and support black English, but the preceding sentence has given that responsibility to teachers. This confusion results from what is usually called a *dangling modifier*. The adverb modifier "By acknowledging the existence and supporting the use of black English" should modify teachers' behavior, not children's, but because the teachers are not mentioned in the main clause of the sentence, the modifier is left to dangle and confuse the readers.

One way to make this sentence less confusing is to bring "teachers" into the main clause:

> By acknowledging the existence and supporting the use of black English, teachers can help children retain their cultural and personal identity.

Omitting the actual subject of a modifier from the main clause of a sentence causes many dangling modifiers, and as you revise sentences, you can prevent confusion by checking to see that the phrase modifiers are included in the main clauses.

> To me the most important thing about writing is that after writing a paper, the reader should clearly understand what exactly the writer was trying to point out or convey to him.

The confusion in this sentence hinges on the subject that follows "after writing a paper." As it stands, the sentence suggests that the reader is writing the paper. One way to change it:

> To me the most important thing about writing is that after reading a paper, the reader should clearly understand what exactly the writer was trying to point out or convey to him.

An alternative:

> To me the most important thing about writing is that afterward, the author should make sure the reader can understand clearly what the writing is trying to point out or convey.

Sentences

In either event, the goal of the revision is to keep the subject of the sentence constant throughout.

Dangling modifiers appear most frequently at the beginning of sentences, but sometimes they appear at the end as well. For example:

> The new tax law will never be ratified, being opposed by union leaders.

By coming after "ratified," the modifier "being opposed by union leaders" seems to introduce a new idea when it is actually directly related to the preceding clause. To make the sentence clear, we could make the connection between the two more explicit with a connecting word:

> Because it is opposed by union leaders, the new tax law will never be ratified.

or

> The new tax law will never be ratified because it is opposed by union leaders.

Or we could connect the two as short independent clauses:

> The new tax law will never be passed; it is opposed by union leaders.

As these examples demonstrate, dangling modifiers are not always impossibly confusing, but they make the reader stop and take a second look. At the very least, dangling modifiers do not adhere to the conventions of standard written English, which stipulate that modifiers pertain to the nouns or verbs closest to them. By avoiding dangling modifiers, you can do a better job of showing what you have learned.

EXERCISE

The following excerpt from a student paper contains sentences that are confusing because of dangling modifiers. Identify the unclear sentences, explain what is wrong with them, and revise them.

```
     (1) Stopping and looking back on my years of educa-
tion, it could be considered typical for a small
school. (2) The best place to start a summary is at
the beginning. (3) However, before I start, I'd better
explain the local situation and the way my school
system works. (4) Drawing students from two different
towns and their outlying districts, they lie in two
different counties. (5) From kindergarten through
grade 6 the Pacific County kids go to the Naselle
School complex, and the Sahkiakum County kids go to
the Rosberg School, looking forward to junior high at
Naselle. (6) The Naselle complex has a high school
```

wing and a junior high wing, standing apart from the elementary school.

(7) All students share some rooms, the cafeteria, for example. (8) Attending the school in 1982, there were 126 in the high school grades.

Misplaced Modifiers

Sand and gravel are also transported in mass quantities through the locks which are used for much of construction done in the area.

Here again a modifier creates confusion because the reader has no way of knowing whether "which are used for much construction" refers to the locks or the sand and gravel. The general sense of the sentence suggests that sand and gravel are the more likely choices, but the exact meaning remains uncertain. In the first example, the modifier appears at the beginning of the sentence and has an adverbial function, whereas here, it appears at the end of the sentence and functions as an adjective.

To make this sentence clearer, the modifier should be moved closer to the noun(s) it modifies:

Sand and gravel, which are used for much construction in the area, are also transported in mass quantities through the locks.

Unlike the first example, the sentence is not missing something in its main clause but simply needs to be rearranged to become more comprehensible.

EXERCISE

This excerpt from a student paper contains sentences that lack clarity because of misplaced modifiers. Identify the unclear sentences, explain what is wrong with them, and revise them.

(1) Before the field-training exercise, I had no idea what rappeling was which was in the fall. (2) The Field-Training Exercise (FTX) was required for all students enrolled in military science classes. (3) Rappeling means descending a cliff with a rope passed under one thigh, across the body and over the opposite shoulder which supports you. (4) A lot of people don't like heights and are afraid of rappeling. (5) I, on the contrary, like heights and enjoyed rappeling which some people find strange or sick. (6) The FTX was held

Sentences

on a mountain near Fort Lewis that our bus took us to
on Thursday afternoons.

Sentence Fragments

Although there were few exceptions to the insensitive instructors who intimidated me rather than encouraged me.

This is a sentence fragment because it lacks an independent clause. *Although* signals subordination or a dependent clause, but no main or independent clause follows it. In addition to representing a grammar fault, this sentence is confusing because it introduces an idea (insensitive instructors) without developing it. Frequently, sentence fragments create ambiguity because they fail to explain themselves completely. To clarify this sentence, add a main clause such as

I did find some supportive teachers, or I managed to get an education.

The task of the main clause is to explain the consequences of the idea expressed in the fragment.

If you are concerned about locating fragments in your own writing, one way to find them is through reading your writing aloud. In a sentence such as the one above, the subordinating conjunction *although* changes your intonation so that you end the clause on an unfinished note. Reading aloud cannot always, however, identify sentence fragments because we are so accustomed to fragments in oral language. Another alternative is to learn to "see" sentence fragments by becoming familiar with the sentence grammar in Chapter 15.

EXERCISE

Read the following excerpt and identify the sentence fragments in it. When you have found them, revise them for clarity.

(1) When I arrived at Ketchikan, I had a substitute teacher for two months. (2) One of two teachers I had for an entire year. (3) Students in my school came from all over the country, but I still felt like an outsider. (4) I decided to begin playing Dragons and Dungeons. (5) Because the game is too complicated to explain here. (6) Basically there are four character groups: clerics, fighters, magic-users, and thieves. (7) Alignments combine these groups. (8) Lawful or chaotic, good or evil, and neutral.

Unclear References

The ambiguity of this sentence derives from a shift in number; the plural *their* refers back to the singular *friend*. Although we assume that the friend is

The Structure of Writing

the one whose opinion is sought, the sentence leaves some doubt. The uncertainty can be removed in one of two ways:

I read the letter out loud to a friend, asking his opinion.

or

I read the letter out loud to friends, asking their opinion.

As I explained in Chapter 9, reference, particularly pronoun reference, creates cohesion in writing, but when the reference is unclear, confusion rather than cohesion will be the result. A good way to ensure clear reference in your writing is to do a special check of the pronouns as you revise.

EXERCISE

The following excerpt contains sentences that are confusing because of unclear reference. Identify them, explain what is unclear, and revise them.

(1) When I had trouble with the tractor, Mike encouraged me by sending me back out into the field. (2) In no more than an hour I felt I had control over it. (3) I realized that it takes confidence in a person to help a person with their job. (4) Now that I've become an expert in handling small tractors, I teach other people how to drive them. (5) Each person has a different approach to their driving. (6) When I teach them I let them do what's comfortable as long as it's safe, and I end up by giving them a test where you drive between the rows with a sprayer on the back.

Run-on Sentences. I find relatively few run-on sentences in my students' papers, but when they do occur, they obscure meaning, because one idea merges with another. Run-on sentences use conjunctions to connect thoughts, which should be separated into independent sentences:

```
    In high school I was asked to do some analysis,
and I had to read a story, and on the test I had to
point out what motivated the characters, and I couldn't
do it because I hadn't studied enough.
```

As you can see, this sentence is hard to follow because it does not give you any space for stopping and assessing what has gone before. You could improve it by dividing it into two sentences:

```
    In high school I had to do some analysis of a
story I read. The test that followed asked me to point
```

Sentences

```
out what motivated the characters, and I couldn't
because I hadn't studied enough.
```

An alternative revision is:

```
    In high school I had to analyze a story I read and
the test that followed asked me to point out what
motivated the characters. Because I hadn't studied
enough, I couldn't do it.
```

EXERCISE

Here are some run-on sentences for you to revise; try to do at least two different revisions for each.

1. We walked down the street and saw a clown on the corner and a crowd had gathered around him and the police were standing nearby watching.
2. The student who wants to get good grades must learn to manage time and she needs to think about establishing priorities for using her time so it will be spent productively and she should be sure she doesn't allow herself to get distracted.
3. I finally got the paper back and I had part of one day and a morning left to accomplish the last four steps and I had other assignments due, and so I ran into problems.

Fused Sentences. Fused sentences, like run-ons, merge several independent ideas. The difference is that fused sentences do not use conjunctions or punctuation to connect their independent clauses. A fused sentence is even less clear than a run-on, as you can see in this example:

   Parent dissatisfaction with public schools has led to the establishment of several private schools in this city among them are University Prep and Northside School.

One way to revise this sentence is

   Parent dissatisfaction with public schools has led to the establishment of several private schools in this city. Among them are University Prep and Northside School.

An alternative is

   Parent dissatisfaction with public schools has led to the establishment of several private schools in this city; among them are University Prep and Northside School.

The Structure of Writing

As you see, the semicolon can take the place of a conjunction and can serve equally well in revising fused sentences.

EXERCISE

Here are some fused sentences for you to revise with both conjunctions and punctuation.

1. Horses are not cars. I came to this conclusion about a year ago when I first started taking riding lessons.
2. It is little wonder that cars have gained such wide acceptance as people's conveyance of choice they do not leave smelly piles of burned up gasoline around, they don't turn a straw hat into a ragged beanie cap, and I've never seen a car that's tried to eject me out of the seat.
3. Eventually I learned that horses are not inanimate objects like scooters and bicycles they have personalities, bad days, and personal preferences just like people.

Comma Splices. As you revised run-on and fused sentences, you may have been tempted to insert commas between the independent clauses. To do this would create a comma splice or a comma fault. When commas are used between two independent clasues, they confuse the reader because they do not signal a strong enough stop between the two, as this example illustrates:

> The composition class was canceled at the last minute, because students were unable to fulfill the requirement, a number of them signed a written protest.

The two separate ideas presented here tend to blur together because nothing but the comma separates them; they would be clearer this way:

> The composition class was canceled at the last minute; because students were unable to fulfill the requirement, a number of them signed a written protest.

or this:

> The composition class was canceled at the last minute. Because students were unable to fulfill the requirement, a number of them signed a written protest.

EXERCISE

Revise these sentences to eliminate the confusion caused by comma splices.

1. People learn the quickest and forget the least when they have to figure something out for themselves, they also sometimes need a little help to get pointed in the right direction.
2. The heart of any learning experience is remembering what has been

Sentences

taught, both theory and practice, theory reminds me of wet clay that still needs a potter's hands before it can become something useful.
3. When a graduate is handed that much-coveted sheepskin, he's scared because he knows he has little practical experience, his real-world education is about to begin.

These features—dangling modifiers, misplaced modifiers, unclear references, run-on sentences, fused sentences, and comma splices—all detract from clarity in sentences, and as you revise, you will want to eliminate them. Of course, when you revise your own writing, the sentence problems will not be arranged according to type. Part of writing to show learning is recognizing the lack of clarity as it occurs in the midst of your prose. And by recognizing it, you can eliminate it as a problem for your reader.

EXERCISE

Read the following excerpt from a student paper, noting those sentences that seem unclear. Identify the type of problem in each, and revise it.

```
    (1) In looking back at my school experiences I
find a few key things that stick out in my mind, these
are my preparation for college, the validity of tests,
grading systems, and teaching consistency. (2) I find
these subjects to be the ones that have made the
biggest impact on my school experiences. (3) School
had never been challenging until I reached the univer-
sity last year. (4) In my thirteen previous years of
education I never felt anything I was assigned pushed
me to work hard and I became bored with most classes,
although some were interesting, and did just enough
work to get A's and B's. (5) Of course I did learn a
lot in school, but I feel that I could have learned
more if we covered the material deeper and at an in-
creased rate. (6) Upon arriving at the university last
year unprepared for the challenge I would face. (7) In
high school I neither developed my potential academi-
cally nor developed any study habits. (8) These two
points became very real when I received my first quar-
ter's grades at the university.
    (9) In my experience with classes I have found
that I fare better in classes with either laboratory
work or oral presentations than I do in classes that
require tests and papers. (10) I'm far better at ex-
pressing myself orally than I am at expressing myself
on paper when I can get feedback from the audience.
```

The Structure of Writing

(11) An example in which I showed I knew more than a test score showed was back in seventh grade where we took a test to find what level math class we should be placed in, I was placed in the middle. (12) But by the second semester I showed that the material we were going to study the next semester I already knew. (13) As a result I was placed in the high math class. (14) This showed me the fallacy of standardized tests which all have arbitrary cut-off points.

(15) The question I would like to pose is this: What makes the person who just makes the cut-off point any better than the person on the other side of the cut-off point? (16) The answer to me is "Nothing."

Revising for Variety

Perhaps *interesting* is not a word you usually associate with sentences; rather, you may think of sentences more in terms of *correctness* or *clarity*. Yet, as a reader you have no doubt noticed that some pieces of writing are more fun to read than others are. Of course, the subject matter influences your assessment of the writing, but the author's attention to quality of sentences also contributes to the pleasure you experience as a reader.

Variety makes sentences interesting. Consider this paragraph:

> I graduated last spring. I hope to attend law school next fall. I am using this year to get a second degree. I am also brushing up on neglected skills. I am particularly interested in working on my writing.

There are no problems in clarity here; we can understand exactly what the author is saying. However, it is a boring paragraph to read because every sentence begins with the same pattern, and there is very little variation from one sentence to another.

Sentence combining can transform the preceding paragraph into a somewhat more interesting one. There are a number of possibilities for changing it. The first two sentences can be united with a coordinating conjunction, the second two through subordination, and the last sentence tightened to eliminate extra words. The result might be

> I graduated last spring, and I hope to attend law school next fall. This year I am brushing up on ne-

Sentences

glected skills while I get a second degree. My writing needs work.

But if the author wanted to emphasize the second degree rather than the skills, the second sentence might read:

    This year I am getting a second degree while I brush up on neglected skills.

Another way to revise this paragraph is to connect the first two sentences through subordination and to use a coordinating conjunction with the second:

    When I graduated last spring, I decided to attend law school next fall. This year I am getting a second degree and brushing up on neglected skills. My writing needs work.

Another alternative is to attach the final sentence to the second sentence with a semicolon, as the writing is one of the skills that the author has presumably neglected:

    This year I am getting a second degree and brushing up on neglected skills; my writing needs work.

If the author wants to emphasize her hopes of attending law school, the paragraph might be revised to:

    Because I hope to attend law school next year, I am spending the year after graduation getting a second degree and brushing up on neglected skills. One of these skills is writing.

As you can see, the first four sentences can be combined into one complex sentence by including the fact of graduation in "the year after graduation."

But if the author were more interested in writing skills, the emphasis of this paragraph could be shifted accordingly:

The Structure of Writing

> Because I want to work on neglected skills such as writing, I am spending this year after graduation on a second degree before I start law school in the fall.

Or if the author wanted to give more attention to her second degree, she might revise it in this way:

> Because I wanted a second degree after graduation last spring, I am spending this year brushing up on neglected skills, such as writing, before I start law school in the fall.

The meaning of the paragraph shifts slightly with each revision because the emphasis changes according to what is subordinated. However, each of these variations is more interesting than the original five-sentence paragraph. Deciding on which variation to use is determined by the surrounding paragraphs and sentences and by the author's intentions. For another illustration of this point, consider the following:

The computer has a capacity.
The capacity is for processing data.
The processing is rapid.
The processing makes the computer a tool.
The tool attracts the attention of people.
The people are in nearly every segment.
The segments are of life in America.

The forty-four words of these sentences can be reduced by at least half and, indeed, must be reduced in order to make mature-sounding, cohesive prose. One straightforward way of doing this is the following sentence:

> The computer's capacity for rapidly processing data makes it a tool that attracts the attention of people in nearly every segment of American life.

The sentence has no distinctive rhythm and might be called bland, but at least it is more interesting than the original.

The following version is two words shorter and emphasizes the computer's capacity, thereby strengthening the suggestion of a cause-effect relationship:

> With its capacity for rapid data processing, the computer is a tool attracting attention from people in nearly every segment of American life.

To emphasize the phenomenon of attention, the sentence might be written in this way:

> Attracting attention from people in nearly every segment of American life, the computer is a tool with the capacity for rapid data processing.

Sentences

To distribute the emphasis more equally, the sentence could begin with an absolute and end with a relative clause, leaving the central clause to make an assertion.

With people in nearly every segment of American life paying attention, the computer processes data rapidly, a capacity that makes it a noteworthy tool.

Finally, though other combinations are still possible, in one of most succinct versions, the sentence could achieve its most factually assertive tone:

A rapid data-processing tool, the computer attracts the attention of people throughout America.

E X E R C I S E

Here are other paragraphs that lack interest because there is so little variety in their sentences. Write at least four revisions of each paragraph to demonstrate how the sentences might be made more interesting.

(1) My formal education started on an air force base in Klamath Falls, Oregon. (2) The teacher had had two years of college eduction. (3) The mothers on the base chose her. (4) She was good with children. (5) I started school when I was nearly seven years old. (6) I was really afraid of school. (7) I skipped the first couple of hours of my first day. (8) My father caught me and sent me to school. (9) I came home loving it.

(1) Athletics are the essence of our national image. (2) I think this is a good thing. (3) Sports are intrinsic to Americans of all ages. (4) Almost everybody in America practices sports. (5) Pioneer people didn't have time for sports. (6) The pioneers had to brave harsh elements and endure physical hardships. (7) Today's Americans are free from most physical hardship. (8) Sports take the place of physical hardship. (9) Jogging replaces running away from grizzly bears. (10) Americans love athletics.

(1) Arthur Dimmsdale is one of the main characters in the *Scarlet Letter*. (2) Arthur Dimmsdale is a spineless hypocrite. (3) Dimmsdale is consumed with cowardice. (4) He refuses to reveal his relationship to Hester and Pearl. (5) He endures a life of deception for seven years. (6) Hawthorne reveals Dimmsdale's character through irony. (7) One irony is Dimmsdale's role as a minister. (8) Parishioners confess their sins to Dimmsdale. (9) Dimmsdale does not confess his own sin to anyone. (10) Dimmsdale wears a mask of respectability.

(1) Those of us who knew Mark were stunned. (2) Word of his death came unexpectedly. (3) The weekend turned into a nightmare. (4) We sat at home trying to understand our loss. (5) We were only beginning to realize the hurt. (6) It started when we entered school. (7) The building was quiet. (8) No one spoke or hurried. (9) The bell rang. (10) We were at our desks. (11) The teacher was late. (12) We squirmed as she opened her roll book. (13) She saw us watching her. (14) She put the book away. (15) There was only one empty seat.

The Structure of Writing

Limiting use of Passive Voice. The passive voice shifts the emphasis of the sentence from the action to the result of the action, and this can be a useful strategy for making some sentences interesting. But when the passive voice is used too often, it gives writing a heavy, plodding quality. Consider this paragraph by a student.

    Women of our generation are found to be working out of the home more than in it. This fact has been documented by a number of studies and has been found to represent a change in women's roles. No longer are women seen as only wives, mothers, and housekeepers. They are now recognized as part of the work force. Advertisements have been modified to appeal to working women, and magazines have been developed specifically to address this population. Despite all the changes, it has not yet been revealed whether there have been corresponding changes within the families of which working women are members.

Although there is some variation here in sentence pattern, this cannot be described as an interesting paragraph. It is boring, in part because every sentence is in the passive voice. The reader gets no sense of immediacy or energy from this passage; rather, the subject of women's position in society seems distant and unimportant. One way to make this group of sentences more interesting is to shift some of them into active voice:

    Women of our generation work out of the home more often than in it. A number of studies document this fact and describe it as a change in women's roles. No longer are women only wives, mothers, and housekeepers; they are also part of the work force. Some advertisements are written to appeal to working women, and new magazines specifically address this population. Despite all the changes, we do not yet know whether the families to which working women belong have changed correspondingly.

EXERCISE

Here is a paragraph containing many verbs in the passive voice. Revise it to make it more interesting.

The type of person seen most frequently in the library is the fellow slouched in a chair with a book on his chest. No studying is being done by this person, and few classes are attended. Sleeping during the day and partying at night are his usual activities. When exam time comes, he is seized by panic and becomes frantic trying to make up for lost time.

REVISING FOR SYMMETRY

If you rarely associate the word *interesting* with sentences, you also may have never thought of them in terms of *pleasure*. Language is the source of much of pleasure. Pleasure was as important as communication when you first learned language and probably continued into your childhood as you delighted in nursery rhymes, without having any idea who "Humpty Dumpty" was or why "Mistress Mary" was "quite contrary."

Even now you probably respond (unconsciously if not consciously) to the aesthetic quality of language as well as its meaning. You no doubt agree that "fourscore and seven years ago" *sounds* better than "eighty-seven years ago." Likewise, you may prefer the poetic language of the King James version of the Bible, even though other translations may communicate more accurately, and you may be able to think of sentences you have liked well enough to copy down or remember.

Just as you respond to aesthetic qualities in language, so will your readers. As Barbara Tuchman reminds us, aesthetic pleasure is one of the goals in writing sentences. Aesthetic quality may seem beside the point for writing in college or at work, but it is not. Writing to show what you have learned is comparable to making an argument on behalf of yourself, and the quality of prose can be a significant part of that argument. To be concerned with giving readers pleasure is like being a good gem cutter. A gem may have good weight and color, but it is the cutting that presents these features to their best advantages. Sentences that give no attention to aesthetic qualities resemble uncut or badly cut gems and cannot show your learning to its best advantage. The reader who can say of your writing, "This passage has all the main ideas and is a delight to read," will respond more favorably than will the reader who notes merely that all the main ideas are present.

The sources of pleasure in writing are various. Previously discussed elements such as organization, cohesion, style, clarity, and interest all contribute to the aesthetic quality of sentences, and there are additional ways to give luster to your sentences.

Keeping Verb Tenses Consistent. Verb tenses indicate time relationships, and in general you should avoid changing them within a piece of writing. Watch for tense shifts within sentences as you revise. It is particularly easy to do this while recounting events, which may be a carry-over from childhood sentences such as "He broke my ray gun and then he goes, 'It's not my fault.'" This tendency to move the conversation into the present tense often appears in relatively mature writing. For example:

The Structure of Writing

My friend walked into my room without knocking, just barges in and demands his stereo.

Although the meaning of this sentence is clear enough, and it cannot be faulted for being excessively boring, it gives the reader an unpleasant jolt to switch from *walked* to *barges in* and *demands*. Possible revision include

My friend walked into my room without knocking, just barged in and demanded his stereo.

or

My friend walks into my room without knocking, just barges in and demands his stereo.

EXERCISE

Revise these sentences to remove the abrupt shifts in verb tense.

1. When I finally got the paper back, I had part of a day and a morning to accomplish the last four steps, then I run into problems.
2. She walked down the aisle, automatically avoiding the place where his feet had always stuck out, before she realizes those feet will never be there again.
3. Thompson was impressed by the power of Carnot's theory, especially by the rationalization it affords, and he draws on Carnot for describing thermal processes.

Maintaining Parallel and Balanced Structure. Symmetry in many forms can give us pleasure, and symmetry in sentences is one source of satisfaction. Parallelism is a form of symmetry achieved by arranging words in grammatically equivalent patterns, and it creates rhythm in sentences. Parallelism can be created by pairing nouns with nouns, verbs with verbs, phrase with phrase, or clause with clause. Here are some examples of sentences with parallel structure:

Singing, sailing, and skiing occupy much of my extra time.
I came, I saw, I conquered
Up, over, and around the steeple the birds flew.

When portions of sentences are parallel, the sentences are often *balanced*, which means they echo one another. The following are examples of balanced sentences with parallel structure:

What lies before us and what lies behind us are tiny matters compared with what lies within us. (phrase with phrase)

Here I am at last, reading *War and Peace* and losing my place among all those sons of vitches. (verb with verb)

He wore a jacket, a tie, and acne ointment. (noun with noun)

Sentences

Do not be over-modest in your own cause, for there is a modesty that leads to sin, as well as a modesty that brings honour and favour. (phrase and phrase)

Alice sings like an angel, and Edith sings like a frog. (clause with clause)

These sentences please the reader because the balanced repetitions create and reward expectations. However, if a sentence fails to complete the parallel structure, it will not be pleasing. These rewritten versions demonstrate the problem:

What lies before us and what lies behind us are tiny matters compared with the things that lie within us.

Here I am at last, reading *War and Peace*, and I lose my place among all those sons of vitches.

He wore a jacket, a tie, and a layer of acne ointment on his face.

Alice sings like an angel, and Edith sings the way a frog does.

EXERCISE

Revise these sentences to create parallel structure.

1. Carnot's theory was founded on the concept that heat is a substance employing a complete cycle of operations, enters the body in a given amount, and at the end of the cycle it is completely removed.
2. Because I am struggling to establish professionalism in my own writing, I didn't like reading or to have around literature of inferior quality.
3. The final exam required us to demonstrate that we had absorbed the content of the course and writing in an acceptable style.

REVISING FOR ECONOMY

Another thing that makes prose lumpish and dull is the baggage of excess language, and in revising you should watch your opportunities to clear out deadwood from your sentences. Among the contributors to sentence deadwood are imprecise words, passive voice, excessive modification, and the use of nouns instead of verbs. The following selections show how eliminating these unnecessary words can increase your readers' pleasure:

The child's gift gave the old man a feeling of great delight.
The child's gift delighted the old man.

The disobedient student was subjected to disciplinary action.
The disobedient student was punished.

The people who completed all the tasks in the study were volunteers.
The subjects in the study were volunteers.

The Structure of Writing

The new insulation had an effect on our health.
The new insulation affected our health.

In each case the second sentence has a more *precise* word and thus is more fun to read. Sometimes, as in the case of "subjects," versus "people who completed all the tasks," the precise language derives from specialized vocabulary, but often it is simply a matter of selecting the most economical form of expression.

E X E R C I S E

Revise each of these sentences by substituting more precise words for those in italics.

1. New energy requirements are *creating heavy demands for* our generator.
2. *The woman in charge of seating people* left the restaurant in a huff.
3. The data *seem to imply* that the hypothesis is correct.

Consider these pairs of sentences:

By the second semester I showed that the material that we were going to study during the next term was material that I already knew.
By the second semester I showed that I already knew the material we were going to study next term.

Subjects that deal in facts that are cut and dried are much easier for me to deal with than subjects that require considerable interpretation.
I find factual subjects easier than interpretive ones.

The note was written in a hasty manner.
The note was written hastily.

She thought about him in a fleeting way.
She thought about him fleetingly.

He took the suggestion offered by his instructor.
He took his instructor's suggestion.

In each case the second version has eliminated the modifying phrases without changing the meaning of the sentence. As you can see, unnecessary modification is frequently introduced by words such as *which* and *that*. Your revising should try to eliminate as many of these phrases as possible. Another source of unnecessary modification is to use a phrase when a word will suffice, as in "in a hasty manner" versus "hastily."

E X E R C I S E

Revise these sentences to eliminate excessive modification.

1. In 1848 Thompson suggested an absolute scale of temperature that was based on Carnot's theory of the native power of heat.

Sentences

2. In order to begin writing I need to find a place in which I can be completely comfortable.
3. The writing to which I refer led me into familiar obstacles that I had to overcome by sheer force of will.

One of the best ways to discipline yourself to avoid excessive language is to read—or write—poetry. The economy of poetry exemplifies language from which all the excess has been removed. And because giving pleasure is one of poetry's chief goals, it also provides a model of offering aesthetic pleasure through words.

IMITATE

Another way to increase the aesthetic quality of your sentences is to imitate sentences you like. If you try to pattern consciously your own sentences after those that give you pleasure, you may increase your reader's sense of delight. Here are some my students have enjoyed imitating:

```
    Because baseball time is measured only in outs,
all you need to do is keep hitting, keep the rally
alive, and you succeed utterly; you suspend time; and
you remain forever young.

In the early morning on the lake, sitting in the stern
of the boat with his father rowing, he felt quite sure
that he would never die.

We begin to climb and my husband catches up with me
again, making one of the brief appearances, framed
memories, he specializes in: a crystal-clear image
enclosed by a blank wall.

In the deformed sedimentary Appalachians, the rock not
only had been compressed like a carpet shoved across a
floor but in places had been squeezed and shoved until
the folds tumbled forward into recumbent positions.
```

EXERCISE

Find four sentences that you enjoy reading, and try writing imitations of them.

Copyright © John R. Brownlie, The National Audubon Society Collection/Photo Researchers, Inc.

Chapter Twelve

Word Choice and Style in Writing

Studies of writers' revisions show that single words are among the elements most frequently changed. Although revision involves much more than simply substituting one word for another, word choice is an important part of writing, and finding exactly the "right" word for what you want to say can be difficult.

Denotation and Connotation

One way to find the "right" word is to consider both its denotation and connotation. Words, as you have probably learned by now, are slippery. They can say one thing and mean another. *Denotation* is the literal meaning of a word, the definition you will find in the dictionary, and *connotation* is what the word says or suggests. Frequently several words have similar denotation or literal meanings, and you will have to decide among them on the basis of their various connotations.

In revising "The Generic Essay," for example, Eva Godwin changed "gratifying" to "satisfying" in the following sentence:

```
    There is something satisfying about picking up a
six-pack of beer and knowing it is just what the label
says.
```

The author substituted the word *satisfying,* meaning "fulfilling needs, expectations, wishes or desires," for *gratifying* (which appeared in the first draft), meaning "giving pleasure or satisfaction." The literal meaning of the two words is very similar; *gratify* is listed as a synonym for *satisfy* in some dictionaries, just as satisfaction appears in the definition for *gratify*. Among the other words, the author might have chosen are

fulfilling—satisfying conditions, filling requirements.
pleasing—giving pleasure, being agreeable or satisfying.
delightful—giving great joy or pleasure.
contenting—desiring nothing more, satisfying.

As you can see, the denotation or dictionary meaning of all these words is very close, and so denotation alone could not guide her choice.

The connotation of *satisfying* seemed, the author explained, to come closest to her point about wanting labels to correspond more closely to their products. *Gratifying* seemed more sensual than she wanted to be, as did *fulfilling*. *Pleasing* seemed too bland, *delightful* was too exuberant, and *contenting* struck her as awkward.

These distinctions and the corresponding change in word choice are rather subtle, and choosing the "right" word is often difficult. Connotations of words are based on the feelings, attitudes, and associations that the word conveys, and these are not easy to define.

As was true for the author choosing between *satisfying* and *gratifying*, the overall purpose and content of the writing usually influence word choice and help writers sort out the denotations and connotations of their language. Sometimes, of course, the differences in connotation are much more obvious and can shape the style considerably. For example, the restaurant review that appears later in this chapter contains the phrase: "An owner who does all the cooking and is an assertive, omnipresent personality." If the author were writing a less flattering review, substituting *aggressive* for *assertive* and *overbearing* for *omnipresent* would change the style of the review dramatically.

EXERCISE

In each of the following passages, substitute the word in italics with a word that has a slightly different connotation but nearly the same denotation. Explain how each change affects the style of the passage.

1. After several minutes of *contemplation*, I gave up trying to decide between Cheerios and Grape Nuts and settled on some store-brand bran flakes.
2. Leo Buscaglia is a very *powerful* yet *intimate* speaker.
3. I don't know about everybody else, but I *hate* this time, mainly because I haven't the *foggiest* notion of what classes to take.
4. Confucianism, Taoism, and Legalism, three of these philosphies, took very different approaches to the *achievement of social order*.

Word Choice and Style in Writing

Abstract and Concrete Language

Another aid in finding the "right" word when writing is to distinguish between abstract and concrete language. *Abstract* words refer to feelings, states of being, ideas, theories, fields of inquiry, and other inclusive categories of things. *Concrete* words refer to what you can apprehend with your senses of touch, taste, smell, sight, and hearing. To understand the difference between the two, consider these two lists:

Abstract	*Concrete*
embarrassment	spider
exhaustion	meadow
awkwardness	golf ball
kindness	grape
terror	binoculars
fun	dime
nervousness	toast
humor	gravel
innocence	strawberry
fool	snail
trust	trout
sadness	milk
affection	Boeing 767
exaltation	eraser
witticism	VW bug

Most people who read these two lists respond by saying that the words on the right put vivid images in their heads, whereas those on the left are much more diffuse; they evoke lots of things, but nothing in particular. This demonstrates one of the differences between abstract and concrete words. Concrete words can help you convey specific details about real situations while abstract words enable discussions of ideas and theories.

To see this difference in practice, consider these two versions from the final paragraph of "The Generic Essay."

```
    In a way I get a secret thrill out of generic
products. I find peace, somehow, in their simplicity.
I know what is in the package, and you know what is in
the package. There is something gratifying about pick-
ing up a six-pack of beer and knowing it is just what
the label says.
```

In this version Eva relies on the abstract word "simplicity" to convey her point

The Structure of Writing

about generic products. This word carries the general meaning, but it does little to show exactly what Eva means. Now look at the revised version:

```
     I get a secret thrill out of generic products. I
wish we had generic everything. Shopping would become
so much easier if you didn't have to sort through
aisles of eye-catching packages and screaming slogans.
I wouldn't have to choose between Cheerios and Grape
Nuts. With their simple wrappers and "bare bones"
labeling, generics don't mislead consumers or make
false connections through association with nonrelated
items and made-up words. I know what is in the package,
you know what is in the package. There is something
satisfying about picking up a six-pack of beer and
knowing it is just what the label says.
```

The word "simple" appears in this version also, but here it is accompanied by concrete words such as "eye-catching packages," "Grape Nuts," "bare bones labeling," and six-pack of *beer*" that make Eva's meaning much more clear. Abstract words often require the reader to do more work than do concrete words. When you consider word choice, be sure you include enough concrete words to guide your readers. As one student put it, "Choosing the right word can turn a hard place into a rock."

Clichés

In casual writing here and elsewhere, you have probably noticed familiar phrases, the dead metaphors known as *clichés*. A cliché is a bit of tired and predictable language that resembles a precooked and packaged TV dinner rather than a zesty combination of freshly cooked food. TV dinners exist because people sometimes need them, and the same is true for clichés. Clichés are a kind of shorthand language to express complicated ideas, and they, like TV dinners, can save time. Generally, though, clichés give writing a monotonous style, and so you should avoid them if you can. An essential part of avoiding clichés is recognizing them.

The following list of phrases contains familiar clichés. Test your knowledge of clichés by attempting to fill in the blank at the end of each phrase. Your ability to supply the missing word will show that the phrase is one you have heard many times before and should avoid.

a tempest in a _____
at loose _____
at death's _____

bite off more than you can _____
by the sweat of one's _____

Word Choice and Style in Writing

a good time was had
  by _____
beat a hasty _____
bury the _____
clear as _____
the depths of _____
doomed to _____
a gala _____
none the worse for _____
abreast of the _____
the agony of _____
cool as a _____
the acid _____
beyond the shadow
  of a _____

few and far _____
in no uncertain _____
last but not _____
long arm of the _____
from the frying pan into
  the _____
straight and narrow _____
trials and _____
the other side of the _____
more than meets the _____
like a needle in a _____
from every walk of _____
from the bottom of
  my _____

Clichés can occasionally, however, enliven writing if they are given a new twist. Not long ago, I read this in a student paper: "She is a professor who is mindful of the absent." The student had taken the clichéd "absent-minded professor" and given it new life.

EXERCISE

List five clichés (do not draw on the preceding list) and rearrange one of them to give it new meaning.

Consider Audience

Without thinking about it, you probably do a considerable amount of style shifting in your daily language use. In recounting the same car accident to your parents, your roommate, and your instructor you probably choose very different words for each audience. With your parents you might choose words like "the other guy wasn't watching," "the car swerved," and "the police got there 20 minutes later." With your roommate you might select words like "this jerk was spaced out," "I did a wheelie," and "the cops took their own sweet time to get there." With an instructor you might say something like "the driver of the other car was distracted," "my vehicle went out of control," and "the police officers arrived about 20 minutes after the accident." In each case, word choice is guided by the audience. Similar considerations of audience can guide some word choices in writing.

JARGON

Jargon is the specialized langauge of occupations and fields of inquiry. To the car mechanic, words such as *differential, shoes,* and *king pin* have special meanings. For someone interested in mountain climbing, terms such as *screeing,*

305

The Structure of Writing

belay, and *cliffhanger* refer to specific techniques and equipment, and for someone in computer science, words such as *file, input,* and *document* specify computer activity.

When such language is used in its own sphere, it can make communication more effective, but when it is extended to other realms, it makes writing more difficult for the average reader to understand. This sentence illustrates the problem: "The car came screeing down the hill." The writer has appropriated the language of mountaineering and used it in a completely different context. To someone who knows that screeing refers to sliding downhill on a slope of loose gravel, the sentence has meaning, but to many readers it has little. The risk in using jargon is that it will make writing incomprehensible.

Of course, the other side of the risk is the benefit of being able to use language common to a given group. Whether it is the language of auto repair or the language of literary studies, knowing precise terms can make writing easier. Revising writing requires that you learn to recognize jargon, use it when appropriate, and eliminate it when it is not. Learning the specialized vocabulary of a discipline is part of learning about discipline. In English literature classes, you will be expected to use terms such as *synecdoche, caesura,* and *structuralism* to describe what you read; in sociology class you will have to use terms such as *social islet, upward mobility,* and *normative*. Nearly every course you take will require that you assimilate some of its specialized vocabulary, and your writing in the course should reflect this.

At the same time, you need to avoid using specialized terminology in situations in which your readers are unlikely to be familiar with it. I cannot be very sympathetic with writing that includes terms such as *feedback* and *glitch* because I think of that as language for computer scientists, not for students of English literature, and I assume that my colleagues in the computer science department would be equally inhospitable to terms such as *foreshadowing, new criticism,* and *mimesis*.

EXERCISE

Think of a course you are currently taking, and list the specialized vocabulary of that course.

1. Compare your list with someone else's. What similarities and differences do you notice?
2. Write a paragraph using this specialized language in an inappropriate context. What do you notice about this writing?

PRETENTIOUS LANGUAGE

On some occasions formal clothing such as a dinner jacket or a long dress are appropriate, but in many situations this kind of clothing would be pretentious, as if one were trying to appear more sophisticated than everyone else. Similarly, failure to choose words appropriate to one's audience and context can lead to a phony quality in writing. Selecting words for the length of their syllables rather than their clarity can lead to pretentious language. Here is an example:

> It would please me exceedingly if you would be so kind as to accompany me to this evening's performance at the local cinema.

Early in their freshman year some college students fall into the habit of using pretentious language because they have the idea that college instructors will be impressed with a display of polysyllabic words such as "superannuated homosapiens" and "omniscient oligarchies obfuscate." Although it is true that using language specific to a given discipline can make writing much more effective, there is no advantage in trying to overwhelm readers with inflated language.

EUPHEMISMS

Euphemisms are related to pretentious language in that they, too, often obscure meaning. However, whereas pretentious language aims at overwhelming or at least impressing the audience, euphemisms try to soften or in some cases distort reality by using less specific words. When I was a child, people never died, they "passed away" or were "gone," and a hysterectomy was termed a "woman's operation." You can probably think of a number of euphemisms from your own life experience.

Euphemisms such as "sanitation engineer" for garbage collector or "intimate relations" for sexual intercourse cause no particular harm because they merely gloss over the reality to make it seem more attractive. But some euphemisms are deliberately calculated to obscure the truth. When the Pentagon, for example, began its early discussion of funding for the neutron bomb, the bomb was described as an "antipersonnel weapon." This terminology made it difficult for legislators or the press to understand exactly what was being discussed. An alert and persistent reporter eventually ascertained that "antipersonnel weapon" meant "neutron bomb" and brought the issue to public attention. But had this reporter not investigated, the "antipersonnel weapon" might have been approved without its supporters recognizing its true nature.

As a writer you should avoid euphemisms designed to obscure the truth. Euphemisms' effect on the style of writing is similar to that of pretentious language. Of course, as is true with jargon, there may be occasions when euphemisms serve your purposes. For instance, if you are describing a child who has been horribly scarred by a fire, you may wish to say "disfigured" instead of "horribly scarred." Balancing sensitivity to your subject and to your audience will usually guide you to appropriate decisions about euphemisms.

SEXIST LANGUAGE

Most contemporary audiences are sensitive to sexist language, and another way of considering your audience is to avoid using masculine pronouns to refer to both men and women, to avoid perpetuating stereotypes of male and female roles through images created by words, and to avoid other forms of gender bias in the words you choose.

Man. One of the current topics of debate in language concerns the generic term *man*. Some people maintain that *man* (and masculine pronouns such as *he* and *him*) includes women, and other people call this sexist language. Efforts to make language less sexist have led to substitutions such as *chairperson* or *chair* for *chairman* and *salesperson* for *salesman*. As you revise your writing, you will want to consider ways to avoid gender bias without creating awkward constructions. The use of *he/she* and *his/her* ("Everyone should get *his* or *her* books") often calls attention to itself. The guidelines below provide graceful alternatives to sexist language.

1. Use gender-neutral terms when speaking of other people. These include substituting the *human race, humankind, work force* or *personnel,* and *average person* for words such as *man, mankind, manpower,* and *man on the street.*
2. Avoid gender-marked titles when good alternatives are available. Substitute *speaker* or *representative* for *spokesman,* *police officer* for *policeman,* and *flight attendant* for *stewardess.*
3. If you know the gender of the person being discussed, use it ("The student who wrote this paper began by determining what was required of *HER*").
4. Rewrite sentences to avoid using gender pronouns, by using the appropriate title instead. (Substitute "You should see your doctor first, and *the doctor* should call the emergency room directly" for "You should see your doctor first, and *he* should call the emergency room directly.")
5. Recast sentences in the plural to avoid third-person singular pronouns. (Substitute "All students should bring *their* texts to class" for "Each student should bring *his* text to class.")
6. Address your reader directly in the second person if you can do so appropriately. (Substitute "Send in *your* application by the final deadline date" for "The student must send in *his* application by the final deadline date.")
7. Replace third-person singular possessives with articles. (Substitute "Every proctor should draft a preliminary schedule by Friday" for "Every proctor should draft *his* preliminary schedule by Friday.")
8. Remember that the primary goal is to avoid distracting your reader with constructions that offend because they show gender bias or that interfere with reading because they are awkward.

C. Landing Areas

All FAA-authorized demonstration jumps are classified as Open Field, Level 1, Level 2, or Stadium. With the FAA's concurrence, USPA defines these areas as described in Table 6.A, Size and Definition of Landing Areas.

Minimum landing areas for PRO Rating holders:

- For PRO Rating holders, there should be no less than 5,000 square feet of landing area per four jumpers.
- An additional 800 square feet per jumper is required for any jumper landing within 30 seconds of the last of any four jumpers.

When evaluating a demonstration jump, the jumper must consider alternate landing areas, such as run-offs or escape areas. Open bodies of water may be included when measuring landing-area requirements for open-field, level 1 and level 2 landing areas—however, the vertical and horizontal distance limits from any spectator outlined in Table 6.A still applies.

Table 6.A— Size and Definition of Landing Areas
Open Field
1. A minimum-sized area that will accommodate a landing area no less than 500,000 square feet.
2. Allows a jumper to drift over the spectators with sufficient altitude (250 feet) so as not to create a hazard to persons or property on the ground
3. Will accommodate landing no closer than 100 feet from the spectators
Level 1
1. An area that will accommodate a landing area no smaller than 250,000 square feet up to 500,000 square feet
2. Or an area with the sum total that equals 250,000 square feet, up to 500,000 square feet) with a one-sided linear crowd line
3. Allows jumpers to drift over the spectators with sufficient altitude (250 feet) so as not to create a hazard to persons or property on the ground
4. Will accommodate landing no closer than 50 feet from the spectators
5. Many Open-Field athletic areas constitute a Level 1 area.
Level 2
1. An area that will not accommodate a 250,000 square-foot landing area but will allow an area no smaller than 5,000 square feet per four jumpers
2. Allows jumpers to fly under canopy no lower than 50 feet above the crowd and land no closer than 15 feet from the crowd line
3. Parachutists who certify that they will use both ram-air main and ram-air reserve parachutes will be permitted to exit over or into a congested area but not exit over an open-air assembly of people.
4. This area would require an FAA Form 7711-2 to conduct an approved demo.
Stadium
1. A Level 2 landing area smaller than 450 feet in length by 240 feet in width and bounded on two or more sides by bleachers, walls, or buildings in excess of 50 feet high
2. This area would also require an FAA Form 7711-2 to conduct an approved demonstration jump.

D. Experience and Ability

Jumpers must have all the following experience and ability when jumping into an Open Field and Level 1 area, as defined by USPA and accepted by the FAA:

- C license or higher
- 50 jumps within the past 12 months
- five jumps within the previous 60 days using the same model and size canopy to be used on the demonstration jump
- For tandem jumps, the above requirements do not apply to the tandem student

Jumpers must have all the following experience and ability when jumping into a Level 2 and Stadium area, as defined by USPA and accepted by the FAA:

- hold the PRO rating (required by the BSRs)
- 50 jumps within the past 12 months
- five jumps within the previous 60 days using the same model and size canopy to be used on the demonstration jump

Word Choice and Style in Writing

Style in Writing

Many elements including denotation and connotation, abstract and concrete words, jargon, pretentious language, cliché, and euphemism contribute to what we call style in writing. Style is both paradoxical and difficult to define.

The paradox in style is that it requires writers to be unconsciously self-conscious. It is not sufficient to many weak habits, for example, but attention to these three can lead to new discoveries in writing. As you look at the following two opening paragraphs by the same student, you can see how an individual can shift from one writing task to another.

[example paragraphs partially obscured, discussing mastering individual movements in sports—the arc of a tennis swing or the crouch of downhill skiing. However, if you continue to think consciously about these movements while you are performing them, your body will become rigid and awkward. For that matter, notice what happens when you start concentrating on each step as you walk downstairs. The same is true for style in writing, because a mechanical approach will lead...]

Style is difficult to define, as we can recognize it much more easily than we can explain it. You have probably described people as "having style" or commented on the style of music or art, but you would have a hard time explaining exactly what you meant by this. Still, you would probably claim that you recognize style when you see it. Truman Capote defined style in this way:

> ...No one really *knows*. Yet either you *know* or you don't. For myself, if you will excuse a rather cheap little image, I suppose style is the mirror of an artist's sensibility—more so than the content of his work.
> —*Paris Review*, vol. 1, p. 295

Words closely associated with style include tone, voice, and persona. *Tone* can be described as the emotional coloration or attitude toward the subject...

Voice in writing refers to the way the writing "sounds" and is influenced by pronoun usage and other word choice. For example, "I think the book is lost" sounds different from "It appears that the book has vanished." You may encounter instructors who give you specific instructions about voice in writing. They may tell you to use an "authentic" voice, or they may direct you to use an objective or disinterested voice. More commonly, instructors will give you no direct advice about voice in writing, but you will need to consider it as you revise for style.

Persona is the personality revealed in writing. Sometimes writers try to project a personality that closely resembles their own, and sometimes they take on a quite different one. The word *persona* comes from the Greek word

309

addition, the second selection is more tightly structured because it avoids personal commentary, and this contributes to the feeling of formality.

Even though we can point to these differences between the two, we have not yet accounted entirely for the difference in style. The subject matter itself and the circumstances of writing also contribute to the differences. The assignment for the first paragraph was to describe an ideal class for a writing instructor, and the class had practiced using a personal voice in writing. The assignment for the second paragraph was to describe how each of the three philosophical schools approaches problems of society and to compare their effectiveness. The instructor had demonstrated no interest in personal views. Accordingly, the student modified his tone in response to the constraints of the two writing tasks.

These subtle differences between the two passages suggest that some aspects of style deserve more attention. The first of these is the issue of *formality*. There are a number of ways to describe different levels of formality in writing: One rhetorician describes them as sweet, tough, and stuffy, and another describes them as a series of clocks. Here I shall talk about three levels, casual, informal, and formal.

Casual, Informal, and Formal Styles

One way to think of levels of style is in terms of clothing. You have probably been in a few situations in which formal dress was required; perhaps it was a wedding or a dance. The clothes you wore may have been rented for the occasion, or they may still hang in your closet, waiting for the next formal occasion. These clothes, like a formal tone in writing, indicate importance, significance, and respect. In contrast, you probably have clothes that you wear every day, for work, classes, and most social events. These everyday clothes are analogous to an informal tone in writing. Informal writing spans considerable range, just as your general wardrobe does. Finally, you probably have some very comfortable clothes that you wear only for working on projects or lounging around. These very comfortable clothes resemble a casual tone in writing, the kind of writing appropriate among close friends and family, but not usually acceptable in college classes.

The exact boundaries of these distinctions are difficult to determine. Is the green turtleneck informal or casual? Does the word *sucker* belong in informal writing? However, just as you have developed ways of dressing appropriately for different occasions, so you will learn to manage levels of formality in writing. A formal tone, like formal clothing, is for special occasions. It is appropriate for some essays, answers to essay questions, formal reports, and research papers. It uses words and structures that rarely appear in conversation, and its sentences are often more elaborate and longer than those of informal writing. Contractions and slang rarely appear in formal English; it uses "refined" language.

Informal writing is what most educated people use for communicating with people other than personal friends. It is the language of magazines, newspapers, most books, most business letters, and writing intended for general audiences. Informal English adheres to less rigid rules and forms than does formal English; contractions and slang do appear, although in moderation. Sentences vary in length, and they often sound more conversational than does the impersonal tone of formal writing.

Casual writing is tied more closely to the "rules" of specific people, communities, times, places, and circumstances. Slang expressions, contractions, and nonstandard dialect appear frequently, and often casual writing is incomprehensible to someone not familiar with the situation in which the writing is done. "Back in ten" may make no sense to the general reader but is a clear explanation to students who find it tacked on my office door.

The following three letters illustrate formal, informal, and casual styles:

```
Dear Sir:

I wish to bring to your attention the fact that my
performance has improved immeasurably in terms of
increased contract production and unique customer
generation. Therefore, in the interest of fairness, I
request an appropriate monetary reward.

                                    Sincerely,

                                    Joe Humble


Dear Mr. Jones:

I think I've done a good job during the past six
months. I've filled more contracts than ever before,
and I've brought more new customers to the company
than anyone else in the division has. I would ap-
preciate a raise.

                                    Sincerely,

                                    Joe Humble


Frank--

The way I figure it, I'm about the best you've got in
this company. I'm hustling contracts and pulling in
customers like crazy. How about crossing my palm with
a little more coin next month?

                                    Joe
```

Word Choice and Style in Writing

These three letters demonstrate formal, informal, and casual style in writing. As was the case with the two opening paragraphs, the stylistic effect is achieved by a number of features in the writing, but the central difference is in Joe's attitude toward the subject of his salary and his audience, Mr. Jones.

E X E R C I S E

The following paragraph contains material for a communications paper on television violence.

> TV violence is getting out of hand. "Cheyenne" started it all in the fifties with shooting and stuff. Then some of the other guys got the idea and "Sugarfoot," "Maverick," and "Gunsmoke" got into the act. Pretty soon along came the "Wagon Train," "Tales of Wells Fargo," and "Tombstone Territory." In the sixties, violence cropped up in police and detective shows. "The Untouchables" was one of the goriest shows of all time. It played until the early 1970s.

Much of what appears here could be described as casual writing.

1. Try rewriting it in an informal style.
2. Now write the same paragraph in a formal style.

Copyright © Grant Haist, The National Audubon Society Collection/Photo Researchers, Inc.

PART FOUR

SPECIAL APPLICATIONS

Copyright © Martin Litton, The National Audubon Society Collection/Photo Researchers, Inc.

Chapter Thirteen

Getting Ready to Write Research Papers

WRITING a research paper resembles other types of writing. In this, as in all writing tasks, you need to understand the assignment, consider your audience; generate ideas; develop a thesis; write a draft; revise organization; check for coherence and cohesion; and edit mechanics of writing. Yet, writing a research paper is different from other types of writing. Among the differences are these: research papers are usually longer than other types of college writing and are produced over an extended period of time; research papers rely extensively on sources of information outside the individual writer; research papers employ special forms of documentation. This chapter will help you integrate what you already know about writing with the special requirements of research papers.

Length and Time

Research papers vary in length, but most are between ten and twenty typewritten pages. Many students report that research papers are the longest pieces of writing they do, and the process of producing a paper of this length requires much more time than does shorter papers, even though the stages in the process are similar in many ways. Consequently, it will be useful to break the task down into smaller parts. One way of doing this is to develop a *plan* for writing a research paper.

Plan

Writers often need more time, and one way to avoid excessive pressure from deadlines is to contruct a plan that breaks the research paper into parts and includes a time for each part to be completed. Elements common to most research papers include these:

Special Applications

> Develop a topic
> Gather information
> Write a draft
> Revise the draft
> Document sources

As is true for most writing, these elements are not usually completed all at once, and writers frequently move from one to the other. As you are gathering information, for example, you will be collecting information that enables you to document your sources in the final draft. Frequently the process of gathering information contributes to topic development, as does writing and revising a draft. But developing a plan based on this list can help you manage what might otherwise become an overwhelming task.

DEVELOP A TOPIC

In some cases, the topic for a research paper is specified. Here, for example, is an assignment from an atmospheric science class:

> Your paper should provide a good meterological description of a weather or climate event. It does not need to be highly technical but should include background information. This paper should contain a minimum of six references, and should be at least ten typewritten pages (excluding references).

Although the exact event is not specified, this assignment gives the student a good deal of guidance about how to proceed. After selecting an event such as a particular tornado or hurricane, the student can proceed directly to gathering information about it.

Frequently, however, research paper assignments lack specificity and require students to develop and refine the topic. Here, for example, is an assignment from a sociology class:

> The final paper should focus on some issue discussed in this class. It should draw on out-of-class readings, use standard documentation and be at least ten typewritten pages.

Here the student must make many more decisions before actually starting to gather information. Which issue should be the focus? How can the issue be narrowed down into a topic that can be covered in a ten-page paper? One student in this class decided that the general issue of *aging* was the issue he wanted to focus on.

He had been interested in class discussions and readings that dealt with gerontology, partly because they reminded him of problems his family faced with his elderly grandparents. But the topic of aging had economic, political, social, and psychological dimensions. He knew that he would have to look at just one part of one of these. As he considered the topic, he thought about his grandfather's depression and decided that he would like to understand more about it. He decided to focus on psychological dimensions of aging,

Getting Ready to Write Research Papers

with particular emphasis on its negative psychological effects. By means of this process, Gordon moved through steps that can be portrayed this way:

```
undefined topic in sociology
aging
psychological effects of aging
negative psychological effects of aging
```

Even though he knew that he would probably refine his topic further, Gordon decided he was ready to gather information.

This process of moving from a general topic to a specific one can be accomplished in a variety of ways. You may find it useful to explore ideas in your journal, to talk about your topic with a friend, to reread selections that interested you especially, or to think about the questions that puzzle you the most. Whatever method you use, try to select a topic that genuinely interests you. A sign on a dirt road clogged with spring mud says, "Choose your rut carefully. You will be in it for the next 17 miles." Similarly, you will spend considerable time with the research topic you choose, so it is worth considering your choice carefully.

Here are some examples of how other students have developed their topics from general to more specific terms:

```
sexually transmitted diseases
AIDS
effects of AIDS on social behavior
effects of AIDs on heterosexual relations among
  college students
```

```
media
film distribution
distribution of films by independent studios
distribution of "independent" films in Seattle
```

EXERCISE

Select one of the general topics below and develop it into a topic suitable for a research paper.

>   Science fiction
>   London during World War II
>   The 1984 election
>   Teenage pregnancy

Gather Information

Once you have specified the topic for your research paper, you are ready to begin gathering information about it. Frequently this process will lead you to change your topic slightly, but without some specific idea for a topic, you will find it impossible to gather useful information.

319

Special Applications

INTERVIEWS

The first impulse of most students who need more information on a topic is to rush to the library and start reading books and articles on the subject.

This is often a very good way to gather more information, but it is not the only way. People are often excellent sources of information, and interviews can often supply writers with considerable information for writing. For example, a student who planned to write about a tornado for the atmospheric science class lived in Lubbock, Texas, where a major tornado had struck on May 11, 1970. Many of the people in Lubbock vividly remembered events from the tornado, and so they provided an important source of information for her paper. You may not find yourself in a community filled with people who have direct experience with your topic, but it is surprising how often people can offer valuable ideas. In addition, every college campus houses experts on a variety of subjects, and usually some of them are willing to talk with students about their work.

The success of an interview depends on preparation, and the most important preparation is to decide what you want from the person you will be interviewing. If you have no clear questions in mind, it will be difficult to get much useful information. In order to know what you want from an interview, you need to have some idea of what that person can provide. What worthwhile knowledge or experience does this person have? If you plan to talk with a biology instructor who specializes in plants, try to find out whether her expertise is in the plants of India or in the flora of the tundra. If you can read something written by that person, you will have an even better idea of what you can learn.

One good way to get ready for an interview is to practice your questions with a friend. Often the process of asking the questions will show you how the questions can be improved so that you can obtain the information you seek. The student who planned to write about the Lubbock tornado prepared this list of questions:

```
1. Did you have any advance warning of the tor-
   nado's approach? How did you learn about the
   tornado? What preparations did you make?
2. If you have no prior warning, how did you first
   become aware of the tornado?
3. What did you observe as the tornado occurred?
   What did you see, hear or feel?
4. After the tornado was over, what did your im-
   mediate area look like?
5. What were the long-term effects of the tornado
   on your life?
6. Where can I learn more about the 1970 tornado?
```

As she tried out these questions with friends, she realized that she was not asking people about their prior knowledge of tornados. People who had experienced or read about tornadoes had different responses than did those for whom the 1970 tornado was a new experience. Accordingly, she added this question: What did you know about tornadoes before 1970?

Asking for sources of further information adds to the effectiveness of an interview. With experts such as college instructors or specialists in the field, the best procedure is often to ask for a recommendation of the one most important thing to read on the subject. A longer bibliography, particularly from a specialist in the field, may be overwhelming, but one important source can often provide valuable ideas. As you no doubt noticed, the student investigating the Lubbock tornado likewise included a question about further information in her interview plan, which allowed her to go from one person to another for addition information.

The information received during an interview can be recorded in several ways. One way is to use a tape recorder and transcribe all the answers after the interview is over. This method frees you from taking notes while you are talking, but many people find the machinery intimidating and talk unnaturally if they know they are being recorded. Indeed, there are some people who refuse to have an interview recorded. An alternative is to take notes either during or immediately after an interview. Taking notes during an interview allows you to record comments word for word and specific information such as names and dates. But recording your impressions immediately after an interview gives you a chance to think about the whole interview, not just focus on parts of it.

Whatever method you use, recording information from interviews will require strategies of narration. Except in rare instances, when you want to get exact words, you will not copy what you hear; you will put down in your own words what the person is saying. This process of translating another's language into your own helps you learn more about your topic.

In addition to recording what is said, be sure to record the name of the person, the date, and the place of the interview. If you decide to use the interview material in a paper, you will want to footnote it just as you would a book or article. The footnote should look like this:

```
Elizabeth Nichols, personal interview, May 1, 1987,
Lubbock, Texas.
```

EXERCISE

Imagine that you wish to interview practicing sociologists and laypeople on the subject of occupational prestige. Construct a list of questions for each group.

1. What differences do you notice in the questions?
2. Try your questions out on a friend. What changes do you need to make?

Special Applications

E X E R C I S E

Picture the library on your campus. Think about where it is in relation to other buildings, imagine the entrance, and focus on what you see as you walk through the entrance. Now draw a floor plan of the library, much as you would draw a floor plan of your house. Label all the rooms you can identify. Then look at the following list, and add places to your plan. If you cannot find any of them, it is time for a field trip to the library.

1. Card catalogue.
2. "Stacks" or book collection.
3. Reserve desk.
4. Circulation desk (where you check out books).
5. Reference desk (where is the reference collection in relation to this desk?).
6. Periodicals area (indicate where both bound periodicals and current periodicals are kept).
7. Copy machines (and change machines).
8. Microfilm collection and microfilm readers.
9. Study areas.
10. Media collection, computer terminals, special collections, typing room.

LIBRARY RESOURCES

The library will be the scene of some of your most important exploration during college, and the first step is to know where everything is located, much as a detective "cases a joint." Indeed, using a library resembles detective work in many ways, and effective recording of library resources requires that you search and evaluate as detectives do. Libraries contain more information than you can use in a lifetime, but you have to know how to find it. The organization of libraries varies tremendously. Some library catalogues use the Dewey Decimal system (the call number begins with a number such as 808.42), and others use the Library of Congress system (the call number begins with a letter such as LB 201.2). Other libraries use a combination of the two. Some library card catalogues include books only; others list both books and periodicals; and some show books, periodicals, and government documents. The holdings and facilities also vary from one library to another, and so it is important to learn how your library works.

The one safe generalization about all libraries is that they are not self-service institutions. Librarians are trained to help students find information; thinking of them as teachers can help you use their expertise most effectively. Many librarians teach library orientation courses. Sometimes these orientations are tied to specific disciplines and sometimes they are general introductions to the library. Perhaps even more valuable than the courses are the "individual tutorials" that librarians can offer when you ask your particular question.

Getting Ready to Write Research Papers

As is true with interviews, you will get the most from librarians if you do your homework and answer the mundane questions for yourself. Although these questions are important, the answers can usually be found posted on walls or in pamphlets provided by the library.

1. What are the library hours? If there is more than one library on campus, are the hours for all libraries the same? Do these hours change during vacations?
2. How long may you keep the books you have checked out? (And what is the fine if you return them late?)
3. What are the procedures for checking out a book from the reserve desk?
4. What are the search/hold procedures for getting a book that has been checked out by someone else?
5. Are there any unusual features about the card catalogue system? (Some libraries, for example, require users to check a location file as well as the card catalogue.)
6. How are abstracts, bibliographies, and indexes arranged in the reference area? Where are the encyclopedias and dictionaries?
7. Where can you find out which periodicals the library has? (And how do you find call numbers for bound periodicals?)
8. Where do you report broken copy machines?
9. What is included in the library's microfilm collection? (Usually newspapers are on microfilm. Which ones? Are there other kinds of information on microfilm?)
10. Does the library have facilities for making "hard copies" of microfilms?
11. Does your library have facilities for computer information searches? What are the procedures and costs?
12. Can you check out tapes or records from the library or listen to them in a media center?
13. What other nonprint resources does your library contain?
14. What do you do if you lose your library card?

You will probably not find the answers to all these questions at one time but will discover them when they become important to you. These are not the most useful questions you can ask a librarian. Rather, the best questions to ask a librarian are those that help you with actual exploration.

The Search Strategy

Recall the assignment to write about a meterological event. The student who interviewed witnesses of the Lubbock tornado realized that she needed more technical information about tornadoes in general and about the Lubbock tornado in particular, and so she went to the library.

Her first stop was the reference area where she looked up the word *tornado* in an encyclopedia. She found a general introductory article that described tornadoes, gave accounts of some specific ones, provided charts and maps showing the occurrence and distribution of tornadoes, listed the physical

Special Applications

characteristics of the vortices, and contained a bibliography of other introductory sources to consult. She took notes on the article, paying particular attention to the accounts of two especially destructive tornado series in 1925 and 1965. Her note card appears below.

> Encyclopedia Britanica "Tornadoes, Whirldwinds and Water Sports" pp. 514-520.
> - Word "tornado" from Latin "tornare" - "to make round by turning"
> - Speeds 300-500 mph (rotational) 30-70 mph (forward)
> - Analysis of surface & upper air weather + detection
> - 1953-65 average 628 tornadoes per year in U.S. May usually highest month - Oklahoma most
> - 1965: 898 tornadoes in U.S.
> - 1925: tornado 1 m. x 219 m.

The annotated bibliography with the encyclopedia article listed six technical books and two popular ones and briefly described each. It also listed and described thirteen technical articles. She decided to look up two of the books, one technical and one popular, and because the encyclopedia was published in 1970 and listed articles that had been published before 1967, she decided to look also for more recent information in periodicals.

She wrote down the titles and authors of the books she planned to check and went to the card catalogue, where she looked at the *Library of Congress Subject Headings* under tornadoes to find which terms to look up in the card catalogue. She found the listing shown in the illustration below. She then

```
      Tornado warning systems   (Indirect)
          (QC955) ◄──────────────────── Library of Congress call number
        x Warning systems, Tornado
       xx Civil defense—Warning systems
          Emergency communication systems
          Meteorological services
          Natural disaster warning systems
          Tornadoes
      Tornadoes   (QC955)
see also ──────► sa Cyclones
          Storms
          Tornado warning systems
          subdivision Tornado, (year) or
             Tornadoes under names of countries,
             cities, etc.
       xx Meteorology
          Storms
          Winds
      Note under Cyclones
```

decided to look under the *tornadoes* heading because that seemed the most directly related to her topic. Then she looked in the card catalogue for books listed under *tornadoes*. Ten books were listed there, including one novel, one book on mental illness, and several on tornadoes in places such as Canada, India, and various parts of the United States. Because there was nothing on the Lubbock tornado itself, she decided to look for general texts that would tell her more about the nature of tornadoes. She selected three to examine and made source cards for each of them. One of her source cards appears below.

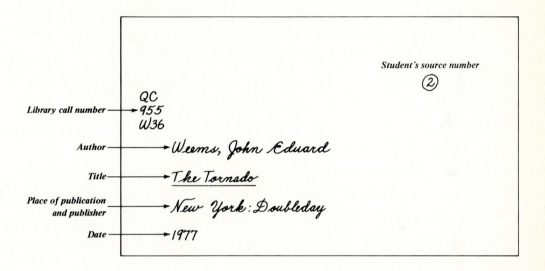

When she had finished her source cards, she went to the stacks to look for the three books. She found two on the shelves; the third was not there, and she concluded that it was either missing or checked out and made a note to ask about it at the circulation desk. She scanned the two other books to see whether they would be useful. The Flora book, although it was published in 1953, contained a great deal of useful information about tornadoes in general, including causes, force, unusual cases, and a summary of especially destructive tornadoes in the United States and the rest of the world. She decided to check out the book. The popular book contained a ten-page list of acknowledgements and an annotated bibliography that named several more articles. Because the book was published in 1977 and contained more recent entries than the encyclopedia did, she decided to check it out also. Browsing among the books located nearby, she found a monograph entitled *Storm Data*, published by the U.S. Department of Commerce. It listed storms by state and included their location, path, damage, and characteristics. She decided to take it along and reminded herself that she should check other government documents for more information.

Special Applications

Then she turned to the reference section in search of articles on the Lubbock tornado specifically. She checked the *Reader's Guide to Periodical Literature* for 1970 and found this entry:

```
TORNADO detection. See Tornadoes
TORNADOES
    Can TV really detect tornadoes? W. G. Biggs
      and P. J. Waite. bibliog il Weatherwise 23:
      120-5 Je '70
    Eyewitness tornado observations obtained
      with telephone and tape recorder. R. T.
      Ryan and B. Vonnegut. bibliog il Weather-
      wise 23:126-30+ Je '70
    Lubbock tornadoes: a study of suction spots.
      T. T. Fujita. bibliog il Weatherwise 23:
      161-73 Ag '70
    Miniature whirlwinds produced in the labo-
      ratory by high—voltage electrical dis-
      charges. R. T. Ryan and B. Vonnegut.
      bibliog il Science 168:1349-51 Je 12 '70
    News from the world of space exploration;
      satellite photographs in predicting torna-
      does. Space World G-10-82:43+ O '70
    Tornado at Kent, Washington, on 12 Decem-
      ber 1969. C. Feris. il Weatherwise 23:75-7+
      Ap '70
    Tornado season of 1969. A. D. Pearson and
      R. P. Krebs. il Weatherwise 23:18-23 F '70
```

She decided to look at the "eyewitness" and "Lubbock" articles. Then she looked at the *General Science Index* but found that it began in 1980 and would not have anything on the Lubbock tornado. She did not know what other indexes to check, and so she asked the reference librarian for help, and together they looked at *Ulrich's International Periodicals Directory* and found other listings. The librarian also suggested that she look at the *Applied Science and Technology Index* and *Meteorological and Geoastrophysical Abstracts*. She checked both and found these entries:

from Applied Science and Technology Index

```
TORNADOES
    Dynamical analysis of outflow from tornado-
      producing thunderstorms as revealed by
      ATS III pictures. K. Ninomiya. bibliog
      maps diags J Ap Meteorology 10:275-94 Ap
      '71
    Lubbock tornado. il QST 54:70-1 S '70
    Nuclear power plant tornado design considera-
      tions. J. A. Dunlap and K. Wiedner.
      bibliog map Am Soc C E Proc 97 [PO 2 no
      7949]:407-17 Mr '71
      See also
    Storms
```

Getting Ready to Write Research Papers

from Meteorlogical and Geophysical Abstracts

21.1-242   551.509.327 :551.501.81

Waldheuser, Harry W. and Hughes, Lawrence A., **Aid for tornado warnings.** *U. S. Weather Bureau, Central Region Technical Memorandum WBTM CR-29, April 1969.* 10 p. Figs., refs. (*U. S. Weather Bureau, Technical Memorandum WBTM CR-29*) (*U. S. ESSA, Technical Memorandum WBTM CR-29*) DAS (M(055) U587cet)—This memorandum describes an aid for tornado warnings and documents it with several cases. It provides an aid to the radar operator so that, in conjunction with the radar scanning procedures suggested in *WBTM CR-20* and elsewhere, he might assist the forecaster with decisions, or cause more warnings to be issued on the basis of radar information alone. A majority of tornadoes moves from the southwest quadrant. The area selected for warning usually lies to the northeast of the known location. The selection of a warning area is also influenced by the direction of movement of radar echoes, since tornadoes are generally associated with a particular thunderstorm cell, or by the wind direction in the mid-levels of the atmosphere, since radar echoes usually move with nearly the mean mid-level wind vector. A likely place for initiation of another tornado is along or near a line perpendicular to a squall line or cold front and passing through the point of initiation of a previous tornado. *Subject Headings:* 1. Tornado warnings 2. Radar observation of tornadoes 3. Radar forecast aids.—E.S.

She decided to look at the articles in *Quest* and the *Journal of Applied Meterology* and added their publication information to her list before she went to the periodicals room. Because the articles she sought were published more than a year ago, she knew that they would be in bound periodicals not in the periodical display area, and fortunately, they were not at the bindery. One of the articles she wanted to look at had been cut out with a razor blade, but she located the others and made notes on them. One of her note cards appears below.

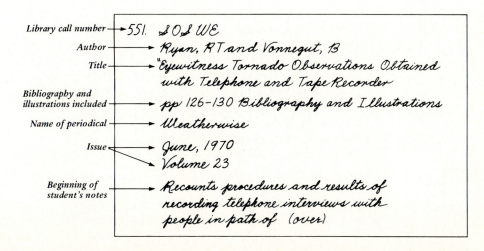

Special Applications

After she finished taking notes in the periodicals area, she returned to the reference area where she checked the 1970 *New York Times Index* and found these entries:

> **TORNADOES**
> Pres Nixon grants Ohio $2.5-million more to spur recovery from tornado and flood damage last July, Ja 6,10:3
> Lanett, Ala, hit; 1 killed, Mr 20,8:1
> 6 villages in E Pakistan hit; 17 killed, 110 hurt, Ap 15,15:1
> **Tornadoes hit 200-mi area of Tex Panhandle; 25 killed, hundreds hurt;** millions of dollars of property damage reptd in 11 towns; map; SBA designates secs as disaster areas, Ap 19,41:1
> Naylor, Mo, hit; extensive damage, My 2,30:1; Okla City and nearby communities hit by series of tornadoes; 8 hurt; extensive damage, My 2,65:7
> **Lubbock, Tex, hit,** My 12,32:4; Lubbock damage illus, My 13,1:3; **20 killed, over 300 seriously hurt;** extensive damage, including derailment of train, described; winds put at over 200 mph; Lt Gov Barnes in city to direct rescue work; damage illus; map, My 13,82:1; Pres Nixon declares Lubbock major disaster area; families begin moving into homes repossessed by FHA and leased to city for $1; damage put at $102-million; rescue operations and cleanup pushed, My 14, 23:1
> Theories on storm behavior discussed (W Sullivan rept); he notes tornado-watching systems, including new ATS (Applied Tech Satellites); map showing US sites where storms are most common and number of storms in '69, My 17,IV,11:1
> Lubbock, Tex, death toll at 23, My 18,11:1; at 26, My 22,46:2; 2 tornadoes hit Zapata, Tex; cause up to $400,000 damage, My 25,27:1
> Comment on Topeka, Kan, tornado season; '66 storm that caused estimated $100-million damage revd; scene illus, Je 11,58:1; US had nearly 100 tornadoes in 6-day period ending June 16, including 25 in Kan, Je 17,45:5
> 3 homes destroyed, Tallahassee, Fla, Jl 23,62:8
> Device patented to protect bldgs from 'exploding' from drop in atmospheric pressure assoc with tornadoes, Jl 25,31:3
> SW France hit; 9 killed, 29 hurt and 11 reptd missing; storm causes heavy damage in Landes and Gironde regions, Ag 5,17:8
> Bridgeport, W Va, hit; 25 homes destroyed, Ag 24, 66:3
> Shawnee, Okla, hit; 3 dead and about 40 hurt; damage put at $3.5- to $4-million; tornado also hits Prague, 15 miles to northeast; map, O 6,93:7; death toll at 4; damage put at $33-million, O 7,50:8

After carefully noting the publication dates and pages, she went to the microfilm room to read all the Lubbock articles.

Finally, she looked in the 1971 volume of the *U.S. Monthly Catalog* for U.S. government publications on the tornado. Here she found several entries from the U.S. Department of Commerce, and she decided to look at one entitled "Lubbock Tornado: A Survey of Building Damage in an Urban Area." N.B.S. Technical Note 558. National Bureau of Standards, U.S. Department of Commerce, Washington, D.C., March, 1971.

This student followed a *search strategy,* which is a combination of gathering and evaluating library information. By beginning in the reference section with an encyclopedia, she was able to locate the most general sources and progress from these to more specialized and technical information. At every stage in the search she decided what to use and what to reject. Her decisions were based on what each source added to her information about tornadoes.

Getting Ready to Write Research Papers

Paper References

Regardless of the topic, the search strategy is the best method for exploring in the library. Start with the encyclopedias in the reference section, use the *Library of Congress Subject Headings* to find card catalogue subject headings, browse among related books in the stacks, locate journal articles in periodical indexes, use newspaper indexes, and finally check government documents. The following chart suggests sources and strategies for a wide variety of topics:

When you need	*Look at*	*But remember*
a basic introduction to your topic, with some suggestions for additional reading.	a subject encyclopedia covering your field.	Use an index first to locate all material on your topic; keep in mind that the references may not be up to date.
to identify the subject headings used for a topic in the card catalogue.	*Library of Congress Subject Headings.*	Use the most specific term that you can find, and remember that new headings are being added to the catalogue all the time.
to find books on a topic.	the main card catalogue.	*See* and *see also* references in the catalog will help you locate material.
to browse through some books on a topic.	the stacks.	Only books *not* checked out will be on the shelves, and so you may not see all the books that are available.
to look at critical reviews of some books.	book review indexes.	Reviews usually appear within one or two years of *first* publication date; paperbacks are not usually included in these indexes.

329

Special Applications

When you need	*Look at*	*But remember*
to identify some periodicals in a specific field.	Katz, *Magazines for Libraries,* or *Ulrich's International Periodicals Directory.*	Both are arranged by broad subject areas; Katz gives more information about the journals, but Ulrich's is the more comprehensive list.
to identify periodical indexes that will include material on a topic.	Kujoth, *Subject Guide to Periodical Indexes.*	New indexes and abstracts have appeared since this guide was compiled.
to find articles on a topic.	*Reader's Guide* (for popular articles) or an index that covers your subject, as listed in Kujoth.	Use as specific a subject heading as possible; start with the most recent volumes and work back.
to get an overview of the information sources in a subject area.	a basic guide to the field	Check the publication date of your guide—newer materials in the field will not be included.
to find some recent bibliographies on a topic.	*Bibliographic Index.*	This index covers bibliographies in a variety of forms, including books, journal articles, and pamphlets.
to learn about the current state and possible future of research in a field.	a publication of the "Advances in . . ." or "Annual Review of . . ." type (located by using *Ulrich's Irregular Serials and Annuals*).	These publications generally cover some topics in the field each year, but not the same ones every year.

Getting Ready to Write Research Papers

When you need	Look at	But remember
to see what books have been published recently on a topic.	Subject Guide to Books in Print (for U.S. publications); Cumulative Book Index (for English-language publications generally).	These list *all* books published, academic and popular.
to locate U.S. government publications on a topic.	U.S. Monthly Catalog or Android Guide to Government Publications.	This is most useful when the topic has been studied by some government body.
to see what doctoral dissertations have been written on a topic.	Dissertation Abstracts International.	Complete dissertations will probably not be available.
to locate ephemeral (pamphlet-type) material on a topic.	the branch library or special collection most closely related to your subject.	Ask a librarian whether there are any special files of material on the topic.

This search strategy is modeled on materials developed by the University of Washington Undergraduate Library. If any of these resources are unfamiliar to you, see the accompanying charts for further details.

Typical Encyclopedias

GENERAL ENCYCLOPEDIAS

Colliers Encyclopedia
Encyclopedia Americana
Encyclopedia Britannica
Encyclopedia Britannica: The New Britannica (15th ed.)

SUBJECT ENCYCLOPEDIAS

A. *Fine Arts & Literature*
    Enclopedia of Photography (20 vols.)
    Enclopedia of World Art (15 vols.)
    Grove's Dictionary of Music and Musicians (10 vols.)
    McGraw-Hill Encyclopedia of World Drama (4 vols.)
    Cassell's Encyclopedia of World Literature (3 vols.)

Special Applications

B. *Philosophy and Religion*
   Dictionary of the History of Ideas (5 vols.)
   Encyclopedia of Philosophy (8 vols.)
   Encyclopedia of Religion & Ethics (13 vols.)
   Encyclopedia Judaica (16 vols.)
   Jewish Encyclopedia (12 vols.)
   New Catholic Encyclopedia (16 vols.)

C. *Psychology*
   Encyclopedia of Human Behavior (2 vols.)
   Encyclopedia of Mental Health (6 vols.)
   Encyclopedia of Psychology (3 vols.)
   International Encyclopedia of Psychiatry
     Psychology, Psychoanalysis and Neurology (12 vols.)

D. *Science*
   Grizimck's Animal Life Encyclopedia (13 vols.)
   McGraw-Hill Encyclopedia of Science & Technology (15 vols.)
   New Illustrated Encyclopedia of Gardening (6 vols.)
   Standard Encyclopedia of Horticulture (3 vols.)

E. *Social Sciences and Education*
   Dictionary of American History (8 vols.)
   Encyclopedia of Social Work (2 vols.)
   International Encyclopedia of the Social Sciences (17 vols.)
   Encyclopedia of Education (10 vols.)
   International Encyclopedia of Higher Education (10 vols.)

Getting Ready to Write Research Papers

Library of Congress Subject Headings

(More specific heading)

Social problems *(HN)*
   sa Buddhism and social problems
      Charities
      Children—Employment
      Church and social problems
      Civilization
      Community centers
      Cost and standard of living
      Crime and criminals
      Delinquents
      Discrimination
      Divorce
      Emigration and immigration
      Eugenics
      Euthenics
      Family size
      Homelessness ───────────┐
      Housing
      Judaism and social problems
      Juvenile delinquency
      Liquor problem
      Migrant labor
      Migration, Internal
      Mutualism
      Old age pensions
      Parasitism (Social sciences)
      Poor
   x Reform, Social
      Social reform
      Social welfare
  xx Civilization
      Ethics
      Social ethics
      Social history
      Sociology ────────────┐
      Technology and civilization

Homelessness *(Indirect)*
   sa Children, Vagrant
      Domicile in public welfare
      Migrant labor
      Poor
      Refugees
      Relief stations (for the poor)
      Rogues and vagabonds
      Runaway children
      Runaway youth
      Tramps

(Broader heading)

Sociology
      Here and with local subdivision are entered works on the discipline of sociology. Works on the social conditions of particular regions, countries, cities, etc., are entered under the name of the place subdivided by Social conditions.
   sa Age groups
      Anomy
      Aristocracy
      Atomic warfare and society
      Charities
      Chicago school of sociology
      Cities and towns
      War and society
      Wealth, Ethics of
      Women
      Women—Health and hygiene—Sociological aspects
   x Science, Social
      Social science
  xx Human ecology
   —Authorship
      Notes under Authorship; Technical writing
   —Comparative method
     xx Methodology

NOTE: **Boldface type** indicates a subject term that *is* used in the card catalog.

     sa   (see also) Indicates a related topic, usually a narrower one.

     x   Indicates a term not used in the card catalog. There will be a reference from this term in the card catalog to the term that *is* used.

     xx   Indicates a related heading from which a "see also" (sa) reference is made in the card catalog. In this case, at the beginning of a group of catalog cards on a particular subject, there will be a list of related subject headings which will include this term.

   (Indirect)   This term used after a subject heading or subdivision means that the heading may be further subdivided geographically.

Special Applications

Anatomy of a Catalog Card

```
     PN       Zinsser, William Knowlton.
     171         Writing with a word processor /
A    D37         William Zinsser. -- 1st ed. -- New York      B
     Z56         : Harper & Row, c1983.
     1983        viii, 117 p. ; 22 cm.
                 ISBN 0-06-015055-6

                 1. Authorship--Data processing.
                 2. Word processing (Office practice)
                 I. Title                                     C

     WaU      19 AUG 83      9111502    WAUWdc     82-48140
```

The main (usually author) card for a book provides three kinds of information:

1. The *call number,* assigned according to subject, which locates the book on the shelf.
2. A *description* of the book, including author, title, publisher, number of pages, and presence or absence of illustrations and bibliography.
3. *"Tracings,"* which indicate what additional cards have been filed in the catalog for this book. In this case, there are additional cards filed under:

```
                          Subject
                WORD PROCESSING (OFFICE PRACTICE)

     PN       Zinsser, William Knowlton.
     171         Writing with a word processor /
     D37         William Zinsser. -- 1st ed. -- New York
     Z56         : Harper & Row, c1983.
     1983        viii, 117 p. ; 22 cm.
                 ISBN 0-06-015055-6

                 1. Authorship--Data processing.
                 2. Word processing (Office practice)
                 I. Title

     WaU      19 AUG 83      9111502    WAUWdc     82-48140

                           Title
                 Writing with a word processor

     PN       Zinsser, William Knowlton.
     171         Writing with a word processor /
     D37         William Zinsser. -- 1st ed. -- New York
     Z56         : Harper & Row, c1983.
     1983        viii, 117 p. ; 22 cm.
                 ISBN 0-06-015055-6

                 1. Authorship--Data processing.
                 2. Word processing (Office practice)
                 I. Title

     WaU      19 AUG 83      9111502    WAUWdc     82-48140
```

Getting Ready to Write Research Papers

The subject tracing ("word processing") is especially useful because it indicates which subject heading to look under for more books on the same subject. Many books will have more than one subject tracing. The use of several catalog cards for each book lets you locate a book whether you know only the author, only the title, or only the subject you are interested in.

Book Review Digest and Book Review Index. These two reference sources index the book reviews that appear in selected journals. Each annual volume of the *Digest* and the *Index* lists the reviews published that year, alphabetically by the authors of the reviewed books.

Book Review Digest began in 1905, and indexes about 70 journals. *Book Review Index* began much later, in 1965, but it indexes over 300 journals. In general, the *Book Review Index* will list more reviews of a wider variety of books, while the *Digest's* advantages are that it includes summaries of most reviews, and covers books published before 1965.

The reviews of Edwin P. Hoyt's book, *The Phantom Raider,* appear this way in:

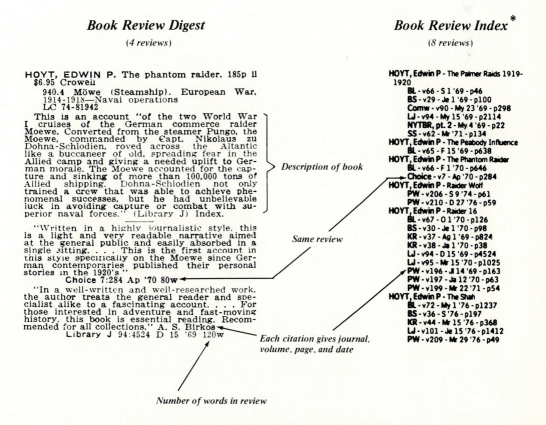

*The example from *Book Review Index* is from the 1983 edition. A more recent edition, 1987, appeared too late to be included.

Special Applications

Psychological Abstracts. *Psychological Abstracts,* which began publication in 1927, is a monthly index listing periodical articles, dissertations, and books in the field of psychology. A brief summary article, or abstract, is included for most items indexed. The entries are arranged under broad subject headings such as experimental psychology, animal psychology, and personality. For research on specific topics, there are six-month cumulated subject indexes published in June and December of each year. Two or three bound volumes are used together as sets; each of the volumes will be labelled with the same number on the spine. For example, the three volumes in the set for the first half of 1980 will be labelled #63.

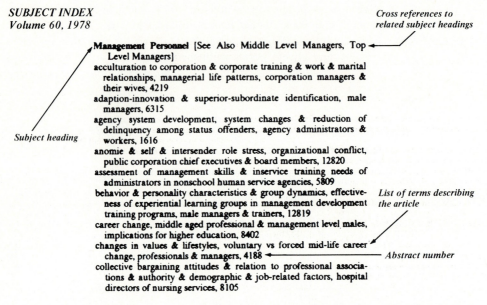

In the subject index, each entry is followed by a paragraph or abstract number. To find the abstract #4188, shown above in the subject index, look for it in the abstract volumes that are also labelled volume #60 on the spine.

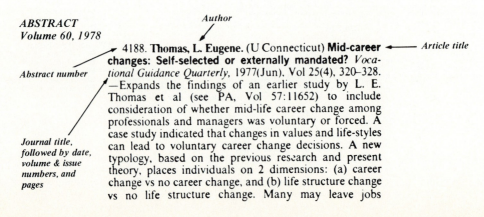

Getting Ready to Write Research Papers

resembling "empty shell" marriages, and need exists to help job-alienated individuals locate new professional and individual growth opportunities. —C. A. Heikkinen. ← Author

Indexes

Indexes to Reviews of Books
Book Review Digest
Book Review Index
Index to Book Reviews in the Humanities

Since 1974, book reviews have also been listed at the end of volumes of *Humanities Index, Readers' Guide to Periodical Literature, Education Index, Business Periodicals Index, General Science Index,* and other periodical indexes published by the Wilson Company.

Indexes to Periodical Articles.
  A. Indexes. These list periodical articles by subject and author.
   Art Index
   Business Periodicals Index
   Education Index
   General Science Index
   Humanities Index
   Public Affairs Information Service (Economics, political science, sociology, and public affairs.)
   Readers' Guide to Periodical Literature (Use for current events.)
   Social Sciences Index

Here is a sample entry from such an index:

Humanities Index

VICKREY, Robert Remsen
  about
   Robert Vickrey. B. Gallati. il Arts Mag 56:32 F '82
VICO, Giovanni Battista
  about
   From Machiavelli to Vico: three books by Rocco Montano [review article] E. G. Caserta. Comp Lit Stud 19:67-75 Spr '82
   Genetic interpretation of divine providence in Vico's New science. S. R. Luft. J Hist Philos 20:151-69 Ap '82
   Twelve tables and their origins: an eighteenth-century debate. M. Steinberg. J Hist Ideas 43:379-96 Jl/S '82
   Vico, Auerbach and literary history. T. Bahti. Philol Q 60:239-55 Spr '81
   Vico's notion of divine providence and the limits of human knowledge, freedom, and will. G. L. Lucente. MLN 97:183-91 Ja '82
   Was Vico's theory of history a true social science? H. Liebel-Weckowicz. Historian 44:466-82 Ag '82
VICTIMS of crimes
   Armenian survivors: a typological analysis of victim response. D. E. Miller and L. T. Miller. Oral Hist R 10:47-72 '82
VICTOR, David
   Life guard [poem] Mich Q R 21:169 Wint '82
VICTOR, Sextus Aurelius

Continued

Special Applications

```
                    Sources
        Sources of the De caesaribus. H. W. Bird. Class
          Q ns31 no2:457-63 '81
    VICTORY
        Second reading of Pindar: The fourth Nemean.
          M. M. Willcock. Greece & Rome 29:1-10 Ap
          '82
        Victorious charioteer on mosaics and related
          monuments. K. M. D. Dunbabin il Am J
          Archaeol 86:65-89 Ja '82
        Winners and losers: the limits of pragmatism
          and moralism in politics. I. L. Horowitz. New
          Lit Hist 13:515-32 Spr '82
        La VIDA de Lazarillo de Tormes y de sus
          fortunas y adversidades (novel) See Lazarillo
          de Tormes (novel)
    VIDEO art
        Growing up wired. D. Boyle. il Am Film 7:21-3
          Jl/Ag '82
        Video guru. M. Sturken. il Am Film 7:13-16 My
          '82
    VIDEO discs. See Video records
    VIDEO display terminal. See Information display
        systems
    VIDEO recorders and recording
            See also
        Household electronics
        Video art
        Video records
    VIDEO records
        Hi-fi: on the beam. H. Fantel. Opera News 46:
          34-5 Ap 17 '82
    VIDEO tapes. See Videotapes
    VIDEOTAPES
            See also
        Video art

        Caught in the act: video performance. A. Greene.
          Am Film 7:66-70+ Je '82
        Common carrier: performance by artists. P.
          Monk. il Mod Drama 25:163-9 Mr '82
        Mondo video. J. Waters. il Am Film 7:17-20+
          Je '82
        Movies on tape. L. P. Robley. Am Film 7:20+
          Ap '82
    VIDEOTAPES in courtroom proceedings
        Trial by tape. M. J. Weiss. Am Film 7:61-4 Je
          '82
```

    B. Abstracts. These index journal articles and some books by author and subject, and include a brief summary (abstract) for each item.
        America: History and Life
        Communication Abstracts
        Psychological Abstracts
        Sociological Abstracts
        Women Studies Abstracts

Other Indexes

Bibliographic Index. Subject list of separately published bibliographies as well as bibliographies appearing at the end of books and journal articles.

Essay and General Literature Index. Indexes chapters and essays in books by subject and author in the fields of philosophy, literature, political science, economics, education, history, and science.

Monthly Catalog of United States Government Publications. Indexes government documents by subject, author and title.

Getting Ready to Write Research Papers

New York Times Index. Subject index to the *New York Times* newspaper, giving the date, page, and column as well as a brief synopsis of each article.

New York Times Index. The *New York Times Index* is an annual subject index to articles published in the *New York Times Newspaper*. Each volume covers one year's articles. References are arranged chronologically under each subject heading and give the date, page, column, and a brief synopsis of the article.

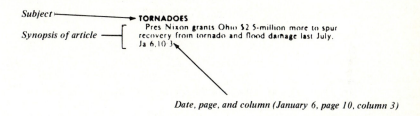

Note that no year is given with the rest of the date. The year is marked on the outside of each volume and is not repeated within the volume.

Sources of Biographical Information. This selective listing includes some of the most useful tools for locating information about people living and dead. For book-length biographies on individuals, check the library's card catalog under the subject heading: "[person's name]—Biography"

I. Persons from all geographical areas and all time periods:
Biography Index
Chambers Biographical Dictionary
Encyclopedia Britannica
Webster's Biographical Dictionary

II. Living or recently deceased persons, all geographical areas:
Current Biography
International Who's Who
New York Times Biographical Edition

III. Persons of specific nationalities:
American:
Dictionary of American Biography (historical)
Notable American Women 1607–1950 (contemporary)
Who's Who in America (contemporary)
Who's Who Among Black Americans (contemporary)
British:
Dictionary of National Biography (historical)
Who's Who (contemporary)

Special Applications

IV. Persons in specific occupational fields:
    Art:
        Contemporary Artists (contemporary)
        Index to Artistic Biography (historical)
    Literature:
        Cassell's Encyclopedia of World Literature (historical)
        Contemporary Authors (contemporary)
    Music:
        Baker's Biographical Dictionary of Musicians (historical & contemporary)
    Science:
        American Men & Women of Science (contemporary)
        Dictionary of Scientific Biography (historical)
    Social Sciences:
        Directory of American Scholars (contemporary)
        International Encyclopedia of the Social Sciences (historical)
        Names in the History of Psychology (historical)
        Political Profiles (contemporary, since 1940)

Sources of Statistical Information

Europa Yearbook. Statistical, political, financial, and trade information on individual countries. Also contains information on the United Nations and other International organizations.

Historical Statistics of the United States From Colonial Times to 1970. Published by the U.S. Census Bureau, this reference book includes statistics about agriculture, transportation, housing, income, prices, migration, media and other areas in which the government has collected information.

Statistical Abstracts of the United States. Published annually by the U.S. Census Bureau. Shows the latest political, economic, and social statistics for the United States.

UNESCO Statistical Yearbook. Education, science, publishing, and media statistics from UNESCO countries.

World Almanac. Annually updated compendium of statistics on all subjects, facts about events, and information on personalities and organizations, etc.

NONPAPER RESOURCES

As I mentioned in the section on interviews, some of the most valuable information may be found by talking to people rather than looking in a book. But paper resources in the library can help you find people who will answer questions for you. The reference librarian can tell you where to find information about local research centers, professional organizations, and government offices that may have information on your topic. You may want to interview the members of such groups. In addition, many libraries include telephone directories in their collections, which can tell you about other local and national groups and individuals who can help you with your topic.

Information continues to expand at geometric rates, and as the quality and durability of paper decrease, libraries are turning to other forms of technology for storing information. Some microform collections extend beyond newspapers to include journal articles and even book-length manuscripts. Audio and video tapes offer additional resources. But perhaps the most revolutionary technology is provided by computers in the library.

In addition to facilitating administrative tasks such as circulation, computers can search for information. Some libraries have facilities for computer-based reference services that use key words to search for information and to compile bibliographies. Besides being faster than manual search methods, computerized searches are more thorough and efficient. Computerized searches are particularly effective when your topic requires the coordination of two or more sets of subject terms; when your topic is so new or obscure that it may not appear as a subject heading in printed indexes; when little about your topic has been published, or it is very narrow; when your topic is so broad that it would be listed under many synonymous headings, making a manual search of printed indexes extremely time-consuming.

Of course, there are both financial and time costs attached to computer-based reference services. The charges vary according to the complexity of the topic and the number of references printed in the bibliography, but a specialized reference librarian can usually estimate the cost of a specific search. A computerized search may take a week or more, whereas a manual search can be done immediately. And, of course, there is no guarantee that the information provided by a computerized search will be useful to you. As is true with most aspects of writing, decisions about manual versus computerized searches will involve juggling constraints and will ultimately be up to you.

EVALUATING LIBRARY RESOURCES

The evaluation of library resources takes several forms, but the most important is your continuing dialogue with yourself as you read titles, scan articles, and examine books, constantly taking notes and asking yourself whether what you read will inform your writing. A continuing evaluation of information ensures that the eventual collection will be useful. At the same time the dialogue of evaluation can help you refine and shape your topic, because the additional information will give you a new way of viewing your ideas. Evaluating information in the library resembles standing on the other side of an argument and pretending you are the audience to be convinced. The convincing information will survive the evaluation process.

Checking the Quality of Periodicals. The internal process of constantly asking yourself questions and deciding which information to keep and which to discard is primary, but there are other things to consider. For example, the library contains tools that can help you evaluate the sources of your

Special Applications

information. You know that an article in *Family Circle Magazine* will not be as scholarly as one from the *Journal of Verbal Learning,* and you would probably include information from the latter and omit the former. However, it is often difficult to make more subtle discriminations among journals. Fortunately, the library's reference section contains tools to aid in this process of evaluation. Katz's *Magazines for Libraries* and Farber's *Classified List of Periodicals for the College Library* both evaluate periodicals and can help you decide which journals will be the most helpful.

Evaluating Books. Although there is no equivalent to Katz or Farber for books, there are a number of ways to determine which will serve you best. The documentation in the book provides a major clue. Books containing bibliographies can lead you to other sources, and if the bibliographies include annotations or descriptions, you have an important resource. Because bibliographies can look backward only, the most recent books will be the most valuable because they will offer the most current bibliography. As you become more familiar with the library, you may begin to distinguish among publishers and recognize those that produce quality work. If you are interested in the merits of a particular book, you can check the *Book Review Index* to see what reviewers have said about it.

Primary and Secondary Sources. Another approach to evaluation is to distinguish between primary and secondary sources. A primary source is the original document, statement, record, or narrative. A secondary source is something written about it. For example, Jean Piaget's *The Language and Thought of the Child* is a primary source, whereas a book such as Formaneck's and Gurian's *Charting Intellectual Development: A Practical Guide to Piagetian Tasks,* which describes Piaget's work, is a secondary source. However, the definition of primary sources can be slippery, depending on your topic. If your topic is Piaget's theory of psychology, then his own book will be a primary source, but if your topic is implementing Piaget's theories in the classroom, then the Formaneck and Gurian will be a primary source. In general, primary sources are better than secondary ones, and knowing how to distinguish between the two contributes to evaluative skill.

Plagiarism

When you read a book or an article, you assume that the author is representing facts correctly, is reporting results accurately, is repeating the words of others fairly. Similarly, your readers trust you to be truthful. They assume that your writing represents your own work, and that you will indicate where you have borrowed the words or ideas of others. Plagiarism breaks this trust between writer and reader because writers claim others' work as their own when they plagiarize.

Many colleges have stiff penalties for plagiarism, which can include automatic failure in the course in which the plagiarism occurs, academic probation,

Getting Ready to Write Research Papers

expulsion, or even denial of a degree. One of the most publicized plagiarism cases in recent history involved a graduating senior at an ivy league university. Because one of her professors accused her of plagiarizing in a paper, the university refused to grant her a degree, and when she took the case to court, the judge refused to override the university's decision.

Plagiarism can occur in a variety of ways, and you should avoid all forms of it. One form is using a passage word for word without enclosing it in quotation marks or acknowledging the author's name. This is the easiest form to find, but there are others. Plagiarism also occurs if you use words and phrases without enclosing them in quotation marks or acknowledging the author. Paraphrasing ideas without acknowledgment is also plagiarizing. Your instructor can help you if you have further questions about plagiarism.

NOTE CARDS

Although it is always essential to document your sources, the method may vary according to your audience. In writing this book, for instance, I drew on a variety of sources, but I avoided including footnotes in the text because I thought they would distract the readers who are more interested in learning and writing than in current theories of composition. Accordingly, I noted sources in the preface. Your instructors may have specific instructions about the forms of documentation for their papers. For an explanation of typical footnote and bibliography documentation, see Chapter 14.

The best way to avoid plagiarism is to take careful notes on your sources of information. Look again at the source card for the Flora book and at the note card for the article on the Lubbock tornado to see how bibliographical information is recorded.

QC
955
F33
Flora, Snowden D.
Tornadoes of the United States
Norman, OK: University of Oklahoma Press
1953

①551.505 WE
Fugita, L.T.
"Lubbock Tornadoes: A Study of Suction Spots"
pp. 161–73 bibliog.
Weatherwise
August 1970
Volume 23

Special Applications

As you can see, the student has included all the information that will be needed for documentation in her paper. The notes on the card appear in two forms: summaries and exact quotations. As you probably recall from Chapter 4, narration provides the foundation for many other kinds of learning and writing. The best way to find out what you know about material found in the library is to put it in your own words rather than to copy it in the author's words. Yet, you will undoubtedly find phrases or sentences that express your ideas very effectively and that lend authority to your argument. These should be copied exactly and enclosed in quotation marks so that you will remember that they are actual quotations.

Having said all this, I must confess that my own notes are never completely adequate. I jot down the complete information about the source, read through the article, summarize it for myself, and copy quotations that strike me as important. However, when I begin writing I frequently find that I need another quotation, just above or just below the one I have written down, and so I have to look at the article again. Accordingly, to avoid making extra trips to the library, I take the article to a copy machine after I read it for the first time. Making the copy does not substitute for taking notes, because the process of note taking helps me learn more about my topic, but the copy saves me time later and also helps me verify facts for my bibliography.

EXERCISE

The following exercises ask you to follow search strategies in the library on your campus. If the books mentioned are not in your library or if you are currently working on a research paper, substitute others.

1. A book called *Weasel Words: The Art of Saying What You Don't Mean,* by Mario A. Pei, was published in 1978. Find the author card for this book in the card catalogue. The information at the bottom of the card includes the subject headings assigned to the book, which are headings you could look under to find more books on the same subject. List the subject headings used for this book. Now look for another book under one of these headings. Note its title and author. Next use the cumulated *Book Review Index* to find a review of Pei's book. Note the journal, volume, date, and page of the review. Find the review in the periodicals section and read it. Finally, write a paragraph sumarizing the review.
2. Imagine that you need information on the Norse discovery of Greenland. Use the *Social Sciences Index* in the reference area to find three articles on this subject. What subject heading must you use to find this information? List the article title, journal title, volume, pages, and date for the three articles.
3. Imagine that you are writing a paper on euthenasia. Go to the *Encyclopedia of Bioethics* and find an article on the right to refuse medical care. What is the fundamental objective of the "doctrine of informed consent?" There is a list of related articles at the end of this one; which

Getting Ready to Write Research Papers

one will you read next? Why? Check the *Library of Congress Subject Headings*. Under what headings will you find books on your topic?

4. Suppose that you are writing a paper about the American artist Milton Avery. What information can you find in the *Encyclopedia of World Art*? Avery died in 1965. Which reference source would tell you more about his biography? You know that during his lifetime, Avery was overshadowed by other artists. What have critics written about his work since his death? Check the *New York Times Index* for articles.

Assimilate Information

As you gather information from other people and from library resources, you will need to develop ways of assimilating it into your thinking about your topic. Various forms of writing can help you incorporate new information into your thinking.

ANNOTATE READINGS

With books you own or with photocopies of articles or chapters, you may find it helpful to make notes in the margins of the text. This is called *annotating*. The process of annotating allows you to "talk back" to what you read. You can note repetitions, ask questions, make comments, draw lines from one selection to another, and use many other forms of writing to respond to what you read. The example below illustrates several types of annotation. The marginal brackets highlight key points, the circles note repetitions, the boxes mark key terms, and the marginal questions suggest new departures.

Annotating texts offers a basic means of assimilating new information. Using several forms of annotation will help you see patterns in what you read, help you, for example, identify new terms, note places where you need further information, and make connections between main ideas. Annotating can also be used effectively with activities such as paraphrasing and summarizing.

CREATE DIALOGUES

An alternative to writing in the text itself is to take notes in your journal. Effective notes record the most important parts of a selection so you can retrieve the information later. Although notes by themselves are useful, a dialogue between notes and your responses to the reading can be even more effective. Writing both notes and responses to reading creates an internal dialogue about the material. One format for this kind of internal discussion is to use the left page for note taking or putting reading material in your own words and the right page for writing your response to what appears on the left page.

Writing this kind of dialogue resembles the internal discussion you might have with yourself about whether or not to do something of which your family

345

Special Applications

What about Van Gogh et al. impressed the younger painters?

Does this relate to minimalistic art?

Is this a purely aesthetic view?

The twentieth century may be said, so far as painting is concerned, to have begun five years late. Between 1901 and 1906, several comprehensive exhibitions of the work of Van Gogh, Gauguin, and Cézanne were held in Paris. Thus, for the first time the achievements of these masters became accessible to a broad public. The young painters who had grown up in the "decadent," morbid mood of the 1890s were profoundly impressed, and several of them developed a radical new style, full of violent color and bold distortions. On their first public appearance, in 1905, they so shocked critical opinion that they were dubbed the *Fauves* (the wild beasts), a label they wore with pride. Actually, it was not a common program that brought them together, but their shared sense of liberation and experiment. As a movement, Fauvism comprised numerous loosely related, individual styles, and the group dissolved after a few years.

Its leading member was Henri Matisse (1869–1954), the oldest of the founding fathers of twentieth-century painting. *The Joy of Life* (fig. 770), probably the most important picture of his long career, sums up the spirit of Fauvism better than any other single work. It obviously derives its flat planes of color, heavy undulating outlines, and the "primitive" flavor of its forms from Gauguin (see colorplate 69); even its subject suggests the vision of Man in a state of Nature that Gauguin had pursued in Tahiti (see fig. 761). But we soon realize that these figures are not Noble Savages under the spell of a native god; the subject is a pagan scene in the Classical sense—a bacchanal, like Titian's (compare colorplate 41). Even the poses of the figures have for the most part a Classical origin, and in the apparently careless draughtsmanship resides a profound knowledge of the human body (Matisse had been trained in the academic tradition). What makes the picture so revolutionary is its radical simplicity, its "genius of omission": everything that possibly can be, has been left out or stated by implication only, yet the scene retains the essentials of plastic form and spatial depth. Painting, Matisse seems to say, is the rhythmic arrangement of line and color on a flat plane, but it is not only that; how far can the image of nature be pared down without destroying its basic properties and thus reducing it to mere surface ornament? "What I am after, above all," he once explained, "is expression . . . [But] . . . expression does not consist of the passion mirrored upon a human face . . . The whole arrangement of my picture is expressive. The placement of figures or objects, the empty spaces around them, the proportions, everything plays a part." But what, we wonder, does *The Joy of Life* express? Exactly what its title says. Whatever his debt to Gauguin, Matisse was never stirred by the same agonized discontent with the "decadence" of our civilization. He had strong feelings about only one thing—the act of painting: this to him was an experience so profoundly joyous that he wanted to transmit it to the beholder in all its freshness and immediacy. The purpose of his pictures, he always asserted, was to give pleasure.

H. W. Janson, *History of Art*

Getting Ready to Write Research Papers

would disapprove. One part of your mind takes the family side, and the other takes "your" side as you consider the alternatives and consequences. A dialogue with reading material is less emotional, but the process is similar. To assimilate information is only half the job of reading. The other half is to respond, to ask questions, to look for places where the information does not make sense, to compare it with other things you have read or heard, and to connect it to various ideas in the reading. The following is a dialogue written by a student who read an article about the history of religion.

Notes
At the time of Christ's birth, there were four major civilizations, Roman Empire, Persian Empire, India, and China. Religions flourished in each of these. The cult of the Emperor; Greek philosophies such as Stoicism and Platonism; and Eastern mystery religions based on figures such as Mithra and Dionysius existed in the Roman Empire. Zoroastrianism was the official religion in the Persian Empire. (It resisted Christianity much more than did any of the religions of the Roman Empire.) Hinduism and later Buddhism were strong in India, and in China under the Han dynasty, Confucianism was the prominent religion, although Buddhism came later.

Response
It's funny, I know there was a Persian Empire, and I know the civilizations in India and China are very old, but somehow I don't think of them as contemporary with the Roman Empire. In fact, I don't think about them much at all. I know much more about the Roman Empire than the other three. I wonder if that is the result of my own religious history? I wonder what it was about Zoroastrianism that made it resist Christianity, and I wonder if Zoroastrianism still exists today if it was so strong then. I can't think of any countries that practice Zoroastrianism. I still don't understand the differences between Confucianism and Buddhism well enough. And where do the Hari Krishnas fit in?

As you can see, this response includes reflections on the writer's own knowledge and experience, questions that ask for further information about world religions, and comparisons between familiar and unfamiliar traditions. This response, in combination with the notes to the left, demonstrates that the writer is actively involved in learning about world religions. In addition

Special Applications

to facilitating learning, writing the responses helps the writer explore issues that may later be used in the research paper.

Paraphrase

When you read longer selections, you may find that annotations or notes are not enough to help you remember all the important points in what you read. You may find it helpful to paraphrase or write all the main points of a selection in your own words. The process of paraphrasing can help you assimilate new ideas because as you translate material into your own words you will become more conscious of special vocabulary, of how an argument is made, of the development of ideas within a piece of writing. The following is from an introduction to a text about essays. Read it carefully, and then go on to the paraphrase that follows.

What Is an Essay?

If you ask "What is an essay?" Michael de Montaigne should be allowed to answer first. Born into a wealthy, aristocratic French family in 1533, Montaigne retired into his study at the age of 38, after twenty years' work as counselor-at-law. He did so, he later explained, because he had decided that "To compose our character is our duty, not to compose books, and to win, not battles and provinces, but order and tranquility in our conduct." Too many men, he observed, sell themselves into servitude; "They seek business only for busyness," and in the course of attending to "men's affairs," they lose the independence of their soul.

At first his plan for retirement was "rest and seclusion," but in total idleness his mind grew distracted—frivolous, he thought—so that ultimately he determined to bridle it by setting his thoughts in writing. The result was three volumes of the world's first (and possibly best) essays. Two were published in 1580 and then republished—with revisions, additions, and a new third volume—in 1588, four years before his death. In 1603 John Florio translated Montaigne into English, but even before that Francis Bacon had already borrowed the term *essay,* and between 1597 and 1625 he wrote the first great essays in a rich English tradition.

To the reader who picked up his first essays, Montaigne frankly declared: "I have no thought of serving either you or my own glory." Furthermore, he warned, you will find here no formal elegance or studied posture: "I want to be seen . . . in my simple, natural ordinary fashion, without straining or artifice; for it is myself that I portray." Even for the Renaissance, this is a bold assertion of individualism, and coinciding as it does with the Protestant Reformation, political revolution, the discovery of the New World, and the advent of empirical science, the newborn essay reaffirms man's dignity and power even while it questions what new fortune freedom will bring.

The man portrayed in Montaigne's essays (and he believed any man might stand for Everyman) has, first of all, "an honest curiosity to inquire into all things." Montaigne wrote, he claimed, on the first subject that came to mind, thinking all subjects equally good and never intending to exhaust any of them. He believed that a subject might be tried, tested, assayed, but never exhausted, for no single man could contain the whole truth, only solitary bits and pieces.

Getting Ready to Write Research Papers

"Only the fools," he wrote, "are certain and assured." Yet despite his strong sense of human limitation, "I love life," he exclaimed, "and cultivate it just as God has been pleased to grant it to us." In Montaigne's mind, the surest sign of wisdom was "constant cheerfulness; her state is . . . ever serene."

Given this tolerance for life's ambiguities and such willingness to rest in uncertainty, it is not surprising that Montaigne should write *essays* "tests" or "trials" of human experience. "If my mind could gain a firm footing," he explained, "I would not make essays, I would make decisions; but it is always in apprenticeship and on trial."

—Paul Connolly, *On Essays*

Here is how one student paraphrased this passage:

    Michael de Montaigne, a Frenchman born in 1533, can tell us what an essay is. Montaigne retired from law at age 38 because he decided that "To compose our character is our duty, not to compose books, and to win, not battles and provinces, but order and tranquility in our conduct." This composing would, he felt, prevent people from losing their independence of soul.
    Distracted by idleness, Montaigne set his thoughts in writing. He wrote three volumes of the world's first essays. These were published between 1580 and 1588. Francis Bacon borrowed the term essay and wrote the first English essays between 1597 and 1625, some even before John Florio translated Montaigne into English in 1603.
    Montaigne warned his readers: "I have no thought of serving you or my own glory." He also announced that he wanted to appear natural and ordinary without formal elegance or artifice. This assertion of individualism coincided with the Protestant Reformation, political revolution, the discovery of the New World, and the advent of empirical science, thereby investing the essay with a reaffirmation of human dignity and power while questioning the new fortunes of freedom.
    Montaigne's essays portray a man with honest curiosity about all things. He wrote about many things, believing all subjects equally good and inexhaustable. Montaigne believed that no single essayist could portray the whole truth about a subject and he mocked those who were certain and assured. Despite this sense of human limitation, Montaigne loved life and found serenity in wisdom.
    Montaigne's essays or "trials" expressed his toler-

Special Applications

```
ance for ambiguity. He claimed that the difficulty of
gaining a firm mental footing led him to make essays
rather than decisions.
```

As you can see, this paraphrase contains all the information in the original. It reproduces completely, in the student's words, all the ideas that appeared in "What Is An Essay." This inclusion of all information marks one of the differences between a summary and a paraphrase. Summaries extract main ideas while paraphrases include all of them. Usually paraphrases avoid using the language of the original, but occasionally quotations or striking phrases are copied exactly. Paraphrases usually offer a more clear and simple version of the original.

Paraphrasing is frequently useful in writing research papers. It enables you to put a complicated argument in your own language or to explain difficult material. Putting ideas in your own words does not free you from the obligation to acknowledge your sources. It is just as important to document paraphrased sources as direct quotations.

SUMMARIZE

Another way to assimilate information from a long selection is to summarize it in your own words. While a paraphrase attempts to repeat all the ideas contained within a selection, a summary emphasizes the main ideas. It is usually considerably shorter than the original, and it is very selective. Here, for example, is a summary of "What Is An Essay":

```
    Michael de Montaigne, a Frenchman born in 1533,
originated the essay. After retiring from law at the
age of 38, Montaigne "composed himself" by writing
unaffectedly about a variety of subjects. Publication
and later translation of his essays or "trials" in-
itiated the tradition of English essays.
```

This summary includes the main ideas of the original but omits details and illustrations. Like the paraphrase, it translates the original into the student's own language, but it avoids repeating all the ideas of the original.

Documen-tation

Because research papers rely so heavily upon sources outside the writer's mind, they require writers to indicate the sources of their ideas as well as of quotations. This process of crediting sources is called *documentation*. Usually documentation appears both within the text (either in the form of footnotes

Getting Ready to Write Research Papers

or endnotes or in parenthetical references) and at the end in a bibliography or list of references. Your instructors will probably indicate which style of documentation they expect you to use, but three of the major styles are described in *The Chicago Manual of Style,* the *Publication Manual of the American Psychological Association,* and the Modern Language Association's *Handbook for Writers of Research Papers.*

You can consult these manuals for detailed information about documentation, but an introduction to the essentials of each appears in Chapter 11. Documentation in research papers depends upon keeping good records as you gather information. The source card on page 325 provides a model for keeping the data you will need for documentation. Getting in the habit of noting the author, title, and publication information of all the materials you consult can save you hours of retracing your steps in the library.

Copyright © G. E. Kirkpatrick, The National Audubon Society Collection/Photo Researchers, Inc.

Chapter Fourteen

Writing Research Papers

ONCE information for a research paper is gathered, it is time to follow the same processes that go with writing any paper. These processes include writing a first draft and then revising it by developing the thesis, considering the audience, developing an original plan, evaluating coherence and cohesion, editing, and documenting sources. Although most of these processes contribute to the writing of any paper, the length of typical research papers makes them more time-consuming.

The First Draft Because gathering information for research papers takes a long time, it may be tempting to try to save time by eliminating the first draft. The first-draft/last-draft research paper is rarely, however, effective. As is true with other forms of writing, the process of drafting leads to new insights into the material. Frequently, in writing the last sentence of a draft, you will discover what you really want to say about your subject. Drafting, in other words, can help you refine your thesis.

Writing to Show Learning Once you have written a draft of a research paper, you can begin the process of revising it to show your work to best advantage. The hours you have spent tracking down information on your topic will pay dividends if you give attention to revising your draft. Many of the same revising strategies that improve other types of drafts will work effectively with research papers.

Special Applications

RECONSIDER THE ASSIGNMENT

Just as is true with other types of school-sponsored writing, the assignment for a research paper can provide guidance as you revise. The two assignments discussed in Chapter 10 suggest the range of specificity. If it is like this sociology assignment for a research paper can provide guidance as you revise. The two assignments discussed in Chapter 10 suggest the range of specificity. If it is like this sociology assignment

> The final paper should focus on some issue discussed in this class. It should draw on out-of-class readings, use standard documentation and be at least ten typewritten pages.

you will not find much to guide your revision except the reminder to document your reading and adhere to the specified length. On the other hand, if the assignment is like this one from an atmospheric science class

> Your paper should provide a good meterological description of a weather or climate event. It does not need to be highly technical but should include background information. This paper should contain a minimum of six references, and should be at least ten typewritten pages (excluding references)

you will have more criteria against which to check your draft. Not only is the general topic (weather or climate event) specified, but a draft can be checked for background information, a minimum of six references, and the specified length.

In addition to considering the specifications of a particular assignment, this is also a good time to rethink the priorities of the discipline in which the research paper is being written. If the paper is for a course in the arts and humanities, more attention should be given to individual interpretation, direct perception, and the uniqueness and innate qualities of the item being considered. If it is for a course in the natural sciences, criteria of factual descriptions, observation, experimentation, and scientific laws should be considered. If it is for a course in the social sciences, considerations of interpreting how human beings act, along with observation, evidence, and verification, should be prominent. You may find it useful to return to pages 40–42 in Chapter 3 for further information about the priorities of various disciplines.

CONSIDER AUDIENCE

Thinking about disciplinary priorities is, of course, one way of considering the audience for your research paper. As you take account of what various disciplines value, you are considering the priorities of your audience. Similarly, the specifics of the assignment will lead you to consider your audience because the instructor who wrote the assignment will be your primary audience.

Writing Research Papers

Documentation is one special feature of research papers, and this, too, has implications for thinking about your audience. Many instructors will specify the documentation style they prefer, but if no style is indicated, you may need to choose one. Generally, audiences in the social sciences (and sometimes in the natural sciences) prefer the forms described in the *Publication Manual of the American Psychological Association,* and audiences in the arts and humanities would like you to use *The Chicago Manual of Style* or the Modern Language Association's *Handbook for Writers of Research Papers.* If you are uncertain, check with your instructor because appropriate documentation style indicates that you are interested in suiting your work to your audience's expections.

DEVELOP AN ORGANIZATIONAL PLAN

In looking at the first draft of your research paper, you will undoubtedly see the skeleton of some organizational structure. Perhaps your paper follows chronological order, reporting events as they occurred; perhaps it uses a classificatory structure, organizing information according to type or kind—grouping several composers of the romantic period together, for example, and comparing them with a group from the classical period; perhaps it looks at causes and effects, moving from cause to effect or the reverse; or perhaps it moves from specific cases to general patterns or it may do the reverse by starting with a general principle and moving to individual cases.

Whatever skeletal organizational plan you find, the process of revising should include a refining of it. Consider which organizational structure or combination of structures will work best with your material, and find ways to highlight your plan.

CONSIDER SUBHEADINGS

As is true for all writing, issues of coherence and cohesion should be considered during revision. After you have decided upon an organizational plan and developed a general structure for your writing, you will need to evaluate the coherence of the whole paper, ascertaining that all the sections work together to create a united effect. Similarly, check for cohesion to be sure that individual paragraphs connect to one another.

Because of their length, research papers can sometimes be divided into sections with subheadings designating the contents of each part. You may, for example, indicate sections of a political science paper with headings such as "introduction," "historical background," "recent developments," "conclusion." A biology paper might include subheadings such as "review of the literature," "methodology," "results," and "conclusion." Your subheadings may, alternatively, serve to introduce topics in your paper. For an example of subheadings used in a research paper, turn to "Grayout: Societal Hazards of Aging" on page 389. As with documentation style, your instructor may provide specific instructions.

355

Special Applications

INSERT QUOTATIONS

One of the special problems of writing research papers concerns the use of quotations. In most cases it is better to paraphrase or summarize information and ideas, using appropriate citations to credit the author, because too many quotations give your paper a cluttered quality. But there will be some occasions when you will want to use the exact words of one of your sources. You may find language that is particularly striking or you may want to call upon the authority of a given author. In these cases you should duplicate the source exactly. If there is an error in the source, copy it exactly and insert the Latin word *sic* in brackets immediately after the error to indicate that it comes from the source:

```
    A recent magazine article claims, "Drug use sepa-
rates young people from their familes [sic] and
friends."
```

Even though quotations should be reproduced exactly as they appear in the original, you may modify them in the following ways: emphasis, deletion, and insertion.

If you wish to emphasize specific words in a quotation, you can underline or use italics, adding a phrase such as (*emphasis added*) or (*italics added*):

```
    Harry Simon, an expert in crowd control, asserted,
"over 600 people participated in the demonstration at
the capitol" (emphasis added).
```

With long quotations, you may find it useful to delete parts that are not essential to your paper. Ellipsis marks of three periods with spaces before and after (. . .) indicate deletions in a quotation:

```
    Mary Kelley explains the problem with most portray-
als of women writers of the nineteenth century: "The
result has been not only to place them outside of
history . . . but also implicitly to deny the existence
of positive and substantive elements in the domestic
experience and thus in women's experience."
```

Writing Research Papers

If the grammar of a quotation does not fit your sentence, you may change it, indicating the changed words with brackets:

> The committee chair, who had served three terms in office, expressed his displeasure by explaining that the group "has . . . avoid[ed] yet another decision. If we continue in this fashion we will soon have nothing to decide about" (<u>News</u> 3).

Short quotations may be inserted into your text as shown in the examples above. Quotation marks indicate the words are quoted exactly, and the source can appear at the beginning, middle, or end of the quotation (see Kelley quotation above for an illustration of inserting the source at the beginning):

> Women writers of the nineteenth century have received little attention. "The result," writes Mary Kelley, "has been not only to place them outside of history . . . but also implicitly to deny the existence of positive and substantive elements in the domestic experience and thus in women's experience."
>
> Women writers of the nineteenth century have received little attention. "The result has been not only to place them outside of history . . . but also implicitly to deny the existence of positive and substantive elements in the domestic experience and thus in women's experience," writes Mary Kelley.

Longer quotations (more than five typed lines) are set off from the text and indented. No quotation marks are used with these blocks of text:

> George Eliot shows how the flood leads Maggie to row in search of her family:
>
> > The first thing that waked her to fuller consciousness was the cessation of the rain and a perception that the darkness was divided by the faintest light, which parted the over-

Special Applications

> hanging gloom from the immeasurable watery
> level below. She was driven out upon the flood,
> that awful visitation of God which her father
> used to talk of, which had made the nightmare
> of her childish dreams. And with that thought
> there rushed in the vision of the old home,
> and Tom, and her mother--they had all listened
> together.

As the examples above demonstrate, quotations may be introduced in several different ways:

- The colon (:) can be used to set the quotation off from the rest of the sentence.
- A comma (,) can be used to introduce a quotation.
- A statement using *that* can be used to introduce a quotation.

Regardless of what punctuation you use, try to avoid grammatical tangles and awkward phrasing as you insert quotations into your research paper. Be sure that verb tenses of your text and the quotation agree, that the introductory phrase or sentence moves smoothly into the quotation, and that changes in the quotation (such as additions and deletions) do not obscure its meaning.

Documentation

Sources for both quotations and paraphrased versions of what you have read should be acknowledged in your research paper. Citations of your sources help distinguish between your work and that of the individuals from whom you borrow, and they enable your readers to return to your sources if they want more information. In most cases your instructor will specify the documentation style to be used, but the three major styles are: the *Chicago Manual of Style's* system of footnotes (numbered notes that appear on the bottom of the page on which the information appears) or endnotes (a separate numerical listing of all the notes in the paper); the American Psychological Association's system of parenthetical citations (described in the *Publication Manual of the American Psychological Association*); and the new parenthetical documentation described in the 1984 Modern Language Association's *Handbook for Writers of Research Papers*; the following section introduces the main features of each system, but you should consult the appropriate handbook for more detailed information. For an example of a paper using APA style, see "The Lubbock Tornado," and see "Greyout: Societal Hazards of Aging," for an example of MLA style.

Writing Research Papers

Footnotes and endotes. Footnotes and endnotes are indicated in the text by a number slightly raised above the line. These numbers should be consecutive throughout the paper, rather than beginning with number one on each new page. See the following examples of both footnotes and endnotes.

Placement of Footnotes

    Six hundred to twelve hundred tornadoes occur in the United States each year. Approximately two-thirds of these are small tornadoes whose winds range from 40 to 112 m.p.h. The normal lifespan of these small tornadoes is usually one to three minutes, and their damage paths are generally less than one mile long and 100 yards wide.[1] In contrast, the Lubbock tornado of 1970 was a combination of one small and one extremely large tornado which contained winds of over 290 m.p.h. and had a damage path over two miles wide.[2]

    [1]Snowden F. Flora, <u>Tornadoes of the United States</u> (Norman, OK: University of Oklahoma Press, 1953), p. 32.

    [2]Thomas T. Fujita, "Lubbock Tornadoes: A Study of Suction Spots," <u>Weatherwise</u>, 23 (August 1970), 162.

— Notes indicated by raised numbers in the text

— Four spaces between text and first note

— Double space within and between notes

Note numbers indented five spaces and raised

Special Applications

Sample Endnotes

Numbers indented five spaces and raised → NOTES ← *Triple space between title and first note*

¹Snowden F. Flora, Tornadoes of the United States (Norman, OK: University of Oklahoma Press, 1953), pp. 32-34. ← *Double space within and between notes*

²Thomas T. Fujita, "Lubbock Tornadoes: A Study of Suction Spots," Weatherwise, 23 (August 1970), 162.

*Form Guide for Footnotes**

Type of Entry	Footnote Form (first footnote)
Book (single author)	¹Lucy Komisar, The New Feminism (New York: Franklin Watts, 1971), p. 79.
Book (more than one author)	²Ell Ginzberg and Robert M. Solow, eds., The Great Society (New York: Basic Books, 1974), p. 11.
Book (corporate author)	³Council of Europe, Handbook of European Organizations (Strasbourg: Secretariat-General of the Council of Europe, 1956), p. 9.
Article from book	⁴Jean-Pierre Worms, "The French Student Movement." In Student Activism, Alexander De Conde, ed. (New York: Scribner, 1971), p. 79.
Article from journal	⁵Patrick Brantlinger, "Dickens and the Factories." Nineteenth Century Fiction 26 (December 1971), 271.
Article from newspaper	⁶Editorial, Wall Street Journal, November 1, 1966, p. 8.

*Based on: A Manual of Style, 13 ed. rev. (Chicago: Univ. of Chicago Press, 1982).

Writing Research Papers

Place the note number at the end of the sentence(s) in which you have used a source, as the following example indicates:

Small tornadoes behave very much like suction vortices and actually cannot be differentiated from suction vortices. The rotation of the individual vortices within the tornado "determines the tornado's damage pattern."[1]

One footnote can be used for more than one source; to do this, put a semicolon between the sources.

---

[2]Theodore Fujita and G. S. Forbes, "Three Scales of Motion Involving Tornadoes," in L. B. Snowden, <u>Photogrammetric Analysis of Tornados</u> (Chicago: University of Chicago Press, 1972), p. 32; Allen Pearson, Symposium on Tornadoes (Columbia; University of Missouri Press, 1969), pp. 54-56.

Notes can also offer additional information that if included in the text would distract readers from your central point.

Violence on television has increased dramatically since it first appeared on "Cheyenne" in the mid-1950s.[2] This increase has led to protests from television viewers, and the protests have forced the networks to take some programs off the air.

[2]I define violence as an overt expression of physical force against self or other, action against one's will or pain of being hurt or killed, or actual hurting or killing.

Once you have made reference to a source, you do not need to provide all of the publication information a second time. Second and all later references to the same source may be made in abbreviated form. This can be done with a numbered note:

361

Special Applications

> ³Pearson, p. 83.

If you use more than one publication by the same author, include the title (or a shortened form of a very long title) in your abbreviated note:

> ³Pearson, p. 83, Symposium on Tornadoes, p. 83.

APA Parenthetical Citations. Courses in the social and physical sciences frequently use parenthetical documentation. There are several styles, but the American Psychological Association's is a common one. APA style documents sources with parenthetical references within the text. If you use a source without mentioning the author's name in the text, the parenthetical reference should include the author's name, date of publication, and page(s) of the source. You can insert the parenthetical reference just before the cited material in a way that does not interrupt the flow of your statement:

> One researcher (Pearson, 1969, pp. 54-55) found that damage results from three features of the tornado: pressure differences, airborne missles, and wind intensity.

Or you can insert the parenthetical reference just after the cited material:

> Recent research on tornadoes indicates that damage results from three features of the tornado: pressure differences, airborn missiles, and wind intensity (Pearson, 1969, pp. 54-55).

As is true with abbreviated footnotes, including the date in the parenthetical reference allows you to distinguish between two or more works by the same author. If you cite two publications by the same author dated in the same year, put a lower-case *a* after the date of the one whose title comes first alphabetically, *b* after the next one, and so on.

> (1968a; 1968b).

Writing Research Papers

If you include the author's name in the text, you need include only the date and page number(s) in your parenthetical reference:

```
According to Pearson (1969, pp. 54-55), tornado
damage results from three features of the tornado:
"pressure differences, airborne missiles, and wind
intensity."
```

The following guide indicates the appropriate parenthetical form for various types of sources.

Form Guide for Parenthetical Citations*

Type of Entry	Reference Citation in Text
Book (single author)	(Komlsar, 1971, p. 79)
Book (more than one author)	(Strunk & White, 1972, Chap. 3)
Article from book	(Riesen, 1966, p. 236)
Article from journal (two authors)	(Atkinson & Shiffrin, 1971, p. 90)
Article from journal (no author)	("The Blood Business," 1972)
Article from newspaper	("Amazing Amazon Region," 1969)

*Based on *Publication Manual*, 3rd ed. (American Psychological Association, 1983)

MLA Parenthetical Citations. Courses in arts and humanities are moving toward parenthetical documentation similar to that used in the social and physical sciences. The most recent edition of the *MLA Handbook* describes this new style in detail. As is true of APA style, MLA documentation identifies the location of the borrowed information as specifically and concisely as possible. The form and content of parenthetical citations vary according to what is included in the text. For example, if you include the author's name in the text, the parenthetical citation need include only the page number:

```
Burke takes exception to this view (191-232).
```

But if the author's name is not included in the text, it should be included in the citation:

Special Applications

> At least one prominent rhetorician has taken exception to this view (Burke 191-232).

Note that no comma appears between the author's name and the page numbers and that neither the word *page* nor its abbreviation is used. As the examples above illustrate, the parenthetical reference should appear where a pause would naturally occur, usually at the end of a sentence, and if a quotation comes at the end of a sentence, insert the parenthetical citation between the closing quotation mark and the concluding punctuation mark:

> James Moffett writes, "I must use a vocabulary, style, logic and rhetoric that anybody in that mass audience can understand and respond to" (37).

If you refer to an entire work, you should include the author's name in the text, and it is not necessary to use a parenthetical reference:

> Elizabeth Eisenstein wrote the most comprehensive study of this subject.

Form Guide for MLA Parenthetical Citations. For the above reference, as for all parenthetical citations, the *List of Works Consulted* (which will be discussed in a later section) provides complete publication information. The following guide illustrates appropriate MLA form for various types of sources. It is based on the *MLA Handbook for Writer's of Research Papers,* 2nd edition (MLA, 1984).

Type of Entry	*Reference Citation in Text*
Book (single author)	When author's name appears in text: (131–132)
	When author's name does not appear in text: (Smith 131–132)
Book (more than one author)	When authors' names appear in text: (29)
	When authors' names do not appear in text: (Gilbert and Gubar 29)
Book (corporate author)	When author's name appears in text: (62)

Writing Research Papers

	When author's name does not appear in text: (Commission on the Humanities 62)
Article from book	When author's name appears in text: (175)
	When author's name does not appear in text: (Scribner 175)
Article from journal	When author's name appears in text: (234)
	When author's name does not appear in text: (Cooper 234)
Article from journal (no author)	When title of article appears in text: (182)
	When title of article does not appear in text: ("Modern Art" 182)
Article from newspaper	When author's name appears in text: (5)
	When author's name does not appear in text: (Boren 5)

Bibliography. The bibliography is usually the last part of the research paper and contains a list of all the works cited in the footnotes. In research appears using footnotes or endnotes, a bibliography is often superfluous because it repeats what has already been stated in the notes, but you should check your instructor's preferences. The following lists contain sample bibliography entries which follow the *Chicago Manual of Style*:

Sample Bibliography

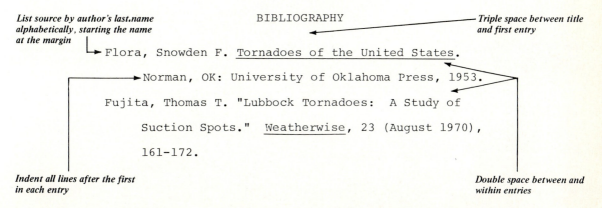

365

Special Applications

*Form Guide for Bibliographies**

Type of Entry	Bibliography Form
Book (single author)	Komisar, Lucy. <u>The New Feminism</u>. New York: Franklin Watts, 1971.
Book (more than one author)	Ginsberg, Eli and Solow, Robert M., eds. <u>The Great Society</u>. New York: Basic Books, 1974.
Book (corporate author)	Council of Europe. <u>Handbook of European Organizations</u>. Strasbourg: Secretariat-General of the Council of Europe, 1956.
Article from book	Worms, Jean-Pierre. "The French Student Movement," in <u>Student Activism</u>, Alexander De Conde, ed. New York: Scribner, 1971, p. 72-86.
Article from journal	Brantlinger, Patrick. "Dickens and the Factories." <u>Nineteenth Century Fiction</u> 26 (<u>December 1971</u>): 270-85.
Article from newspaper	<u>Wall Street Journal</u>. Editorial, November 1, 1966, p. 8.

List of Works Cited (APA Style). If you use parenthetical citations, a *List of Works Cited* is an essential part of your paper, because this is the only place where full publication information will appear. The following guide shows APA style for listing various types of entries:

Sample List of References
(for Parenthetical Citations—APA style)

REFERENCES

List sources alphabetically by author's last name → *Triple space between title and first entry*

Flora, S.F. <u>Tornadoes of the United States</u>. Norman, OK: University of Oklahoma Press, 1953.

Fujita, T.T. Lubbock tornadoes: A study of suction spots. <u>Weatherwise</u>, 1970, 23, 161-172.

Indent all lines after the first in each entry — *Double space within and between entries*

Writing Research Papers

Form Guide for List of References (APA Style)

Type of Entry	Form of Entry
Book (single author)	Bernstein, T.M. (1965). *The careful writer: A modern guide to English usage.* New York: Atheneum.
Book (more than one author)	Gilbert, S. M. & Gubar, S. (1979). *The madwoman in the attic: The woman writer and the nineteenth-century imagination.* Bloomington: Indiana University Press.
Book (corporate author)	American Psychiatric Association. (1980). *Diagnostic and statistical manual of mental disorders* (3rd ed.). Washington, DC: Author.
Article from book	Hartley, J. T., Harker, J. O., & Walsh, D. A. (1980). Contemporary issues and new directions in adult development of learning and memory. In L. W. Poon (Ed.) *Aging in the 1980s: Psychological issues* (pp. 239-252). Washington, DC: American Psychological Association.
Article from journal	Paivio, A. (1975). Perceptual comparisons through the mind's eye. *Memory & Cognition.* 3, 635-647.
Article from newspaper	Lublin, J. S. (1980, December 5). On idle: The unemployed shun much mundane work, at least for a while. *The Wall Street Journal,* p. 1.

List of Works Cited (MLA Style). Because parenthetical citations following MLA style do not include publication date as do those following APA style, the *List of Works Consulted* is even more important to readers. This list provides the only source of complete publication information and should be attached

367

Special Applications

to the end of your research paper. Each entry has three main parts—author, title and publication information—each followed by a period and two spaces. The following guide illustrates MLA style for entries in this list:

Sample List of Works Cited
(for Parenthetical Citations—MLA Style)

List sources alphabetically by author's last name or, where there is no author, by first word in the title.

```
            LIST OF WORKS CITED
Booth, Wayne C. "Kenneth Burke's Way if Knowing."  Critical

    Inquiry 1 (1974):1-22.

Commission on the Humanities.  The Humanities in American

    Life:  Report of the Commission on the Humanities.

    Berkeley:  U of California P, 1980.

Gilbert, Sandra M., and Susan Gubar.  The Madwoman in the Attic:

    The Woman Writer and the Nineteenth-Century Literary

    Imagination.  New Haven:  Yale UP, 1979.

O'Connor, Flannery.  "The Life You Save May Be Your Own."

    The Realm of Fiction:  Seventy-Four Stories.  Ed. James B.

    Hall and Elizabeth C. Hall. 3rd ed. New York:  McGraw,

    1977. 479-88.
```

Indent all lines after the first line in each entry

Double space within and between entries

Form Guide for Works Consulted (MLA Style)

Type of Entry	Form of Entry
Book (single author)	Clark, Kenneth. *What Is a Masterpiece?* London: Thames, 1979.
Book (more than one author)	Scholes, Robert, and Eric Rabkin. *Science Fiction: History, Science, Vision.* New York: Oxford UP, 1977.

Book (corporate author)	Commission on the Humanities. *The Humanities in American Life: Report of the Commission on the Humanities.* Berkeley: U of California P, 1980.
Article from book	Schafer, John. "The Linguistic Analysis of Spoken and Written Texts." *Exploring Speaking-Writing Relationships: Connections and Contrasts.* Ed. Barry M. Kroll and Roberta Vann. Urbana: NCTE, 1981. 1-31.
Article from journal	Spear, Karen. "Building Cognitive Skills in Basic Writers." *Teaching English in the Two-Year College* 9 (1983): 91-98.
Article from newspaper	Greenberg, Daniel S. "Ridding American Politics of Polls." *Washington Post* 16 Sept. 1980: A 17.

Special Applications

Sample Research Paper (APA Style)

The following paper, written for an atmospheric science class, uses parenthetical citations and a list of references in APA style. You may recall the Lubbock tornado topic from Chapter 13. As you read this paper, notice how the sources located through search strategies have been integrated with additional information in order to produce a unified paper. This paper, like all finished writing, went through several revisions before the author began to think about the format used here.

The Lubbock Tornado: May 11, 1970

Ruth E. Nicholson
Atmospheric Science 101
February 23, 1983

GENERAL CHARACTERISTICS OF TORNADOES:

Six hundred to twelve hundred tornadoes occur in the United States each year. Approximately two-thirds of these are small tornadoes whose winds range from 40 to 112 m.p.h. The normal lifespan of these small tornadoes is usually one to three minutes, and their damage paths are generally less than one mile long and 100 yards wide. The other third of these tornadoes is mostly comprised of medium-sized tornadoes whose winds vary from 113 to 206 m.p.h. Their damage paths usually are in the range of ten miles long and 300 yards wide. "Maximum tornadoes" make up one to five percent of all

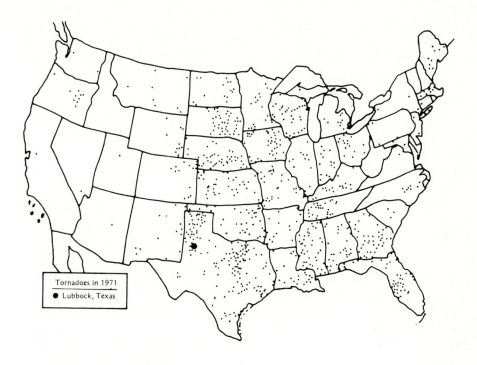

Figure 1. Typical Tornado Distribution in the United States

reported tornadoes. These tornadoes are rare, but they account for 70% of all tornado-related deaths. Although they are the easiest to detect, maximum tornadoes are the most destructive of all tornadoes. The wind-speeds in a maximum tornado can be as much as 300 m.p.h. They may exist as long as three hours and leave damage paths up to 200 miles long and a mile and a half wide (Flora, 1953, pp. 40-42). No area is more favorable to the formation of tornadoes than the midcontinent of North America (see Figure 1). No month is free of these violent storms, but the number of tornadoes reaches a peak in May. The second largest number of tornadoes occurs in April and June. The "tornado season" runs from April to June because two-thirds of all tornadoes occur in these months. September is also a "good" month for tornadoes, but fall tornadoes are a bit different from spring tornadoes and are generally weaker. The lowest frequency of tornadoes is found in the months of December and January. Generally, the best time of day for tornado formation is in the late afternoon and early evening (Weems, 1977, p. 132).

In order for a tornado to form, some specific meterological conditions must be met. These conditions are:

1. mass convergence near surface
2. mass divergence aloft
3. a buoyant air mass
4. wind sheer in the vertical
5. moist air mass in the lower layers
6. a "trigger" mechanism
7. surface cyclogenesis (NOAA, 1978)

Tornadoes form in the middle portion of very intense

thunderstorms. Warm, moist air feeds the thunderstorm at the rear of the storm while wind, rain, and hail are produced at the front. The usual weather sequence preceding a tornado is high winds, rain, and then hail. The tornado itself is a center of extremely low pressure surrounded by high winds. These winds rotate counter-clockwise in the northern hemisphere due to the Coriolis force. Eighty percent of tornadoes are formed from a wall cloud that is located near the rain-free base of the storm. The wall cloud is usually one to three miles wide and often forms 20 to 30 minutes before a tornado appears. If and when the wall cloud begins to rotate, it is called a funnel. A tornado that is formed from a funnel or wall cloud may form as much as 20 to 30 minutes before it descends to the ground. Note that a funnel or funnel cloud differs from a tornado in that a funnel is a violently rotating column of air that does not touch the ground or cause any damage. The visible part of a tornado is comprised of small water droplets, dust, and debris, but tornadoes are not always visible. The tornado has a characteristic life cycle. During the first half of its "life" the tornado increases in size and intensity; the second half, it contracts into a rope-like structure and tilts before dissipating. Tornadoes are capable of splitting into two separate tornadoes or forming

Special Applications

five or six smaller tornadoes inside the main tornado. Separate tornadoes can also combine to form a single tornado (Gaston, 1974, p. 516).

Tornadoes have three scales of motion: the movement of the tornado as a whole, the tornado cyclone, and suction vortices. Generally, tornadoes move from the southwest to the northeast. The tornado cyclone is the parent cyclone from which tornadoes form. Suction vortices form inside large tornadoes. A suction vortex is a small, spinning mass of air usually less than 30 feet in diameter. Suction vortices are accompanied by an excessive rate of pressure change due to their small size and fast travelling speed. The pressure in a suction vortex often differs from the pressure of the tornado as a whole. Suction vortices are capable of picking up debris but are unable to carry debris for long distances. Therefore, suction vortices usually leave a litter line in their damage path. Small tornadoes behave very much like suction vortices and actually cannot be differentiated from suction vortices. The rotation of the individual vortices within the tornado is believed to determine the tornado's damage pattern (Golden, 1976, pp. 75-78).

There are four causes of tornado damage: pressure differences that cause wall and roof failure, airborn "missiles", collapse of high structures such as chimneys, and high winds. Wind intensity is classified according to the F-scale as shown below.

(F-) 40 m.p.h. or less. Little or no damage. Doubtful tornado.

(F0) 40-72 m.p.h. Light damage. Very weak tornado.

(F1) 73-112 m.p.h. Moderate damage. Weak tornado.

(F2) 113-157 m.p.h. Considerable damage. Strong tornado.

(F3) 158-206 m.p.h. Severe damage. Severe tornado.

(F4) 207-260 m.p.h. Devastating damage. Devastating tornado.

(F5) 207-318 m.p.h. Incredible damage. Incredible tornado.

(F6)-(F12) 319 m.p.h. to sonic speed. Inconceivable damage. Inconceivable tornado.

Although winds in the lower F-scale range are the most common, flying debris is the cause of most tornado-related deaths (NOAA, 1978).

The four methods of tornado detection are weather radar, spotters (visual sightings), satellite detection from geostationary satellites, and detection of sferics (electrical discharges emitted from tornadoes--not all tornadoes give off sferics, though). The National Weather Bureau issues two types of bulletins concerning tornadoes. One is the Tornado Watch which is issued after determining that there is a potential for a tornado-bearing storm to develop in a particular area. Tornado Watches are issued from one to eight hours in advance of any development. The Tornado Warning is the second type of bulletin. It is issued only after an existing tornado or tornado-bearing storm has been detected. (NWB, 1977) When a tornado has been sighted, it is wise to take shelter immediately. If you are out in the open, find a ditch, ravine, or culvert to lie in. Do not stay in an automobile. If you are in or near a building, go to the nearet tornado shelter, basement, stairwell, central closet, bathroom, or hallway. These structures usually have more reinforce-ment than other parts of the building and are safer (NOAA, 1978).

Below are some Spotter Rules and Clues.

1. Overshooting tops are indicators of a very strong storms.
2. A rain-free base denotes the storm's intake area, the place to watch.
3. Wall clouds form from the rain-free base often 20-30 minutes before a tornado.
4. Differentiate tornadoes and funnels! Funnels don't touch the ground or do damage.

5. Large hail often falls just in advance of a tornado.
6. The direction of the storm's movement is generally indicated by the cirrus anvil.
7. Tornadoes generally move toward the northeast at 25-35 miles per hour.
8. Poor visibility, ponding, and running bar ditches are indicators of heavy rain.
9. The first gust of wind from a thunderstorm is usually the strongest.
10. Cars are safe places in case of lightning, but not in case of tornadoes.

Always Have a Fraidy-Hole Picked and Handy (ESSA, 1970).

THE LUBBOCK TORNADO: MAY 11, 1970

Lubbock, Texas is a city of 150,000 people located on the South Plains of West Texas. (see Figure 1) The city itself covers an area of 10 by 8.5 miles. It is a major trade center for sorghum and cotton grown in the area. The Lubbock tornado of May 11, 1970 was unique in four ways:

the meterological conditions which gave rise to the tornado

Special Applications

> the widespread severity of the wind
>
> the disorganized patterns of structural damage
>
> the magnitude of the impact of the tornado on the economic, sociological, and political systems in the Lubbock area.

Because the storm occurred after dark, no photographs or films were taken of the tornado. Instead, information on the storm was taken from radar, verified spotter observations, and analysis of the damage. There are three meterological views on the configuration and path of the storm. An additional engineering viewpoint focuses on the disorganized damage patterns and differs somewhat with the meterological views of the storm. (Miner, 1983).

An average of two tornadoes a year touch down in the Lubbock area. The meteorologist in charge of the Lubbock Weather Bureau Office has said that tornadoes are a way of life at the office. Personnel are scheduled so that a professional meterologist and two meteorological technicians are on duty from mid-afternoon until midnight in the time of greatest danger (Smith, 1983). The sequence of events in Lubbock on May 11, 1970 were as follows. (All times are given in Central Daylight Time.)

6:00 P.M. Cumulus clouds began to gather
6:55 P.M. Thunderstorm spotted five miles south of city
7:50 P.M. Severe Thunderstorm Warning issued to be in effect until 9:00 pm
8:00 P.M. Egg-sized hail reported south of city
8:10 P.M. Grapefruit-sized hail reported five miles south of city

           Baseball-sized hail reported in southeast Lubbock

           Funnel cloud reported seven miles southeast of airport

8:15 P.M. Storm moving northeast at 25 m.p.h. with large hail and possibly a tornado

           Two more thunderstorms spotted eight miles southwest of the airport moving northeast at 25 m.p.h.

           Tornado Warning issued to be in effect until 9:00 pm

9:00 P.M. Funnel in southeast Lubbock moving north at 15 m.p.h.

           Funnel cloud reported seven miles south-southeast of airport moving northeast at 15 m.p.h.

           Tornado Warning extended until 10:00 pm

Special Applications

   9:35 P.M. New funnel spotted seven miles south of airport
               Warning sirens sounded in Lubbock (not all the sirens sounded due to powerline damage due to tornado)
   9:50 P.M. All communications lost at Lubbock Weather Bureau Office
11:30 P.M. All tornado warnings cancelled (ESSA, 1970)

The maximum estimated windspeeds vary from 163 m.p.h. to 290 m.p.h. The difference in opinion in interpreting the damage patterns have also led to differing opinions concerning the tornado's structure and windspeeds.

One of the meterological views on the Lubbock tornado is given by T. T. Fujita (1970, p. 165) a recognized authority on tornadoes from the University of Chicago. His "two tornado theory" says that Lubbock was hit first by a small tornado and then by a giant one that traveled between downtown and the airport. The tornadoes were formed behind an advancing moist front that had a very small temperature difference across it. It was not a front where moist air was meeting cold air as is usually the case with tornadoes. The first tornado was a forerunner of the second. It had approximately 75 m.p.h. winds and left a two mile long damage path. Fujita claims that the first tornado occurred at around 8:10 pm, but the Weather Bureau did not report a hook formation until 9:00 pm and never received confirmation on that report (Kishor et al., 1970). The larger tornado that followed touched down in downtown Lubbock. The storm's core shrank from two miles to 0.4 miles in diameter while over the downtown area. This increased the windspeed. The tornado made a loop just north of Texas Tech University and then headed northeast at 21 m.p.h. When the tornado passed the Weather Bureau Office in northeast Lubbock, the pressure of the tornado was recorded at 996.9 mb, and the pressure field around the tornado extended for ten miles. Fujita estimates that the tornado contained three to five suction vortices, and that the tornado's rotational speed was between 145 m.p.h. and 290 m.p.h., depending on how many suction vortices actually existed. The disorganized pattern of structural damage is believed to have been caused by these suction vortices. Because there are no films of the tornado, there is no direct physical evidence of the suction vortices in the Lubbock storm, but 95% of the deaths due to the tornado (i.e., all but one) occurred along the path of Fujita's suction vortices that led from the downtown area to the airport.

    Another meterological theory on the Lubbock storm

Special Applications

was proposed by Somes et al. (1971, pp. 14-17). This two tornado theory holds that two tornadoes touched down simultaneously east of Texas Tech University: one right near Jones Stadium and another southeast of the stadium. Both tornadoes headed for downtown Lubbock and were in discontinuous contact with the ground. The tornadoes merged just north of the city center and continued traveling northeast. This large combination tornado stayed in contact with the ground until it passed the airport and the Weather Bureau Office.

The third meterological theory was hypothesized by Thompson et al. (1970, pp. 21-25). This theory considers the possibility of three different tornadoes. According to this theory, the storm lasted from 9:35 pm to 10:06 pm. The first tornado was formed aloft and moved from the south-southwest to the north-northeast of downtown Lubbock. This tornado damaged tall buildings but left short ones relatively untouched. It reached its greatest intensity just north of the downtown area. The second tornado formed just northeast of Jones Stadium. It moved eastward, leaving a one mile wide damage area until it joined the first tornado just north of downtown. This newly-formed tornado then moved north, leaving a one and a half mile wide damage path. A third tornado could have formed just north of the merger point and would have then been responsible for the damage in north Lubbock. The existence of a third tornado is supported by observations of damage patterns and the recorded times of arrival of severe winds at various locations. (ESSA, 1970).

The Institute of Disaster Research at Texas Tech University has its own viewpoint concerning the damage patterns of the Lubbock tornado. The meterological data supports all three meterological views, but after surveying the damage, the Institute concluded that the disorganized pattern of structural damage was due to the differing abilities of different structures to resist wind forces. The damage patterns do not seem to support theories that assume that the storm was a "clean," axis-symmetric funnel. The Institute believes that the Lubbock storm was intense but disorganized over the downtown area. It intensified and became more organized as it moved to the northeast. Using information from the damage survey, the maximum windspeed was between 163 m.p.h. and 200 m.p.h. Most of the damage was believed to have been caused by winds between 75 m.p.h. and 125 m.p.h. (Minor, 1983).

The May 11, 1970 tornado was the worst in Lubbock's history. The damaged areas were classified into three destruction zones: scattered, moderate, and extensive (Somes et al. 1971, pp. 25-29). The scattered zone contained only a small percentage of structures that

Special Applications

were significantly damaged, whereas in the moderate zone, about half the structures were significantly damaged. In the extensive zone, a high percentage of structures were affected and a majority of these were either destroyed or severely damaged. The extensive zone in Lubbock stretched seven miles between the downtown area and the airport, an area which included downtown, an industrial section of town, and medium and low density residential areas. The damage area ranged from a quarter mile to a mile and a half in width. The zones grew progressively narrower as the storm moved northeastward. The most extensive destruction was found in the northernmost portion of the tornado's path due to the progressively intensifying storm. The severe damage covered nine square miles, and other damage covered an additional six square miles. A total of fifteen square miles was affected, which is roughly 1/4 of the city of Lubbock.

Property damage estimates range from $125 million to $200 million. These figures include:

damaged utilities
119 small aircraft
thousands of private automobiles
600 commercial structures
100 mobile homes

- 1,000 totally destroyed family units
- 9,000 damaged family units
- 220 street light poles
- 25,000 telephone stations
- destroyed long distances lines
- power plant damage
- cut off water supply

An example of some of the damage in the downtown area lies in the 20-story Great Plains Life Building. The building's steel frame was bent so that the top of the building is now twelve inches out of plumb. The building is still standing, and in addition to office space, it now has a restaurant on the top floor.

Twenty-six persons died as a result of the tornado, and another 1,500 persons were injured. Most of the casulties were due to flying debris. The storm left 3,000 people homeless. These people were sheltered and fed in the municipal coliseum. President Nixon declared the city of Lubbock a disaster area on May 14, 1970.

One of the social impacts of the Lubbock tornado was its effect on the segregation found in north Lubbock. The tornado path crossed a low-income, predominately Mexican-American, community on the north side of the city. This community was a highly segregated, close-knit section of town, and the tornado shattered its way of life. Seven hundred homes were destroyed, leaving only 83 homes in Lubbock's "barrio." The damage was so extensive that many families were relocated to the northeast side of town made up of predominately Negro and Anglo families. This "natural" integration provided not only some problems, but some unforeseen benefits as well. (Minnis, 1971, p. 92; Smith, 1983).

REFERENCES

Environmental Science Services Administration (ESSA), U.S. Department of Commerce (1970) The Lubbock, Texas Tornado: May 11, 1970. Natural Disaster Survey Report 70-1. Rockville, Md: Author.

Flora, S. W. (1953): Tornadoes of the United States. Norman; University of Oklahoma Press.

Fujita, T. T. (1970): The Lubbock tornado: A study of suction spots. Weatherwise, 23, 161-173.

Gaston, G. (1974) Tornadoes, whirlwinds and water spouts. Encyclopedia Brittanica: Macropedia, 514-520.

Golden, J. H. (1976) Assessment of windspeeds in tornadoes. Symposium on Tornadoes: Assessment of Knowledge and Implications for Man. Lubbock: Texas Tech University.

Kishor, C. M., Mcdonald, J. E., Minor, J. E., and Sanger, A. J. (1971) <u>The Lubbock Storm, May 11, 1970: Response of Structural Systems to the Lubbock Storm.</u> Texas Tech University Storm Research Report 03. Department of Civil Engineering, Texas Tech University.

Minnis, M. S., and McWillians, A. P. (1971) <u>Tornado: The Voice of the People in Disaster and After: A Study in Residential Integration.</u> Lubbock: Texas Tech University.

Minor, J. E. (1983) Institute for Disaster Research. Personal correspondence.

National Oceanic and Atmospheric Administration (NOAA) (1978) <u>Tornado.</u> U.S. Department of Commerce Bulletin 003-018-00085-7.

National Weather Bureau (NWB) (1977) <u>Tornado Watch and Tornado Warning.</u> Washington, DC: U.S. Department of Commerce.

Ross, D. (1970) President Nixon declares Lubbock disaster area. <u>New York Times,</u> May 14, p. 23.

Somes, N. F., Dikkers, R. D., and Boone, T. M. (1971) <u>Lubbock Tornado: A Survey of Buiding Damage in an Urban Area.</u> Washington, D.C.: National Bureau of Standards Technical note 558.

Smith, W. (1983) Personal Interview. Lubbock, Texas.

Thompson, J. N., Kiesling, E. W., Goldman, J. L., Mehta, K. C., Wittman, J., and Johnson, F. B. (1970) *The Lubbock Storm of May 11, 1970.* Washington D.C.: National Academy of Sciences.

Weems, J. E. (1977) *The Tornado,* New York: Doubleday.

Sample Research Paper (MLA Style)

Grayout: Societal Hazards of Aging

Gordon Knight
Social Stratification
March 4, 1987

Introduction

Aging. It begins the moment of conception and continues, at least physiologically, until our bodies return to dust. Aging is a universal happening that occurs for every human being, and this lifelong event can greatly influence the quality and quantity of one's life.

In my paper I have chosen to cover only the psycho-social aspects of aging, specifically the negative aspects. A main assumption underlying my research is a theory put forth by Vern Bengston. He maintains that there are three critical needs of elderly individuals: identity, connectedness, and effect (25).

Identity covers the area of self-concept. The interaction and interrelationship between elderly people and society as a whole is dealt with under connectedness. Effect refers to the amount and type of influence that elderly people are able to wield upon the world around them. Aging and the societal consequences that it brings can and do have a very grave effect upon these three important needs.

Identity

Each person develops a sense of self, separated from the surrounding environment. This concept of "me" is very important for the individual's functioning in society. The self can have a great influence upon behavior and attitudes.

Although there is little agreement among sociologists about the exact nature of the self, I have chosen a model of the self outlined by Robert Atchley. In this model the self is composed of two elements, one cognitive and one emotional. The cognitive element, self-concept, is concerned with individuals' description of who they are and what they are like. Self-esteem, the emotional element, focuses upon how individuals feel about the comparison of their self-concept with some sort of ideal (86-87).

Much of the self-concept is formed through the actions and reactions of others to us. The reflexive, or "looking glass," self is marked by three elements: an imagined idea of how one appears to others, the imagination of the judgment rendered by these others, and some self-feelings (Hess and Markson 67).

The first two elements in the reflexive self can be very strongly influenced by the ideals and stereotypes of a society. Our society, with its strong emphasis upon youth and usefulness demands that old age be dreaded. Belief in activism has shaped the image of old age that our society holds (Hess and Markson 60). Old age, and its inevitable partner, death, is doubly unwelcome because it represents the cessation of life as well as the epitome of inactivity; the end of becoming and being.

The close tie between old age and death conferred by society can be traced to the medical and technological advances that have insured that all but the weakest have a good life expectancy and most people will avoid death until time catches up with their bodies. These advances have also brought about a great change in societal attitude toward death and the aged. As medical advances made death less of an everyday event, the thought of dying has become terrifying and the elderly (the closest to death) have become feared. They stand as living proof of our eventual demise (Hess and Markson 60).

The aged are regarded very unfavorably by both stereotypical thought and by extensions of that thought, as seen in the media. Studies conducted to evaluate ideas about the elderly have found that many people perceive old people as stubborn, touchy, bossy, meddling, and engaging in frequent quarrels with their families or friends (Hess and Markson 65). Television views the aged along very similar lines. The elderly are seen as increasingly evil, failures, or as being very unhappy. Few programs include portrayals of effective old people, and televised romance between aged adults is nonexistent. Novels, while not openly stereotyping oldsters, tend to view the aged as only partial people. Old people are rarely the main characters and they are often useful only for their relationship to the "important" characters (Barrett 72).

Old people are therefore caught in a double bind as they age. All around them are negative attitudes and portrayals of the aged, some of these attitudes may even be coming from inside. The old people can't stop their constant aging but if they adhere to society's standards, they can't stand their aging. The incredible conflict should be evident by now.

The overwhelming amount of negativism toward aging can have a very strong effect upon a person's self-esteem. There is little positive information on which to model an ideal self, and so aging persons are left trying to meet an ideal image that time has taken away from them.

Because the prescriptions and proscriptions of society have a strong influence upon the ideal self, role performance becomes very important to self-esteem (Atchley 89). And because self-esteem is emotional in content, it can be more responsive to moods and bodily states (Atchley 89). These two factors place the self-esteem of elderly people in a very shaky position. As people age their bodies inevitably begin to slow down and this slowing process tends to make them much more vulnerable to sickness and disability. Sickness tends to limit the ability of an aging person to effectively play certain roles and disability in its most extreme forms usually turns into dependency, a role few people willingly assume.

The role shift from independent to dependent is dreaded by many people. From childhood forward we receive societal messages about the value of independence and self-sufficiency, and this makes a shift to dependence extremely difficult. Dependency is further complicated because of the expectations attached. A dependent person is expected to defer to benefactors, give up personal rights, and exhibit eternal gratitude for what they've received--a hard role for anyone young or old. Clearly individuals' self-esteem can take a beating as they age.

Connectedness

As people move toward old age they experience constraints in maintaining social networks. The natural process of biological aging brings about a reduction in energy in most individuals. These aging people may choose to conserve their remaining energy by disengaging themselves from certain roles (Atchley 201). They withdraw from various social roles and move toward ever-increasing concern with self and an increasing isolation from the world around them. With increasing age, preoccupation with inner life tends to increase while interest in the outside world slowly begins to decrease.

This shift in perspective creates a reduction in the ability of the aged to relate emotionally and in their readiness to perceive the people around them as active and feeling. After a short time older people can become trapped in a vicious circle: their inability to relate or positively perceive people leads to a greater withdrawal which in turn creates an even greater inability to relate, and the cycle continues until the person has totally withdrawn from the world.

One of the major causes of preoccupation with self is the presence of disease. Diseases usually have at least one of two socially undesirable consequences--they are painful to the individual and/or they handicap individuals in exercising their faculties, mental or physical, for the performance of social roles (Hess and Markson 91). If the handicap or pain becomes great enough, an individual may be placed in an institution. While the institution may offer some advantages to an aging person, once put in an institution the elderly become even more isolated than they were previously. They are separated--spatially, socially and physically --from their everyday lives.

Those elderly who can avoid placement in an institution are still affected by disease or physical disability. Several environmental constraints affect connectedness for the elderly, the largest being a lack of mobility. This limited ability to get around may result from physical disability, the inability to pay the high cost of transportation, or it may be the result of fear (Hess and Markson 279). The high incidence of crime has created a high level of fear among the aged, especially minorities and females (Townsend 136). This fear may keep the elderly from going out into the community in order to keep up with contacts. They stay confined within their homes or apartments totally excluded from the mainstream of life.

In old age the role of friends becomes particularly important. Friends can supplement social networks or even become the basis of such a network. The group of relatives, friends, and/or neighbors with whom the old person interacts is called an "informal" support system (Atchley 129). These support systems can be very important for promoting the well-being of elderly people. The great majority of older people report at least one non-family friend whom they look to for assistance and companionship (Townsend 219). But these support systems do have limitations in terms of knowledge and ability to provide for an aging person. A small group cannot undo what a very large group, society as a whole, has done.

Social institutions outlive the people who comprise them, and thus most institutions are constantly phasing young people in and old people out. Society withdraws from the individual and no longer seeks the individual's efforts. The term social disengagement refers to this withdrawal. Older people are no longer sought to lead organizations, provide labor, or to involve themselves in the lives of their children or other close relatives. Government and banks become unresponsive to their needs or desires.

Each institution in society accomplishes disengagement in different ways at different times. For example, while retirement is a formalized event that usually occurs between the ages of 65 and 70, withdrawal from the family often doesn't happen until individuals lose their mental faculties, regardless of the individual's age (Townsend 219). Societal disengagement may be inflicted unintentionally and often it goes unrecognized but it is a reality for older people.

Effect

> One third of older Americans are living in quiet despair, stemming both from physical and spiritual poverty that in turn stems from the chilling realization of powerlessness and non-participation (Townsend).

The above quote unfortunately is very accurate when it describes older Americans as "powerless." Public esteem of the aged has varied greatly from society to society. In tribal societies being old was an advantage that was considered synonymous with power and rank (Hess and Markson 57). But the industrialization of American society changed all that. Industrialized society demanded that the place of business be relocated from the home or farm to a separate business district. When this relocation occured the material base of power was shifted from the home, where the oldest members of a family were generally held in high regard, to a separate area where anyone regardless of age could be in charge. Thus the material base of power and of authority for the elderly was substantially reduced or given out to social agencies (Townsend 58).

Sources of traditional authority have been parceled out to social institutions while continued technological advances have made the labor of old people less and less necessary. As western cultural values and social institutions have been recast, secularization and rational law-based authority have emerged. All of these changes have brought one concept to the forefront. No longer is the skill or knowledge of the past, one of the greatest gifts the elderly have to offer, particularly needed by society (Hess and Markson 57).

Many other problems related to the shift of social power have a direct influence upon the ability of people to affect change in the world around them. One of the most important is a lack of money. Some seven million older people, more than one-third of the population over the age of 65, are impoverished and must depend upon someone else for income assistance

(Townsend 136). This assistance may come from either family or the government. One such source of income is Social Security. Based upon work-related deposits into the system, a person receives a monthly allotment. The government has proudly proclaimed the virtue of this program but has failed to adequately inform the elderly of what their benefits really are.

The system discriminates against women and minorities who either work irregularly or at low-paying jobs and are therefore unable to collect more than the minimum benefits. Since women are much more likely to live to an advanced age and require assistance, many women now make up the over 65 population but are collecting only the bare minimum for existence. Today minimum monthly benefits are about $260 per month, hardly enough to provide a decent way of life let alone wield great monetary power.

Unlike other segments of the population, the elderly rarely form a coherent political force. Although older Americans make up 15 to 17 percent of the voters, they almost never vote as a block and the elderly take part in very few political organizations in order to further their special causes (Townsend 96).

The relative prestige of the elderly and their ability to exert their influence may be colored by the fact that elderly women now comprise the great majority of the elderly (Hess and Markson 58). Women have always been awarded less authority and influence than men, and older women are no different. In fact, they have lost what little influence they might have had because they no longer can bear children to contribute to society. Overall aging does have an influence upon the effect of all people, and unfortunately this influence is almost entirely negative.

Conclusion

    Throughout this paper I have focused upon the negative aspects of aging and by now the picture I've painted appears to be quite depressing. But it need not stay that way.

    There are three very important steps which every person can take in order to change the grim picture of aging that I have presented. The first is for people to try and put themselves into the place of the elderly. Look closely at their lives and imagine what people would do or how they might feel in such a position. Examining personal perspectives would be a second step in removing hazards for the aged. Are social values designed to help the aged or do these values confine and degrade people solely on the basis of their chronological age? And last, but by no means least, people should explore ways of changing the social institutions that serve and discriminate against the elderly. Find out what might be done and then resolve to do it.

    All of these steps have one thing in common: People must be aware of the problems that confront the aging person before they can begin to bring about changes. With the full knowledge that, with a little luck, I too will grow old, I have written this paper in the hope of sharing some of that knowledge.

Works Cited

Atchley, Robert D. *The Social Forces in Later Life: An Introduction to Social Gerentology.* Belmont, CA: Wadsworth, 1972.

Barrett, James H. *Gerentological Psychology.* Springfield, IL: Thomas, 1972.

Bengton, Vern L. "The Institutionalized Aged and Their Social Needs." *Psychosocial Needs of the Aged: Selected Papers.* Los Angeles: U.S.C., 1973.

Hess, Beth B. and Elizabeth W. Markson. *Aging and Old Age: An Introduction to Social Gerontology.* New York: Macmillan, 1980.

Townsend, Clair. *Old Age: The Last Segregation.* New York: Grossman, 1971.

Copyright © Bucky and Avis Reeves, The National Audubon Society Collection/Photo Researchers, Inc.

Chapter Fifteen

Writing on Demand

Most of the writing you do in school imposes some constraints. An assignment usually specifies a deadline, something about required length, and it may also provide directives about format. These specifications do, of course, constrain your writing in certain ways, but you still have considerable latitude for making decisions about when you will write, what processes you will follow, and the exact form of your writing.

Some writing situations, however, allow considerably less latitude. Sometimes the constraints are temporal, as in essay examinations. When you write in response to questions on an essay examination, time pressures you to work quickly, and you may not be able to go through your normal processes of drafting and revising. Sometimes the constraints are formal, as in business letters and resumes. Business letters and resumes follow prescribed patterns, and writing effective ones does not leave you much latitude for innovation.

The Essay Examination

If your experience is like that of most students, the essay exam will be the most common form of writing you do in college, and it is one for which you will be given virtually no instruction on format. You will be given one or two questions, or perhaps a series of questions, and told to answer them within a specified amount of time. Here is a typical essay exam question from a biology class:

> Write a short essay on the extent to which Darwin was original and the extent to which he made use of the work of others.

This one is from a history class:

> The years between 1918 and 1939 have been called the "years of the long armistice." In your opinion, is this evaluation justified or unjustified? Support

Special Applications

your judgment with specific references to events, circumstances, and the like that occurred or were present in Europe during the years between the two world wars.

Like most essay exam questions, these two make clear what information the instructor requires, but provide no guidance on how to proceed.

An essay exam represents compressed writing. You go through many of the same steps you would go through in a longer piece of writing, but you must do them much more quickly. This compression dictates the form of an essay exam, and preparing for it can make your performance on essay exams more successful. Of course, the most important preparation for an essay exam is mastering the material to be covered. Cramming facts into your head the night before may help with an objective test like true-false or fill-in-the-blank, but cramming does not usually improve the quality of an essay exam.

Getting Ready to Write Essay Exams

Essay exams ask you to write to show learning, and the best preparation for them is writing to learn. Using strategies such as those described in Chapter 2 helps you prepare for an essay exam, because writing about what you are studying helps you assimilate it, as well as discover what you need to know.

As the time of an exam approaches, you can make writing to learn more productive by imagining the kinds of questions you are likely to be asked and writing in response to them. This kind of rehearsal will make your actual performance on the essay exam less nerve wracking. Another form of preparation is to go over the *spelling* of key terms for the exam. To write, *Hemmingway* throughout a literature exam or *behavoristic* throughout a psychology exam does nothing to enhance the format of the completed essay.

Allocate Time

When you actually take the exam, remember that you are compressing your writing but are writing all the same. As is true with any writing, then, the first thing to organize is your *time*. Scan the exam quickly to see how many questions you must answer, and then figure out how much time you can allocate to each. Even if you have a great deal to say on one question and less on another, do not let yourself spend all the available time on one or two questions and then run out of time at the end. Next to each question or section on the exam, write the time when you must begin in order to complete the exam. Be sure to allow a few minutes at the end for reading through what you have written so that you can check writing conventions.

Read the Question Carefully

Once you have allocated your time, reread the exam to determine what it asks of you. If you have to choose one of several questions, make your

Writing on Demand

selection, and begin focusing on what the question asks of you. This means you need to *read the question carefully* to see exactly what it asks. Return to the preceding biology question, and see how it suggests approaches for the writer. By asking you to consider Darwin's originality and his use of others' work, the question does not ask you to take a position or make an argument for or against Darwin's originality. Rather, it asks you to *explain* the originality and borrowing in his work. Strategies of explanation such as defining, recognizing similarities and differences, categorizing, identifying priorities, illustrating, and considering cause and effect will be helpful here.

In contrast, the history question asks for an *argument;* it requires you to take a position on the "long armistice" and to justify it. Although strategies of explanation can help you here, you will also need to concentrate on the quality of your evidence, possible oppositions to what you say, priorities of the discipline, and potential fallacies.

Plan Your Answer

Once you have determined what the question asks for and which strategies will be most helpful to you, do some initial planning. This does not mean actually writing the exam, but making preliminary notes about what to include in your answers. Exclusion is as important as inclusion in an essay exam, and you will need to think about what belongs in your answer. A student planning to answer the question about Darwin's originality made these notes:

```
Original                    Not Original
first to collect fac-       Grandfather's state-
  tual evidence for           ment on evolution
  theory                    Alfred Wallace's
Beagle expedition             statement
Galapagos islands
fossils, plants,
  animals, geology
```

He realized that his knowledge of Darwin's methodology, the controversy surrounding his work, and the details of Darwin's biography should not be included in the answer. This process did not take more than a minute, but it helped the student plan the form of his response to the essay question. Another student made a list to plan his response to a question on a history exam. The question was "The Indian warfare that was an adjunct of the War of 1812 had rather distinct northern and southern phases. Write an essay describing the action in the North and in the South, beginning your essay with the Tippecanoe episode of 1811." The student made this list:

```
Tippecanoe incident         Northern phase
causes                      those involved
the battle                    (Indians)
```

405

Special Applications

```
the actions              those involved
aftermath                redstick faction
government counter-      government counter-
  measures                 measures
southern phase
```

Each of these words had considerable meaning for the student, enabling him to collect ideas quickly and see what he could include when answering the question. This list will work to the extent that the student has adequate information for each item. As you can see, some of the items in the list come directly from the question, and others come from the student's own knowledge of the topic, but the two are woven together to produce a piece of prewriting from which he can work.

Not only does this list give the student a quick overview of how to approach the essay, but it also provides an organizational structure. Like many lists, this one suggests an order for discussing the various topics included. The difference between this and a traditional outline is that the content, not proper outline form, shapes the list. This student is not concerned about ways to fit information about Indian warfare in 1811 into a set of roman numerals with letters and numbers following each. Rather, the constraints of the question and his knowledge of the topic determine how the student organizes the list.

This procedure of writing to learn in advance of the exam, rehearsing in writing before the exam, organizing your time during the exam, and planning the form of your response before you actually begin writing will make your essay exams much more successful than if you follow the common procedure of cramming facts into your head and writing them down frantically before you have found out what the exam actually requires. Thinking of the form of the exam will make your writing show your learning to its best advantage.

The following checklist can help you both before and during an essay exam.

Before an Essay Exam:
1. Write to learn the material.
2. Rehearse in writing before the exam to anticipate questions, and make sure your spelling is under control.

During an Essay Exam:
3. Allocate time for each question and follow this schedule.
4. Plan the form of your responses before you begin writing.

ACCOMMODATE LENGTH

Essay exams come in various forms. Some ask you to spend an entire class period responding to one or two questions, and others include a number of questions for which shorter answers are appropriate. A key identifier for the length of response expected by the instructor is the number of points or the amount of time indicated for each question. If you read through a whole

Writing on Demand

examination before you begin, you will be able to gauge your time, allowing enough time for all questions.

Short Answers

This question and response from a speech communication class illustrate one common type of short essay question, the question that focuses on a definition.

> How does the Aristotelian definition of rhetoric relate directly to the necessity for audience analysis?

```
     Aristotle defines rhetoric as finding "the avail-
able means of persuasion." By analyzing the audience,
the speaker can use the available means of persuasion
that would apply to that audience and be most effective
with that audience. One method of persuasion does not
apply to every audience. For example, asking the
rhetorical question "couldn't an aborted child be your
child's best friend right now?" of an anti-abortion
group of mothers wouldn't be the same as asking the
same question of a group of teenaged girls.
```

Even though the instructor does not ask for Aristotle's definition explicitly, the question cannot be answered effectively without providing the definition. By beginning with the definition, Casey Anderson, the author of the response, establishes the basis of her discussion immediately. Then she moves quickly to explain its application. The concluding example demonstrates that Casey understands the concept of audience analysis.

Here are a question and response from a history class:

Identify this term: *Norman Conquest of England*

```
     The Normans were Vikings who had settled in Nor-
mandy, France, in the 10th century. They were expert
administrators. Early in the 10th century, Ethelred of
England married Emme, sister of the Duke of Normandy.
When their son Edward III was king he had no sons. He
died in 1065, leaving no heir to the throne. William
the Conqueror (a Norman) claimed the throne, along
with two others. One of the Harolds took the throne,
the others attacked, and William won in the Battle of
Hastings (1066). He replaced all Saxon nobility and
clergy with Normans. He built up the most powerful
empire at the time. The Norman kings died out soon
after, but England was made Norman.
```

Special Applications

Identification is another common short answer form. In responding to identification questions, it is important to provide enough information to identify the term completely. Suzanne Johnson, the author of this response, includes a great deal of detailed information about the Norman Conquest, and all of this detail contributes to the identification of the term.

LONG ANSWERS

In addition to the obvious markers of time or points allocated, key terms in essay examinations provide clues about the appropriate length for an answer. Words such as "discuss," "explain," and "argue" frequently appear in questions that demand longer answers. The following question and response from a political science class illustrate:

Discuss the political implications of the beast metaphor in *Lord of the Flies*.

> The beast metaphor in Lord of the Flies represents evil in humans, the evil that, according to Hobbes, can be altered by good government. It also represents fear and insecurity.
> In the beginning of the book, the boys, led by Ralph, attempt to set up a democratic society. They soon realize, however, that this ideology, however well it may work for civilization, does not provide a sense of security or belonging on the unfamiliar island.
> Jack's plan--that of fascism--turns the boys' minds away from the beast (their fears) by joining them in a ritual in which they ceremonially kill it. Banded together, they feel safe. When the boys are in a group, they do not need to think for themselves, nor do any of them feel personally responsible for committing violent acts. This is exemplified when the ritual killing of the beast turns into reality in the murder of Simon.
> The beast which comes from everywhere (the sky, water, mountains) cannot be properly contained in a democratic society which upholds individualism because these boys feel that it is too big to combat alone. As the boys become more and more scared, they are pressured into fascism by the situation.

Jerry Noe, the student who wrote this response, develops the relationship between the beast metaphor and fascism, offering a number of examples from the book to support the claims he makes. By making the correlation between the beast and fascism, he shows how the metaphor can have very explicit political dimensions. In making the connection with Hobbes, the opening paragraph connects this metaphor with politics immediately. The following paragraphs, organized around the chronology of the book, develop these ideas more fully.

The Business Letter

There will probably be relatively few occasions when an instructor will ask you to write a letter for an assignment, but you will undoubtedly find that you need to write business letters during your college career. If nothing else, you will probably need to write letters to prospective employers as you begin looking for employment after college. While you are a student you may write letters requesting financial aid, protesting or affirming some political action, seeking assistance with a project, asking for information, or explaining something you have done.

For your letter to have the greatest possible effect, it should adhere to conventional business letter format. Use standard (8½ by 11 inches) typing paper, and center the letter on the page. The paragraphs should be single spaced with double spaces between them. Double spaces should also be used between the inside address and the salutation, between the salutation and the body, and between the body and the complimentary close. Leave at least four spaces between the complimentary close and the typed name. Fold the letter in thirds and insert in a standard (4⅛ by 7½ inches) business envelope, addressed as indicated.

Adhering to appropriate format is, of course, only one aspect of writing an effective business letter. Issues of context, audience, and strategies of development are as important in business letters as in any other writing. You need to consider purposes and circumstances of writing, as did Frank Gatelli when he wrote the letter on the following page.

As you can see, Frank Gatelli has assembled information designed to convince the Blunden Foundation of his need and intent. His expenses of the past year might have included paying for a car he wrecked or posting bail for a friend, but he does not include such things because he recognizes that they will not favorably impress his audience.

GETTING READY TO WRITE A BUSINESS LETTER

You may have any one of several purposes for writing a business letter. You may, for example, write a letter of *application,* either for a job or a scholarship; you may write a letter of *complaint,* asserting your rights as a consumer; you may write a letter of *inquiry,* requesting information about employment, products, or services; you may write a letter of *response,* answering questions or providing information. Whatever your purpose in writing, you can prepare for writing by doing an inventory of the ideas and information you wish to include.

Special Applications

Sample Business Letter

Sender's address → 24 Hagget Hall
Commonwealth College
Mountainview, N.J. 08920
Date → April 3, 1987

Inside address →
Mr. Frank Blunden, President
Blunden Foundation
842 Third Avenue
New York, N.Y. 10092

Salutation → Dear Mr. Blunden:

Body →
I am writing at the suggestion of Mr. George Worth, President of the Rotary Club in Mountainview, New Jersey. Mr. Worth suggested that I apply to the Blunden Foundation for financial aid to complete my education at Commonwealth College.

As the enclosed transcript shows, I graduated from Marysville High School in 1984 and came to Commonwealth College in the fall of that year. During my freshman and sophomore years I received a scholarship from the Mountainview Rotary Club to help defray tuition. That scholarship expired after the second year, I depleted all my savings to pay for the expenses of this past year, and my family is unable to help me.

I have a job for the summer with McDonald Trucking where I will earn approximately $1000, but I need an additional $1000 to remain at Commonwealth College for my senior year. Mr. Worth told me that the Blunden Foundation is interested in assisting young people who plan to pursue a career in business, and since I am majoring in economics and plan to seek employment as a trainee in management, I hope the Blunden Foundation will be able to provide the $1000 necessary for me to complete my education.

Complimentary close → Sincerely yours,
Signature → *Frederick Gatelli*
Typed name → Frederick Gatelli

enc: transcript

Writing on Demand

Sample Business Envelope

```
Frederick Gatelli
24 Hagget Hall
Commonwealth College
Mountainview, N.J. 08920




                              Mr. Frank Blunden, President
                              Blunden Foundation
                              842 Third Avenue
                              New York, N.Y. 10092
```

In preparing to write his letter of application, for example, Frederick Gatelli made this list:

```
-George Worth suggested I write
-Rotary scholarship for two years
-father laid off from business
-used my savings
-summer job with McDonald--earning about $1000
-business major
-Blunden Foundation interested in business majors
```

Using this list, Frederick was able to develop a plan for the letter he ultimately wrote. He decided that referring to Mr. Worth would attract his reader's attention, so he elected to put that in the first paragraph. The explanation of his previous scholarship and present financial situation seemed the best thing to put next. Frederick decided not to go into detail about his family's financial situation and his father's unemployment. He decided that the information about his major and intended employment would provide a good ending because they would speak directly to Mr. Blunden's interests. With this general plan in mind, Frederick was ready to write his letter.

FORMAT

Once you know what you want to include and have developed a general plan for your letter, you are ready to think about the demands of format. Business letters include the following parts:

Heading: This part includes the sender's full mailing address—but *not* the sender's name because that appears at the end of the letter—and the date. If you have letterhead stationery on which your return address appears, simply type the date.

Special Applications

Inside Address: The recipient's title, full name, position, and complete mailing address appears here.

Salutation: This part addresses the recipient by title and last name. If you do not know the name of the person to whom your letter should be directed, you may be able to indicate the person's function. For example, the salutation may be:

```
Dear Consumer Relations Director:
Dear Personnel Director:
Dear Maintainence Director:
```

If you cannot specify a function for the individual to whom you are writing, you can use a more general salutation such as:

```
Dear Sir or Madam:
To Whom It May Concern:
```

Whatever salutation you use should be followed by a colon(:) and it should appear two spaces below the inside address.

Body: The body may consist of one or several paragraphs. All paragraphs should be single-spaced, with double spaces between them.

Complimentary Close: Typical complimentary closes include these:

```
Sincerely,
Sincerely yours,
Yours sincerely,
```

If you know the recipient well and want to indicate greater informality, you can use a complimentary close such as:

```
Cordially,
Cordially yours,
Best regards,
```

Any complimentary close should be followed by a comma(,), and it should appear two spaces below the last line of the body.

Signature: The full name of the sender is typed four spaces below the complimentary close, and a handwritten signature should be inserted in the space between closing and typed name. The sender's title may appear below the typed name.

Special Notations: Three types of notations may appear next to the left margin below the sender's typed signature. These include:

> Enclosure: This notation indicates that something has been included in the envelope with the letter and specifies what it is—enc: transcript
>
> Recipient of Copy: This notation informs the recipient of anyone else receiving a copy of the letter—cc: James Smitherman
>
> Typist: If someone other than the author types the letter, the typist's initials appear after the author's with a colon (:)—ARG:SMR

The Résumé

When you begin to apply for employment after college, you will probably want to send a resumé, or a summary of your education and experience, along with your letter of application. One conventional format for a resumé is shown in the accompanying illustration.

Because this student is applying for a position in forest resources management, she emphasized those aspects of her background that apply directly to her employment objective. During the summer of 1980, for example, she worked at a fast-food restaurant, and she had jobs cleaning houses and taking care of children during most of her college career. She omitted these things from her resumé because she assumed they would not impress prospective employers in forest management. Both the content and the format of a resumé can be shaped to suit the specifics of a particular situation. For example, if your grades are more impressive than your work experience, or vice versa, you can select and arrange elements in your resumé to highlight your strongest points.

Getting Ready to Write a Resumé

The first step in writing your resumé is to gather all the information you wish to include. Getting the correct dates, names, and places together will make your task easier. Once you have gathered all the relevant information, you will need to decide what to include and how to organize it. As was true for Elizabeth, you may find that some information is not relevant, at least not for certain audiences. If you are applying for several different types of jobs, you may want to consider developing a resumé for each type. Elizabeth, for example, discovered that there were very few positions for forest resources management specialists, so she developed another resumé that listed her employment objective as general land management and used that resumé for applying for positions with city park departments.

Format

The format of a resumé varies both according to the individual writing it and the position being applied for. If you feel you are overeducated for a given position, for example, you may want to give less prominence to your education, or if your employment record is uneven, you may want to summarize positions held rather than listing each one with dates.

In general, however, a resumé will include these elements:

Heading: The word *resumé* should be centered at the top of the first sheet, and the heading should include your full name, mailing address and telephone number.

Employment Objective: If you are applying for several types of jobs, you may wish to omit this item from your resumé, or you may develop multiple resumés to convey your various career goals. If you are applying for a specific job, you may wish to mention it specifically here.

Special Applications

Sample Resumé

```
                    Elizabeth Nickerson
                    329 Meridian Street
               Westmoreland, Minnesota 56792
                      (312) 928-7929
```

<u>Employment Objective</u>	Forest resources management position (Date available: July 1, 1988)
<u>Education</u>	
1984-1988	Augusta University, Augusta, North Dakota Degree: B.S. (expected in June, 1988) Major: Forest resources
1980-1984	Westmoreland High School, Westmoreland, MN Highest Honor Graduate
<u>Work Experience</u>	
Summer 1987	Joint Information Office: U.S. Forest Service/National Park Service, Seattle, Washington. Handled Park and Forest Service information for the Pacific Northwest Region including permit and policy interpretation, recreational opportunities, current campground, road, backcountry and avalanche conditions, and sales.
Summer 1986	Glacier National Park. Naturalist/Interpreter.
Summer 1985	Rocky Mountain National Park. Backcountry construction and conservation projects.
<u>Extracurricular Activities</u>	Student Conservation Association American Forestry Association Forest Club, College of Forest Resources Augusta University
<u>Special Interests</u>	Photography, guitar, backpacking
<u>References</u>	For academic references: Office of Student Placement Augusta University Augusta, North Dakota 63654 Ms. Penny Flaman, Manager Joint Information Office 1293 Fourth Avenue Seattle, Washington 92354 Ms. Caroline Rind, Supervisor St. Mary Ranger Station Glacier National Park Browning, Montana 59417

Education: This part should include schools (both high school and college) you attended. List the dates you attended each one, any degrees received, your major, and any honors you received.

Work Experience: List your work experience, starting with the most recent and working backward. If some of your jobs bear no relation to the position you are seeking, you may wish to summarize them, but for any job related to the one you seek, be sure to give the name of your employer and a brief description of your duties.

References: After you have ascertained that individuals who know you and your work are willing to serve as references, list their names, addresses and telephone numbers, so a potential employer will know how to reach them. Alternatively, your college placement office may be willing to establish a file in which all letters of recommendation can be kept. This system avoids the inconvenience of asking your referees to write many letters on your behalf.

In addition to observing the demands of format for resumés, it is especially important to attend to the physical appearance of this document. Issues of spacing, margins, and quality of type face are worth considerable attention because your resumé will make the first impression upon a potential employer.

Copyright © Jack Dermid, The National Audubon Society Collection/Photo Researchers, Inc.

PART FIVE

HANDBOOK OF USAGE AND GRAMMAR

Perspective on Conventions

THE Book of Judges in the Old Testament recounts how Gileadite sentries protected their newly conquered territory on the Jordan River against enemies from Ephriam:

> And when any of the fugitives of Ephriam said, "Let me go over," the men of Gilead said to him, "Are you an Ephriamite?" When he said "no," they said to him, "Then say Shibboleth," and he said "Sibboleth," for he could not pronounce it right; then they seized him and slew him at the fords of the Jordan. (12:5–6)

This account explains the derivation of our modern use of *shibboleth* as a test of class or group, and it also illustrates an important point about conventions. Conventions are customs or practices agreed upon by an established group of people. It may be a convention of pronunciation, as with the Gileadites who preferred *shibboleth* over *sibboleth*, or it may be a convention of driving on the right side of the road rather than on the left, but membership in a particular group, whether club or culture, requires adherence to certain conventions. This is not to say that all conventions must be adhered to at all times, but a general agreement on them helps groups cohere.

To understand the role of conventions in your own life, you might think of a few you take for granted. You are probably accustomed to place settings that put the fork at the left of the plate and the knife and spoon on the right. When you answer the telephone, you speak first rather than waiting for the person on the other end to initiate conversation. You probably use forms of greeting such as "Hi" or "How are you?" when you meet people you know. In European cultures, the fork, knife, and spoon are placed differently and are substituted in many Asian ones by chopsticks. The caller rather than the receiver initiates the conversation on French and Japanese telephones, and the appropriate greeting in Hong Kong is "Have you eaten rice today?" whereas in Accra, it is "How is your mother?" These differences suggest that conventions are essentially arbitrary. There is nothing inherently better about forks or chopsticks or about a particular form of greeting. In addition, some conventions are more important than others. To put forks on the right side of the plate will probably attract no more than a second look from dinner guests, but to drive on the left side of the road in the United States will almost surely lead to a fatal accident.

Writing is, among other things, a highly conventionalized form. Like the conventions of driving or pronunciation, many of the customs of writing are arbitrary. There is nothing inherently better about using quotation marks (as we do) rather than parentheses (as Italians do) to mark direct discourse, but because it is an agreed-upon practice, a deviation from it is perceived as "wrong" by readers and writers of English. Adherence to conventions of writing make reading easier, just as the conventions of answering and responding make telephone conversations more effective. In addition, adherence to conventions in writing shows your learning to its best advantage.

In the largest sense, conventions shape all levels of writing, from whole

Handbook of Usage and Grammar

books to individual punctuation marks. From your own reading, you know that telephone books are organized according to one set of conventions, whereas textbooks are organized according to another.

This handbook explains conventions of sentences, usage, punctuation, capitalization, abbreviating, hyphenating, italics, numbers, and spelling. To ignore these conventions will not lead to a head-on collision or death at the hands of a Gileadite, but it will make it harder for your readers to understand what you are saying. Some people like to describe writing as a computer program that always produces the same information no matter who is on the receiving end. I prefer to think of writing as a musical score for which the basic outline is provided, but each performance is subject to individual interpretation and variation. If you think of writing as a musical score, then the importance of conventions will become evident immediately. Your task as a writer is to guide the reader to the interpretation you intend, and conventions can help you do this.

To be sure, some deviations from conventions can be effective. You might think of the poetry of e.e. cummings, which ignores the conventions of capitalization, or the prose of James Joyce, which contains page-long sentences and in which deliberate deviations work well. Accidental lapses from writing conventions, however, can be distracting and confusing to the reader. In addition, conventions depend to some extent on the context of the writing. Degree of formality depends on circumstances, and so do conventions. For example, in this book I sometimes use the word 'alternatives' when more than two choices are available, but if I were writing for a legal audience or for a very formal publication, I would limit my use of *alternatives* to two-choice situations.

As is true with other conventional forms, some written conventions are taken more seriously than others are. For example, to misspell the word *forgetting* as *forgeting* will usually be viewed as a more serious fault than failing to capitalize the word *east* in a sentence such as "She returned to the East" or failing to put commas around a modifier as in "Josh, the second of eight sons, had plenty of experience with children." Even the same types of deviations from convention may be viewed with differing degrees of seriousness. For example, "My friend and me went to the show," is usually seen as a more serious deviation than is "The box office sent tickets to my friend and I." In both instances a pronoun of the wrong case is used, but the first seems the more obvious fault to most speakers and writers of English. This handbook is designed to help you avoid such lapses in conventions.

Parts of Speech

It is entirely possible to use conventions of standard written English effectively without knowing names for the parts of speech, but these terms, like the specialized language of any discipline enable you to discuss writing more effectively. Just as dentists find it more convenient to discuss teeth by using a common numbering code rather than saying something like "The upper molar on the right side, five teeth back from the center, has a cavity," so writers find it useful to have precise terms to describe language. Parts of speech include these: noun, pronoun, verb, adjective, adverb, preposition, conjunction, and interjection.

Noun

Nouns are usually described as words that name people, places, things, ideas, actions, or qualities.

Common nouns refer to any one class of people, places, or things such as priest, computer, event, and continent.

Proper nouns are always capitalized and refer to particular persons, places, or things such as Father Flanagan, Apple 2E, the World Series, and Australia.

Abstract nouns refer to intangibles such as ideas or concepts like peace, friendship, prosperity, and destiny.

Concrete Nouns refer to groups of people who can be regarded as a unit, groups such as committee, orchestra, family, and legislature.

To see more about how nouns function, turn to the sections on *complements* and *agreement* in the "Sentences" section of this Handbook.

Pronoun

Pronouns take the place of nouns, noun phrases, or other pronouns. Types of pronouns include personal, indefinite, demonstrative, relative, reflexive, interrogative, and reciprocal.

Personal Pronouns

I	he	you	them
me	him	they	their
mine	his	we	theirs
my	she	us	it
you	her	our	its
yours	hers	ours	

Personal pronouns refer to beings or objects.

Indefinite Pronouns

all	many	each	one
another	many a	each one	other
any	much	either	several
anybody	neither	everybody	some
anyone	nobody	everyone	somebody
anything	none		someone
both	no one		something

Indefinite pronouns make only third-person (he, it, they, and the like) references.

Handbook of Usage and Grammar

Demonstrative Pronouns
this	these
that	those

Demonstrative pronouns focus on or point to something that has appeared earlier.

Relative Pronouns
who	which
whom	that
whose	what

Relative pronouns introduce clauses that act as nouns or modifiers and refer to other clauses or sentences.

Reflexive Pronouns
myself	ourselves
yourself	yourselves
herself	themselves

Reflexive pronouns refer to another noun or pronoun in the sentence, usually the subject.

Interrogative Pronouns
who
what
which

Interrogative pronouns introduce questions.

Reciprocal Pronouns
each other
one another

Reciprocal pronouns indicate a mutual relationship.

VERB

Verbs express actions or states of being. *Transitive verbs* require an object or word that indicates where the verb's action is directed. *Intransitive verbs* do not require objects.

Linking verbs connect a subject to its complement and are intransitive. The most common linking verbs are *become, seem, appear,* and forms of the word *be*.

For more information on how verbs function, see these sections in the "Sentences" portion of this Handbook: *complements, tense, number, person, aspect, mood, voice, agreement,* and *modifier*.

Adjective

Adjectives describe nouns or pronouns. They answer questions such as *Which? What kind of?* and *How many?*

For more information on how adjectives function, see the *modifier, phrases,* and *clauses* sections of the "Sentences" portion of this handbook.

Adverb

Adverbs modify, describe, or limit verbs, adjectives, other adverbs, or whole clauses. They answer questions such as *How? Where? When? and Why?*

For more information on how adverbs function, see *modifier, phrases* and *clauses* sections of the "Sentences" portion of this Handbook.

Preposition

Prepositions connect their objects (usually nouns or pronouns) to other words in a sentence. Common propositions include: *above, across, among, around, at, before, beside, between, by, from, in, of, on, over, through, to, toward, under, up,* and *with*. Prepositional phrases consist of prepositions and their objects.

For more information on how prepositions function see the *phrases* section of the "Sentences" portion of this Handbook.

Conjunction

Conjunctions connect words, phrases, and clauses.

Coordinating conjunctions connect words, phrases, or clauses of equal grammatical rank and include *and, or, but, nor, for, so,* and *yet*.

Subordinating conjunctions introduce dependent clauses and include *since, because, although, after, when, while, before,* and *unless*.

For more information on how coordinating and subordinating conjunctions function, see Chapter Eleven.

Interjection

Interjections indicate exclamations such as *yea, wow, alas,* and *oh* and are set off from sentences with either commas or a period.

Sentences

The most common definition of a sentence is "a group of words that expresses a complete thought." In Chapter 11 you were asked to identify the sentences in the following groups of words:

1. although the consequences have not yet been assessed.
2. stop.
3. having begun the process.
4. the data are incomplete.

If you immediately selected the second and fourth items as sentences, you made the choice with more knowledge of the nature of a sentence than the definition supplies. Each group carries a different criterion for completeness, as long as meaning is uppermost in the choice. If the first and third items seem incomplete, it is not because you do not understand their meanings but because you sense their grammatical incompleteness. Something must be added to make them "feel" like sentences. Yet the second item, with its single word, does feel complete as a sentence.

To explain the grammatical knowledge that you bring to test sentences, you need two concepts: *subject* and *predicate*. If a group of words contains both parts, explicitly as in the case of the first and fourth items, and implicitly as in the second item, you will recognize it as a potential sentence. The subject contains the person, thing, or abstraction that the sentence is about, and the predicate contains the assertion made or the question asked about the subject. These two essential parts of every sentence are its nuclei, and those nuclei must seem to be related. Through that relationship, you infer what we call the sense of a sentence.

In the second item, you recognize an implied subject—*you*—which combines with *stop* to create the sense of a command to someone: he, she, or they must stop doing something, the assertion made about the subject.

In the fourth item, *the data* is the subject, though the writer of this sentence has not specified which data he means. A preceding part of the discourse must have clarified which data are intended. The assertion made about the data is expressed with a verb—*are*—and an adjective—*incomplete*—that together comprise the predicate.

The subject and predicate in the first item are, respectively, *the consequences* and *have not been assessed*. Yet, this whole group of words may seem "incomplete" because it is introduced by *although*, a word that changes the grammatical status and sense of this "sentence." It has become subordinate to or dependent on some other sentence, and the reader awaits its insertion into another subject-predicate combination before calling it a sentence.

Similarly, the third item lacks a subject, though it is a different kind of subject omission from that of the second item. *You* could be the subject of the third item if *having* were changed to *have* or *had*, but many other nouns or pronouns could also fit that subject slot.

These variations in the forms that subjects and predicates can take illustrate the almost infinite possibilities for expanding on the basic concept of a sentence—a concept without which grammar could not exist, and writing would be incapable of conveying meanings.

COMPLEMENTS

Though English has many verbs that are sufficient to complete the predication of a subject—they are called *intransitive verbs*—the sense conveyed by many other verbs is incomplete without a *complement*. Meaning literally "to complete," this term includes the following types:

Direct object: for example, Students write *essays*.
Indirect object (always appears with a direct object): for example, The instructor offered the *students* several options.
Object complement (always appears with a direct object): for example, I consider Conrad a *fine novelist*.

In each of these three examples, the verb is transitive because its meaning is not complete without a complement; the meaning proceeds across (*trans*) the verb to be completed later in the sentence. (Note, however, that some verbs can be used either transitively or intransitively. We can write "Students write," leaving the *what* of the writing unspecified, and not confuse the reader. But to write "The instructor offered" and "I consider" without complements leaves the reader waiting for more information. The natural question is "Offered what?" or "Considered what?" thus probing for the complements.) Indirect objects are very common and follow prescribed limits for placement. If the indirect object is a noun, it will appear between the verb and the direct object or else right after the direct object with another word such as *to* ("The instructor offered several options to the students"). If the direct object is a pronoun, however, the indirect object must appear after the direct object and with a word like *to* ("The instructor offered it to the students" not "The instructor offered it the students" or "The instructor offered the students it.").

Another type of verb, called *linking* or *copula*, takes a different category of complement, called the *subject complement* because it refers directly to the subject of the sentence. This term includes the following types:

Predicate noun: for example, Students should be *writers*.
Predicate adjectives: for example, Good writing is not *easy*.

Whether the complement is a noun (or pronoun) or an adjective, the linking verb indicates its relationship to the subject, renaming it, putting it in a category, or describing it. The forms of the verb *to be* are common linking verbs, though many other verbs can also perform that function. The crucial distinction between the complements of linking verbs and the complements of transitive verbs is the former's special relationship with the subject. The object complement is similar to the subject complement except that no linking verb joins it to its partner, the direct object preceding it. Object complements can also be adjectives ("We considered him *intelligent*").

MODIFIERS

Although the term *modifier* is very common in grammatical descriptions, the words *qualifier* or *limiter* might better be used to name the functions in question. Single words, phrases, and clauses may be added to the subject-predicate base of a sentence, permitting the writer to play endless variations on sentence meanings.

Adjective modifiers qualify or limit the meanings of nouns, as in "*fine* novelist," "*incomplete* data," "*enlarged* understanding," and "*running* commentary." These adjectives are typically in front of the noun. Phrase and clause modifiers of nouns usually appear after the noun, as in "notes *from reading*," "and essay *to satisfy the assignment*," and "a book *that I admire*."

Adverb modifiers are more slippery in their modification relationships. They express several kinds of meaning, represented by such questions as Where? When? Why? How? How much? Under what conditions? They may join the verb of a clause (as in "He wrote *industriously*"), to another adverb (as in "He wrote *very* industriously"), to an adjective (as in "*almost* empty"), or even to an entire sentence (as in "*indeed*, the responsibility has not been met"). Phrase and clause modifiers used adverbially also tend to be flexible in their placement, as in "The assignment must be finished *by noon today*" versus "*By noon today,* the assignment must be finished" and "*After you finish the assignment,* put it in the instructor's mailbox" versus "Put the assignment in the instructor's mailbox *after you finish it.*" (Note that to make it clear, moving the adverb clause requires changing the use of the noun *assignment* and the pronoun *it.*

PHRASES

Two or more words that form a sequence and, as a unit, express a meaning constitute a *phrase*. They are identified by structure and function.

In the preceding section, *from reading* and *by noon today* are examples of *prepositional phrases*, used in their two most characteristic ways—as adjectives and as adverbs. They may be expanded with their own modifiers, including other prepositional phrases ("in a time *of stress*"), single words ("from *extensive* reading") or clauses ("in a time *when resources are limited*"). The identifying structure of this kind of phrase is its preposition headword (though some prepositions are really two or more words, like *because of, thanks to, in compliance with,* and *as far back as*) and the noun or noun unit following it.

Infinitives, which usually begin with *to* (not to be confused with *to* used as a preposition), are the simple or uninflected forms of verbs. Every verb has an infinitive form except for certain auxiliary verbs like *ought* and *must*. In the example "an essay *to satisfy the assignment*" the infinitive is *to satisfy* with its complement *the assignment;* the whole infinitive phrase qualifies *an essay*, limiting its meaning in its sentence.

Infinitive phrases may also be used adverbially, as in "The student revised her essay *to improve its organization*" (modifying the verb *revised* and answering the question why); "The essay was difficult *to revise*" (modifying the adjective *difficult*); "She revised well enough *to satisfy the instructor*" (modifying the adverb *enough*).

Infinitive phrases are also commonly used as nouns in any of the usual sentence positions for nouns: as a subject ("*To err* is human"); as a direct object ("He began *to write*"); as a subject complement ("His aim is *to succeed*"); and as an object of preposition ("My aim is for you *to succeed*"), though this last infinitive phrase also has the subject *you,* the entire infinitive phrase there being *you to succeed*.

Sometimes infinitives appear with an auxiliary to form the main verb in a clause, as in "The student ought *to revise*" and, without *to*, "The student must *revise*."

Verbs can also serve as modifiers when their form changes from *revise* to *revising* or *revised*, for example. These are participles that, with their own complements and modifiers, become participial phrases. In "a *revised* essay" and "*revising his essay*, the student succeeded in improving it," both participles are used as adjectives. Writers who use participial phrases as adjective modifiers need to be careful to include prominently in the main clause the noun that the phrase modifies. In the preceding example, *the student* is the noun; its meaning relationship to *revising his essay* is implied by the reader's recognition that it is the implied subject of the participle *revising*. (Compare "*revising his essay*, it was improved.") Making sure that this relationship is clear allows writers to avoid dangling participles. The same principle applies to infinitive phrases used as adverbs, as in "*To improve his essay*, the student revised it" versus "*To improve his essay*, it was revised." (In the second version, *it*, meaning "the essay," is not the implied subject of *to improve*.)

The *-ing* form of verbs can also be used as nouns. This first example in the preceding paragraph contains such a use; *improving it* functions as object of the preposition *in*. Whenever the *-ing* verb form can serve as a noun, it becomes a gerund rather than a participle. Gerunds are extremely common. Like infinitives functioning as nouns, they tend to strengthen a sentence because they convey the concreteness and vividness of the verbs from which they come.

One other type of grammatical phrase—the *absolute phrase*—is special because it seldom appears in oral language. In fact, only more mature writers ever use it. The absolute phrase allows writers to add narrative and descriptive detail, but with a very loose grammatical connection to the main sentence. "The student left the room, *his head lowered, the exam paper a token of his exhaustion*." The two absolutes in this sentence do not modify any one part of the sentence and can be moved to other positions in the sentence. Their structure consists of a noun introducing the phrase plus a modifying word or phrase, in this example a participle (*lowered*) and a noun (*token*) with its modifying prepositional phrase.

CLAUSES

Sentences are clauses because they contain a subject and a predicate, but not all clauses are sentences. The addition of a connecting word at the beginning of a clause converts it into a grammatically dependent status, thus nullifying its claim to being a sentence. The first example at the beginning of this section ("although the consequences have not yet been assessed") is an adverb clause because *although*, a subordinating conjunction, makes it an answer to the question "Under what condition?" If it is combined with an independent clause, such as "Should we consider his action blameless?" the sense of concession conveyed by the adverb clause will be evident.

If the connecting word is an adverb (like *when, where, why*) or a relative pronoun (like *who, which, that*), the clause will function as an adjective. Examples include "Economic assumptions become especially evident in a time *when resources are limited*" and "*Crime and Punishment* is a book *that I admire.*" Variations on the adjective clause include the omission of the relative pronoun (as in "*Crime and Punishment* is a book *I admire*") and the change of *who* to *whom* (as in "Dostoyevsky is an author *whom I admire*"), a change necessitated by the grammatical function, the adjective clause, of *whom* as the direct object of *admire*.

Clauses also function as noun units, just as infinitive and gerund phrases can. In "*That the student revised her essay* surprised her instructor" the noun clause is the subject of *surprised*. In addition to being used as a direct object, a subject complement, and an object of preposition, the noun clause can often function as an appositive, a restatement, or a renaming of another noun in the sentence. Example: "The fact *that no revision is evident* makes the essay less good than it could be." The appositive specifies what the fact is, rather than merely modifying or qualifying it. (Single words can also function as appositives.)

The preceding example also illustrates a common way of attaching clauses to independent clauses, namely, with correlative conjunctions. In the adverb clause *than it could be, than* is the other half of the pair *less . . . than*, with comparative degree as the meaning conveyed by the pair of words.

SENTENCE TYPES

Sentences are classified in two main ways, one arising from the writer's intent with respect to meaning and the other from grammatical structure. Previous examples included these three writer's intentions:

Declarative—to make a statement of fact or opinion ("The data are incomplete.").
Imperative—to make a request or command ("Desist").
Interrogative—to frame a question ("Should we consider his actions blameless, although the consequences have not been assessed?").

The possible grammatical structures include *simple* (one independent clause plus its modifiers, including all phrases, as in "That the student revised her essay was no surprise"); *compound* (two or more independent clauses joined by a conjunction such as *and, but, however,* and *moreover,* as in "My aim is for you to succeed, and I shall do everything I can to help you"); and *complex* (one or more dependent clauses joined to one or more independent clauses, as in "After you have finished the assignment, put in your instructor's mailbox, which is in Room 10").

Given the fundamental grammatical structure and definition of a sentence, any group of words that does not meet these criteria is technically not a sentence. Yet, accomplished writers do often intentionally omit a subject or a verb, thereby producing a fragment. Examples: "no," "certainly not," "overcoming even the most potent objections." When these fragments appear in context, however, they can be interpreted as if they were complete sentences, and their rhetorical effectiveness often outweighs the seeming grammatical deficiency. For example, "Shall we continue this absurd arms buildup? No. It is ruining our economy and undermining our stamina." "I admire his acumen and his tenacity. He isolates the issues astutely. Marshaling the resources necessary to pursue them. Debating every opponent who dares confront him. Overcoming even the most potent objections." This string of three fragments gives the prose additional momentum that grammatically complete sentences might not have and underscores the vehemence of the assertions. Although intentional sentence fragments can improve writing, unintended ones weaken it considerably. Be sure you know the difference.

TENSE, NUMBER, AND PERSON

The main verb in a clause must be inflected—that is, changed—to show three properties: tense, number, and person. The rub in English is that these inflections often do not literally change the form of the verb. We often have to infer the inflections from the position of the verb and from our store of knowledge of particular verbs' forms.

English words have only two tense inflections, although they can be combined with other words to show many time relationships, the present and the past forms: *see/saw, wait/waited, go/went, keep/kept.* Though there is some correlation between the tense form and the actual time of the action to which the writer refers, the correspondence is not perfect. "Dostoyevsky writes about characters with emotional disturbances" is not meant to refer to a time concurrent with the writer's present. This is called the *historical present tense*. So-called universal truths are also expressed in the present tense: "Time flies," "A rolling stone gathers no moss." Even an action that has not yet occurred is often expressed with a present tense verb: "The author arrives tomorrow."

When they are part of the verb phase, infinitives do not bear a tense marker; the auxiliary verb does that, as in "The story *has* to end," "The student *must* revise." It is for that reason that the verb or an auxiliary that appears first in the predicate is called *finite*, that is, limited by inflections.

When used with any noun and such pronouns as *she, it* and *he*, present tense verbs have a unique inflection: *she writes, he reads, it computes, the reader comprehends.* This is the sole inflection for person, namely, the third-person singular. It is the only remaining manifestation in English of inflections for the first, second, and third persons and for number, either singular or plural. Several other languages, of course, still retain inflections to indicate those grammatical distinctions.

Although English verbs have only two tense inflections, there are other means for conveying complex time relationships. Among them are adverbs that overtly signal time, as in "The author arrives *tomorrow*." The time of the event is clearly in the future, though there is no future tense in English.

Another means to denote time is the addition of certain auxiliaries, like *will, shall,* and *might.* When these words precede a main verb, they suggest future action. Examples: "The ceremony *will* begin at 7:00 P.M." "John Updike *might* win a Pulitzer Prize."

ASPECT

Other kinds of auxiliaries change the power of verbs to convey still more complex time relationships. The word *aspect* covers these more elusive meanings, and the words *perfect* and *progressive* specify the categories. *Perfect* means action completed before some designated time in the past, present, or future.

> *Examples*
> *Past Perfect*: "Even before the nineteenth century, English literature *had established* its eminence." (Auxiliary is always *had*.)
> *Present Perfect*: "Until now, no one *has disputed* the evidence. (Auxiliary is always *have* or *has*.)
> *Future Perfect*: "By 1990, enrollment trends *will have changed* drastically. (Auxiliary is always *will* or an equivalent future-time-bearing word plus *have*.)

Another identifying feature of the aspect-bearing verb structure is the past participle form of the main verb: *established, disputed, changed, eaten, given, kept.*

The progressive aspect signals events occurring over a span of time, from a few billionths of a second to eons, as in "These computer episodes *are occurring* in six nanoseconds," "Glaciers *were depositing* moraines in the Northwest." The progressive forms can combine with perfect forms, as in "The computer *has been malfunctioning*," "Can we predict whether the metal *will have been bearing* too much stress?" The progressive aspect always uses an *-ing* form of the main verb.

MOOD

Verbs also undergo changes to convey the writer's intentions about the possibility or likelihood of events and about the writer's attitude toward those events. *Mood, mode,* and *modality* are the almost-interchangeable terms for these verb states. The indicative mood is used to make an assertion, as in the declarative sentence. The imperative mood, of course, corresponds to the intention to request or command. The subjunctive mood reflects doubt, uncertainty, or even impossibility, as in "If the author *were* shrewd, she *would* alter the tone of her essay," "If you be so minded, consider joining our society," "If I were God, I *would* reconsider my decision to create humankind."

Because the few subjunctive forms remaining in English sound rather formal, modal auxiliaries often are used to express subjunctive intention, as in "If you should be so minded, consider joining our society," "Though the argument may be weak, he continues his effort to advance it."

Distinctions among the three moods blur when other modal auxiliaries combine with main verbs, as in "The essay *ought to be* completely *revised*,"

"*Can* geologists *predict* future earthquakes?" "Volcanic eruptions *may affect* worldwide weather conditions."

Modality is also expressed by adverbs, as in "*Perhaps* the effort will fail," "Her essay is *conceivably* the best of any I have read." (Compare "The effort *might* fail" and "Her essay may be the best . . . ")

Voice

Still another manipulation of verbs reflects changes in the writer's intentions. When the actual subject of a verb is moved to another part of the sentence (or is deleted) and the verb is converted from the active to the passive voice, the emphasis in the sentence changes. When "The writer *should revise* her essay" becomes "The essay *should be revised*," the emphasis shifts from the writer who does something to the object of that action—the essay—and what happens to it.

The mechanism of creating passive voice, which works only with transitive verbs, requires the direct or the indirect object to become the subject, the subject to disappear or to be incorporated in a prepositional phrase (beginning with *by*), the verb to collect another auxiliary (a form of *be* or *get*), and the main verb to become a past participle. Example: "The command *has been given by* the sergeant."

Agreement

Grammatically tidy sentences exhibit the property of agreement of certain specially related sentence parts. The subject and verb must agree in person and number, though because of the relative lack of inflections for English verbs, this becomes an issue only in the third person singular, in which *-s* must appear, as in "The issue looms." Achieving this kind of agreement is seldom a problem for writers unless certain phrases intervene between a singular noun and verb or unless the subject consists of certain pronouns. Examples: "None of the authors represented in this anthology *is* American," "The doubt aroused by the many errors of fact and the demonstrable lapses in logic *renders* the manuscript suspect."

When collective nouns, such as *data, criteria, people*, and *committee*, are used as subjects, agreement becomes more problematical. *Data* and *criteria* are plural forms and therefore should not be used with the *-s* verb form, but informal usage sometimes makes them singular. The choice of verb form therefore depends on the level of formality. Nouns like *people* and *committee* may appear formally with either a singular or a plural verb form, according to the writer's intention to stress singularity or plurality. Examples: "The committee *has* published its report," "The committee *expect* their report to be scrutinized and attached." The governing principle of choice is the writer's intention to stress either the collectivity of the group or the actions of the individuals in the group. This decision transcends grammar.

Agreement must also unite pronouns with their antecedent nouns—an agreement of person, number, and gender. Example: "The authors of the text explain *their* assumptions in the introduction." There is likely to be confusion in these choices only when an indefinite pronoun, like *everyone*, or a singular noun meant to include both men and women, like *author*, is the antecedent. Agreement may be achieved in this way: "Everyone who writes seriously must document *his* sources." Why not "*their* sources"? Or "*her* sources"? The answer is that preferences are changing. A writer must be sensitive to the issue of agreement, often recasting the sentence to avoid a possibly controversial choice. For example, the preceding example could be written "All serious writers must document *their* sources," thereby achieving unquestionable agreement in person, number, and gender.

Usage

The term *usage* refers to the actual use of language, what living people do with language, rather than the grammatical principles that describe its structure. You have probably encountered many variations in usage. For example, you may have noticed differences in pronunciations by speakers from different parts of the United States and the world. You can understand an English-speaking person from Nigeria, say, but you are aware that the person pronounces English words differently from the way you do. Speakers from the northeastern part of the United States and those from the Southeast can likewise understand one another but are aware of distinct differences in pronunciation. These differences refer to the phonological, or auditory, variations in usage. Linguists have studied pronunciation throughout the United States and have produced maps indicating where certain pronunciations occur (such as *creek* with an /I/, as in *pick* or with an /i/, as in *peak*). With a well-trained ear, you can locate speakers' origins from the way they pronounce words such as

greasy
park the car
first/bird
wash/water/Washington
on/off/dog/oft/lot/log/sorry
horse/hoarse.

Although the phonological dimensions of usage are interesting, they are not as important to writers as are their *lexical* and *syntactic* aspects. Lexical issues of usage refer to vocabulary or word choice. Depending on the area of the country where you live, you may use one of several terms to describe the strip of grass between sidewalk and street (parking strip, easement, boulevard) or nonalcoholic, carbonated drinks (soft drink, pop, tonic, soda). You may have heard speakers of English from other countries using words such as *queue up* ("to stand in line") or *lorry* ("truck") or *shroff* ("cashier"). Word choice also extends to selections between *it is I* and *it is me* or *he's got it* and *he has it* or *who are you talking to* and *whom are you talking to* or *the concert was pretty good* and *the concert was very good*. As you revise your writing, you will undoubtedly face lexical choices.

Syntax refers to word order or the way words are arranged to create meaning in English. In my discussion of sentence revision, I touched on syntax's importance to revising writing. Dangling modifiers and misplaced modifiers represent poor syntactic choices because they can cloud meaning. As you revise your writing, you will want to attend to syntax that obscures meaning. In addition, you will probably find yourself puzzling about the placement of the word *only* in a sentence such as

The fly ball hit one spectator.

Should it be

The fly ball hit one spectator only.

or

The fly ball only hit one spectator.

or

The fly ball hit only one spectator.

Dialect

Taken together, usage patterns of phonology, lexicon, and syntax form a *dialect*. Dialects can be described in personal, social or national terms. You may, for example, use forms or words that have meaning to you and those closest to you; a term such as *raccoon bread* or *'khead* may have developed within your immediate group and be common to a select few. Your individual collection of phonological, lexical, and syntactic choices can be described as your *idiolect*. Likewise, similar choices common to groups of people within specific geographical boundaries, such as the northeastern section of the United States, can be called a *regional dialect*. In a larger scope still we can talk of national dialects when distinguishing between the English spoken in Australia and that in Scotland.

Dialect has a social as well as geographical dimension. People of differing educational and socioeconomic backgrounds often make different phonological, lexical, and syntactic choices in their speech and writing. You have probably noticed that judges express themselves differently than welders do. The standard written English that I discussed earlier is a dialect of English, and as a college student you will be held accountable for the usages that come under this general heading. Some features of standard written English are, from the perspective of conventions, merely interesting as are variations in place settings, whereas other patterns of usage are taken very seriously, and ignoring them leads to the academic equivalent of a fatal accident. Part of your task as a writer is to decide which is which. To help you make this decision, I have listed items of usage that may puzzle you as you revise your writing, and with each I have provided a brief explanation to help you make your choice.

Handbook of Usage and Grammar

Puzzling Usages

Among. (see *between*).

Amount/number. *Amount* is usually used with uncountable things.

> We have no way to calculate the *amount* of damage the tornado did in this town.

> *Number* is usually used with countable things or people.

> The *number* of subscribers has increased dramatically during this theater season.

Anywheres. *Anywheres* is occasionally used in casual writing and does not appear in informal or formal writing; use *anywhere* instead.

As/like. *As* is used to introduce clauses and can substitute for such words as *when, while, since,* and *because.* Often one of these other words makes a more emphatic statement of cause or time.

> *As* we walked out of the room, we saw the broken statue in the corner.

> During last night's performance Louise sang *as* if she were inspired.

> *Like* means "similar to." The use of *like* as a conjunction ("Few people sing *like* she does.") is controversial; the more acceptable form is to use *as* ("Few people sing *as* she does.)

> The animal in that cage looks *like* an antelope.

Awfully. *Awfully* is used as an intensifier in casual writing ("This pie is *awfully* good"), but it is not usually in informal or formal writing. A better alternative is *very* ("This pie is *very* good.")

Being that/being as. Both *being that* and *being as* are used in casual writing as a variation of *because.* ("*Being that* I am already here, I may as well join you for dinner.") Neither of these forms is used in informal or formal writing. The better alternative is *because* or *since* (*Since* I am already here I may as well join you for dinner.")

Between/among. *Between* is generally used for two people or objects, and *among* is used for three or more. This distinction is not always maintained in casual writing ("Just *between* the three of us, he failed"), but it is maintained in informal and formal writing.

> The final game of the World Series will decide *between* the Brewers and the Cardinals.

> I wouldn't say this publicly, but *among* friends I will admit that I don't support his plan.

Can/may. In formal writing *can* means "ability" or "power," and *may* means "permission" or "chance."

    I *can* climb this mountain.

    May I have your ticket? I *may* go to the show tomorrow.

    This distinction is not observed in casual writing or in most speech.

Can't help but. *Can't help but* is acceptable for casual and informal writing. If you want to be formal, you will do better to omit the *but*. Transform "I *can't help but* sympathize with these hungry people" to "I *can't help sympathizing* with these hungry people."

Center around, about. Some people object to *center around* or *center about* because it seems illogical. Things usually revolve around a center, not the reverse. If you want your writing to be formal, use *center on* instead.

Contact. *Contact* is frequently used as a verb (I will *contact* you sometime next week) meaning "to get in touch with." If you check the usage ratings in dictionaries, you will probably find that panels are divided on whether *contact* should be used this way. If you are writing formally, you should avoid using *contact* as a verb. Instead, substitute "get in touch with" ("I shall *get in touch with* you next week").

Contractions. *Contractions* are abbreviated forms that combine two words into one, in an imitation of speech (I'm for I am, it's for it is or it has, should've for should have). Contractions are used frequently in casual writing but should be used more sparingly in informal writing. Formal writing usually contains no contractions.

Could of/might of/should of/would of. *Of* is not a verb and should not be used in combination with could, might, should, or would. The word *have*, particularly in its contracted form (should've) sounds like *of*, which may explain why you occasionally see forms such as *could of*.

Disinterested/uninterested. *Disinterested* means "impartial" or "objective."

    The players and management sought a *disinterested* arbitrator.

    Uninterested means "indifferent" or "not interested."

    My father is so *uninterested* in sports that he doesn't even know which team is playing.

    The distinction between these two words is not always observed, and you will probably find occasions when *disinterested* is used to mean "having no interest." However, in formal writing you should maintain the distinction.

Handbook of Usage and Grammar

Enthuse/enthused. *Enthuse* and *enthused* are formed from *enthusiasm* and carry the same meaning. However, despite their relatively wide usage, they are not completely accepted, and if you are writing a formal piece, you should avoid them.

Etc.. *Etc.* means "and other things" and is an abbreviation of the Latin *et cetera*. It is used in casual writing to indicate that a list goes on beyond the given words. *Etc.* is not usally used in informal or formal writing because it appears to be a lazy substitute for continuing the list or writing "and so forth" or "and so on."

Fewer/less. *Fewer* is generally used with countable nouns ("This bowl contains *fewer* apples than that one does"), and *less* is used with uncountable nouns ("After his surgery John had *less* energy than he had before"). In casual writing, *less* is often used with countable nouns ("Use *less* words"), but in formal and informal writing, the distinction is usually preserved.

Good/well. *Good* and *well* both mean "in a sound state of health." ("I feel *good*/I feel *well*"). *Good* is usually used as an adjective ("This is a *good* start, now revise your work"), and *well* is usually used as an adverb ("You write very *well*"). In casual writing, *good* is often substituted for *well* ("The car runs *good*), but this usage should be avoided.

Hopefully. *Hopefully* means "full of hope."

When the dessert cart approached, Sally looked *hopefully* at her mother.

Hopefully often appears in casual and informal writing to express the idea "we hope that" or "I hope that" ("*Hopefully* the rain will stop tomorrow"). The difficulty with this usage is that it lacks the precision of "I hope" or "we hope" because it does not make clear who is doing the hoping. In informal writing on which precision is important, it is a good idea to avoid using *hopefully* to mean "I hope."

I/me. *I* is used when the pronoun appears in the *subject* position in a sentence ("I am going tomorrow"). *Me* is used when the pronoun is used in the *object* position in a sentence ("The conductor gave the ticket to ME"). I is also used afte the verb "to be" ("It is I"), but frequently in casual writing *me* is substituted. In informal or formal writing, you should avoid the "It is me" construction.

-ize. The suffix *-ize* is frequently added to nouns to create verbs (finalize, operationalize). Although these formations are common in speech and casual writing, they can obscure meaning because they allow the actor (or noun or subject) to disappear into the verb. Plans can be "operationalized" with no visible operator. If you are in doubt about a particular *-ize* word, check your dictionary.

435

Kind of/sort of. Kind of and sort of both appear in casual writing to mean "rather" or "somewhat." ("You made me *kind of* angry just then"). This form does not usually appear in informal or formal writing. Substitute *rather* or *somewhat*. ("You made me *rather* angry just then")

Less. (see *fewer*).

Like. (see *as*).

Me. (see *I*).

Might of. (see *could of*).

Number. (see *amount*).

Only. The placement of *only* can influence the meaning of a sentence, and so as you revise make sure that *only* says what you intend.

    The irate fans threw garbage into the field, but it hit *only* an umpire. (not a player)

    The irate fans threw garbage into the field, but it *only* hit an umpire. (did not kill him)

    The irate fans threw garbage into the field, but it hit *only* one umpire. (not more)

Real/really. Real is usually used as an adjective in informal and formal writing ("Pollution is a real problem in this city"). It means "actual."

    Really is usually used as an adverb ("We have a *really* active council here"). It also means "actually."

    In casual writing, real is sometimes substituted for really ("We have a real active council here"), but it is not usually acceptable in informal and formal writing.

Should of (see *could of*).

Sort of (see *kind of*).

Toward/towards. Both *toward* and *towards* are acceptable usages for writing at all levels of formality.

-wise. The suffix *-wise* is sometimes added to nouns to turn them into adjectives ("How are we doing *timewise?*"). This usage is appropriate for casual writing but should be used with caution in formal and informal writing because it adds bulk to words without giving any additional meaning.

Would of (see *could of*).

Unique. *Unique* means "singular." To write *very unique* is repetitive.

Uninterested (see disinterested).

Punctuation

The most important thing to remember about punctuation is its contribution to meaning. It is not merely a set of mechanical rules but also can indicate relationships of meaning within sentences.

Even though decisions about particular uses of punctuation are somewhat flexible, there are certain conventions within which those choices must be made. This section explains many of those conventions, using subsections to emphasize the reasons for using specific types of punctuation. Throughout this discussion of punctuation, function is emphasized because punctuation's main usefulness rests in what it can help writers do.

PUNCTUATING TO ENCLOSE

If you are unfamiliar with the punctuation system used in standard written English, you might begin to discern the logic of the system by noticing pairings:

(with); "with" *or* 'with' [with]

You may observe that they enclose either a single word or a group of words and that the enclosed material receives special attention. For example, paired quotation marks highlight someone else's exact words.

> Dostoyevsky's biographer calls *The Brothers Karamazov* "far more a novel of ideas than is any of his other fictional works."

The reader of this quotation infers the writer's belief by quoting the exact words, not paraphrasing them, presumably because they are so apt or so significant to the writer's argument.

A single word or phrase is enclosed in quotation marks usually because it has a special meaning or use in that context. For example, in *The Soul of a New Machine,* Tracy Kidder wrote at the end of a paragraph: This was a system of "rings." The words *rings* is being used metaphorically to help the non-specialist reader visualize and understand how the system works.

Similarly, if a word is mismatched tonally with the rest of the passage, it will need quotation marks to signal the writer's awareness of its potential inappropriateness. Words like *goofed* and *ditched* are clearly slang, which does not ordinarily belong in formal or informal writing, and so if they are used, they will be less jarring to the reader if they are enclosed in quotation marks.

Sometimes it is necessary to call attention to a word or other symbol, perhaps to question the frequency of its use

> The paragraph contains too many "ands."

or to call attention to a spelling error

> She spelled it "committment."

or to correct an error

> The author wrote "H_2O" when he meant "H_2O_2."

In other words, quotation marks enclose words referred to for themselves.

As is true of all punctuation, too many quotation marks are worse than none at all. If you start enclosing many words in quotation marks, they will lose their effect and distract rather than enlighten your readers. In addition, the injudicious use of quotation marks can have exactly the opposite effect from what you intend. For example, describing restaurant fare as "home-cooked food" may arouse readers' suspicions rather than appetites.

Single quotation marks are reserved for calling attention to words and phrases within double quotation marks. These may be titles, as in

> The review ended with the comment, "The diction of 'The Whale's Tail' was unfortunate."

or words that deserve special emphasis

> "It was De Castro who said, 'no mode bit.'"

A parenthesis is, literally, an inset or an interpolation, an item that interrupts the normal flow of meaning in the sentence. Sometimes the addition is a definition or explanation that the writer considers of secondary importance, yet likely to be helpful to the reader's understanding. For example:

> The heat radiation from its surface then appears mainly in a band of wavelengths around ten microns (about twenty times the wavelength of visible light).

Or the writer may wish to insert a technical term or a non-English word:

> In Fiji there is a special name (*Kana Lama*) for the disease supposed to be caused by eating out of the chief's dishes or wearing his clothes.

Often, the material enclosed in parenthesis will seem like the writer's afterthought or something spoken as though it were a commentary on the main idea. For example:

> For if it is trampled on, struck, or stabbed, he will feel injury as if it were done to his person; and if it detached from him entirely (as he believes that it may be) he will die.

Parenthetical insertions have a way of multiplying themselves. Once you discover their usefulness for qualifying and elaborating, you may be tempted to use them frequently, but writing littered with parenthetical units is hard to read. For example:

> Students who violate copyright provisions (as outlined in the student handbook) will be subject to disciplinary action (ranging from receiving no credit to academic probation) by the dean of academic affairs (or a repre-

sentative of that office) before the end of the term in which the violation (or violations) occurs.

The excessive number of parenthesis in this sentence makes it difficult for readers to keep the main point in mind.

Brackets have a similar, though more limited, function. Within quoted material, they mark insertions when parentheses might be interpreted as being part of the original quotations. In the preceding quoted sentence, if one wanted to indicate what *it* refers to, this would be a good method:

Frazier states, "for if it [one's shadow or reflection] is trampled on...."

They also have a use special to academic writing. If a writer quotes another writer and believes that an error exists, the material can be quoted and the suspected error marked by [*sic*] (a Latin word meaning "so," "thus," "in this manner"). When used after a misspelling

The writer accused me of "faulty grammar" [*sic*], an accusation of dubious merit.

the effect on the reader can be humor. Most often, the use of [*sic*] conveys the writer's concern for precision.

Pairs of commas and dashes can also be used to enclose, though they are less easy to identify visually than are pairs of parentheses and quotation marks. The purpose for the enclosing is much the same, however, it shows the special relationship of the enclosed material to another part of the sentence.

A parenthetical interruption may be enclosed in dashes when it suddenly and forcefully breaks the continuity. For example:

It had not been much over a century from the time when the United States had begged for its very existence to the time when it had broken every treaty—except the Pickering treaty—and made the tribes beggars on their ancestral lands.

Either commas or parenthesis could have been used here, but neither gives quite the degree of separation and, therefore, emphasis that dashes do. (Also note that a dash is made on a typewriter with two hyphens and that there is no space between the words separated by dashes.)

Pairs of commas are most often used to enclose *nonrestrictive* modifiers: words, phrases, and clauses that if omitted will not change the meaning of the main clause. The judgment about necessity depends on context. Consider this sentence:

The idea of cost effectiveness, so central to our thinking, was absent from this view of the world.

The phrase that is enclosed is "extra" information about cost effectiveness, a fact that the context makes apparent. For example, in writing about your family, you could say

My sister, who has three children, lives in California.

Handbook of Usage and Grammar

if the fact that she had three children was extra information, was parenthetical. But if you wanted to specify that it was your sister with three children who lived in California, and not your sister with two children, you would say

My sister who has three children lives in California.

Meaning is another vehicle for distinguishing between restrictive and nonrestrictive modifiers. For example, consider the following sentence:

In our negotiations with the Soviet Union we should seek limitations only on offensive weapons *that would be threatening to us* and should avoid any prohibition of deployment of ABM systems.

Note that the clause in italic is essential to specifying or identifying exactly which offensive weapons the writer means. Note too that because it is a restrictive clause, it uses *that* instead of *which* and is *not* enclosed by commas.

Appositives are another kind of modifier to which the principle of restrictiveness applies. Most appositives simply supply another name for a noun, as in Khrushchev, the Soviet leader, on the assumption that the reader may not immediately recognize who Khrushchev was. But if you need to distinguish between two different people, Khrushchev the leader and Khrushchev the writer, however, no commas should separate the identifying (that is, restrictive) appositive from the proper noun.

As you can see, the choice of punctuation depends on the meaning you seek. Although there are some clear rules (quotation marks set off direct quotations), you have choices of whether to use parenthesis, dashes, or commas to enclose certain words, and part of revising is making these decisions.

EXERCISE

All the enclosing punctuation has been left out of the following passage. Revise it by inserting enclosing punctuation when you find it necessary, and be prepared to explain each of your choices.

The Monongahela controversy a debate which focused on clear-cutting practices in the Monongahela National Forest in West Virginia forced Congress to define the forest service's professional discretion.(1) As one person put it, this country needed new legislation for forest management to be effective.(2) National environmental organizations the Izaak Walton League and the Sierra Club became involved in the controversy because of their concern about unclear management guidelines.(3) The organic act established in 1897 specified conditions for timber harvest, and even it had been violated by the forest service.(4) The resulting legislation the National Forest Management Act of 1976 is not only concerned with timber production in national forests but also addresses public participation and decision making as they relate to these forestlands.(5)

Handbook of Usage and Grammar

Punctuating to Separate

Although punctuation to enclose also has the effect of separating grammatical units, other kinds of separation involve only one punctuation mark.

Two words that might be mistakenly read together need to be separated by commas as in

> While she was painting, the chair on which she was sitting collapsed.

A comma would be desirable after this introductory clause modifier even if the noun following *painting* could not be construed as its object. Most introductory words, like *furthermore* and *thus,* as well as phrases and clauses, like "in fact," "from two until four," and "when he decided to write his final chapter," gain emphasis and clarity if they are followed by commas. When such emphasis is not needed or when the meaning does not seem to suffer, however, you can omit the comma.

When two or more adjectives precede a noun, the placement of a separating comma depends on the meaning relationship of those adjectives to the noun. If the adjectives are *coordinate,* that is, equal in their modifying force, a comma separates them, as in

> a protracted, difficult negotiation

You can test for this relationship by seeing whether you can replace the comma with *and* and reverse the order of the adjectives without changing the meaning. If the adjectives are not coordinate, as in

> a difficult legal negotiation

no comma separates the adjective that identifies the particular noun and the adjective preceding it.

Words and phrases that appear in series also need commas to separate them, as in

> Migration to the cities has meant an emphasis on land sales, little development of existing resources, and abandonment of tribal traditions.

When single words appear in a series, some writers omit the comma before *and,* assuming that the reader will easily perceive the series principle of separation. Series separation becomes more complicated when commas appear for other reasons within the items of the series, as in

> These talismans are three: the fruit of a creeper called *cui,* gathered ages ago at the time of the last deluge, but still fresh and green; a rattan, also very old but bearing flowers that never fade; and lastly, a sword containing a *yan,* or spirit, who guards it constantly and works miracles with it.

Note that semicolons take the place of commas to separate units containing commas.

Dashes separate or set off a word or phrase at the ends of a sentence:

There was only one person in the room who understood the lecture—the instructor.

Despite the airline's new promptness policy, the plane left at 9:00—two hours after the scheduled departure time.

Commas separate whole quoted sentences from the name of the source, as in

"I think I wanted to see how complicated things happen," West said years later.

Some writers use a colon instead of a comma when the quotation follows the name of the source, as in

West said: "Yes, Rosemarie. It's going to be good."

though the comma is more commonly used there. If the identification of the source breaks up the quoted sentence, as in

"What," people often ask, "Did you expect to happen? After all, the continent had to be settled, didn't it?"

separation occurs on both sides of the source name. Writers may separate a sentence in this way to achieve a special emphasis that the intact sentence may lack.

Quoted words and phrases are not separated from the sentences in which they appear except by quotation marks:

Succeeding treaties generally provided for lands to be held "as Indian lands are held."

When quoted material exceeds 150 words, it is separated from the text by indentation and is not enclosed in quotation marks. For example:

The Treaty of the United Sac and Fox Tribe of November 3, 1804, is a case in point. Article I states:
> The United States receive the United Sac and Fox tribes into their friendship and protection, and the said tribes agree to consider themselves under the protection of the United States, and of no other power whatsoever.

Commas separate names and titles (Roger Rumpole, Ph.D.), cities and states (Wichita, Kansas), and various insertions

You completed the revision, didn't you?

We took the freeway, not the arterial.

Dates may appear either with commas (March 31, 1889) or without them (31 March 1889). As you can see, separating with commas or dashes enhances the clarity of your writing, and revising should include attention to ways of eliminating ambiguity through punctuation.

Handbook of Usage and Grammar

EXERCISE

All separating commas and dashes have been eliminated from the following excerpt. Insert them where you think they belong, and be prepared to explain your choices.

One day while I was studying history intervened and changed my life.(1) The date was October 22, 1982.(2) I was in a dormitory room at Colby College in Waterville Maine preparing for a chemistry exam to be given by Robert Marsden Ph.D.(3) I was busy going over my notes checking to be sure I knew all the formulas and memorizing technical terms.(4) Suddenly the door of my room burst open and a short fat fellow I had never seen before came in.(5) He was carrying a tape recorder a microcomputer and he had a pair of skiis on his shoulder.(6) "Get out of here" he shouted "The building is on fire."(7)

Punctuating to Join

Although commas and other punctuation can be seen as separating sentence units, they also can join them. In the preceding examples of items in series, the commas and semicolons were also performing the implicit function of supplying the word *and*. When the conjunctions *and* and *but* join two independent clauses, it is customary to precede the conjunction by a comma except when the clauses are very short:

He had formed the scheme of setting up there in trade, and somehow or other Sam had blocked it.

If the conjunction is omitted or if words like *moreover, however, indeed,* and *furthermore* join the independent clauses, a semicolon replaces the comma as a signal of joining:

They tell one what there is; they make an inventory. Any photograph has multiple meanings; indeed, to see something in the form of a photograph is to encounter a potential object of fascination.

Note that the semicolon always joins two or more grammatically equal units—clauses or phrases.

Simultaneous separation and joining is also achieved by the colon and the dash in examples like these:

I heard them coming before I saw them—two huge watchdogs from the mine property.
So far this point has been entirely theoretical: paradigms could determine normal science without the intervention of discoverable rules.

In both instances, the punctuation links a specific instance on the right to a more general statement on the left.

Dashes are also used by many writers to establish a loose conjunctive relationship, often in imitation of the rhythms of speech. For example:

443

Handbook of Usage and Grammar

One has the right to, may feel compelled to, give voice to one's own pain—which is, in any case, one's own property.

This use can easily be abused, however, substituting a purported linking of sentence units for carefully thought-out links.

The slash / is used as joining punctuations:

He photographed New York in the 1910s in an almost quixotic spirit—camera/lance against skyscraper/windmill.

The writer wishes to show two or more words or phrases as intimately related, as even closer than a conjunction, a comma, or a hyphen would suggest. Abuse of the slash can occur for reasons similar to those applying to the dash.

E X E R C I S E

You can test your control of punctuation that joins by inserting the appropriate marks in the following excerpt:

(1) About a year ago I took a writing course in which I was taught to get the main idea down and forget the lesser aspects. (2) It's a lesson I learned well. (3) I assume no one wants to read more than a few brief paragraphs about something and then I get my paper back with a low grade. (4) The margins are filled with comments such as vague unclear or unfinished undeveloped. (5) It goes against my nature to write at length on one subject and so English 271 is quite a change for me a change I am finding more difficult than I first thought.

PUNCTUATING TO END

The apparently simplest use of punctuation is to end sentences. The period, of course, is the most common terminal punctuation, and the exclamation point (!) is the least common. A useful rule of thumb for the exclamation point is to avoid using it except when there is absolutely no other way to show surprise or intensity of feeling. Frequent use of the exclamation point is considered a mark of immature writing.

Question marks should follow so-called direct questions:

Should the sales tax be repealed?

but not indirect questions:

The politician questioned whether the sales tax should be repealed.

Similar to the use of *sic* in academic writing, a question mark inside parentheses can indicate the writer's doubt about the accuracy of some detail or the lack of authenticating information, perhaps about a date:

After the law was repealed in 1972 (?) there was a marked increase in crime.

But a question mark inserted to bring a word into question is likely to seem juvenile:

> The writer made several interesting (?) assertions.

PUNCTUATING TO SHOW OMISSION

When quoting another writer, a writer often will need to shift a sentence to eliminate material unnecessary to the immediate context. A series of three spaced periods (. . .) shows this omission. Because they indicate an ellision, or shortening, they are called *elliptical periods.* The following example shows a mid-sentence ellision within a passage in which one writer is quoting another:

> "I do not doubt but the majesty and beauty of the world are latent in any idea of the world . . . I do not doubt there is far more in trivialities, insects, vulgar persons, slaves, dwarfs, wrecks, rejected refuse, than I have supposed."

When a full sentence from the original source is quoted, followed by an ellision and then a resumption of the quoted source, the period that ends the first quoted sentence is followed by three ellision dots.

> "We particularly need young men and women who work in our factories. . . . Housewives in their kitchens or in their yards picking flowers."

PUNCTUATING WITH THE APOSTROPHE

Like ellision dots, the apostrophe can show omission. When two words are joined together in a *contraction,* the apostrophe indicates the missing letters: *it's* (*it is* or *it has*), *doesn't* (*does not*); *you're* (*you are*). Contractions are used frequently in casual writing, sparingly in informal writing, and rarely in formal writing.

The second use of the apostrophe is to indicate possession, and the conventions for this are worth reviewing. The simplest case is to make a singular noun possessive by adding an *'s: car's; Frank's; everyone's, Charles's.* If the noun is plural and ends in *s*, just add an apostrophe: *boys'.* But, if the plural noun does not end in *s*, add an apostrophe and *s: children's.*

The apostrophe is also used to form the plural of a number, a letter, or a word treated as a word, if adding *s* alone would lead to confusion.

> He received two A's last term.
> There were four large 55's on the wall.
> There are no but's about it.

As you can see, punctuation adheres to general conventions, but you frequently have choices. Part of revising is selecting the punctuation which will convey your meaning most effectively. When you wish to enclose parts of sentences, you need to decide whether parentheses, quotation marks, brackets, commas, or dashes serve your purposes best. To separate parts of sentences you can choose between commas and semicolons. When you are joining words, phrases and clauses, you can select from commas, semicolons, colons, dashes, and slashes.

EXERCISE

All punctuation has been omitted from the following passage. Read it through, and then copy and punctuate it.

GOLD

Gold can be taken from such veins with dynamite blasts pneumatic drills but that requires the funds and efforts of a large corporation the deepest mine in the Western Hemisphere the Homestake gold mine in Lead South Dakota goes down into the earth more than a mile and a half its capital cost to date has been upward of a billion dollars Alaskan lone miners people who have or who have had names like Pete the Pig Pistolgrip Jim Groundsluice Bill Coolgardie Smith Codfish Tom Doc La Booze the Evaporated Kid Fisty McDonald John the Baptist Cheeseham Sam the Man with the Big Nugget prefer to wait for God to break open the rock to lift up and expose something like the Sierra Nevada and with epochal weathers blast it and spill it and tear it apart until the gold rolls out into the rubble of the streams placer mining separating gold from stream gravels is difficult work but beside any other method it is comparatively easy placer in Spanish means pleasure.

After you have decided on you own punctuation, compare your choices with someone else's, and discuss the differences. Then you may want to turn to the end of the next section to see punctuation that the author of this selection chose.

Mechanics

Compared with the conventions of sentences, usage, and punctuation, other conventions of standard written English seem relatively uncomplicated and easy to manage, but their simplicity makes them no less important. These conventions include capitalization, italics, underlining, titles, abbreviations, numbers, and spelling.

CAPITALIZATION

Ever since you learned to make upper- and lower-case letters, you have probably known that the first words of sentences, proper nouns, and most of the words in titles should be capitalized. This general understanding of conventions of capitalization is probably evident in your writing, and you need help for only the more uncommon uses of capitalization.

As is true for other conventional forms, capitalization is best used sparingly. Avoid using capital letters to call attention to words, and if you are in doubt about whether or not to capitalize, check the conventions.

1. Capitalize the first word in a sentence, a fragment written as a sentence, and each line of poetry, unless the lower case is used in the original.

The Senate's decision is irrational. Absolutely irrational.

> Slow, slow as a fish she came,
> Slow as a fish coming forward,
> Swaying in a long wave;
> Her skirts not touching a leaf,
> Her white arms reaching towards me.
> —Theodore Roethke

2. Capitalize the pronoun I.

When I arrived in Paris, I was exhausted.

3. Capitalize proper nouns such as people's names, place names, names of countries and businesses, and initials and abbreviations of proper names.

Ken Green drove west to California in his Mazda. When he arrived on the West Coast, he helped resettle Amerasian children with money from Washington, D.C. Then he enrolled in college and studied biology, Korean, and mathematics.

4. Capitalize the first and last words in titles and all the principal words in between, excluding articles (a, an, the), prepositions of fewer than five letters and conjunctions (such as and, but, or).

There, on the bookshelf, is a copy of *Excellent Women* by Barbara Pym.

EXERCISE

Revise the capitalization in the following excerpt to conform to the conventions:

Last fall I took political science 101 and read to kill a mockingbird, a book which deals with racism in the south. Now that I am a sophomore I am interested in learning more about other cultures, so I am studying french and anthropology and hope to travel in europe.

ABBREVIATIONS

Abbreviations shorten long names, titles, and some words. You have probably seen abbreviations used frequently in advertising and informal writing. However, in college writing and in other more formal writing, use abbreviations cautiously, and if you are in doubt, do not abbreviate.

Many abbreviations are followed by periods, but abbreviations pronounced as words or sounded as letters tend to be written without periods. As is true with most conventions of writing, consistency is especially important. Use the same pattern of abbreviation throughout a piece of writing. The best time to check for consistency is during the last stages of revising, because before then you will have too many other things on your mind. Knowing when not to use abbreviations is nearly as important as knowing when to use them. In writing essays, you should not abbreviate place names: Canterbury Street, Wilmington, Virginia. However, it is appropriate to use abbreviations such as St. (for street or saint) and Va. (for Virginia) in addresses. Likewise, avoid abbreviations of days of the week and months of the year:

We shall meet on Sunday in December,

not

we shall meet on Sun. in Dec.

The following section summarizes the conventions of abbreviation.

1. Abbreviate titles accompanying a name.

The list of donors included James Brown, M.D.; Mrs. Cynthia Chadwick; Robert D. Downs, Jr.; Dr. Abigail Eaton; and Denis Smith, D.D.

However, full titles should be used for religious, governmental, and military leaders.

The Reverend Alexander H. Tisbet, the Honorable Richard T. Watson, governor of Oregon, and General Malcolm F. Scott offered their opinions on nuclear armaments.

2. Abbreviate references to well-known firms and organizations.

The YWCA study group is investigating programming on CBS with a grant from TWA.

If you are writing about a less well-known firm or organization, you may write it out in full and then abbreviate subsequent references.

The economic woes of the Washington Public Power Supply System (WPPSS) have implications for the whole nation. Utility companies everywhere are feeling the effects of the WPPSS drama.

3. Abbreviate measures that appear with numerals.

In A.D. 1884, the term "55 MPG" made no sense, but one hundred years later vehicles driven by fossil fuels dominate our economy. Today at 5:30 P.M. I saw an example of this dominance.

Hyphens

Unlike conventions of capitalization or punctuation that are relatively fixed, the conventions of the hyphen change quickly. Words that start as a hyphenated compound often become compound words, and you will need to check a recent dictionary to determine the current preference. For example, when the word *pre-writing* was first used (nearly twenty years ago), it appeared with a hyphen, but now it is commonly written *prewriting*.

The most common and fixed use of the hyphen is to divide words at the end of a line. Hyphens also appear in compounds and with written numbers below one hundred.

1. Hyphenate words at the end of a line, being sure to divide the word into syllables. (If you are uncertain about where the word is divided, check your dictionary.)

Sitting there on the other side of the recreation room was an enor-mous rat who looked very hungry.

2. Hyphenate words that are divided into syllables.

Chris learned the meaning of the word vac-ci-nate the day before school began.

3. Hyphenate common compound words.

The daughter-in-law was a twenty-year-old who read self-help books.

4. Hyphenate after the prefix *ex* and after prefixes that precede proper nouns or proper adjectives.

The ex-football player was pro-Asian in his business dealings.

5. Hyphenate written numbers below one hundred.

Our club recruited twenty-two new members, and three-quarters of them joined committees.

6. Hyphenate compounds that function as grammatical units.

The first prize is a round-the-world voyage on a cruise ship.

Italics

Italics are used to give special status to words such as titles, foreign phrases, words as words, or words that you wish to emphasize. Your decision about which foreign phrases to italicize depends on the experience and sophistication of your audience. A word such as *avant-garde* might be italicized for some audiences and not for others. The best rule about using italics for emphasis is to be sparing; if you italicize too many words, the effect of the emphasis will be lost.

In printed books such as this one, italics are indicated by *italics* which contrast with the regular or roman type. When you are writing or typing, you can indicate italics by *underlining*.

1. Italicize names of books, magazines, newspapers, movies, plays, long poems, musical, compositions, ships, and airplanes.

Kesey's *One Flew over the Cuckoo's Nest* was made into a film which received good reviews in The *New York Times*.

The *Atlantic Monthly* carried an article about the blockade of the *S.S. Ohio*.

2. Italicize foreign phrases if you think your audience will regard them as unusual.

The president's statement became a *cause célèbre* on campus.

Leonardo provided the *deus ex machina* of the plot.

3. Italicize words or phrases you wish to emphasize.

I will do it if you insist, but I *prefer* not to.

An *editorial decision*, not censorship, is at issue here.

4. Italicize words, letters, and numbers that are referred to for themselves.

I spell my name with an *e*.

The word *effect* is often used incorrectly.

The graffiti on the wall included a large *7*.

NUMBERS

The conventions of numbers vary according to the type of writing. In business, scientific, technical, and legal writing, numbers are often written as figures, whereas in general prose, numbers of fewer than three words are usually written out. As you become familiar with an area of study, you will learn about how it deals with numbers. The following conventions apply to general prose, and if you are uncertain about what standard to use, it is better to err on the side of writing out numbers rather than using figures.

1. All numbers should always be written out when they occur at the beginning of a sentence.

Seventy-two people signed the petition in one day.
Five monkeys wriggled in the same cage.

2. Numbers that can be written in one or two words should be written out; use figures if writing out requires more than two words.

According to seven different accouts, there were 36,000 people at the rally.

3. Numbers referring to like items in the same paragraph should be represented the same way to ensure consistency.

The suite down the hall holds 15 people, and there is room for a total of 125 in this area.

4. Numbers should be represented as figures in addresses, dates, time of

Handbook of Usage and Grammar

day, exact sums of money, decimals, measurements, code numbers, percentages, and page numbers.

2315 Easton Avenue
September 9, 1884
3:42 P.M. (but half-past three)
$9.32 (but one million dollars)
significant at 0.78

use a 3 by 5 card
a ratio of 3 to 2
4 percent
page 32

Here is the "Gold" selection as punctuated by the author

> Gold can be taken from such veins with dynamite blasts, pneumatic drills. But that requires the funds and efforts of a large corporation. The deepest mine in the Western Hemisphere—the Homestake gold mine, in Lead, South Dakota—goes down into the earth more than a mile and a half. Its capital cost to date has been upward of a billion dollars. Alaskan lone miners—people who have, or who have had, names like Pete the Pig, Pistolgrip Jim, Groundsluice Bill, Coolgardie Smith, Codfish Tom, Doc La Booze, the Evaporated Kid, Fisty McDonald, John the Baptist, Cheeseham Sam, The Man with the Big Nugget—prefer to wait for God to break open the rock, to lift up and expose something like the Sierra Nevada and with epochal weathers blast it and spill it and tear it apart until the gold rolls out into the rubble of the streams. Placer mining—separating gold from stream gravels—is difficult work, but beside any other method it is comparatively easy. "*Placer*," in Spanish, means "pleasure."
>
> —John McPhee, *Coming into the Country*

Spelling

Spelling is both the most simple and the most difficult of the conventions of writing. It is simple because words are spelled either correctly or incorrectly. But, spelling in English is very difficult because there is so little correspondence between the sounds of the words and their spellings. We are told to spell words the way they sound, but those hoo spel fonetikly hev truble. Spelling is based on conventions of what words are supposed to sound like rather than what they actually sound like. For example, 70 percent of the words containing the sound [a] are spelled with *o*. Many English words contain the schwa [ə], a short *e* or *uh* sound that is represented by several different letters. The pronunciation of words such as *grammar, independence, attendance, separate*, and *benefit* provides no clue as to which letter represents the schwa sound.

You probably have your own funny stories of how the lack of correspondence between letters and sounds has tricked you. My own concerns the word *erudite*. I was a freshman in college before I realized the word *erudite* that I had been reading as (e-ru-dite) had anything to do with the word (airyudite) that I heard in conversations. Although stories like this can be amusing in retrospect, the experiences they represent are not pleasant ones. It is frustrating and embarrassing to realize that you do not have any idea how to spell a word.

Handbook of Usage and Grammar

Another problem with spelling is that there are not always absolute answers about correctness. A number of English words have variant spellings, and writers must decide which to use. For example, each word in the following pairs is listed as the preferred spelling in at least two major dictionaries: hearken and harken, vendor and vender, fjord and fiord, and incrust and encrust. Once you have decided which spelling to use, *consistency* is crucial. A variant spelling of the same word within a piece of writing will distract your readers.

SELF-ASSESSMENT

Because spelling can be tricky, the way to revise spelling in your writing is not to begin by searching for what you think are misspelled words and looking them up in the dictionary. A first step is to assess your own abilities in spelling. Because you are a college student, you have a number of years of education behind you, and you probably have a general idea of your ability to spell.

Begin by writing a paragraph-length statement about your spelling ability, starting with "As a speller I . . ." and then find an old paper, something you wrote a while ago and turned in for a grade. It should be a piece of writing in which the instructor marked all the misspelled words. Make a list of your spelling errors in this paper. As you look at this list you will probably begin to see patterns of misspelling. You may find that you have trouble knowing whether to double a consonant at the end of a word when adding a suffix (*forgeting* versus *forgetting*.) You may have problems with word confusion (*off* for *of*), or with homophones (*their, there,* and *they're*). You may have difficulty with long-vowel sounds (*eather* for *either*). To be able to recognize your problems, identify and put each spelling word on a chart on which you list the correct spelling, the spelling you used, the letters that caused the error, and the type of error. Here is an example from one student's paper:

Word	Misspelling	Letters or Syllables	Type of Misspelling
deceiving	deciving	ei/i	long-vowel sound
grenade	granade	a/e	short-vowel sound
asset	assett	t/tt	final consonant
definitely	definitly	e	omission of silent *e*
aisle	isle	i/ai	word confusion
perceive	percieve	ei/i	long-vowel sound
capable	capible	-able/-ible	suffix

By completing this chart, the student got a much better idea of the kinds of spelling errors he was likely to make and could be alert for them.

Another part of your self-assessment should include checking your dictionary skills. The standard response to people who have difficulty with spelling is that they should use a dictionary. But can you use a dictionary? Do words

Handbook of Usage and Grammar

such as *accent, syllable, prefix,* and *suffix* have meaning for you? To check your dictionary skills, look at the following chart. If you see unfamiliar words and symbols, you are probably not using a dictionary effectively.

Sample Dictionary Entry

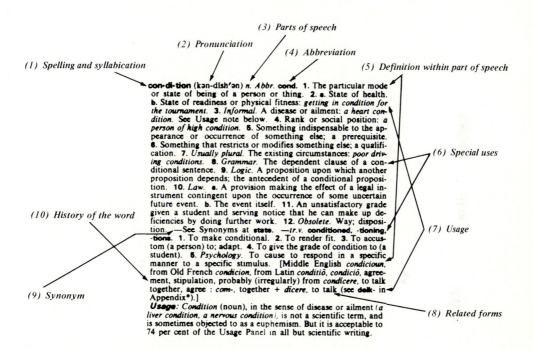

Explanation of Dictionary Entry

1. *Spelling and syllabication.* In addition to providing the correct spelling for the word, this portion of the entry tells you where the syllable divisions occur. This information can be very useful for hyphenating words at the end of a line. Some words have more than one spelling, and the spelling preferred by the dictionary is given first.
2. *Pronunciation.* The pronunciation appears immediately after the entry word and is usually in parentheses. The accent mark tells you which syllable is accented (in the word *condition,* it is the first syllable). The pronunciation key at the bottom of the page tells you how to make the sounds suggested by this phonetic spelling.
3. *Parts of speech.* An abbreviation of the part of speech appears next in the entry. *Condition,* like many words, is used as more than one part of speech (it is used as a noun, transitive verb, and intransitive verb). As you can see, all definitions for the first part of speech are grouped together, then the meanings for other parts are grouped in succession.
4. *Abbreviation.* Most dictionaries list common abbreviations of entry words, but the placement of these abbreviations varies from one dictionary to another.

5. *Definitions.* Some dictionaries list definitions historically, starting with the earliest, and others (like this one) list them in order of usage with the most common appearing first. The front of the dictionary will tell you which system it uses.
6. *Special uses.* Some words have special meanings within certain disciplines. *Condition,* as you can see, has special meaning in grammar, logic, and law.
7. *Usage.* Some dictionaries include usage labels such as "slang" or (in this case) "informal" to help you decide whether your use of the word is appropriate for the level of diction your writing reflects. This dictionary also includes a rating of questionable usages by a panel of prominent people.
8. *Related forms.* Variations on the entry word include verb forms, plurals, and words formed from the entry word. Sometimes these words formed have entries of their own.
9. *Synonyms.* Words which have similar meanings are often included in the description of the entry word. Careful reading of synonyms and definitions can help you distinguish between words with similar connotations.
10. *History of the word.* The etymology or history of the word is given in brackets. Often this history includes a definition of root words (here the Latin *conditio*) which can help you expand your vocabulary because if you know the definition of a root word you can often decipher the meaning of more complex words that contain root words.

Of course, a dictionary can tell you much more than the correct spelling of a word; it can also provide information on parts of speech, pronunciation, forms, definition, level of usage, related forms, synonyms, and etymology. If you were to have only one book on your college bookshelf, I would recommend that it be a dictionary. Yet a dictionary will be useful in spelling only if you know how and have the self-discipline to use it.

Still another way to assess your abilities as a speller is to determine the most effective learning style for you. There are a variety of ways to learn the spellings of words: you may learn from their sounds (once you have sorted out the deceptive ones); you may learn from reading or seeing them; you may learn from writing them; or you may associate their spellings with their meanings. Because undoubtedly you use all of the strategies to some extent, the question is whether any one strategy seems to be the most effective for you. When someone asks you how to spell a word, do you write it out, listen to its sounds, or think of its meaning? If you can discover how you best learn spelling, you can increase the efficiency of your memorization of correct spellings.

Learning Appropriate Rules

Once you have assessed your abilities in spelling and have an idea of the kinds of words that give you trouble, you may benefit from learning a few rules of spelling. Your assessment may suggest the best ones to learn, but here are some common ones that have helped my students.

1. i before e
   except after c
   or when sounded like a
   as in *neighbor* and *weigh*.

This is probably the most well-known rule of spelling, and it can help confusions between *ie* and *ei*, but for other spellings of the *e* sound (as in *reach* or *extreme*), it is no help. Furthermore, in order to apply the rule effectively, you need to know that the word to be spelled involves the *e* sound spelled either *ie* or *ei*. But the *e* sound is spelled *ie* in only 2 percent of all English words, and so this rule does not have wide applicability.

2. Drop the silent *e* when adding a suffix that begins with a vowel, as in *inflate* to *inflatable*. This rule, like many in spelling, has its exceptions. If the silent *e* is preceded by *c* or *g* and the suffix begins with *a, o,* or *u*, the *e* will remain, as in *manageable* and *peaceable*.
3. When adding a suffix to a word that ends with *y*, change the *y* to *i* and add the suffix, as in *deny* to *denied*. However, if the suffix is *-ing*, keep the *y*, as in *denying*.
4. Double the final consonant if the word ends in one vowel plus one consonant, if the accent is on the last syllable of the word, and if the suffix begins with a vowel, as in *control* to *controlling* and *begin* to *beginning*.

CONFUSING HOMOPHONES

Once you have assessed your abilities in spelling and learned a few rules, you are ready to begin revising the spelling in your own writing. One of the most common problems for unpracticed writers is confusing *homophones*, or words that sound the same, such as the following list:

Ascent/assent. *Ascent* means "a rising," "an advancement," or "a climbing."

The *ascent* of Mount Rainier took two days.

Assent means "to consent" or "to agree."

With the *assent* of this committee, we can allocate the funds.

Bear/bare. When used as a noun, *bear* refers to the furry mammal.

I saw a brown *bear* in the zoo.

When used as a verb, *bear* means "to carry," "to give birth to," or "to support."

The family budget cannot *bear* any more unnecessary expense.

When used as a verb, *bare* means "to expose" or "to strip."

The encounter group expected all of its members to *bare* their souls.

When used as an adjective, *bare* means "uncovered" or "simple."

They lived in a *bare* room on Second Avenue.

Capital/capitol. *Capital* means "a seat of government," "upper-case letter," or "accumulated wealth."

Salem is the *capital* of Oregon.
Use a *capital* letter to begin a quotation.
The *capital* funds drive was successful.

Capitol means "the building that houses governmental bodies."

Standing on the steps of the *capitol* was a thrilling experience for the high school seniors.

Council/counsel. *Council* means "a group that deliberates and decides issues."

The city *council* opposed redevelopment of the waterfront.

When used as a verb, *counsel* means "advise."

My high school English teacher *counseled* me to major in computer programming.

When used as a noun, *counsel* means "advice" or "lawyer."

His suggestion that I spend a year in Mexico was good *counsel*.

Pray/prey. *Pray* means "implore," "beseech," or "make supplication."

We *pray* that there will be no more war in our world.

When used as a noun, *prey* means "plunder" or "victim."

The lion seized his *prey* from the pack of zebras.

When used as a verb, *prey* means "to hunt or kill for food," "to make a profit by swindling," or "to have a destructive influence."

Loan sharks *prey* on the indigent in our city.

Principal/principle. When used as a noun, *principal* means "administrator" or "sum of money."

The *principal* of the school endorsed the smoking policy. Interest from the *principal* provides a good scholarship each year.

When used as a adjective, *principal* means "most important."

The athletics deparment showed the *principal* effects of the budget cut.

Principle means "basic truth," "rule of behavior," or "general law of nature."

The *principle* of gravity shapes life on the planet Earth.

To/too/two. *To* refers to direction, place, or position. It is also used to form infinitives.

Pine Street is perpendicular *to* Fifth Avenue.

Too means "excessively" or "also."

Bring your friend along *too*.

She ate *too* much and was uncomfortable.

Two refers to the number.

Next to the table stood *two* chairs.

Their/they're/there. *Their* is the possessive form of the pronoun they. They will take *their* picnic basket when they leave the park.

They're is the contraction of "they are."

They're off to the city for the weekend.

There indicates location or direction.

The tool you are looking for is sitting over *there* in the corner.

EXERCISE

The following list contains other homophones that can cause spelling problems. Select five pairs, and distinguish between them. Be sure to define all the words in the group and to use each in a sentence.

allowed/aloud	earnest/ernest	knew/new
altar/alter	fair/fare	lead/led
base/bass	fore/four	right/write/rite/wright
board/bored	forward/foreward	sole/soul
cannon/canon	foul/fowl	threw/through
cast/caste	grate/great	waist/waste
die/dye	hole/whole	who's/whose

Some homophones are relatively easy to distinguish because their meanings are so different. Once you think about the differences between words such as *prey* and *pray* or *waist* and *waste,* you will probably find it easy not to confuse them in your writing. However, *its* and *it's* may be more difficult because the meaning is not obvious in the word. Because you are accustomed to using an *'s* to show possession, it seems natural to write sentences such as "The boat lost it's sail" but according to conventions of standard written English, that is *wrong*.

It's is a contraction of *it is* or *it has*.
It's too bad she couldn't be here.
It's been a long day.

Handbook of Usage and Grammar

Its indicates possession.
The door is off *its* hinges.

Knowing that other possessive pronouns also lack apostrophes may help you remember this distinction. Forms such as *hers, yours,* and *theirs* are like *its* in indicating possession without an apostrophe.

ELIMINATING WORD CONFUSIONS

In addition to homophones, the English language contains a number of words that are confusing because they look or sound somewhat alike. Distinguishing between them as you revise will bring your writing closer to the norms of standard written English. Among those words often confused are

Accept/except. *Accept* means "to receive" or "to agree to."

Mr. Jones will *accept* the plaque on behalf of his wife.

When used as a verb, *except* means "to exclude," "to leave out," or "to omit."

If you *except* the incomplete from last term, your record is very good.

When used as a preposition, *except* means "other than."

Everyone *except* John was invited.

Advise/advice. *Advice* (a noun) means "guidance."

Parents seem to enjoy giving their children *advice.*

Advise (a verb) means "to give advice," "to recommend," "to counsel," or "to notify."

The board will *advise* the president on which contracts to accept.

Affect/effect. *Affect* means "change," "disturb," or "influence."

The changing climate *affects* agriculture throughout the world.

Affect also means "to pretend to feel" or "to feign."

Even though she had witnessed the crime, she *affected* innocence when asked about it.

When used as a verb, *effect* means "to perform," "to accomplish," or "to bring about."

The new director *effected* a change in the whole organization.

When used as a noun, *effect* means result or impact.

The lack of snow had a disastrous *effect* on the ski industry.

All ready/already. *All ready* refers to the readiness of people or things.

The refreshments were all ready *when the party began.*

Already means "by this time" or "by that time."

He had already *heard the news by the time my message reached him.*

Allusion/delusion/illusion. *Allusion* means "indirect reference."

In his opening speech, the president made several allusions *to the previous administration.*

Delusion means "false belief or opinion" and is often associated with mental illness.

The psychopathic killer suffered from the delusion *that women are evil.*

Illusion means "a false impression" or "a false perception," often resulting from visual confusion or wishful thinking.

The oasis we saw from afar turned out to be an optical illusion.

All right (alright). *All right* means "satisfactory," "safe," or "completely correct."

If you arrive after dinner it will be all right.

When Joe took his written exam for a driver's license, his answers were all right.

Alright is a less common form that is accepted by some people but is usually considered incorrect.

All together/altogether. *All together* refers to things or people.

The audience stood all together *to give the performer a standing ovation.*

Altogether means "entirely" or "wholly."

This is an altogether *new idea.*

A lot (alot). *A lot* means "a great amount" or "a great number."

Members of the press received a lot *of free passes to the show.*

Alot is a misspelling of *a lot*.

Amoral/immoral. *Amoral* means "without morals" or "outside the moral sphere."

The street children we met in Peru were completely amoral.

Immoral means "wicked."

    Murder is an *immoral* act.

Choose/chose. *Choose* means "select."

    The coach will *choose* the first line for the game.

    Chose is the past tense of *choose*.

    Yesterday she *chose* me, but now she has changed her mind.

Censor/censure. When used as a verb, *censor* means "to exercise censorship."

    The school board *censored* the English department's book list.

    When used as a noun, *censor* means "one who censors."

    The *censors* read all our mail before it was delivered to us.

    When used as a verb, *censure* means "to reprimand" or "to find fault with."

    The chemist who falsified his results was *censured* by the university.

    When used as a noun, *censure* means "disapproval" or "blame."

    The quick-tempered baseball player received the umpire's *censure*.

Complement/compliment. When used as a noun, *complement* means the "total number of persons needed in a group."

    Despite the storm, a full *complement* of players appeared on the field.

    When used as a verb, *complement* means "to bring to perfection."

    The wine *complements* the delicate flavor of the fish.

    When used as a verb, *compliment* means "to praise."

    Chuck *complimented* Edgar on his performance.

Elicit/illicit. *Elicit* means "to evoke" or "to draw forth."

    None of the electronic machines could *elicit* a response from the comatose patient.

    Illicit means "unlawful" or "improper."

    He was accused of possessing an *illicit* substance.

Emigrate/immigrate. *Emigrate* means "to leave one country to live in another."

    Many people have *emigrated* from Southeast Asia since the war there.

    Immigrate means "to enter a country to live permanently."

    Their son-in-law *immigrated* to the United States when he was a child.

Handbook of Usage and Grammar

Formally/formerly. *Formally* means "in a ceremonious manner."

Everyone at the reception behaved very *formally* until the band began to play.

Formerly means "at an earlier time."

Now we must walk down the hall to receive a call; *formerly* we had telephones in the rooms.

Human/humane. *Human* refers to human beings.

Darwin offered a logical account of *human* evolution.

Humane means "merciful," "considerate," or "kindhearted."

I think termination is the only *humane* action we can take.

Imply/infer. *Imply* means "to suggest" or "to hint at."

She *implied* that the will contained a bequest for us.

Infer means "to reach a conclusion based on evidence."

From your statement, I *infer* that you prefer not to accept the position.

Later/latter. *Later* refers to time.

Hortense arrived *later* than Eloise did.

First the lettuce will come up; *later* the other vegetables will appear in the garden.

Latter refers to the second of two previously mentioned people or things.

We have before us two choices; we can accept this proposal or wait for another to emerge. I prefer the *latter* option.

Lead/led. When used as a noun, *lead* refers to the metal.

This mine contains *lead*.

When used as a verb, *lead* (rhymes with bead) means "to guide," "to be first," "to begin, open with," and "to tend toward."

We need a president who can *lead* everyone toward unity.

One thing *leads* to another.

Led is the past tense of *lead*.

When Lincoln was president he *led* a very different country than the one that faces today's leaders.

Leave/let. *Leave* means "to go away" or "to put in a place."

I think it is time for everyone to *leave*.

Please *leave* your umbrella in a corner.

Let means "to permit" or "to allow."

Please *let* us go through.

Lie/lay. *Lie* (lie, lying, lay, lain) means "to recline" or "to stay."

Don't *lie* in the sun too long or you will damage your skin.

I was *lying* down when the telephone rang.

When Jack broke his leg, he *lay* for days looking at the ceiling.

The book has *lain* on my desk for days, but I haven't read a word of it.

Lay (lay, laying, laid) means "to place" or "to put into a certain position."

Lay the pencil on the table.

He has been *laying* bricks all afternoon.

The previous speaker *laid* the foundation for what I want to say.

Loose/lose. *Loose* means "not securely fastened" or "free."

The *loose* shutter banged all night.

The bull was *loose* under the stands during the bull fight.

Lose means the opposite of win or "to fail to keep."

If you don't start playing more aggressively, we shall *lose* the game.

I think I shall *lose* my mind.

Moral/morale. *Moral* (the first syllable is accented) means "ethical" or "virtuous."

This is not a legal decision; it is a *moral* one.

She has lived a *moral* and upright life.

Morale (the second syllable is accented) means "attitude" or "spirit."

During the budget cuts, the *morale* in our company was very low.

Off/of. *Off* means "no longer on" or "away."

He took *off* his coat and hung it in the closet.

She was standing *off* to one side.

Of means "derived from."

The table is made *of* pure gold and weighs three hundred pounds.

Handbook of Usage and Grammar

Personal/personnel. *Personal* (the first syllable is accented) means "individual" or "private."

Please send all *personal* mail to my home address.

Personnel (the last syllable is accented) means "persons employed in a firm or military group."

The director of *personnel* will handle your application for a position with this company.

Quiet/quite/quit. *Quiet* means "no noise," or "still."

The moon rose over the lake, and the woods were *quiet*.

Quite means "completely" or "positively."

Sarah is not *quite* finished with her work.

Quit means "to stop" or "to go away."

I wish Max would *quit* smoking.

Raise/rise. *Raise (raise, raising, raised)* takes an object because it is a transitive verb.

Let's *raise* the shades and let the sun in.

In that field he is *raising* wheat.

My cousin was *raised* by her grandparents.

Rise, (rise, rising, rose, risen). takes no object because it is an intransitive verb.

The bread will *rise* in two hours.

The sun is *rising* in the East.

Yesterday I *rose* at 5:00 A.M., but the sun had already *risen*.

Regardless (irregardless). *Regardless* means "unmindful" or "in spite of."

Regardless of his feelings, she slammed the door and walked out.

Irregardless is a redundancy and is incorrect.

Stationary/stationery. *Stationary* means "not moving."

Even though all the passengers were on board, the train was *stationary*.

Stationery means "writing paper."

Elizabeth's personal *stationery* is embossed with her monogram.

Statue/statute/stature. *Statue* means "sculpted figure."

The new *statue* in the quad has puzzled everyone.

Statute means "law."

According to this *statute,* you are required to secure your neighbor's permission before you build the fence.

Stature means "height" or "growth achieved" (in a moral sense).

Someone of your *stature* should have no trouble fitting through the opening.

Her moral *stature* in the community makes her a natural leader.

Were/we're/where. *Were* is the past plural form of the verb *to be* and is used in verb phrases.

The young children *were* playing outside in the rainstorm.

We're is the contraction of *we are*.

After we finish building the house, *we're* going to add a garage.

Where means "in a certain place."

This is the corner *where* the accident occurred last week.

ELIMINATING MISSPELLED WORDS

If you have assessed your spelling abilities, learned a few rules of spelling, and distinguished between homophones that confuse you, you are well on your way to avoid misspellings in your writing. The process of eliminating spelling errors from writing is a long one, however, so you may want to give spelling additional attention as you revise.

If you keep a *spelling log* of words that give you trouble, you can use it to check questionable spellings in your final copy. A spelling log is a list that contains, in alphabetical order, those words that you have difficulty spelling. Recording the correct spellings and looking at them frequently to check your work will help you memorize them, and at the same time, you have a handy reference that is less cumbersome than a dictionary. Here is one student's spelling log:

absence	commitment
accommodate	connoisseur
acquaintance	curiosity
amateur	deficient
analogous	diaphragm
appearance	erroneous
argument	exhilaration
carburetor	financier
colonel	gaiety

Handbook of Usage and Grammar

grammar	permissible
grandeur	rendezvous
hygiene	reservoir
innoculate	separate
khaki	sergeant
lightning	tangible
medieval	vengeance
miniature	weird
noticeable	

Another advantage of the spelling log is that it makes you aware of your own areas of weakness. If you know which words you are likely to misspell, you can learn to avoid them when you will not have an opportunity to use a dictionary or spelling log. During an essay exam or when you are asked to fill out a form on the spot or on other occasions when you cannot check spellings, you may substitute a word you are sure of rather than write one you cannot spell. One student who used this strategy chose the word *underwear* because he was not sure of the spelling of *lingerie*.

Author and Title Index

A

The Adventures of Huckleberry Finn, 21
Androit Guide to Government Publications, 331
Applied Science and Technology Index, 326
The Ascent of Man, 252

B

Bibliographic Index, 330
Book Review Digest, 335
Book Review Index, 335
Brewster, David, 23, 219, 220–221
Brownowski, Joseph, 20, 253

C

"Can Men Mother?" 123–126
Caoli, Monica, 35, 36, 65, 156, 161
Capote, Truman, 309
Carroll, Jeff, 48–51
Chem One, 253–255
Chicago Manual of Style, 358
"Cinematypes," 174–176
Connally, Paul, 349
Conroy, Frank, 110, 11, 113, 114
Cooney, Adam, 179, 184, 189
Cumulative Book Index, 331

D

Daley, John and Wayne Shamo, 81
"The Death of a Friend," 213

Didion, Joan, 273
Dissertation Abstracts International, 331
A Distant Mirror, 57, 114–119
"Drug Abuse," 241–247

E

Edison, Thomas, 31–32
Eisley, Loren, 257, 259, 260, 262

F

"Fear of Dearth," 199–201
"Fog," 167
"Fun Anger," 136–138

G

General Science Index, 326
"The Generic Essay," 63
Godwin, Eva, 60, 63
"Gold," 451
Greenberg, Dan, 24–36

H

Hall, Donald, 55, 146–148
Handbook for Writers of Research Papers, (MLA), 351, 358
History of Art, 76, 346

I

"I Want a Wife," 222–223

J

Janson, H.W., 76, 346
Johnson, Patrick, 232, 241
Johnson, Robert, 202, 207
Jordon, Suzanne Britt, 57, 142–144

L

"Land of One Thousand Seasons," 146–148
"Language Essay," 63
Lawton, Jim, 136, 138
"Learning a Foreign Language," 89–90
Lee, Harper, 43–44
Library of Congress Subject Headings, 324, 329, 333
Lives of a Cell, 24
Luepnitz, Deborah Anna, 123

M

Magazines for Libraries, 330
McPhee, John, 451

N

New York Times Index, 328, 339

O

O'Brien, James, 79
Oceanus, 78–79

467

Author and Title Index

P

Practising History, 275
"Problems and Solutions," 232–235
Psychological Abstracts, 337
Publication Manual of the American Psychological Association (APA), 351, 358

R

Reader's Digest Condensed Version of the Bible, 128–129
Reader's Guide to Periodical Literature, 326
"The Redesigning of a Deathtrap," 207
"Revenge Can Be Sweet," 136–139
"Reversing the Downward Drift of American Education," 219–221
Revised Standard Version of the Bible, 127–128
The Right Stuff, 20–21
Roethke, Theodore, 447

S

"Savages," 110–113
Sandburg, Carl, 167
"Science," 196–199
A Sense of the Future, 20
The 60's—A Time for a College Education," 156–158, 161–163
"Skokie," 129–130
The Starthrower, 257, 259, 260, 262
Subject Guide to Books in Print, 331
Subject Guide to Periodical Indexes, 330
Swenson, May, 194
Syfers, Judy, 222, 223, 224

T

"That Lean and Hungry Look," 57, 142–144
Thomas, Lewis, 24
Thoreau, Henry David, 31
"Three Boys," 169–172
To Kill a Mockingbird, 43–44
Toth, Susan Allen, 147, 175, 176, 196, 198, 199
Tuchman, Barbara, 57, 114, 116, 118, 119, 275
Tucker, Carll, 57, 199, 200, 201
Twain, Mark, 21

U

Ulrich's International Periodicals Directory, 326
Ulrich's Irregular Serials and Annuals, 330
"The Unfortunate Encounter," 65
"The Universe," 194
Updike, John, 123, 169, 170, *172*
U.S. Monthly Catalog, 328

W

Waser, Jung, 255
"What Is An Essay?" 348–349
White, E.B., 18, 23
Wolfe, Tom, 20–21
The Writer on Her Work, 273
"Writing Apprehension and Occupational Choice," 80–81

Subject Index

A

A LOT (alot), 459
Abbreviations, 447–448
Absolute phrase, 426
Abstract language, 303–304
Abstract terms, defining, 152
ACCEPT/EXCEPT, 458
Active voice, 430
AD HOMINEM, argument, 237–238
Adjectives, 422
Adverbs, 422
ADVISE/ADVICE, 458
AFFECT/EFFECT, 458
Argument of sentence parts
    noun/pronouns, 431
    subject/verb, 430
ALL READY/ALREADY, 459
ALL RIGHT (alright), 459
ALL TOGETHER/ALTOGETHER, 459
ALLUSION/DELUSION/ILLUSION, 459
ALREADY/ALL READY, 459
ALTOGETHER/ALL TOGETHER, 459
AMONG/BETWEEN, 433
AMORAL/IMMORAL, 459–460
AMOUNT/NUMBER, 433
Annotation, 327, 345
Anywheres, 433
APA style, 370–388
APA style manual. *See Publication Manual of the American Psychological Association*
Apostrophe, 445–446
Appeal to emotions argument, 239
Appeal to false authority argument, 239

Appositives, 440
AS/LIKE, 433
ASCENT/ASSENT, 455
Assertions
    support of, 142–158
        written illustrations, 145–149, 153–156
Assignments, 39–67
    clarifying, 42–43
    cues in, 40–42
Attitudes of writer, 6–8
Audience, 43–53
    perception of, 45–52
    priorities of, 74–83
        arts and humanities, 75–77
        natural sciences, 78–79
        social sciences, 80–83
    questions regarding, 46–52
    recognizing otherness, 43–45
Audience response
    writing groups, 70–74
AWFULLY, 433

B

BARE/BEAR, 455–456
Begging the question, 239
BEING AS/BEING THAT, 433
BETWEEN/AMONG, 433
Bibliography format, 365–366
    APA, 366–367
    MLA, 367–369
Biographical dictionaries and encyclopedias, 339–340
Biopoem 27–30
Brackets, 439
Business letters, 409–412

C

CAN/MAY, 434
CAN'T HELP BUT, 434
CAPITAL/CAPITOL, 456
Capitalization, 446–447
Card catalog, 329–334
Casual writing style, 311–313
Causes and effects, 193–215
Cause/effect patterns, 196–199
    questions about events or processes, 195–196, 203–205
CENSOR/CENSURE, 460
CENTER AROUND/About, 434
CHOOSE/CHOSE, 460
Clarity through context, 230–231
Clauses, 426–427
Cliches, 304–305
Cloze test for cohesion, 102–103
Clustering, 27
Cohesion, evaluation of, 93–94
Cohesive ties, 94–102
    comparatives, 98–99
    conjunctions, 99–102
    demonstrative adverbs, 97–98
    pronouns, 94
    punctuation, 101
Colon, 442
Comma, 439, 440, 441, 442, 443
Comma splices, 288–289
COMPLEMENT/COMPLIMENT, 460
Complements to verbs, 423–424
Computers in information gathering, 341
Concrete language, 303–304
Conjunctions, 422
Connotation, 301–302
CONTACT, 434

469

Subject Index

Contractions, 434
Coordinate adjectives, 441
COULD OF, 434
COUNCIL/COUNSEL, 456

D

Dashes, 439, 441–442, 443
Declarative sentence, 427
Defining, methods of, 145
DELUSION/ILLUSION/ALLUSION, 459
Demonstrative pronouns, 421
Denotation, 301
Dialect, 432
Dictionary skills, 452–454
Direct objects, 424
DISINTERESTED/UNINTERESTED, 434
Documentation
    research papers, 350–351

E

EFFECT/AFFECT, 458
Effect/cause patterns, 199–201
ELICIT/ILLICIT, 460
EMIGRATE/IMMIGRATE, 460
Encyclopedias, 329, 331–332
Endnotes and footnotes, 359–362
ENTHUSE/ENTHUSED, 435
Essay examinations, 403–409
ETC., 435
Euphemisms, 307
EXCEPT/ACCEPT, 458
Experiences of writer, 4

F

Fallacies in argument, 237–239
FEWER/LESS, 435
Finite verb/auxiliary, 428
Five Ws of journalism, 224–226
Footnotes and endnotes, 359–362
Formal writing style, 311–313
FORMALLY/FORMERLY, 461
Format, 103–105
Fused sentences, 287–288

G

Gender bias, *See* Sexist language
GOOD/WELL, 435
Gerunds, 426

H

Homophones, 455–457
HOPEFULLY, 453
HUMAN/HUMANE, 461
Hyphens, 448–449

I

I/ME, 435
ILLICIT/ELICIT, 460
ILLUSION/ALLUSION/DELUSION, 459
Illustrations, use of written, 145–149, 153–156
Imitation, 21–26, 299
IMMIGRATE/EMIGRATE, 460
IMMORAL/AMORAL, 459–460
Imperative sentence, 427
IMPLY/INFER, 461
Indefinite pronouns, 420
Indexes, 338
Indirect objects, 424
Infinitives, 425–426
Inflection of verbs, 428–429
    number, 428
    person, 428
    tense, 428
Informal writing style, 311–313
Information analysis, 165–191
    categories, 167–176
    coherence and cohesion, 188–189
    memory, 176
    organization, 188
    parts and wholes, 168–172, 180–182
    similarities and differences, 172–176, 182–186
    word arrangement, 173
Interjections, 422
Interrogative pronouns, 421
Interrogative sentence, 427
Interviewing, 320–321
Interviews, 320–321
Intransitive, verbs, 421

Italics, 449–450
ITS/IT'S, 457–458

J

Jargon, 305–306
Journals, 13–14, 18–21

K

KIND OF/SORT OF, 436

L

LATER/LATTER, 461
LEAD/LED, 461
LEAVE/LET, 461–462
LESS/FEWER, 435
Library resources, 322–341
    evaluation of, 341–342
LIE/LAY, 462
LIKE/AS, 433
Linking verbs, 421
LOOSE/LOSE, 462

M

MAY/CAN, 434
ME/I, 435
Memory chain, 120–121
Metaphor, 166–167
MIGHT OF, 434
MLA Style, example, 398–401
MLA style manual. *See Handbook for Writers of Research Papers*
Modifiers, 424, 427, 439–440
    dangling, 282–284
    misplaced, 284–285
MORAL/MORALE, 462

N

Narrative
    definition, 109
    memory, 110–114, 119–121
    selection, 126–131
Nonpaper resources, 340–341
Note cards, 327, 343–344
Noun/pronoun agreement, 431

Subject Index

Nouns, 420
NUMBER/AMOUNT, 433
Numbers, 450–451

O

Object complement, 424
Objects
   direct/indirect, 424
OFF/OF, 462
ONLY, 436
Organizational patterns, 83–85
   combined, 85–89
Organizational plan
   cause/effect, 206
Outline, chain, 195, 202
Outlines, 89–93

P

Paragraphs
   concluding, 261–263
   important parts, 253–256
   introductory, 257–258
   length, 251–253
   revising, 263–273
      for cohesion, 269–271
      for organization, 266–269
      for purpose, 263–266
      for style, 271–272
   topical, 260–261
   transitional, 259–260
Paraphasing, 348–350
Parenthesis, 438–439
Parenthetical citations
   APA, 362–363
   MLA, 363–365
Parts of speech, 419–422
Passive voice, 430
Periodicals, evaluation of, 341–342
PERSONAL/PERSONNEL, 463
Personal pronouns, 420
Phrases, 425–426
Plagiarism, 342–343
PRAY/PREY, 456
Predicates and subjects, 422–423, 424
Prepositional phrases, 424
Prepositions, 422
Pretentious language, 306–307
Prewriting, 17–37
   biopoem, 27–30
   circular lists, 27–28
   clustering, 27
   definition, 17
   drafts, 35–37
   experimentation, 27–30
   explaining material, 33–34
   journals, 18–21
   lists, 26–30
   recording observations, 30–32
   uses, 17–18
Primary/secondary resources, 342
PRINCIPAL/principle, 456
Pronoun/noun agreement, 431
Pronouns, 420–421
Punctuation, types of
   apostrophe, 445–446
   brackets, 439
   colon, 442
   comma, 439, 440, 441, 442, 443
   dashes, 439, 441–442, 443
   to enclose, 437–440
   to end, 444–445
   to join, 443–444
   parenthesis, 438–439
   quotation marks, 437–440
   semicolon, 441–442, 443
   to separate, 441–443
   to show omission, 445
   slash, 444

Q

QUITE/QUITE/QUIT, 463
Quotation marks, 437–440
Quotation placement, 356–358

R

RAISE/RISE, 463
Reading, as an aid to writing, 10–12
REAL/REALLY, 436
Reciprocal pronouns, 421
Red herring argument, 238
Reflexive pronouns, 421
REGARDLESS (irregardless), 463
Relative pronouns, 421
Resumes, 413–415
Revision
   reviewing a draft, 133–139
      checking the organization, 135
      considering the audience, 133–134
      editing and proofreading, 136–139, 417–465
      evaluating coherence and cohesion, 135–136
      identifying the thesis, 134–135
      reconsidering the assignment, 133
   sentences
      for aesthetic quality, 299
      for clarity, 282–290
      for economy, 297–299
      nouns and adjectives, 279
      parallel predicates, 279
      prepositional phrases, 279
      participial phrases, 279
      for symmetry, 295–297
      for variety, 290–295
Revision of drafts, 57–67
   checklists, 59–60, 61, 62–63
   plan for writing, 317–318
   questions to ask, 59–60
   reseeing, 59
Research papers
   assimilating information
      annotation, 345
      creating dialogue, 345–346
   revising
      considering audience, 354–355
      considering subheadings, 355
      development of organizational plan, 355
      first draft, 353
      gathering information, 319–345
      integration of quotations, 356–358
      reconsidering assignment, 354
      topic development, 318–319
Run-on sentences, 286–287

S

Search strategy, 328–332
Semicolon, 441–442, 443
Sentences, 422–423, 428
   clauses, 280–281
   combining, 276
      coordination, 279–280
      modification, 276–278
      subordination, 280–281
   comma splices, 288–289
   dangling modifiers, 282–284

Subject Index

Sentences (*Continued*)
  fragments, 285
  fused, 287–288
  limiting passive voice in, 294–295
  misplaced modifiers, 284–285
  parallel structure 279, 296–297
  revising for aesthetic quality, 299
  revising for clarity, 282–290
  revising for economy, 297–299
  revising for symmetry, 295–297
  revising for variety, 290–295
  run-on, 286–287
  unclear references, 285–286
Sentence fragments, intentional, 427–428
Sexist language, 308
SHOULD OF, 434
Slash, 444
SORT OF/KIND OF, 436
Spatial order, organization, 84
Spelling, 451–465
  rules, 454–455
Spelling log, 464–465
STATIONARY/STATIONERY, 463
STATUE/STATUTE/STATURE, 464
Style manuals, 351

Subheadings, 355
Subjects and predicates, 422–423, 424
Subject/verb agreement, 430

T

THEIR/THEY'RE/THERE, 457
Thesis, 53–57
  compared to subject, 53
  definition, 53
  development, 53–54
  placement, 55–57
  statement of, 54–55
Time order organization, 83–86
TO/TOO/TWO, 457
Tone, 309
Topic development, 318–319
TOWARD/TOWARDS, 436
Transitive verbs, 421
TWO/TO/TOO, 457

U

UNINTERESTED/DISINTERESTED, 434

UNIQUE, 437
Usage, 431–437

V

Verbs, 421, 426, 428–431
  aspects, 429
  complements to, 423–424
  mood, mode, modality, 429–430
Verb/subject agreement, 430
Voice, 309

W

WELL/GOOD, 435
WERE/WE'RE/WHERE, 464
Word choice, 301–308
WOULD OF, 434
Writing environment, 14–15
Writing folders, 13
Writing groups
  guidelines, 70–72
  size, 70
Writing habits, 4–6